The Regions of Spain

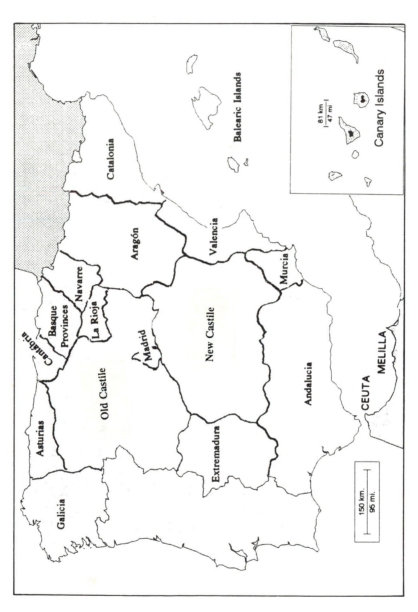

REGIONS OF SPAIN

The Regions of Spain

A Reference Guide to History and Culture

Robert W. Kern

Photographs by Chuck Smith

Greenwood Press
Westport, Connecticut • London

Library of Congress Cataloging-in-Publication Data

Kern, Robert.
   The regions of Spain : a reference guide to history and culture /
Robert W. Kern.
      p.   cm.
   Includes bibliographical references (p.   ) and index.
   ISBN 0–313–29224–8 (alk. paper)
   1. Spain—Civilization.   2. Spain—History, Local.
3. Regionalism—Spain.   I. Title.
DP48.K45   1995
946—dc20   95–6481

British Library Cataloguing in Publication Data is available.

Library of Congress Catalog Card Number: 95–6481
ISBN: 0–313–29224–8

First published in 1995

Greenwood Press, 88 Post Road West, Westport, CT 06881
An imprint of Greenwood Publishing Group, Inc.

Printed in the United States of America

The paper used in this book complies with the
Permanent Paper Standard issued by the National
Information Standards Organization (Z39.48–1984).

10 9 8 7 6 5 4 3 2 1

CONTENTS

Photo essay follows p. 174.

ACKNOWLEDGMENTS

I owe a special debt of thanks to my wife, Susan L. Brake, for her assistance on this book. I am also deeply grateful to Stanley G. Payne of the University of Wisconsin for reading the manuscript so thoroughly, and to Meredith D. Dodge of the University of New Mexico for her early encouragement. James W. Cortada read the Catalan section, while Neddy A. Vigil and Alfred Rodríguez of the Spanish Department at the University of New Mexico were particularly kind in giving me such long hours and good advice and counsel on Spanish literature. Susan Benforado Bakewell read the art sections, and William A. Douglass and staff of the Basque Studies Center at the University of Nevada at Reno provided some pointed criticism that helped me improve the Basque section. Donald C. Cutter also gave me the benefit of his long acquaintanceship with Spain.

Martha E. Heard of the Spanish Department at Highland High School in Albuquerque, a former national teacher of the year, was my sounding board for what high school Spanish courses need in the way of reference material. Special thanks go to Francine Cronshaw of East Mountain Graphics, who did the maps, and Chuck Smith of San Francisco, who provided the photographs. Despite such able associates, any mistakes that remain are mine alone.

Finally, I am grateful to Robert Bello for helping by proofreading the manuscript, and Aurora Morcillo for the cover photograph.

STYLE

The place-name spellings used in this book come from *Webster's New Geographical Dictionary*. Seville, Navarre, Andalusia, Castile, Catalonia, Majorca, and Minorca (instead of Mallorca or Menorca) are conventionally anglicized, but not Zaragoza or Aragón, which are left unchanged by the dictionary. Extremadura, which the dictionary anglicizes as Estremadura, is left unchanged here, since there is an Estremadura in Portugal.

In some cases, historic regional names have been retained to avoid confusing English-language readers. Old Castile and New Castile are used in place of the current Castilla y León or Castilla y La Mancha, and the Basque Provinces rather than Euskadi or País Vascos.

Castilian is used for place names except for the major cities and provinces of the Basque Provinces and Catalonia, where Euskara or Catalàn, the Basque and Catalan languages, have replaced Castilian, or in Valencia, where the regional dialect Valenciano has also caused a fair number of place-name changes. Galicia, which speaks its own language of Galego, has made fewer changes. No reference work published late in the twentieth century should fail to acknowledge the linguistic changes recently adopted in Spain, even if to do so makes the narrative process slightly more cluttered.

I note the alternative spellings for Basque provinces (Araba for Alava, Gipuzkoa for Guipúzcoa, Bizkaia for Vizcaya) in the title of provincial entries, with the Castilian name second. I have also used Euskara for major Basque cities (Bilbo for Bilbao, Gasteiz for Vitoria, or Donostiá for San Sebastián), but I still use the pre-1978 Castilian names in the historical and literary sections to indicate that these cities once officially were known as Bilbao, Vitoria, or San Sebastián. My only intent is to try to combine new and old place names in a way that makes best sense for American or English readers.

Changes in place names are also numerous in Catalonia, Valencia, and the Balearics. Català is used for geographic terms such as Girona (Gerona) and Lleida (Lérida) in Catalonia. Barcelona and Tarragona remain unchanged. In all other place-name matters, I have used the standard *España: atlas e indices de sus terminos municipales.*

Given names of Spanish rulers (Carlos or Felipe rather than Charles or Philip) have not been anglicized in order to avoid contrast with other Spanish names in print. I have also kept the Castilian spellings and accents for aristocratic titles, since terms of address differ considerably in Spanish. Noble titles are never capitalized.

Titles of books, dramatic, cinematic, and art works have been italicized in the text. Spanish words now common in English will appear in roman type. Words of the Iberian languages unfamiliar to the reader are italicized, although this does not apply to political parties or organizations.

Finally, inasmuch as possible, I have followed *The Chicago Manual of Style* for the transliteration of Arabic.

The Regions of Spain

INTRODUCTION

The Regions of Spain is designed to provide students and interested readers with concise information on Spanish regional and provincial history, literature, art, music, and other facets of Hispanic civilization.

We live in a postideological age. Empires have departed, nations are losing their monolithic quality, and local regions, states, or provinces assert a new importance. Spain, always a strongly localized society, is now experiencing a new era of devolution from the purely national to the regional or local that makes this reexamination worthwhile. By using a new type of format, *The Regions of Spain* divides the historical, literary, and artistic aspects of Spain by region and province to explain the society within a local context.

REGIONAL CHARACTERISTICS

This will always be the first entry in each chapter. It provides essential information pertaining to the regions, such as census data from 1990 and 1992. Spain is composed of eighteen regions, encompassing fifty provinces. Each of the eighteen chapters of this book follows exactly the same format.

To understand the importance of regionalism, a historical digression is necessary to provide perspective on this new unit of administration, which has existed only since 1978. In early times, Spanish society was a collection of scattered tribes colonized by Carthage, Greece, and Rome. After the long Roman period, civilization declined under the Goths but rose under the Muslims, at least until antagonism between Arabs and Berber newcomers allowed expansion of the Christian north. This development came from the historic regions of Galicia, the Basque homelands, and Catalonia, each of which possessed divergent social patterns and different languages. All lent something of themselves to the new medieval Christian principalities in Asturias, Navarre, Aragón, and León, which sought to reconquer the other two-thirds of the peninsula, which was Muslim. But after 1212, Castile, originally settled by Asturias, Navarre, and León, became the leading principality with its victory over the Muslims at Las Navas de Tolosa.

Castile's dominance among the principalities rose during the reign of Fernando and Isabel to an imperial level. The voyages of Columbus gave Castile world power but also brought problems as political rule grew more absolute. Inheritance of the Spanish throne by the Hapsburg (1517) and Bourbon (1700) dynasties intensified absolutism, although imperial strength wasted away during endless worldwide colonial struggles with England and France, and in Europe against the Turks, Dutch, and Austrians as well as the English and French. Some parts of local Spanish society, such as the Basque Provinces, Navarre, and Aragón, ignored and frightened, zealously defended their *fueros* (local privileges), while the Galicians struggled to obtain basic representation or to overcome famine. Early regionalist efforts of the *juntas* in the War of Independence (1808–13) or the cantonal phase of the First Republic (1873–74) in Andalusia and Valencia exploded briefly in the nineteenth century.

The first major consideration of regional reform started during the Second Republic (1931–39); but five years later, just as initial decentralization was in its infancy, the Spanish Civil War (1936–39) split the nation and created the dictatorship of General Francisco Franco y Bahamonde, who continued rigid centralism until his death in 1975.

Under Franco, Spain diverged in a peculiar corporate way from the social democracy of other European states and remained plagued by old political hatreds. The society steadily grew more restless, and when the dictatorship finally ended, the forward-looking young King Juan Carlos I won widespread support for a new constitution. In his inaugural speech on November 22, 1975, he gave the first official support for regionalism.

> A just order, equal for everyone, makes it possible to recognize, within the unity of the Kingdom and the State, the regional peculiarities which are the expression of the diversity of peoples that make up the sacred reality of Spain.

Thus, during sixteen months of debate in 1977–78, after approving major new articles pertaining to a democratic monarchy, abolition of a formal state religion, and creation of fundamental human liberties, the Constituent Cortes, or parliament, also drew up a set of proposals supporting the "right to autonomy of the nationalities and regions."

Inclusion of these proposals may have been no more than a political maneuver by the premier, the Castilian Adolfo Suárez, to defuse threats of separation made by two independence-minded historic nationalities, the Basques and Catalans. Supported by the left, these regions remained irrevocably convinced that Franco's treatment of their linguistically different northern areas during and after the Spanish Civil War justified regional autonomy. Regionalism was for them the ultimate guarantee to go their own way should Castile and the rest of Spain fail to support future democratic reforms. A smaller number of militants fully expected to secede completely from the national union.

As originally written in the constitution's eighth section, the concept of regionalism inexactly defined cultural or linguistic groups and said little about how to prevent regions from becoming mini-nations in violation of national sovereignty. Moderate and conservative politicians adamantly opposed the entire section, and the Galician Manuel Fraga Iribarne made a counterproposal to recognize the diverse regions of Spain themselves but not the nationalities. When the final version of the constitution was written, these criticisms were brushed aside. Article 143 outlined the autonomous regions and created a process for autonomy statutes requiring two-thirds ratification by town councils of each region, approval by regional referendum, and a final review (with changes, if need be) by the constitutional commission of the Cortes in discussion with regional legislatures.

This process irritated the autonomy bloc, which demanded and got a fast track for Catalonia, the Basque Provinces, and Galicia under Article 151. The article allowed all provincial councils and two-thirds of municipal councils in a cultural/linguistic region to adopt home rule and take over those functions of government (local councils, education, language, culture) not otherwise reserved by the central state (foreign diplomacy, military affairs, welfare, etc.). Regional representatives would have the right to negotiate directly with the constitutional commission on the scope of regional powers. The constitution was ratified by plebiscite in December 1978.

Article 151 was invoked not only by the above three regions but also by Asturias, Valencia, Murcia, Andalusia, Extremadura, the Canary Islands, and the Balearic Islands, all of which expanded autonomy farther and faster than drafters of the constitution had anticipated. On the other hand, some areas initially rejected autonomy altogether. León believed that centuries of historical integration made the autonomy process meaningless. A third group, including Cantabria, Asturias, and La Rioja in the north and Ciudad Real and Extremadura in the south, experienced serious identity crises, since they had no partners to join or little distinct nationality except as Castilians. A few provinces like Albacete felt that it made more economic sense for them to join Murcia than New Castile. At one point, Segovia and Guadalajara threatened to seek individual autonomy if the process could not be resolved quickly.

On February 23, 1981, tension over the regional process provoked an unsuccessful antiregionalist coup d'état staged by elements of the police and the military in Valencia and Madrid. Hurriedly, Suárez put in place a new ministry of territorial administration led by Rodolfo Martín Villa. In July 1981, the awkwardly named Law on the Harmonization of the Autonomy Process (Ley Orgánica de Armonización del Proceso Autonómico or LOAPA) restricted Article 151 to Andalusia alone among areas that had not yet passed regional legislation and put the whole autonomy process under a tighter set of controls.

When LOAPA concluded restructuring in 1983, eighteen regions formally existed. No other European state between World War II and the breakup of the Soviet bloc went quite so far in revising its basic structure. Indeed, in the 1980s, eastern Europeans studied the Spanish experience to better understand the problems involved in making the transition from dictatorship to democracy. Only the slower evolution of the European Community matches what Spain did by itself, and membership in the European Community capped Spain's own transformation in 1986.

While it is impossible to predict the future strength of regionalism, the lesson to be learned from this process is that, if nothing else, localism and regionalism still hold enduring power in the late twentieth century. Futurists in the United States currently discuss the "nine nations of North America" as a way of distinguishing widely divergent regional differences. Who knows? Perhaps the experience of Spain intimates changes far distant in the future of the United States and other large nations.

Under the Constitution of 1978, each region has its own parliament. Leaders of the winning party in provincial elections become provincial council presidents who head commissions that oversee operations of five basic departments delegated to the region: General and Economic Services, Health, Social Services, Culture, Education and Sport, and Municipal Administration. These commissions report to appropriate national authorities in Madrid.

Single-province autonomous communities such as Madrid, Navarre, La Rioja, Asturias, Cantabria, and Murcia let the region assume all powers, responsibilities, and resources of former provinces. Historic regions such as the Basque Provinces, Catalonia, Galicia, and the Balearic and Canary Islands created *diputaciones forales* (governing bodies using local languages) to support linguistic independence and development, granting non-Castilian languages coequal rights or creating special aspects of cultural and institutional diversity. Many of these grants have had awkward aspects, and as a result the regions' power is still debated and occasionally altered.

PROVINCES

This is the next and largest section of each chapter. A province as defined by the Constitution of 1978 serves both the regional and central government by providing essential services and administration. Cultural, educational, and some social services emanate from the region; military, transportation, and other public works come from the central state. All are directly applied by the province, which also serves as a judicial unit.

The history of the old provincial format needs its own brief background. Not all parts of Spain began as principalities or special linguistic/cultural regions. Some existed as a part of Castile or as territory that fell to a principality. Andalusia and Extremadura, for example, ultimately were conquered by Castile. Creation of a thorough system of provinces to achieve uniform governance started in 1707 during the reign of the first Spanish Bourbon, Felipe V (1701–46), when the Nueva Planta decree (literally the new order of the state) revoked traditional rights in Aragón, Catalonia, Valencia, and the Balearic Islands. A new provincial arrangement appeared in the work of José Patiño, the marqués de Castelar (1660–1733), and Zenón de Somodevilla y Bengoechea, the marqués de la Ensenada (1702–81), sometimes using a French-style provincial governor, the *intendant*, in areas where *corregidors* or civil governors did not rule.

During the nineteenth century, liberal reform extended provincial status to smaller and less populated areas and made the title of civil governor uniform by 1837. Change was imposed from the top down. When centralist efforts to promote national solidarity and economic development floundered, intense criticism focused on Madrid's restriction of local autonomy. The cultural bias and corrupt administrative practices used by the national government also clashed with local tradition and caused religious and economic grievances to surface. Two Carlist civil wars (1833–39 and 1874–76) saw northern areas seek to restore local governance, protect traditional Catholicism, and keep their *fueros* (historic laws). During the First Republic (1873–74) the south created short-lived cantons, or city-states, which adopted decentralized regional or anarchist schemes anticipating twentieth-century regionalism and radicalism. Drift to the right and left was exacerbated during the Bourbon Restoration (1876–85) and the Regency (1885–1901), when political bosses and party machines routinely falsified elections, maintaining social hierarchy and political oppression through a corrupt system called *caciquismo* that put decision-making in the hands of a very small political elite.

The failure of this elite to modernize or hold on to what was left of the empire in the Spanish-American War (1898) promoted the further growth of a Spanish left, intent upon industrial and rural change. The economic crisis also stimulated Catalan and Basque regional nationalism. Catalans sought national restructuring because Castilian free-trade policies damaged their infant industries. Madrid depended upon the export sale of agricultural produce and had little confidence that Barcelona alone could supply these needs, much to the distress of the northeast. The Basque intelligentsia had its own economic interests, but reacted more to the human cost and great contrast of industrial life with their idealized and beloved agrarian past.

During the first third of the twentieth century, liberalism collapsed when it could not solve these problems. Against a background of growing military authoritarianism and apocalyptic left-wing revolutionary activity, the Second Republic (1931–39) responded to Basque and Catalan demands by granting autonomy to the provinces of Catalonia in September 1932 and to the Basque Provinces in the fall of 1936. One Basque province rejected the agreement, a second was conquered by Franco's forces before the statute became law, and only one actually benefitted from the short-lived autonomy.

Franco's victory in the Spanish Civil War created an ultra-centralized authoritarian state from April 1939 until November 1975 that was hostile to localism. National syndicalism, the regime's ideology, stressed a type of corporatism emphasizing patriarchy, institutionalism, and indirect control. Its administrative style, almost as overcentralized and culturally imperious as nineteenth-century liberalism, was aggravated further by a military concept of justice and the pursuit of old political grudges. As soon as Franco died in 1975, a flood of demands for regional and provincial autonomy reappeared very quickly. His successor, King Juan Carlos, made it clear that regional autonomy would be an acceptable price for change if unaccompanied by radical revolution or ethnic violence. He also emphasized that not a single province would be destroyed in the process.

Discussion of each province is organized under nine subjects:

1. **Vital Statistics** provides information on population, area (expressed in square kilometers—1 sq. km. is 0.386 of 1 sq. mi.), dominant physical features (rivers, mountain ranges, coastal areas), universities, and location in relation to other regions and provinces.

2. **Economy** summarizes the current provincial economy.

3. **History** contains a broad historical essay on each province. A number of themes about Spanish history are apparent:

   a. the great complexity of rival civilizations that occupied Iberia, ca. 1000 B.C.–A.D. 1000;

   b. the difficult process of emergence experienced by the rival Christian principalities which jockeyed for power, ca. A.D. 1000–1500;

   c. the rise of Castile as an imperial state among the various regions of Spain, 1492–1975;

   d. the deeply held defense of fundamental traditional laws (*fueros*) in some regions that somehow managed to survive during this same period;

   e. social and institutional history, particularly concerning agriculture and grazing, that led to national crises between 1808 and 1975;

f. the impact of modern politics, the Spanish Civil War, the Franco era, and the early constitutional monarchy;

g. and finally, the process leading up to the creation of a new state built upon regions after 1978.

The historical chronology at the end of this volume provides a further overview of Spanish history and will help the reader to understand the juxtaposition of general periods. The glossary also may be of use in defining unfamiliar terms.

4. **Literature** includes major Spanish dramatists, novelists, and poets, or writers of religious, political, and scientific works. The writers are listed by province of birth, although significant periods of creativity spent elsewhere in Spain are cited whenever possible. The intellectual centers of Madrid, Toledo, Barcelona, and Seville attracted many creative persons for varying periods of their careers, but the regional nature of Spanish literature generally makes it sensible to list writers by their home province. Major works are noted, along with genre and stylistic innovations. Names of major writers appear in bold type.

5. **Art** includes the lives of major Spanish artists, discussed in their home provinces. Major centers of art are also included, along with definitions and stylistic developments. Whenever possible, birth and death dates are given for Spanish artists and artisans at the point of first reference to them. The names of major artists of a province appear in bold type in the text.

6. **Music** has a smaller number of contributors than the other arts and will not appear in each province. Folk music also may be noted in the Customs and Society section.

7. **Customs and Society** discusses special institutions, minority groups such as the Jews and the gypsies who have a place in Spanish history, and special practices and holidays.

The main Spanish holidays (not mentioned unless of special importance to a particular province) are Epiphany (January 6); San José (March 19); Holy Thursday, Good Friday, and Easter Sunday; Labor Day (May 1); Corpus Christi (Thursday after Trinity Sunday); Assumption (August 15); Día de Hispanidad, or Columbus Day (October 12); All Souls' Day (November 2), similar to Memorial Day; Constitution Day (December 6); Immaculate Conception (December 8); Christmas; and Día de los Santos Inocentes (December 28), similar to April Fools' Day though not an official holiday.

Another part of this section describes historical dress. For the most part, the clothing styles date from the mid-sixteenth to the late nineteenth century and are the type of costume seen today at occasional fairs and local celebrations. The modern Spaniard, of course, dresses like everyone else in Western society.

Occasionally, this section also explains earlier economic and religious practices typical of Spain to give some perspective and historical dimension to the Spanish character. Again, the great changes in the modern era make this material more historical than contemporary.

8. **Historic Sites** describes the significant towns and historical remains of each province. The first description is of the provincial capital; the directions that follow are from the capital to the other sites in the province. This section can be used to plan trips or simply to understand the tangible physical substance of many areas, with their religious and historical buildings, museums, and historical remains. The choice was selective, since space is not available to give a complete description of every site.

9. **Cuisine** discusses provincial specialties and provides recipes for a few Spanish dishes. Most of these foods are served throughout Spain, but the intent is to indicate dishes original to a province.

It is worth noting that Spanish meals are served at times somewhat different than elsewhere in Western Europe. Breakfast (*desayuno*) is a light repast usually consisting only of coffee and a roll, or the unique *churro*, a tube of flour paste extruded from a machine, fried like a donut, and sprinkled with sugar. Lunch (*merienda* or *comer*) is served from 1:30 to 3:30, during the afternoon siesta. It can be a meal of many courses, especially since dinner (*cena* or *comida*) is served late, between 8:30 and 11:00 P.M., or even later in the summer. Travelers sometimes make the *merienda* the main meal of the day and consume *tapas* as a light evening supper.

This format is uniform throughout the book, so *¡siga leyendo!*—read on.

Chapter 1

ANDALUSIA
(Andalucía)

REGIONAL CHARACTERISTICS. Pop., 6,441,755. Area, 87,166 sq. km., 17 percent of Spanish national territory. Capital: Seville. Andalusia (al-Andalus, literally "land of the Vandals" [Arabic]), united since Roman times, is the ancient center of Roman and medieval Hispano-Muslim civilization.

Geographical features of Andalusia include the Guadalquivir River valley, mountains (Sierra Nevada), and all of Spain's southern Mediterranean coastline bordering the Straits of Gibraltar. The region stretches from the Mediterranean coast of Almería on the east to Portugal on the west, and reaches north to the borders of New Castile and Extremadura. The flag of Andalusia has a field of green with a broad white band in the center. Seville is the regional capital. Andalusia ranks fifteenth in income among the Spanish regions.

During the autonomy process, the case of Andalusia proved complicated. Adolfo Suárez assumed that the region did not qualify for Article 151 because the language and ethnicity had both been Castilian since A.D. 1248. Many opposing politicians, however, rejected these assumptions. While Andalusians speak Castilian, they do not lisp the letter c or z, and they drop as many consonants as possible from their words, creating a regional argot that is very fast and difficult to understand, very much like Cuban or Puerto Rican Spanish. Andalusian culture also retains a flamboyance less com-

ANDALUSIA

Map legend:

Feet / Meters

Feet	Meters
13,123	4,000
6,562	2,000
3,281	1,000
1,640	500
656	200
0	0

Playa

65 km.
41 mi.

N

Provinces and places:

Almería
Mojácar
Almería
Cabo de Gata

Adra
Motril
Salobreña
Almuñecar
Nerja

Granada
Sierra Nevada
Genil River
Santa Fé
Guadix
Granada

Jaén
Úbeda
Baeza
Bailén
Baños de la Encina
Andújar

Córdoba
Medina Azahara
Córdoba
Montilla
Aguilar de la Frontera
Lucena

Ecija
Osuna
Antequera
Málaga
Ronda
Málaga
Marbella

Gulf of Málaga

Seville
Guadalcanal
Alanis
Aznalcóllar
Itálica
Carmona
Alcalá de Guadaira
Seville
Arcos de la Frontera
Jerez de la Frontera

Cádiz
Algeciras
Tarifa
Bay of Algeciras
Strait of Gibraltar

Huelva
Minas de Río Tinto
Niebla
Palos de la Frontera
Huelva
Coto Doñana
Sanlúcar de Barrameda
Puerto de Santa María
Cádiz

Guadalquivir River

Mediterranean Sea

Atlantic Ocean

monly found in the north, causing southerners to complain that they are treated as inferiors by other Spaniards.

These differences led Andalusians to demand autonomy on the same basis as the Basque Provinces, Catalonia, and Galicia. The matter became an issue of honor and caused the emergence of three new regional parties and rediscovery of a former minor regionalist, Blas Infantes. The large Andalusian Socialist Party, which had won no seats in the regional parliament during the first elections of 1977, ultimately used the regional issue to good advantage. While they supported regionalism, they also were known to be committed to keeping the Spanish national structure intact, thereby making autonomy only a symbolic issue.

Technicalities invalidated the first regional vote in February 1980 when Almería's vote indicated no clear preference. Suárez reshuffled his cabinet and began clarifying the autonomy process through LOAPA. On December 30, 1981, after intense campaigning by the socialists, a second referendum approved limited autonomy by 55 percent. Andalusia became the only other region besides the Basque Provinces, Catalonia, and Galicia to be admitted as a historic nationality. Since 1982, when the socialists came to national power with the *sevillano* Felipe González as premier, the popularity of purely regional parties has diminished in Andalusia.

ALMERÍA

VITAL STATISTICS. Pop., 405,313. Area, 8,775 sq. km. Capital: Almería. Diocesan sees: Almería and Granada. As the easternmost province of Andalusia, Almería borders the Gulf of Almería and the southeastern Cabo de Gata and is surrounded by mountains (Sierra de Gádor, Sierra Almahilla, Sierra de Gata) that are an extension of the Sierra Nevadas in Granada. The region touches Murcia on the north, Granada on the west, and the Mediterranean on the east and south. Desertlike areas of the province provided the locale for such movies as *Lawrence of Arabia* and *Patton*. The province is very hot and dry.

ECONOMY. Agriculture, the major activity, uses the *enarenado* system of covered fields and drip irrigation for year-round production of an amazing abundance of crops in an otherwise arid province. Many varieties of winter vegetables and flowers find a lucrative market in northern Europe. Other industries include tourism, sulphur mining, and electrical generation.

HISTORY. (al-Mariyya [Arabic], "mirror of the sea"). Neolithic Almería emerged ca. 3500 to 2000 B.C. as fortified towns (Los Millares) or as farming cultures (El Argar) that showed Egyptian or Minoan cultural influences such as the bronze image of the god Secullus found at Villaricos. Phoenician trade attracted Greeks and Romans to Portus Magnus, today the modern port of Almería.

The Muslim Umayyad period brought other diverse peoples to the region, as shown by ruins of Sephardic synagogues and Yemenite Arab settlements in the interior. Arab pirates used the port of Almería to harass Christian shipping and to trade with Tunisia. The area reached great heights as Abd ar-Rahman III's chief naval base, but the caliphate of Córdoba's collapse caused Almería to pass through a variety of regimes: an independent emirate in the early eleventh century, a Berber regime in 1091, and the ten-year Crusader kingdom of Alfonso VII of Castile and García Ramírez of Navarre in 1147. After this brief period of Christian rule, the Nasrid dynasty of Granada held Almería against Jaume II of Aragón-Catalonia in 1309. Almería fell to Castile only in 1488.

The Reconquest initially kept Almería as a part of Granada. Intense missionary activity swept through the area, and despite a severe earthquake that destroyed the partially built cathedral of Almería in 1502, the area's very popular patron saint, the Virgin of the Sea, was discovered near the beach of Torre García in 1522. The port thrived as a naval base for raids on Algiers and Turkish shipping and in the export of eastern Andalusian crops to Barcelona.

The revolt of Muslims facing conversion to Christianity in 1567–68 intensified racial and religious hatred; deportation to Valencia and Albacete caused the community to disappear by 1609. Maritime traffic increased after English raids on Cádiz, but English ships also harassed the eastern coast during the seventeenth century and blockaded Almería in 1705 during the War of Spanish Succession. Seventy years later, to further stimulate commerce, a branch of the reformist organization, the Real Sociedad de Amigos del País, flourished in Vera and agitated for free trade. On October 12, 1778, when the Bourbon monarchy curtailed Seville's trade monopoly with the colonies, Almería began developing commercial ties with Latin America.

This growing prosperity, only slightly interrupted by the War of Independence, caused the area to be taken away from Granada in 1822 and given its own provincial status, an act that sparked a close relationship with the liberals. But secularization of ecclesiastical properties did not solve the problems of overpopulation or growing peasant poverty. Some peasants of Almería had to emigrate to French-occupied Algeria to find land, while others took jobs in the iron mines. Unrest in 1868–73 promoted the career of Nicolás Salmerón (1838–1908, president of the First Republic), who spent his career advocating republicanism, social reform, and regionalism. Prolonged anarchist violence continued through the period prior to the Second Republic.

Delayed modernization that kept rail service from reaching the area until 1895 was typical of the lack of investment that affected all segments of the economy. While the Second Republic (1931–36) promised positive reform, the murder of provincial officials in 1933 and of the bishop of Almería in 1936 revealed continuing instability and a dark side to change. The province remained republican throughout the civil war (1936–39). In 1937, the German pocket battleship *Admiral Scheer* and four destroyers shelled the port and killed four people. The incident led to diplomatic negotiations to create a safety zone for foreign shipping, but little came of this idea before the province surrendered to the nationalists on March 31, 1939.

During the postwar period, agriculture went through rapid improvement. Backward family farms profited in the 1960s by specializing in exportable produce. During the autonomy process in 1978–80, serious questions arose as to which region Almería should join, and the province invalidated the first Andalusian regional plebiscite by rejecting all possibilities. Talks concerning union with Murcia or New Castile proved inconclusive, and a year later, under considerable pressure, Almería joined Andalusia.

LITERATURE. Almería is one of the few areas in Spain without a strong literary tradition. The only major figure is **Francisco Villaespesa** (1877–1936), a good friend of Huelva's Juan Ramón Jiménez. As a writer, he concentrated on Muslim Spain in works such as *Los nocturnos del Generalife* (1915), a very evocative book about Granada. He also interpreted the Latin American poetry of Rubén Darío and other modernists, but his own poetry tended to be neo-romantic.

ART. The area of Los Millares–El Argar shows the influence of Balearic culture in the remains of cyclopean structures called Talayots. The entire province contains many Mudéjar churches.

CUSTOMS AND SOCIETY. Traditional head coverings in Almería show influence both from Granada and Murcia. Men wore the classical *sombrero de labrador* (worker's hat) made of cheap black velvet with a wide, upturned brim and a conical crown trimmed with pompons of black silk. Field workers imitated the Murcian practice of wearing colored handkerchiefs rolled on the head like a small turban. White pants and colored sashes around the waist were common. Female dress favored long white outer skirts and several bright petticoats. Handkerchiefs stamped in colorful patterns worn around the throat and shoulders (sometimes used to cover the face in public like Muslim women) and light silk mantillas (a lacy head covering) completed their costume.

The annual summer festival, Nuestra Señora del Mar, is held in August. The craft of weaving *harapas* (rag rugs) still continues, and Níjar produces excellent pottery.

HISTORIC SITES. The provincial capital of **Almería** is a quiet Andalusian city and port. Its main structure, overlooking the city, is the Alcazaba, a Muslim fortress built ca. A.D. 900 during the reign of Abd ar-Rahman III and enlarged by Carlos I in the sixteenth century by the addition of the Tower of Homage. The cathedral of Almería follows a design by the Burgos architect Diego de Siloé, with four towers and a Mediterranean touch in the use of Ionic and Corinthian pillars.

Elsewhere in the province, the northeastern town of **Mojácar** contains

Phoenician and Arab ruins and an old Jewish quarter. Outside **Vélez Blanco,** the so-called Cave of the Letters is the site of the prehistoric *indalo* symbol (a stick figure holding an arc).

CUISINE. Lamb dishes are popular, particularly lamb and rice, and many restaurants offer extensive seafood selections. Use of olive oil, wine, and citrus products is common throughout Spanish cuisine.

The Andalusian custom of serving *tapas* (or *pinchos*, picked up with the fingers) is the informal Spanish style of eating bar food to accompany sherry aperitifs, whose 18 percent alcohol content cannot be drunk on an empty stomach. There are many varieties: in sauce, marinades, pâtes or salads, with bread or pastry, fried, or with shrimp or other seafood. *Moros* are small shish kebabs of marinated beef, mutton, or pork.

CÁDIZ

VITAL STATISTICS. Pop., 1,001,716. Area, 7,440 sq. km. Capital: Cádiz. Diocesan see: Cádiz-Cuenta. The province runs north and south from the high elevations of the Sierra Nevada and the province of Seville to the Mediterranean and the Straits of Gibraltar, and on the west from the Guadalquivir River near its mouth to Málaga on the east.

ECONOMY. Some of Spain's largest agricultural enterprises are located in Cádiz. Major crops include sugar beets, cotton, cork (the largest in Spain), and tobacco. Fishing in North African waters and production of sea salt, steel, leather goods, automobile parts, and electronics systems also are important.

HISTORY. (Gades, from Augusta Gaditana, or Gadir, "fortress" [Roman], Jeziret Kadis [Arabic]). Cádiz, with the longest recorded history in Europe, began as a Phoenician colony in the ninth century B.C., passed to Carthage, and finally became Roman at the end of the Second Punic War. Gades grew into an important Roman port, site of a Roman lighthouse, destroyed in A.D. 1146. Other provincial ports included Puerto de Santa María (Portus Menesthei [Roman]) and Algeciras (Cartateia [Greek]). Jerez de la Frontera (Asta Regia [Roman]) became the main inland population center.

In A.D. 480, Cádiz became a part of the Byzantine Empire, which held a fringe of coastal territory stretching all the way to Valencia. The empire remained active in Spain during Justinian the Great's era (527–65), but a Visigothic king, Leovigild, managed to establish a shaky hegemony in 585. During the late seventh century, Visigothic backwardness caused trade and population to decline precipitously.

In 711, the Muslim conquest by Tariq led to greater Arab reliance on Málaga than Cádiz over the next 300 years, but Cádiz's general commerce and proximity to Morocco and other North African territories kept its port busy. While a few towns such as Puerto de Santa María collapsed, others such as Calpe (Gibraltar, from Djehel al Tariq [Arabic]), Medina Arkosh (Arcos de la Frontera), and Jerez (a major fortress protecting the riches of Cádiz) grew prosperous under Muslim rule.

In 1250, Alfonso X conquered Arcos de la Frontera and subinfeudated to the dukes of Arcos, Medina Sidonia, and Osuna, or the counts of Aguila. Cádiz fell in 1262, but while Fernando IV of Castile briefly captured Gibraltar in 1309, Muslim Granada regained it from 1339 to 1461. Jerez fell to the Christians in 1340 and was renamed Jerez de la Frontera, signifying the line of demarcation between Christian Spain and Muslim territory. The capture of Algeciras in 1344 by Alfonso XI of Castile, a crucial victory during the last phase of the Reconquest, cut Granada's closest link with North Africa. Christians poured into the province, and for centuries afterwards a single aristocratic family, the powerful condes de Denia y Tarifa, dominated Tarifa, Spain's southernmost town.

Christian rule promoted trade with the Atlantic coast of Europe, but the discovery of the New World in 1492 for a time made Puerto de Santa María, not Cádiz, into a major Castilian naval center, attracting mariners such as Columbus (one of his ships was named in honor of the port), Amérigo Vespucci (1451–1512), and Alonso de Ojeda (1470?–1515?). Numerous churches and townhouses reflect the cultural and architectural details brought back from the worldwide voyages of the colonial Spanish fleet. At first, treasure ships continued up the Guadalquivir River to Seville, while most ordinary ships anchored in Cádiz harbor. The Castilian monopoly on trade to the New World sent all colonial trade through the two ports, but Cádiz alone faced English retaliation when Sir Francis Drake (1540?–96) burned the city in 1587 and the Earl of Essex, Robert Devereux (1567–1601), destroyed harbor structures in 1596.

By the early eighteenth century, even though Carlos I had improved Gibraltar's defenses to a level that withstood British attack in 1625, Admiral George Rooke (1650–1709) captured Gibraltar in 1704. After the Treaty of Utrecht (1713) permanently awarded Gibraltar to Britain, unsuccessful Spanish sieges failed to retake it in 1727 and 1779–1783. The British retaliated by blockading the port of Cádiz from February 1797 to April 1798, and Admiral Horatio Nelson (1758–1805) destroyed the combined Franco-Spanish navy at Cape Trafalgar not far west of Cádiz in 1805.

Yet somehow Cádiz prospered. River traffic bound for Seville ended when the Guadalquivir River silted and ship drafts grew too large to allow passage of large ocean vessels. As the new terminus for American trade, Cádiz gained a greater share of colonial commerce. Foreign capital revitalized Jerez's wine and sherry industry in the eighteenth century, and the Carthusian monastery of Jerez rose as a center of equine experimentation by crossbreeding Arab and European horses. In 1767 Carlos III gave several to the Austrian empress Maria Theresa, beginning the famous Lipizzaner line of the Vienna Riding School.

Between 1810 and 1812, during the Napoleonic War, Cádiz, defended by a British fleet (now an ally against France), hosted an extraordinary parliament that wrote Spain's first constitution. Six years after the constitution was destroyed by the monarchical restoration of 1814, Colonel Rafael Riego (1785–1823) abandoned a planned campaign against rebellious Latin American colonies to lead the army in a march from Cádiz on Madrid to restore it. During this so-called Triennium (1820–23, literally the "three-year period"), the legislature again briefly met in Cádiz.

Despite the Triennium's failure, Cádiz remained a liberal center, eager to secularize ecclesiastical lands for middle-class ownership. In the regency that followed the king's death, Juan Alvarez Mendizábel (1790–1853), a native of Cádiz, was the premier who facilitated seizure of Church lands in 1837. Later, General Juan Prim y Prats (1814–70), also of Cádiz, overthrew Fernando's daughter, Isabel II, in 1868. Emilio Castelar, one of the more articulate liberals, represented the province in the Cortes.

The middle class, however, grew more conservative when faced with peasant revolt in 1873 and a violent uprising by Jerez vineyard workers in 1893. General Miguel Primo de Rivera y Orbaneja (1870–1930) of Cádiz, leader of a Spanish military dictatorship from 1923 to 1929, expressed this new authoritarianism by condoning peasant illiteracy and high mortality rates as simple facts of life that could never be changed. The peasants responded with murder, church burnings, and membership in the anarcho-syndicalist Confederación Nacional de Trabajo.

Rebelliousness continued during the Second Republic. Despite redistribution of 3,194 hectares by land reform, the massacre of twenty peasants by republican police in the northern provincial hamlet of Casas Viejas in January 1933 discredited Manuel Azaña, architect of the 1931 constitution. Right and left battled one another during the next three years, but General Francisco Franco seized the naval base at Cádiz and the harbor at Algeciras as transport depots for the Spanish Legion of Morocco in the early days of the Spanish Civil War. Radical peasants provided little organized resistance, and the war quickly passed beyond the province.

After 1939, poverty and social unrest did not diminish until the 1960s, when new jobs were provided by the U.S. naval base at Rota, expansion of viticulture, and growth of commercial food processing.

LITERATURE. The literary tradition of Cádiz spreads over many eras. **Abu Abdullah Muhammad Ibn Abbad** (ca. 1371) of Ronda provided Muslim religious writings for the region. During the early Christian era, as the age of exploration began, **Francisco López de Jérez** (1504–39), secretary to Pizzaro and historian of the conquest of Peru, wrote a classic of sixteenth-century travel literature, *Verdadera relación de la conquista del Perú y provincia de Cuzco llamada la Nueva Castilla.*

The Enlightenment poet **José Cadalso y Vázquez** (1741–82) of Cádiz, a satirist and close friend of many Spanish writers, is best known for his amusing *Cartas marruecas* (1793), a satire modeled on the Frenchman Montesquieu's *Persian Letters*, but not published until after Cadalso's death because of his savage criticism of Spanish decadence. He also wrote the romantically gloomy *Noches lúgubres* (1792), the story of a tragic love affair. When the woman of the story dies, her lover misses her so greatly that the plot centers around his efforts to disinter her. Cadalso himself died in battle during the siege of Gibraltar in 1782.

Cádiz grew in importance during the nineteenth century, and literature played a role in its florescence. The romantic writer and revolutionary **Antonio Alcalá Galiano** (1789–1865) was a diplomat for the Cortes of Cádiz who later conspired against Fernando VII and was exiled in 1814 and again in 1823. He began a liberal parliamentary career in 1837 and spent the rest of his life in Madrid as a teacher and writer popularizing English literary and political ideas. Among those he influenced was his nephew, Juan Valera, a well-known Cordoban writer later in the century. **Cecilia Böhl von Faber y Larrea** (1796–1877, pseud. **Fernán Caballero**) wrote sentimental novels about the area such as *La Goviota* (1849), which attracted a large reading audience. This Austrian woman, who had married a Spaniard, was the first modern writer to produce a regional novel, which became a very popular genre later in the century.

Other romantics from the province include **Salvador Bermúdez de Castro y Díez** (1814–83), a poet and diplomat. **Antonio García Gutiérrez** (1813–84) of Chiclana was a playwright friend of Espronceda. **Luis de Eguílaz** (1830–74) of Sanlúcar de Barrameda, a historical novelist and playwright, wrote *La cruz del matrimonio* (1861). **Emilio Castelar** (1832–99), a liberal politician so famous for his rhetorical ability that many of his speeches were later published, occupies a position somewhere between the romantics and later radicals.

Radicalism influenced Padre **Luis Coloma** (1851–1915), whose main work, the novel *Pequeñeces* (1874), makes a vitriolic attack on the landed aristocracy. The poet and playwright **Rafael Alberti** (b. 1902) of Puerto de Santa María, a stylistic rebel, experienced early success by winning the National Prize for Literature in 1925 for *Marinero en tierra*, a surrealistic and nostalgic work exploring his childhood in Cádiz. Alberti, a close friend of Federico García Lorca and also a member of the Generation of 1927, wrote political dramas such as *Fermín Galán* (1931), about a political uprising. His memoir on life during the Second Republic is *El poeta en la calle* (1931–36). He also wrote very surrealistic poetry such as *Sobre los ángeles* (1929), in which angels represent life forces. Close affiliation with communism forced him into Argentine and Italian exile from 1939 to 1976, after which he returned to Spain. *Entre el clavel y la espada* (1941), an elegant celebration of the 1920s and 1930s in Spain, is his best work of this later period.

In recent times, **Mercedes Fórmica** (b. 1918) is a novelist and mystery writer who has dealt with feminism in some of her works. **José Manuel Caballero Bonald** (b. 1926) of Jerez de la Frontera is a leading contemporary poet.

ART. The New Cathedral contains choir stalls attributed to Pedro Duque Cornejo (1678–1757), a statue by Juan Martínez Montañes (1568–1648), a chalice by Benvenuto Cellini (1500–71), and paintings by Alonso Cano (1601–67), **Francisco de Zurbarán** (1598–1664), and Murillo. In the chapel of Santa Catalina, there are paintings by **Bartolomé Esteban Murillo** (1618–82). The church of La Santa Cueva has three paintings by **Francisco de Goya** (1746–1828). The Oratorio de San Felipe Neri contains paintings by Murillo, and the chapel of the Hospital de Nuestra Señora del Carmen has a painting by **El Greco** (1541–1614). The Museo Provincial de Bellas Artes of Cádiz exhibits a major collection of paintings by Francisco de Zurbarán (twenty-two in all), and other works by Murillo, Jusepe de Ribera (1591–1652), Pedro de Campaña (Peter de Kempener, 1503–80?), Cano, Jan van Eyck (1390?–1441), and Rogier van der Weyden (1399?–1464). The most important holding is a Phoenician anthropomorphic sarcophagus unique in its form.

MUSIC. The *bolero* is said to have been invented in Cádiz by **Sebastián Cerezo** (ca. 1780) as a three-part dance by two people. The first and third sections are danced together, with the middle section devoted to complicated solo steps such as the *cuarta*. As in classical ballet, this involves crossing the dancer's feet while in the air. The bolero begins with the *paseo*, a strut of pride and graceful carriage, and concludes in the third section with the *bien parado*, filled with sudden stops and poses.

The composer **Manuel de Falla** (1876–1946) of Cádiz won a prize in Madrid for his first major work, *La vida breve* (1906), and spent the next seven years in Paris, where he became deeply involved in modern music. His later works of importance include *Noches en el jardín española* (1911, Nights in a Spanish Garden), the ballet music *El sombrero de tres picos* (1914–15, The Three-Cornered Hat), and the Ritual Fire Dance for the ballet *El Amor Brujo* (1918–19). He returned to Madrid from 1914 to 1922 and spent 1922 to 1939 in Granada before exiling himself to Argentina. His remains are in the cathedral.

CUSTOMS AND SOCIETY. Jerez de la Frontera is a center for flamenco and *cante jondo*. The Feria de Caballo (horse show) in May and the Fiesta de la Vendima (vintage festival) in September especially bring out the local dress and equestrian character of Jerez. Some of the best horses in the world are exhibited at the fair, and the wine festival goes on for five days of processions, bullfights, livestock shows, flamenco, and sherry drinking. Not surprisingly, this equestrian society has produced a traditional costume still worn on many occasions. Male riders dress in tight trousers decorated on both sides with silver buttons, high boots, a red sash at the waist, and a short jacket sometimes covered with braid. Women wear elaborate lace mantillas over long silk dresses. Their hair is worn up with beautiful combs (sometimes called *tejas*, literally "roof tiles") made of tortoise-shell and many other materials.

On the Guadalquivir River, Sanlúcar de Barrameda celebrates a river festival during the last week of August with decorated boats and river sports. The festival's evenings are filled with some of the best flamenco in Andalusia. Cádiz stages one of Spain's largest and oldest carnivals in February. Troubadours and drum contests are two unique aspects of the carnival. Corpus Christi (usually late May) is also an important event in Cádiz and Zahara de la Sierra.

HISTORIC SITES. The city of **Cádiz** is physically reminiscent of the San Francisco Bay area in California, but is considerably smaller. Both occupy a peninsula between the ocean and an interior bay and possess similar densities of population and sophisticated, lively cultures. Naval bombardments and earthquakes have damaged many of Cádiz's ancient buildings.

The New Cathedral (1838), which replaced a cathedral destroyed earlier, has a nave and two aisles, unusual columns, a dome, and the tomb of Manuel de Falla. Bartolomé Esteban Murillo of Seville died in 1682 while painting its Santa Catalina chapel. Constitutional debates took place in the Oratorio de San Felipe Neri between 1810 and 1812. The church of Nuestra Señora del Carmen has a churrigueresque façade.

Elsewhere in the province, the southernmost point of Spain is **Tarifa**, whose Alcázar (fortress) is the oldest in Spain. On the bay of Algeciras opposite Gibraltar, **Algeciras** is a transportation center for ferries to Ceuta and Tangier in North Africa. The Casa Consistorial housed the Algeciras Conference of 1906, which partitioned Morocco between Spain and France. **Gibraltar** remained a possession of Spain until 1704. The Catholic Cathedral is sixteenth-century Spanish Gothic, reworked from an earlier mosque, while the Franciscan monastery was founded in 1531.

Northeast of Cádiz, **Arcos de la Frontera** contains the church of Santa María de Arbás, which is Romanesque with a plateresque façade. There are a number of gentry town palaces, and the town hall has a local art collection. The architecture is generally Mudéjar. Directly north of Cádiz, **Jerez de la Frontera** is dominated by its main square, the Alameda Fortún de Torres, next to the Alcázar of the eleventh century. The Plaza San Juan possesses two fine buildings, the Palacio de Pemarín and the Fundación Andaluz de Flamenco, the latter full of displays on gypsy culture and music. Another center of special interest is the Real Escuela Andaluza del Arte Ecuestre, a riding school with daily sessions. *Bodegas* (wine bars) of various wine companies are scattered throughout the town and its outskirts.

Also to the north is **Sanlúcar de Barrameda,** on the banks of the Guadalquivir River above the Straits of Gibraltar, thirty kilometers from Cádiz Bay. Treasure ships from the Indies stopped here before going upriver to Seville. Christopher Columbus embarked from Sanlúcar on his third voyage, as did Fernando Magellan (1480–1521) on the first circumnavigation of the world. Magellan died in the Philippine Islands, but his crew finished the voyage and returned to Sanlúcar.

CUISINE. Seafood is a staple and includes *puntillitas* (squid), *cañaillas* (snails), *acedías* (sole), *boquerones* (anchovies), *freidurías* (fish and chips), or *tortillitas de camarones* (shrimp formed into small patties and fried in corn meal). *Jamón al jerez* is ham fried in cornmeal, and *riñones a la jerezana* are kidneys in wine and oil. *Helado de pasas a Viña 25*, an ice cream, contains sherry.

Jerez has produced the famous Spanish sherry since the seventeenth century. Sherry is a blended, aged wine rather than a vintage. To a base of white palomino grapes, smaller amounts of other wines such as muscatel are added. The mixture is aged in oak casks and exposed to oxidation in order for it to mature in a special atmosphere.

The ten types of sherry include *fino* (light, dry, slightly acid, 15 percent alcohol), *manzanilla* (very dry, 15–17 percent alcohol), *amontillado* (yellow, walnut taste, less exposure to atmosphere, 18 percent alcohol), medium (slightly sweeter amontillado), *oloroso* (darkest, most fragrant sherry, 20–25 percent alcohol), *palo cortado* (somewhere between amontillado and oloroso in taste), cream (oloroso with sun-dried pulp added, then strained), pale cream (fino sweetened with wines not fully fermented), and *Pedro Ximénez/muscatel* (very sweet with low alcohol content).

There are many famous brands of sherry, including those of such long-time producers as Pedro Domecq, González Byass, Barbadillo, Duff Gordon, John Harvey, La Riva, Osborne y Cía, and Sandeman. Sherry is the most heavily advertised wine in the world.

CÓRDOBA

VITAL STATISTICS. Pop., 717,213. Area, 13,771 sq. km. Capital and diocesan see: Córdoba. The major geographic feature is the Guadalquivir River and surrounding valley known as La Campiña. The province is bounded by Ciudad Real and Cáceres on the north, Jaén on the east, Seville on the west, and Málaga on the south. Córdoba is very humid and hot in summer, but cool in winter.

ECONOMY. Córdoba produces 13 percent of Spain's olive crop and the fourth-largest cotton crop. Land holdings are third largest in Spain in terms of average size, but among the least improved, dominated by estates over 200 hectares. There are coal mines at Belmez, Peñarroya, and Espiell, while

Rute and Montilla have big distilleries. The valley of La Campiña raises fighting bulls.

HISTORY. (Claudio Marcelo [Roman], but also "across the river" referring to the Guadalquivir Bridge [Spanish]). The original Celtiberian village rose under the Romans as provincial capital of Hispania Ulterior in 152 B.C. but lost out as capital to Seville after creation of the imperial province of Baetica. The bridge over the Guadalquivir River, built ca. A.D. 200 to connect with the Roman road across Andalusia, still stands.

Christianity spread quickly during the later Roman Empire. Zoilus (d. 304) and nineteen others suffered martyrdom by Emperor Diocletian. The Council of Nicea in 325 elevated the archbishop of Córdoba to be primate of all Iberia, but the Visigoths later transferred this title to the archbishop of Toledo. Two other early Christian figures, Prudencio Clemente (ca. 380) and Bishop Hosius, historian of early Christianity, contributed leadership and scholarly insight to the early Church.

After 579, Córdoba fell under the rule of the Vandals, the Suevi, and the Visigoths. Musa Ibn Nusair, an Arab belonging to a tribe from the Yemen in South Arabia, led the Muslim conquest in 712. By the time of Abd ar-Rahman I (756–88), a Syrian noble, Córdoba was made the capital of Muslim Spain under Rahman's Umayyad emirate. Late in its history, the city became capital of a caliphate (empire), which fell in 1031.

The city did not immediately assume a Muslim character; originally less than 4,000 Muslims lived in Córdoba. The Christian population, called Mozarabs (from the Arab word *mustarib*, literally, Christians living under Muslim rule who adopted Arab dress, customs, and language), belonged to the Mozarabic Christian Church, which had only sporadic contact with Rome and thus sometimes adopted heretical Christian doctrines. One of its leaders, Bishop Eulogius (d. 859), reintroduced aspects of Latin culture before suffering martyrdom, but his general acceptance of the Mozarabic rite weakened the authority of the new primate of Toledo and divided the Spanish episcopate.

Córdoba eventually grew into a Muslim city. The construction of the Mezquita, a great mosque begun in 761 by the Syrian Abd ar-Rahman I (785–821) and expanded by Abd ar-Rahman II (822–52), caused the Muslim population to soar. The mosque even possessed a holy relic, the arm of the Prophet Muhammad, making Córdoba a spiritual center almost as important as Mecca. In time, Córdoba was Europe's largest early medieval city, an independent caliphate within the Islamic world. Its population reached 100,000 or more, and the city claimed, perhaps with exaggeration, to have thousands of houses and gardens, 600 mosques, 900 baths, a university, and many public and private libraries by the era of Abd ar-Rahman III (912–61), the first caliph. Its leather processing and textile industries constituted Europe's best, and La Campiña, an extensively irrigated region of the eastern Guadalquivir Valley, far exceeded other European agricultural districts.

The factors that destroyed this magnificent state included unchecked feudal competition, cultural tensions between Berbers and Arabs, and corruption. As the power of Córdoba slipped, Almanzor (al-Mansur billah, or Ibn Abi Amir, "he who is supported by God"), the grand vizier who dominated Abd ar-Rahman III's son, al-Hakam II (961–?), attempted to regain peninsular hegemony by staging annual raids on the Christian north between 985 and 1002, once even bringing the bells of Santiago de Compostela to Córdoba on the backs of Christian captives. In the end, however, his effort to ignite Muslim military zeal backfired by forcing the Christians to unite in the Reconquest of the south.

Two Muslim groups followed the caliphate: Almoravids (1091) and Almohads (1148), both Berber groups from the Maghreb (the western part of the Islamic world, extending from Morocco to Tunisia). Brought in as mercenaries in a futile attempt to preserve Islamic rule, these rural peoples disliked cities and abandoned Córdoba as an imperial center. The shrunken town became a vassal of Alfonso VII of Castile and León in 1148 until liberated in 1236 by Fernando III.

Christian conquest led to neglect or abuse; irrigation systems broke down, and an ill-advised effort to make a Catholic cathedral out of the main mosque defaced the Mezquita. The only early Christian citizen of note was Gonzálo Fernández de Córdoba (1453–1515) of Montilla, "El Gran Capitán," military leader of Fernando and Isabel's Spain who created the most powerful army in sixteenth-century Europe. By 1609, Muslim expulsion from Spain crippled Córdoba's economy and Christian peasants had to be brought from the north to provide a work force. Social conditions became so desperate in 1652 that even this group rebelled against the royal governor (corregidor).

Neglect made Córdoba into a picturesque ruin popular with tourists after romanticism encouraged enthusiasm over antiquarian places, but modern reality essentially held very little romance. The French sacked the city in May 1808, and 60 percent of ecclesiastical property (the Church was the largest landowner) was privatized between 1837 and 1845 without possibility of peasant participation. Carlists from Navarre seized the city briefly in 1836, and the left refashioned Córdoba into a short-lived revolutionary canton during the First Republic in the summer of 1873. These confused circumstances ultimately produced one of the most enigmatic of all Spanish politicians, Alejandro Lerroux García (1864–1949), whose journalistic and political career in Barcelona made him a leader of anti-Catalan forces and later a conservative premier of the Second Republic (1933–35).

Many peasants left the province, but the remainder joined the general strike of 1903 and other anarchist demonstrations of the era. During the Second Republic, violence erupted in September 1931, November 1932, and throughout the first half of 1934. Land reform affected 46.6 percent of all cultivated land in the province. Local republican politicians such as Niceto Alcalá Zamora y Torres (1877–1949), president of the Second Republic from 1931 to 1936, tried to calm political passions through a responsible land redistribution, but he was impeached by the left, leaving local politics in chaos.

The outbreak of the civil war allowed Colonel Ciriaco Cascajo, the military governor, to support Franco openly and execute many republican sympathizers. The International Brigades counterattacked unsuccessfully at Andújar in December 1936, the only sizeable campaign that sought to free the province during the war.

In the postwar period, migration to seek work in the north or in Seville or the Costa del Sol was common. Few persons experienced the success of Manuel Benítez, "El Cordobés" (b. 1936) of Palma del Río, the popular matador of the 1960s and 1970s. Poorly developed farms, a sluggish economy, and a bank collapse with national implications led to new land redistribution efforts in the 1980s.

LITERATURE. There is an ancient intellectual tradition in Córdoba. **Lucius Annaeus Seneca** (2 B.C.–A.D. 65), the Stoic philosopher and author of *De Brevitate vitae*, and his cousin, **Lucian** (A.D. 39–65), came from Roman Córdoba. Seneca took his nine tragedies from Greek drama, but he also wrote philosophy, essays, and poetry as well as being one of Rome's finest orators. Reason, he argued, is the light that guides the individual through life. His Stoic philosophy reflected such a strong sense of honor and ethical moralism that historians see a prefigured Spanish Christianity in Seneca's work. Lucian played a firebrand's role in Roman politics by strongly opposing tyranny and emperor worship. Both died on the orders of Nero.

Another early figure, Bishop **Hosius** (Osio; 265?–358?), is an example of a Christianized Roman who became a church official and participant in the Council of Nicea. His concept of the Christian trinity of Father, Son, and Holy Ghost was crucial in combatting the Arian heresy. Bishop **Eulogius** (d. 859), the last early medieval Christian leader of Córdoba, wrote *Eulogii mementote peccatori* sometime in the ninth century as a work of poetry. His library later passed to the Kingdom of Navarre and helped influence northern Christian culture.

During the Muslim period, **Paulo Alvaro de Córdoba** (800–861?), a Christian writer of possible Jewish origins, defended Christianity against Muslim intellectual attacks. Of greater fame, Abu Muhammad 'Ali ibn Muhammad ibn Sa'ad **Ibn Hazm** (994–1064) of Córdoba rose to become a prime minister during the late Umayyad period. His writings included *The Ring of the Dove*, a work on profane love that spoke quite openly about sex, and *The Book of Religions and Sects*, an attack on several aspects of Muhammadanism. **Ibn Guzmán** (1078?–1160) composed Arab folk songs called *zéjels* that give a personal look into the lives of Arabs in southern Spain of this time. A Jewish poet called **Dunas ibn Labrat** (912–61) composed a new type of Hebrew poetry based on classical Arabic style.

Two brilliant figures particularly dominated the thought of Muslim Córdoba. Moshe ben Maimon, or **Moses Maimonides** (1135–1204) of Córdoba, a Spanish-Hebrew writer of law and philosophy, wrote *Guide for the Perplexed*, an interpretation of Judaism in light of Aristotelian philosophy and a mediation between Judaism and Greek philosophy. Above all, Maimonides believed that science and religion could coexist; he revived the Aristotelian concept of a divinely created and earth-centered universe not rejected until the sixteenth and seventeenth centuries by modern astronomy. Maimonides also abridged the Talmud (sometimes called the Mishneh Torah) for use among the Sephardic Jews of Spain and reawakened their knowledge of ancient Hebrew doctrines, although it also alienated moderates and conservatives who feared alien beliefs and apostasy.

The other major figure was **Averroës** (Ibd Rushd, 1126–98), the Arab translator and interpreter of Aristotle. As Carlos Fuentes has observed, Averroës dared to think of "a double truth," one religiously revealed, the other scientifically found, one of the hallmarks of modern thought. Averroës's Aristotelianism was Neoplatonic in content. Philosophy agrees with religion, and religion recommends philosophy. Religion is true because it is a revelation from God, and philosophy is true because it depends upon the human thought of scholars trained in philosophic reasoning.

During the Renaissance, **Juan de Mena** (1411–56), a Cordoban poet, traveled to Italy to study. He translated works such as the *Iliad* from Latin to Spanish early in the development of the Spanish language. Perhaps his best-known creative work is *Laberinto de fortuna (Las tresicentas)*, an allegorical-historical poem influenced by Dante's *Divine Comedy*. Later, **Francisco Delicado** (1480?–1533?), a former priest expelled from Spain in 1492 as a Jew, who subsequently lived in Italy, wrote *Retrato de la loçana andaluza en lengua española muy claríssa* (1528), a satire about the Renaissance, Rome, and Spain. **Fernán Pérez de Oliva** (1494?–1533) studied and taught humanism at Salamanca and Rome. His influence during the Renaissance came from his major work, *Diálogo de la dignidad del hombre* (1546), a defense of individualism and national culture. He translated a number of classical plays into Spanish and strongly supported the shift from Latin to the vernacular. **Luis Barahona de Soto** (1548–95) of Lucena taught at Alcalá de Henares and reflected new interest in classical and romantic themes in *Las lágrimas de Angelica*, a work based on an Italian poem.

One of the greatest names of the Golden Age, **Luis de Góngora y Argote** (1561–1627), a poet educated at Salamanca, patronized by the duke of Lerma and honorary chaplain to Felipe III, also came from Córdoba. His poems *Polifemo* and *Soledades* (both written in 1613) possessed a Latin style, filled with *culteranismo*, and are still considered a unique early Spanish literary innovation. *Culteranismo*, sometimes called *gongorismo*, can be defined as deliberate use of metaphors, neologisms, and mythological illusions, a poetic vocabulary distinct from ordinary language. Góngora's *Soledades* tells the story of a shipwrecked young man, but the narrative line is less important than the pastoral style of beautiful landscapes and simplicity of rural life. Góngora became a major composer of Castilian ballads while living in Salamanca, Madrid, and Valladolid. Many of his short poems and *romances* charmed the public with their impressionistic style. After his death, Góngora's reputation lapsed into obscurity until the Generation of 1927 rediscovered him.

The nineteenth century witnessed another productive period. Angel de Saavedra, the **duque de Rivas** (1791–1865), a major romantic poet and playwright, wrote *Don Alvaro, o la fuerza del sino* (1835), the period's best romantic drama. It is the story of an elopement that, when discovered, causes Alvaro to kill the father and brother of his love, Leonor, in self-defense. Alvaro then flees to a monastery, where he is attacked again. This time he mortally wounds another of Leonor's brothers, but not before the brother kills Leonor for having dishonored her family. In the end, Alvaro takes his own life. Saavedra's *El desengaño en un sueño* (1844) is a play about Lisardo, a magician's son forced to share his father's isolation. When he complains about wanting to experience real life, his father creates a dream in which Lisardo is visited by all of the major forces in life, who tempt and torment him so much that upon being awakened he is happy to again live in isolation. In 1810, Saavedra helped found the Real Academia de Ciencia, Bellas Artes, y Nobles Artes to promote the arts in Córdoba.

Another nineteenth-century writer, **Juan Valera y Alcalá Galiano** (1824–1905) of Cabra, the nephew of Antonio Alcalá Galiano, established himself with the novel *Pepita Jiménez* (1874), in which a young seminarian's false mysticism disappears after he is seduced by a young widow. Later works of Alcalá Galiano include *Las ilusiones del doctor Faustino* (1875), the retelling of the famous myth in an Andalusian setting with a young nobleman who sells his soul for love; finding that love is not enough, he commits suicide. He also wrote *El Comendador Mendoza* (1877), an adventure set in Latin America and France; *Doña Luz* (1879), in which a priest's love for the heroine, while never consummated, nevertheless influences her life; and *Juanita la larga* (1895), about an old man's love for a young girl. Valera's post-romantic style dealt with Andalusian social issues and the acceleration of cultural decline. Toward the end of his life he went blind.

Among other Spaniards who have written about the province, the twentieth-century agrarian crisis of Córdoba is vividly described by the Valencian **José Más** in *El rebaño hambriento en tierra feraz* (1935).

ART. The painter **Bartolomé Bermejo** (1430?–90?), born in the province, exemplifies the Hispano-Flemish style. **Alejo Fernández** (1475?–1545), a late Gothic painter of Córdoba, did most of his painting in Seville. One of the best artists using Hispano-Flemish style, **Pedro de Córdoba** (ca. 1475), did the great panel of the Annunciation in the cathedral with superb perspective, lighting, and sculptural modeling.

The church of La Campañía has a high altar with statues by Pedro Duque Cornejo, who also did the famous choir stalls in the cathedral. Among the other churches of Córdoba, San Agustín has frescoes by Antonio del Castillo (1603–67); San Pablo contains statues by Cornejo; Santa Marina has paintings by Castillo and other local artists; and the convent of San Francisco displays paintings by Juan de Valdés Leal (1622–90), Alonso Cano (1601–67), and Pedro de Mena y Medrano (1628?–88), Cano's student. A native artist of the later seventeenth century, **Asisclo Antonio Palomino** (1655–1726), became one of the foremost Spanish baroque painters in Salamanca.

The provincial art museum is rich with works of the seventeenth-century Córdoban school by Agustín and Antonio del Castillo and the earlier school of Alejo Fernández and Pedro de Córdoba. There are also works by Murillo, Francisco Pacheco (1564–1654), and Francisco de Goya.

MUSIC. The Italian composer **Giuseppe Verdi** (1814–1901) adopted the duque de Rivas's *Don Alvaro, o la fuerza del sino* as the libretto for his opera *La Forza del Destino*, set at an inn in Hornachuelos, a village nestled against the Sierra Nevada in the southern part of the province.

CUSTOMS AND SOCIETY. Society often shows its rural roots with massive parties at country estates that may include a private bullfight. Traditional dress for women once stressed long black silk dresses. Elaborate mantillas are often still worn, along with a variety of neckerchiefs and shawls. For men, Córdoba invented the tall and wide-brimmed sombrero. The area is also noted for its leather work, and Cordoban shoes and boots are still popular, as are *sajones*, leather aprons worn by workingmen.

The Fiesta de los Patios, held in early May, is a good time to visit the old houses and patios of Córdoba since they are decorated with flowers during this celebration. The Feast Day of Zoilus, an early Christian martyr, is held on June 27.

HISTORIC SITES. The city of **Córdoba** centers around the Mezquita, the Great Mosque, begun in A.D. 761 during the reign of Abd ar-Rahman I. A tall Mudéjar buttressed outer wall encircles the entire complex. Entry is through the Court of Orange Trees (Patio de los Naranjas) and the Gate of Mercy (Puerta del Perdón) to the prayer hall, which is 600 feet long, 430 feet wide, and 38 feet high, with 1,200 columns (only 80 are left) arranged in 38 aisles, linked by red and white horseshoe arches of a striped pattern that is unique. At the end is the Kebla, an area surrounded by incredibly beautiful stucco, arabesques, blind arches, and filigree work with a frieze of script from the Koran at the top of the wall. A horseshoe arch opens into the Mihrâb, a room whose function is to mark the direction to Mecca. The Makkshura (the caliph's room) is beyond.

Unfortunately, these important Muslim ritual rooms are partially separated from the prayer hall by the cathedral of Carlos I, added in the sixteenth century. By taking out hundreds of columns, a Latin cross was inserted in the middle of the Mezquita with a marble altar, churrigueresque choir stall, and baroque pulpits. In technical terms, a transept was erected across the nave of the mosque which, when enclosed, created a small cathedral. This addition did not become locally popular, and even the king allegedly later regretted his order, but the presence of the royal tombs of the Castilian kings Fernando IV and Alfonso XI in the cathedral blocked restoration of the mosque to its original design.

The surrounding neighborhood has narrow streets lined by ancient patio homes, visible through their iron gates. Many patios have fountains and several stories of balconies; all contain a profusion of flowers in the courtyards. There is an archaeological museum on the Plaza don Jerónimo Paéz and a city museum in the Torre de Calahorra, originally a fourteenth-century palace next to the Roman-Moorish bridge on the Guadalquivir River. Between the Mezquita and the Puerta de Almodóvar is a synagogue of the fourteenth century. Much of this area once made up the *judería*, or Jewish quarter.

Elsewhere in the province, six miles west of Córdoba is **Medina Azahara** (also called Medînat az-Zahrâ), royal palace of Abd ar-Rahman III, named for his favorite wife. The original palace, built in 930 and destroyed by the Almoravids in 1010, was enormous; more than 4,000 marble columns once supported the roof, but only the Hall of Viziers has been reconstructed. A short distance away, the monastery of San Jerónimo el Real de Valparaiso has been built from ruins of the castle.

The southern town of **Montilla** witnessed the battle of Munda between Caesar and Pompey in 45 B.C. and is the birthplace of Gonzalo de Córdoba, "El Gran Capitán." **Aguilar** is dominated by the ruins of a large castle. **Lucena** became the place of imprisonment for the last Muslim king of Granada, Boabdil.

CUISINE. Cordoban food includes *cordero mozárabe* (lamb cooked with vinegar and honey) and *pescado mudéjar* (fish with raisins and pine nuts, cooked in local wines). Other unusual dishes are *rabo de toro* (oxtail soup) and partridge.

The Montilla-Moriles wine district (named for the two leading wine towns of the province) produces a sherry-like wine of six varieties (*fino, amontillado, oloroso, palo cortado, Pedro Ximénez, raya*).

GRANADA

VITAL STATISTICS. Pop., 761,734. Area, 12,647 sq. km. Capital: Granada. Diocesan sees: Granada, Guadix. The region lies on the northern slopes of the Sierra Nevada and is well watered by the Río Genil. Granada is surrounded by Jaén on the north, Almería and Málaga on the east and west, and the Mediterranean coast on the south. The eastern region of the province is usually called the Alpujarras district. The University of Granada is the second largest in Andalusia.

ECONOMY. The Vega de Genil area is the largest Spanish sugar beet producer. Granada ranks second in tobacco growing and fourth in cotton. Iron ore production is among the largest in Spain, mercury mining is of some importance, and there are large reserves of lignite. Silk and mineral water bottling are significant manufacturing activities, and dairying from the mountain pastures is the largest in Andalusia.

HISTORY. (Iliberis [Roman], Elvira [Gothic], Albaicín [Arabic]). The statue of *La Dama de Baza*, an earth goddess worshiped for fertility (fifth century B.C., probably of Iberian origin but showing African influences), is a famous relic of Granada's ancient past. Early Iberian people also left burial chambers at Galera that indicate a rich pottery tradition. Visigoths built the town of Elvira, but the desert-dwelling Muslims, particularly attracted to a cool summer climate and verdant landscape, began construction of the Alcazaba castle on the nearby Alhambra hill ca. A.D. 900 and in the process created the village of Albaicín, now Granada's old town. As Córdoba declined, a small Muslim principality created by King Habbus briefly flourished until conquered by the Berbers in 1085. Upon their collapse, an Arab adventurer, Muhammad ibn Yusuf al-Ahmar, founded the Nasrid dynasty of Granada in 1238. By clever use of rugged terrain, payment of bribes, and diplomacy that played off the Christians against each other, the Nasrids remained independent for 250 years as rulers of the last surviving Muslim principality in Spain. To mark the new importance of Granada, the Alhambra Palace (*al-hamra*, the red palace) was built in the early fourteenth century behind the Alcazaba to form a royal city in miniature. It is a celebrated place, "a garden flowing with streams," to paraphrase the Koran's description of paradise.

The Nasrid motto, "And no conqueror but God," inspired courage against considerable odds, but after a high point of Yusuf I's (1333–54) recapture of Gibraltar, the payment of bribes and military expenses consumed the silk and goldsmithing profits of Granada's dependencies, Almería, Motril, and Málaga. Under Muhammad V (1354–91), court plots and conspiracies multiplied each time the Christians defeated the Nasrid army. After Juan II of Castile (1406–54) captured Antequera, Granada lived in growing turmoil, particularly in the 1480s when Isabel of Castile and Fernando of Aragón unified the Christian opposition.

The last Nasrid ruler of Granada, Abu Abd Allah, known to the Christians as Boabdil (1482–92) and to historians as Muhammad XII, ruled under almost continual siege after 1484. Almería surrendered in 1488, Baza in 1489, and the plain of Granada in 1490. When the Muslim position grew untenable, the Treaty of Santafé surrendered Granada to the Christians on January 2, 1492.

Celebration of Granada's fall by Isabel's grant of exploration to Christopher Columbus masked the burning of Arabic books, the beauty of the Alhambra defiled by Carlos I's addition, and fiery conversion sermons of missionaries. When an earlier agreement permitting continuation of Muslim customs expired in 1567, the situation exploded into the revolt of La Alpujarras, led by Abén Humeya and Abén Aboo. The Muslim insurrection killed 90 priests and 1,500 Christians, but don John of Austria retaliated by killing or enslaving 50,000 Muslims and banishing even more. Military masses converted the rest, but in the end the community was expelled from Spain in 1609.

Washington Irving's *Tales of the Alhambra* (1829) rediscovered the area for its romantic, exotic beauty, but the poverty-stricken rural population, 60 percent landless poor peasants (*jornaleros*), did not benefit from liberal land reform. More than 750 properties of above 500 hectares in size passed into private hands. Violence in 1861, 1868, 1873, and later years particularly protested the sale of *vega* lands (very fertile plots) of the irrigated plateau and the dispossession of the peasants. Liberals, made conservative by their land purchases, dominated regional politics. General Ramón María Narváez (1800–1868), a landowner from Loja, actively pursued the secularization of ecclesiastical land; he served seven times as national premier during the mid-nineteenth century and bore considerable responsibility for the era's social crisis.

In the twentieth century, Granada remained a troubled city. Arson, strikes, political fraud, and widespread violence dominated the era of the Second Republic. The city's garrison rebelled in support of Franco in mid-July 1936 at the start of the civil war and managed to hold the city through bloodshed and a reign of terror that included the murder of the famous writer Federico García Lorca. On the other side, republicans murdered the bishop of Guadix. During the war that followed, the province was divided on a north-south line between the republicans and Franco's forces, with the front line running near the city of Granada. Franco controlled everything to the west.

The province remained volatile in the postwar period, with short-lived guerrilla movements in the mountains and violent strikes in the city. Modern economic life has seen the gradual shift from large private estates to more efficient farms, while the surplus agricultural population has taken urban service jobs.

LITERATURE. A Jewish poet born in Granada, **Moses Ben Jacob Ben Ezra** (1055–1138?), and **Recemundus** (ca. 925)—a learned bilingual Christian and bishop of Granada who wrote an Arabic-Christian liturgical calendar—dominated the early period of letters in Granada.

After the Christian conquest, **Diego de Hurtado de Mendoza** (1503–75)

of Granada, last major figure of the famous Mendoza family from Guadalajara, showed a humanist inclination as a historian, poet, and diplomat.
After being barred from the court of Felipe II for a minor indiscretion, he
wrote *La guerra de Granada*, the chief account of Granada's fall in 1492.
His verse shows a strong influence of Italian poetry, and he has been called
the last Renaissance man of Spain. **Francisco Suárez** (1548–1617), son of
a Toledan noble whose father obtained the property of a high-ranking
Muslim lord, attended the University of Salamanca, joined the Jesuit Order,
and taught at Segovia, Valladolid, Alcalá, and Salamanca. His major study,
De Legibus ac de Deo Legislatore (1612), discussed public law from a
legalistic and social-contract view of human society. Another work, *Defen-
sio Fidei* (1614), attacked English absolutism.

Antonio Mira de Amescua (1574?–1644) of Granada, a contemporary
of Lope de Vega, wrote hundreds of plays, few of which have survived or
are still produced. His best-known work is *El esclavo del demonio* (1612),
the story of a man's pact with the devil, which may have influenced one
of the most important later Spanish plays, Tirso's *El burlador de Sevilla*.

Much later, a reawakened interest in literature during the nineteenth
century produced four major writers from Granada. **Francisco Javier de
Burgos** (1778–1849) of Motril became an important neoclassic poet, translator, and editor of *El Imparcial*, one of Madrid's large newspapers.

The second, **Pedro Antonio de Alarcón** (1833–91) of Guadix, a novelist,
journalist, and humorist, is best known for *El Sombrero de Tres Picos*
(1874), set in Guadix. The story, taken from an old ballad, concerns a
miller who enters his home to discover his wife and a naked town official
who, unknown to the miller, had just fallen into the river and was drying
off. The miller, convinced of his wife's infidelity, dresses in the official's
clothes and tries to seduce the official's wife, with disastrous results. The
story is an enduring popular farce later adapted for opera and ballet. Alarcón also wrote *La pródiga* (1882), the epic of a wealthy Andalusian woman
who squanders her fortune, and *El niño de la bola* (1880), the story of a
young man abused by his father's enemy. Seeking revenge, he courts and
wins the man's daughter.

The third, **Francisco Martínez de la Rosa** (1787–1862) of Granada, a
professor and radical deputy to the Cortes in 1813, was imprisoned and
exiled (1814–20) by the Restoration. After he held a cabinet position in
the radical Triennium, he encountered French romantic literature while
again an exile in Paris. Returning to Madrid in 1833, he introduced the
new romanticism into Spanish literature with his popular drama *La con-
juración de Venecia* (1836). The play, set in Venice, concerns a hero who
seeks to lead a revolution, only to be victimized by fate. Martínez's other
major work, *Abén Humeya* (1835), influenced by Victor Hugo, made the
sixteenth-century Muslim revolt of Alpujarras into a swashbuckling adventure.

Last of the nineteenth-century writers from Granada, **Angel Ganivet** (1865–98), a classicist influenced by Miguel de Unamuno to write about contemporary issues, published his *Idearium español* (1897), which defended Spanish culture and called for a renewed national reform effort. During the crisis of the Spanish-American War, emotional depression led to his suicide.

The twentieth century is dominated by **Federico García Lorca** (1898–1936), the well-known dramatist, poet, and leading member of the famous Generation of 1927. García Lorca brought a heightened sense of poetry to the stage in symbolic dramas such as *Boda de sangre* (Blood Wedding, 1933), dealing with the abduction of a bride on her wedding day by a former lover. *Yerma* (1934) is the tragedy of a woman who believed herself to be barren until she learns belatedly that her husband's unwillingness to have children is the true cause. *La casa de Bernarda Alba* (1936) is the story of five sisters kept virginal by a tyrannical mother until one seduces another's sweetheart and then commits suicide. García Lorca's revolutionary impact on Spanish language and ideas can also be seen in *Poeta en Nueva York* (1930), *Poema del cante jondo* (1931), or *Llanto por Ignacio Sánchez Mejías* (1935), which brought popular rhythms, an incredible use of words, and the fulfillment of an Arabic-Andalusian linguistic heritage. His murder by a Franco supporter on August 18 or 19, 1936, came as a chilling shock in the civil war.

Among more recent writers, **Francisco Ayala** (b. 1906) of Granada is a novelist and short-story writer who experienced considerable success with *Cazador en el alba* (1930) until his support of the Republic forced him into exile in Argentina and Puerto Rico. *Los usurpadores* (1949) is a series of dramatic stories taken from Spanish history that try to show the nobility of the people, while *La cabeza del cordero* deals more directly with the civil war. **Luis Rosales Camacho** (b. 1910) of Granada has spent most of his life in Madrid as an editor of *Vértice* and *Cuadernos Hispanoamericanos*. His important collections of poetry include *Abril* (1935), *La casa encedida* (1949), and *Rimas* (1951). His work is religious but also attuned to the sensual pleasure of love, more like Garcilaso than Góngora.

ART. The art history of Granada begins with the anonymous Muslim artisans of the Alhambra and their development of the Nasrid style. Arches and vaults adorned with "stalactites," a form of ornamentation recalling the roofs of limestone caves, are their greatest accomplishment.

The Christian epoch saw the advent of **Pedro Machuca** (1475?–1550), a Toledo-born, Italian-trained painter patronized by Luis Hurtado de Mendoza, the marqués de Mondéjar, who appointed him architect of Carlos I's palace in the Alhambra. Two of his paintings, *Virgin of Souls in Purgatory* and *Deposition*, are in the Prado. Whatever impropriety he caused to the Alhambra, the palace of Carlos is considered a fine piece of Spanish Renaissance architecture due to Machuca's two-tiered concept with rough-cut stone blocks below and finer stone above, divided by pilasters, windows, and porches of gray marble in contrast to the red sandstone used elsewhere.

During the seventeenth century, Granadan-born **Alonso Cano** (1601–67) was the area's leading painter, sculptor, and architect. His passion for beauty created idealized statues of the Virgin that are among the best done in Spain. **Pedro de Mena y Medrano** (1628?–88), Cano's pupil, followed a tradition of extreme naturalism.

The late Gothic cathedral in Granada, begun during the reign of Fernando and Isabel, came from a design by the Toledo architect **Enrique Egas** (1455?–1534?) who had worked with Juan Guas (d. 1495?) at San Juan de los Reyes in Toledo. In 1528, **Diego de Siloé** of Valladolid began the apse and transept using Roman triumphal arches and beautiful ornamental reliefs. His central chapel is 130 feet high and 65 feet wide with Corinthian columns, a carved frieze, and three tiers of windows with round arches that permit an extraordinary amount of light to enter. The royal chapel is furnished from artworks owned by Isabel the Catholic, including a series of illuminated manuscripts and paintings by the Flemish masters Rogier van der Weyden, Hans Memling (1430/40?–94), and Dirk Bouts (1410/20?–75). The forty-seven-panel *Altarpiece of Queen Isabella* is the work of Juan de Flandes (1496?–1519?). There is also a *Pietà* by Fernando Gallego (1440?–1507?).

The Museo Provincial de Bellas Artes in Granada contains sculpture by Jacobo Florentino (d. 1526), Alonso Cano, Pedro de Mena y Mendrano, and Diego de Siloé (1495?–1563); and paintings by Fray Juan Sánchez Cotán (1561–1627), Pedro de Raxis (ca. 1600), Pedro Anastasio Bocanegra (1638–89), Juan Ramírez (ca. 1650), and Juan de Sevilla (1643–95).

MUSIC. "La Caramba," **María Antonia Fernández** (1751–87) of Motril, found fame as an eighteenth-century singer of *tonadillas* (the diminutive of *tonada*, meaning song or tune), often sung in *entreméses*, or short plays. She popularized the *gitanesco* (gypsy-like) style that utilizes Granada's very rich folk music tradition, which includes flamenco, *granadinas, banadinas, peteneras, alegrías, bulerías* (the early source of the *bolero*, the Spanish national dance in ¾ time, accompanied by castanets) and the fandango. The fandango is danced in triple time by two dancers of the opposite sex, accompanied by castanets or tambourine.

In order to utilize these musical traditions, the Spanish composer **Manuel de Falla** (1876–1946) lived for many years near the Paseo de los Cipreses by the Generalife palace. In fact, Granada had attracted classical composers ever since Glinka had visited Granada and Valladolid earlier. The French composers Maurice Ravel (1875–1937), Claude Debussy (1862–1918), and Nikolai Rimsky-Korsakov (1844–1908) were frequent visitors. Inspired by the place, Ravel did *Alborada del Gracioso* (1905), *Rapsodie Español* (1907), the opera *L'Huere espanole* (1911), and the famous *Bolero* (1928), based on a single rhythmic pattern and melody but always increasing in dynamic level. Debussy's *Ibéria* (1901) also had a strong rhythm, while his *Soi-rée dans Granade* is a haunting solo piano piece. Rimsky-Korsakov's *Capriccio Espagnol* likewise captured the essence of southern Spanish music.

CUSTOMS AND SOCIETY. The *tablado flamenco* is rooted in the caves of Sacromonte, near the Albaicín, the old Arab section of Granada. Guitarists provide instrumental music for flamenco songs, which are musical chants called the *cante jondo*, deep and profound songs (García Lorca heard them as a "river of voices") that accompany the dance. Melodies of the *cante jondo* move as a sort of incantation embellished by ornate melodies and an oriental fascination with single notes. Sometimes this takes the form of the *sequiriya gitana*, a gypsy lament that concentrates on a few lines of emotional outburst in ⅜ and ¾ time. It is commonly said in Andalusia that this music is part Oriental, part Gregorian, part Moorish, part Jewish, and best sung by gypsies.

The dances vary from the dignified *alegrías*, the amusing *bulerías*, or the violent *farrucas* where the sensuality of dramatic movement barely represses dancers from lapsing into total passion. *Duene*, or depth of emotion, is the most important quality, like a volcano about to erupt. The male role consists of posturing and heel-and-toe clicking (*zapateado*), while the woman's dance largely is defined by the position of the hands and body. In the *baile grande*, their hand and arm movements resemble classical Hindu dance. Hand claps (*palmadas*) and finger snaps (*pitas*) are also important.

Flamenco has evolved from folk music and dance to the stages of nightclubs and theatres. Performers such as Pastora Imperio, "La Argentina," Vicente Escudero, Carmen Amaya, and "Antonio" have attracted large followings, while in the United States the half-Spanish José Greco (b. 1918) popularized the genre after World War II. Today, Paco de Lucía (b. 1951) has begun to create a fusion between flamenco and other types of music.

Gypsies (*gitanos*) are more common in Granada than elsewhere in Spain, although Madrid and Barcelona also have large populations, and gypsy camps can be found in many places for a short time. The *gitanos*, who originally came from the region of Hindu Kush in northern India, speak a language called Romani or Rom related to Sanskrit, but in Spain they have added Spanish to create the hybrid language Lengua Caló. Most gypsies left India in the Middle Ages and were first recorded being in Barcelona ca. 1447. Spaniards thought them to be Arabs or Egyptians, since they obviously had passed through the Middle East and possessed elements of Arabic culture, particularly in their singing, which became important in flamenco. Persecution of the *gitanos* began in 1492; they became one of the most disliked subgroups in Spanish society, although their culture has somehow survived. They scorn routine or a completely settled life and make their living as horse dealers, coppersmiths, singers, or as fortune-tellers, and by begging.

HISTORIC SITES. The **Alhambra** on Alhambra hill just outside Granada is the dream of the Muslim rulers Yusuf I (1333–54) and Muhammad V (1354–91). Construction of the palace complex used the Torres Bermejas and Alcazaba to provide part of the outward fortifications. The entrance to the Alhambra, with its panoramic views and keyhole arches, is through the Puerta de la Justicia and the Square of Wells. To the east is the palace of Carlos I, and to the north is the Alhambra Palace, royal house of the Nasrid dynasty.

The Alhambra Palace has three main areas, each with separate functions for the royal household: the Mexuar (justice), Diwân (throne room), and Harem (household rooms). All have unique two-dimensional surfaces of stucco arabesques and filigree lines, with texts from the Koran and other Arab proverbs on the walls. Floors and lower walls are covered with original and unique ceramic tiles. Ceilings are treated with massive stalactite domes and honeycombed cupolas. Abstract shapes and forms interact without ever portraying the human form (forbidden by the Koran), and they make surfaces come alive through geometry or natural designs.

The other great feature of the Alhambra is its patios. Of these, the Mexuar, Arrayanes, and Mirtos form the palace's heart, with their arcades leading to rooms deeper in the palace. The Mirtos Patio (the Court of the Myrtles) connects with the Sala de Embajadores, a luxurious room for diplomatic functions. Beyond the Sala is the Court of the Lions, surrounded by magnificent arcades in front of the harem. Here there are several pavilions and the Sala de los Reyes with a number of domed alcoves and honeycombed ceilings.

On the outer wall, twelve towers encircle the palace. Some can be climbed from inside; the Torre de las Infantas has a good view of the surrounding valley and city. At the end of the palace are underground baths for ritual bathing. The last patio of Reja enters the Jardín de Daraxa and is filled with cypresses and orange trees.

Outside the Alhambra, the Palacio del Generalife (the architect's garden) is a real summer palace. The approach from the Avenue of Cypresses to the Patio de la Acequia (Court of the Water Channel) through the main garden's sunken flower beds produces, when the plants grow level with the path, the illusion of walking on a floral carpet. The Hall of Kings is at the end of this patio, with balconies and a superb view. The park extends up the hill beyond the Generalife.

The palace of Carlos I is east of the Square of the Cisterns just before the main section of the Alhambra Palace itself. This unfinished structure has a long, plain façade and a pillared inner courtyard, a two-story rotunda in the lower gallery, and an upper gallery that provides space for the Museo Provincial de Bellas Artes.

The city of **Granada** centers on the cathedral of Santa María de la Encarnación, begun in 1523 as a memorial to the victory of Christian Spain and the first Renaissance church in Spain. Much of the design is by the energetic Diego de Siloé, but Alonso Cano and **José de Granados** (ca. 1570) made later additions. With double aisles and a transept, the cathedral is 390 feet long and 225 feet wide, with a Capilla Mayor 158 feet high. One of the best features of the building is its Flemish windows. Gilded statues of the twelve Apostles and huge statues of Adam and Eve dominate the interior, but the Capilla Real, or royal chapel, is the chief attraction. Inside it are the tombs of Fernando and Isabel, along with those of their daughter, Juana the Mad, and her husband, Philip the Fair (through whom Carlos I inherited a large share of the Hapsburg Empire). The royal chapel is made of Carrara marble, and dozens of paintings hang on the altar walls.

Granada has many other churches. Santo Domingo (on the plaza of the same name) owes its founding to the Catholic Kings, as did San Jerónimo, designed by Diego de Siloé. Isabel also endowed the convent of Santa Isabel la Real.

Arab architecture dominates the convent of Santa Catalina de Zafra, originally a Muslim palace. The Alcaicería is a copy of an old Arab silk bazaar. The Alcázar Genil belonged to the mother of the last Muslim king of Granada, Boabdil. The Arab baths in the city have been restored, and the Casa del Carbón is an Arab *caravanserai*, or hostel, one of the few of its type preserved in Spain. The Casa del Chapiz originated as an Arab country house, the Casa de los Girones, a thirteenth-century Muslim palace, while the Casa de los Tiros is a sixteenth-century Mudéjar house. The Albaicín district of Granada is the former old Arab quarter with narrow, winding streets, small shops, and flamenco clubs.

Elsewhere in the province, just west of Granada, **Santafé** became the headquarters of Fernando and Isabel just prior to the capture of Granada. East of Granada, *pueblos blancos* (whitewashed villages) are very common. To the south, on the Mediterranean coast, **Almuñécar** contains Carthaginian and Roman ruins, including an aqueduct. **Motril** has the church of La Encarnación and ruins of a palace originally built for Boabdil. Northeast of Granada, **Guadix** is well known as the setting for Alarcón's *El Sombrero de Tres Picos*.

CUISINE. The cuisine of Granada features Muslim dishes such as *sopa de almendras* (an exotic almond soup), *olla* (meat and vegetable stew), gazpacho (cold tomato and vinegar soup), and *menudo* (liquid stew made of the internal organs of chickens, sheep, or cows). Desserts include *suspiros de moro* (meringue) and *Tocino de cielo* (a flanlike concoction).

Almost every traveler to Spain comes away with an appreciation of gazpacho. Served ice cold, it is a soup of cucumber, tomatoes, and peppers chopped up in vinegar and oil, sometimes with bread for dipping (for a recipe, see Seville section). Given the high summer temperatures of this region, it is the perfect food for a hot climate.

HUELVA

VITAL STATISTICS. Pop., 414,492. Area, 10,128 sq. km. Capital and diocesan see: Huelva. The province is located west of the Guadalquivir River along its swampy estuary. Portugal lies to the west, the Mediterranean to the south, Extremadura to the north, and Seville to the east. The Coto Doñana National Park is a wildlife preserve on the eastern edge of the province and the biggest area without roads in Europe, created by the estuary of the Río Tinto and the Odiel.

ECONOMY. Huelva is the oldest mining region in Spain. Nationally, of the eight largest mines, six are in Huelva: Cerro Colorado, Sotiel, La Zarza, Tharsis, Filon Sur, and Transacción. Copper has been mined and refined in the province since Roman times, and in 1987 production reached 66,000 tons. Zinc is the second most important mineral, with the Río Tinto mine, once operated by an English company but currently owned by Kuwait (although now in receivership), its most important source. The Río Tinto mine also produces copper, while the Cala mine produces iron pyrite and silver (one of the four silver mines in Spain).

Strawberries are a relatively new horticultural product. While the soil is not rich, the climate is very mild and field improvements have been made wherever possible. Cork production is second largest in Spain. The port of Huelva services part of the Spanish fishing fleet of the South Atlantic, and fish farming is done in coastal waters.

HISTORY. (Area, Niebla, city, Ilipula [Roman], Elepa [Visigothic]). The acropolis at Azaila, decorated with bull heads and astral signs, is typical of the area's many Megalithic and Neolithic remains. Minerals attracted Phoenicians very early, and the oldest known mine, Dolmen del Zancarrón de Soto, dates back 3,000 years. Copper deposits at Río Tinto were exploited for the casting of bronze, which is made by mixing copper with tin. The tin was brought from Cornwall by the Carthaginians and Romans.

Romans allocated mining districts to *publicani* (entrepreneurs) on a private basis. Water wheels controlled drainage, and ore was brought to the surface in pitch-lined baskets made of tough *esparto* grass. Smelting furnaces fueled by charcoal and fanned by huge bellows operated near the mines.

During Visigothic times, lack of technical expertise caused most of the mines to be abandoned by ca. A.D. 500. Muslim artisans of Almería considered Huelva's copper inferior and used the mines of Córdoba and Toledo. Huelva became an independent Muslim principality in 1023, part of Seville in 1051, Almohad in 1150, and Christian after Alfonso X of Castile's conquest in 1261.

To secure the area, the Christian reconquest established great noble estates of Juan Mata de Lara or Alonso Ménendez de Guzmán. In the late fifteenth century, naval activity grew more important. To obtain Castilian backing for his Atlantic voyage, Columbus solicited the aid of the Franciscan monastery of La Rábida through its prior, Juan Pérez de Marchena. Palos de la Frontera, the small harbor closest to La Rábida, was Columbus's last European landfall on August 3, 1492. Ninety men from the town, including Juan de la Cosa, Martín Alonso Pinzón, and Vicente Yáñez Pinzon, captains of the *Santa María*, *Pinta*, and *Niña*, provided the personnel for Columbus's first voyage.

During the Latin American colonial period, the New World's mineral wealth diminished the importance of Huelva's own mines. National self-sufficiency was not considered until the new Bourbon dynasty ordered Swedish engineers to reexplore the Río Tinto area in 1725. The revival, never completely successful, ceased altogether in 1809–12 when France used the province as a base for attacks against Cádiz. In the wake of the War of Independence, however, loss of the American mineral resources led to an 1825 royal decree encouraging domestic mining. New techniques uncovered great amounts of high-grade copper at the Río Tinto mine in 1837, and its purchase by an English company in 1873 eventually made Río Tinto Europe's largest open-pit mine.

By the early twentieth century, serious labor problems brought violence, which limited production. During the general strike of 1919–20, miners evacuated their families to protect them from violence and to publicize the strike. Strikes occurred again early in the Second Republic, and in 1934 four workers died when police opened fire on strikers. The province of Huelva developed a reputation as a radical area, but deep divisions between socialist and anarchist militants and rapid transfer of nationalist troops from Morocco to Cádiz and Huelva at the start of the civil war kept the province from becoming a major theatre of operations. The mines henceforth ran under military discipline, with all strikes or political activity prohibited.

Later in the Franco era, government capital modernized mining operations in the development plan of 1966, but the effort coincided with a downturn of basic metal prices and proved somewhat unsuccessful. Privatization began in 1976, but manipulation of Kuwait's investment in the area has become a scandal in the 1990s.

LITERATURE. The poet **Juan Ramón Jiménez** (1881–1958) of Moguer on the Río Tinto won the 1956 Nobel Prize for Literature. Jiménez founded and edited literary magazines, translated many foreign works, and taught at the Residencia de Estudiantes for exceptional students in Madrid, where he influenced later members of the Generation of 1927. His poetry included the modernist *Nifeas* (1900), *Rimas* (1902), *Pastorales* (1905), or his *poesía desnuda* phase of a more basic style as in *Piedra y cielo* (1919), *Belleza*, and *Poesía* (both 1923). Jiménez's prose poem *Platero y yo* (1914 and 1917), his best-known work, deals with everyday life in Moguer by presenting a timeless picture of life in a small, southern Spanish village.

Jiménez and his wife (who had been educated in the United States) later traveled widely, and travel essays became one of his most delightful outlets. With the coming of the civil war, they left for the United States and lived for a time in Cuba before settling in Puerto Rico for the remainder of their lives.

Another novel written about Huelva, *La rosa de los vientos* (1916) by **Concha Espina de la Serna,** of Santander, is a thinly fictionalized account of hardships suffered by workers at the Río Tinto mine in a strike against a British company.

CUSTOMS AND SOCIETY. The outstanding event is the gypsy Romería del Rocio, held on Whitsunday (fiftieth day after Easter, marking the descent of the Holy Ghost), usually in May. The pilgrimage worships at *Nuestra Señora del Rocio* (Our Lady of the Dew), a statue of the Virgin claimed to have been hidden away from the Muslims and found later near Almonte in the woods at the edge of the swamp. Legend recounts that efforts to move the statue stopped when the Virgin commanded the people to return it to the woods and build a hermitage. The Romería attracts nearly a million worshippers, some of whom come in highly decorated carts pulled by oxen. People make the pilgrimage from all over southern Spain.

Women's clothing in Huelva traditionally has been very elaborate. Linen brocade vests or jackets of a floral design, cut short, were worn over velvet bodices. Silk or velvet skirts trimmed with gold or silver braid were also worn with this costume, set off by dramatic mantillas.

HISTORIC SITES. The city of **Huelva** is small and poor. Two attractions are a seventeenth-century cathedral and an archaeological museum. Elsewhere in the province, **Niebla,** east of Huelva, has kept its ancient walls and towers. The south coast town of **Palos de la Frontera,** last landfall of Christopher Columbus on his first voyage to the Americas in August 1492, has made La Rábida Monastery into a major tourist site. It has an interesting museum about Columbus, the "Cradle of America" room in which Columbus first presented his plans to Fray Marchena, and the *Virgen de la Rábida,* to whom the crew prayed before their departure.

CUISINE. Seafood is widely served. Wine comes from the Condado de Huelva district, a white-wine area that also produces brandy.

JAÉN

VITAL STATISTICS. Pop., 627,598. Area, 13,496 sq. km. Capital and diocesan see: Jaén. The province, 140 miles south of Madrid, includes the Sierras de Alta Coloma and Pandera. Jaén is bordered by Ciudad Real and

Albacete (New Castile) on the north, Albacete and Murcia on the east, Granada on the south, and Córdoba on the west. The recently created Cazorla Nature Reserve is in the Sierra de la Pandera.

ECONOMY. Jaén, a large olive-growing region, produces approximately 15 percent of the world's olive oil, approximately 275,000 tons a year. While many brands are owned by Italian firms, Goya, L'Estornell, and Carbonell are Spanish-owned marketers of olive oil. Unioliva, a 1,200 member producer cooperative of Jaén, also exports to the United States. Another crop used for cooking oil, sunflower seeds, is raised in Jaén as well. Linares is the center of a lead- and silver-mining area and has a factory assembling Suzuki Land Rovers.

HISTORY. (Auringis [Carthaginian], Jayyan [Arabic]). Carthaginians mined silver in the area, but Romans invested in olive cultivation and made the area the largest olive-oil center of the ancient Mediterranean world. This industry declined under the Vandals and Visigoths except at Baeza (Vivatia [Roman]), close to the Guadalquivir River, an important agricultural center and bishop's see of the Visigothic Christian church. Later, the Muslims nearly abandoned Baeza in favor of Jaén, the site of an important *caravanserai* on the route that led from the interior. Baeza fell to Christian knights in 1246 and soon prospered again as a grain market and university town.

Northern areas of Jaén province remained the further limits of the Reconquest until the battle of Las Navas de Tolosa. This victory by Alfonso VIII of Castile came in 1212 when he surprised the Almohad caliph, al-Nasir Miramolín, and inflicted huge casualties on his army, allegedly with the aid of information from a mysterious shepherd that Spaniards took as a sign of divine intervention. Jaén fell under the administration of the Orders of Calatrava and Santiago and the see of Toledo until Granada's fall, when the Castilian monarch distributed land to the Church and many nobles, including the condes de Benavente in Baeza and the condes de Guadiana, marqués de Dávalos, and marqués de Mancera in Ubeda. Life remained feudal for more than four centuries.

Absentee landownership by the Church, however, ultimately harmed the economy by leaving large tracts of land unused or badly farmed. Carlos III sponsored recolonization of the Sierra Morena region in 1767 by founding La Carolina as a model community. As a prototype for other experiments in Galicia and Murcia, foreign and northern Spanish peasants resettled the area from Despeñaperros to Bailén on Jesuit lands seized when the order was expelled from Spain in 1767.

The beneficiaries of this distribution formed the patriotic Spanish army at the battle of Bailén that routed the French units of General Dupont in the War of Independence's early major battle, but civil disentailment and abolition of mortmain (restrictions on the sale of Church lands) embittered social relations later in the nineteenth century. Cholera and famine swept the province in 1859 and 1881–82, and poverty was always a problem. The Carlist invasion of 1836–37 won sympathy and support, but by 1873 local anarchist movements provided a more common form of primitive rebellion. In 1919–20, agricultural unions influenced by the Russian Revolution engaged in bitter social warfare and later made strong land reform demands on the Second Republic. Violence and confusion over land titles permitted only 955 hectares to be redistributed by December 1933, but in the spring of 1936, after the Popular Front election reestablished the left in control of the Second Republic, 8,271 hectares were illegally occupied. The peasants, heavily loyalist during the civil war, lost the southwestern corner of the province to the rebels after the fall of Málaga.

Reprisals followed Franco's final triumph in 1939, and the area remained under control of large military and Civil Guard garrisons for some time. In recent decades, the formation of cooperatives has eased the land crisis somewhat and foreign capital investment has improved agricultural prospects.

LITERATURE. Three writers stand out. **Bernabé Cobo** (1580–1657) of Lopera joined the Jesuit Order and explored the New World, writing one of the best colonial histories of the seventeenth century, *Historia del Nuevo Mundo* (1651). **Francisco Martínez Ortas** (b. 1919), a republican soldier in the civil war, has written several novels of the war such as *Fifty Céntimos* (translated into English) and the autobiographical *Bajo dos banderas*. Of recent note, **Antonio Muñoz Molina** (b. 1956) of Ubeda, university trained in Madrid, has written *Beatus Ille* (1986), *La Córdoba de los Omeyas* (1990), and the libretto for José Garcia Román's opera *El bosque de Diana* (1990).

Among nonnative writers, **Antonio Machado y Ruiz** of Seville taught French in Baeza at the start of the twentieth century and used the province as the setting for several of his works.

ART. The cathedral in Jaén contains a retablo of San Pedro de Osma by Pedro Machuca of Granada, a large candelabra by **Bartolomé de Jaén** (ca. 1560), sculpture by Jacobo Florentino, and paintings by Jusepe de Ribera of Valencia and Juan Martínez Montañes. The church of Santa Magdalena in Jaén possesses a beautiful altar and paintings by José de Mora (1642–1724), Machuca, and Mateo Medína (ca. 1650). In Andújar, the church has paintings by El Greco and Francisco Pacheco (1564–1654).

MUSIC. The self-taught virtuoso **Andrés Segovia** (1893–1987) of Linares gained recognition as the best-known Spanish guitarist of the twentieth century. He attained master status by reintroducing the guitar as a concert instrument, for which he commissioned guitar works by Joaquín Rodrigo of Valencia and other composers. Segovia left Spain after the civil war and lived in southern France and Puerto Rico for the rest of his long life, frequently making tours as the world's most popular classical guitarist during the postwar period.

CUSTOMS AND SOCIETY. Flamenco is almost as important in Jaén as in Granada. One local variant is the *farruca*, danced by males with rhythmic stamping with the heels (*taconeo*) and ending with a *caida*, or fall. The tango is a dance for women in Andalusia, revolving around the *vuelta quebrada* (a broken turn). Women also dance *alegrías*, often wearing a long fancy red dress and using a rhythmic counterpoint of finger snapping and hand clapping.

The *saeta* (literally, an arrow) is a type of expression popular in Jaén. First used by the Franciscans to point out sinners and give moral advice, it is short, designed to express religious contrition through chanted sayings or short songs directed to the Virgin Mary.

The traditional dress worn to dances and fancy occasions was colorful. Men wore tight-fitting knee breeches with silver buttons down the sides, white linen shirts, black waistcoats with silver filigree buttons, and a red woolen sash. Women wore as many as seven petticoats of striped cotton, the top one of particularly colorful design. An apron of striped sateen or bright silk, a silk kerchief, a light shawl, and a mantilla completed the costume.

Shepherds contrasted vividly with genteel society by wearing cloth trousers which in winter were covered with sheepskins and a handsomely worked leather pouch. Rough woolen shirts and leather jackets dyed a russet color completed their wardrobe.

HISTORIC SITES. High above the cliffs to the west of the city of **Jaén** is Santa Catalina Castle, a fortress now converted into a national parador. The cathedral, designed by Andrés Vandelvira (ca. 1525) in early Renaissance style with two towers and a dome, looms over the city. Like so many churches in southern Spain, it occupies the site of an old mosque and has elaborate chapels, appointments, accompanying buildings, and a relic—the scarf of Veronica (claimed to have been used to wipe the face of Christ during crucifixion). Dozens of other churches dot this hilly town, the oldest being Santa Magdalena. Many buildings have Muslim details, and Jaén itself, with its narrow streets, seems genuinely Middle Eastern.

Elsewhere in the province, to the northwest, **Andújar** contains not only the church of Santa María la Mayor, with its Muslim clock tower, but also a Roman bridge across the Guadalquivir River. To the northeast, **Baeza** is a sixteenth- and seventeenth-century town attractive for the Plaza de los Leones, a square surrounded by Renaissance buildings, as well as the Plaza Santa María near the Gothic cathedral of Santa María and the large Palacio Jabalquinto. **Ubeda** has equally good architecture. Sacra Capilla del Salvador is a beautiful chapel built with the aid of Francisco de los Cobos (an advisor to Carlos I) and lavishly designed by Diego de Siloé. The church of San Pablo has a handsome Gothic façade, and the town palaces of Cobos, Dávalos, and Guadiana are very lavish.

Further north, **Linares** is a mining town whose museum has many Phoenician and Carthaginian artifacts, unusual for being so far inland. Near the village of **Bailén** is the battlefield where the Spaniards defeated the French in 1808 at the start of the War of Independence. On the Guadalquivir River, the castle at **Baños de la Encina** (912–61) is made from a handsome pebble and mortar mixture.

CUISINE. *Pipirrana jaenera* is a salad of tomato, peppers, onion, tuna, and hard-boiled eggs in a vinegar and olive-oil dressing. A small part of the Montilla-Moriles wine district is in Jaén.

MÁLAGA

VITAL STATISTICS. Pop., 1,036,261. Area, 7,306 sq. km. Capital and diocesan see: Málaga. The province borders the Mediterranean on the south, Granada and Cádiz on the east and west, and Córdoba and Seville on the north.

Málaga is fast growing, having experienced a 12.2 percent increase of population in the last two decades. More than 70 percent of the population lives in the coastal area with its wonderful Mediterranean climate. Málaga Bay is one of the three most significant on the southern coast. In recent decades, the subtropical western coast has become a tourist mecca. The University of Málaga is third largest in Andalusia.

ECONOMY. Málaga has achieved recent economic diversity. New technology for growing covered crops produces a year-round agriculture. The coastal *vega* is very fertile and raises raisin grapes, figs, bananas, sugarcane, and cotton. Muscatel wine (Pedro Ximenes, Dulce, Lágrimas) may be the most valuable agricultural product. Málaga also has a moderate-sized fishing fleet. Cattle grazing is facilitated by the continued existence of common lands still owned by municipalities in the mountains, although land reform to break up some of the larger tracts began in 1990. Manufacturing is dominated by cotton-spinning mills owned by international companies such as Benetton. Food canning is another large employer, followed by distilling, cigarette companies, and manufacture of telephone components by Siemens and Fujitsu. The province has risen in per capita income, but still ranks only thirty-fourth among the fifty provinces.

HISTORY. (Malac, the word for salt [Phoenician]). The ancient seaport originated as a Phoenician colony to produce salt fish. Carthaginian, Roman, Visigothic, and Byzantine settlements later thrived from production of wheat, wine, and olive oil. The second most important town, Ronda, almost as old as Málaga, is located on a cliff top of the Serranía de Ronda, next to the Gorge of Guadalevina, a natural defensive position Romans and Muslims used to protect the military base that dominated the region.

Tariq, a Muslim adventurer, seized Málaga in A.D. 711 and Ronda two years later. After Muslims poured into the peninsula, the towns belonged to Córdoba in the eighth century and Granada in the eleventh, with Málaga serving as Granada's chief port and commercial center. When Ronda fell to the troops of Fernando and Isabel in 1485, Málaga fell two years later, and its entire population of 15,000 was enslaved and sold. Under Castilian dominance, its harbor was used for attacks on Mers-el-Kebir in 1505 and Orán in 1509. Later in the century, the Hapsburg dynasty invested in iron-forging facilities to attract Christian settlers, but financial difficulties finally ruined the industry.

When Gibraltar was lost in the early eighteenth century, Málaga's fear of English economic competition influenced José Gálvez Gallardo, the marqués de Sonora (1720–87), originally of a poor noble family from the village of Macharavialla near Málaga, to advocate economic reform. He rose to become an early reforming minister who is chiefly remembered for weakening Seville's monopoly on colonial trade. Málaga's commerce with Latin America, which had begun decades before, was formally recognized in 1778. The iron industry reestablished itself, and Málaga's mercantile middle class soon became second only to that of Cádiz.

These burghers, connected by trade with Germany and Britain, developed a taste for independence during the French Wars and sympathized with liberalism during the mid-nineteenth century. Peasants resisted private land sales with violence in 1836, 1841, 1857, and 1861. The canton of Málaga became one of the two most radical city-states of 1873 during the First Republic.

After the Bourbon Restoration calmed national politics in 1876, a *malagueño*, Antonio Cánovas del Castillo (1828–97), dominated national politics for a quarter century. His political system of *caciquismo* minimized liberal party ideological conflict to avoid strengthening the left. Political bosses silenced criticism, rigged elections, and corrupted public administration, while the two liberal parties cooperated in slipping in and out of power as circumstances dictated without ever investigating the scandals that had discredited their predecessors. The assassination of Cánovas by an anarchist on August 8, 1897, came on the eve of the Spanish-American War, a calamity many critics blamed in part on his policies and conduct.

The left's growth became inevitable after the Spanish-American War in 1898. Málaga, one of the six poorest provinces in terms of peasant income and the worst in terms of land scarcity, provided many members of the anarchosyndicalist Confederación Nacional del Trabajo. The reformist policies of the Second Republic did not go far enough for these leftists, but when the right won the elections of November 1933, massive strikes opposed the conservative cabinet of Alejandro Lerroux in 1934. Málaga remained loyal to the Republic at the civil war's start when the city faced heavy forces of Franco based in the provinces of Cádiz and Seville. Republican lines held until the collapse of western Granada in mid-January 1937, which allowed Franco's army to swing southward and enter the city on February 6. Its loss created disunity among the republicans and led to the collapse of Francisco Largo Caballero's Popular Front cabinet in May 1937.

During the Franco era, the province remade itself into a prominent part of Spain's "sun belt." Tourism rose as a focal point of economic development, creating resort complexes such as Torremolinas on the Costa del Sol, which improved Málaga's economy and attracted tourists, retirees, and jobs.

LITERATURE. The earliest contributor to the province's culture, a Jewish poet and philosopher of Muhammadanism, Solomon Ben Judah Ibn Gabirol, better known as **Avicebron** (1021?–57) of Málaga, taught the philosophy of Neoplatonism and composite theology in Zaragoza and traveled extensively through the Middle East. His fame came from *Fons vitae*, a major philosophic work that reestablished Neoplatonic traditions in philosophic discourse.

The major Golden Age figure of the province is **Vicente Espinel** (1550–1624), author of the picaresque novel *Vida del Escudearo Marcos de Obregón* (1618), a happy work filled with discussions of music that is generally ranked as one of the best picaresque stories. But a long period of quiet followed until the nineteenth century, when **Serafín Estébanez Calderón** (1799–1867), a conservative state councilor and senator of considerable local power, also pursued a career as a regional *costumbrista* writer. His chief work, *Escenas andaluzas* (1847), celebrated rural Andalusian values of bucolic paternalism and a noble peasantry. This conservatism influenced Juan Valera of Córdoba and Estébanez's own nephew, Antonio Cánovas del Castillo, who, like his uncle, became a politician and writer of histories such as *Estudios del reinado de Felipe IV* (1868) and *Historia de la decadencia de España desde Felipe II hasta Carlos II* (2nd ed., 1910).

The real heir of Estébanez Calderón, however, may have been **Ricardo León** (1877–1943). As a novelist enamored with the old and traditional, he wrote *Casta de hidalgos* (1908), attacking the ideas of change and modernization popular in early twentieth-century Spain and telling the story of a man so restless that he continually seeks new beginnings without ever finding true happiness. His other works such as *Alcalá de los Zegríes* (1909), *El amor de los amores* (1910), and *Los centauros* (1912) continued to explore traditional Catholic moral values.

The radical tradition of Málaga centered around **Francisco Giner de los Ríos** (1839–1915) of Ronda, a follower of Julián Sanz del Río of Soria. Giner helped to popularize *krausismo*, a doctrine of philosophic modernism, to promote adult education and other notions of popular pedagogy. He lost his professorship during the Bourbon Restoration, fired by Cánovas, but in 1878 he founded the Institución Libre de Enseñanza as the premier private school of Madrid, causing Miguel de Unamuno to call him the Spanish Socrates. His works include *Estudios literarios* (1866), *Bases para el teoría de la propiedad* (1867), *Prolegómenos del Derecho. Principios del derecho natural* (1874), *Lecciones sumarias de Psicología* (1874), and other education studies.

Twentieth-century writers of the province include **José Moreno Villa** (1887–1945), a poet of modernism; **Manuel Altolaguirre** (1905–59), a Góngora-inspired poet and republican exile; and **José Luis Cano** (b. 1912) of Algeciras, who lived in Málaga and wrote extensively about the city and its culture in the review *Litoral*. **Emilio Pardos** (1899–1962), founder and publisher of this journal, also wrote many volumes of poetry about the area.

ART. One of the twentieth century's greatest artists, **Pablo Picasso** (actually Ruiz y Picasso), was born in Málaga in 1881 and spent his first decade of childhood at 15 Plaza de la Merced. Even at this young age, Picasso produced *Toreador on Horseback* and a series of drawings of pigeons good enough to be shown. They are now displayed at the Picasso Museum in Barcelona.

Picasso's family moved from Málaga in 1891 when Pablo's father, José Ruiz Blasco, took a job as an art teacher in La Coruña. After a few years in Galicia, he moved again to teach art in Barcelona, where Pablo Picasso spent his adolescence and began painting professionally. After 1900, he became a full-time resident of France, with Paris and then later the south of France as his home. Picasso's career spanned major involvement in cubism, neoclassic realism, dadaism, and surrealism.

The Museo de Bellas Artes is a national collection of Spanish paintings with a collection of early Picassos, including *Two Old People*, done in La Coruña, ca. 1893. Works of his father, José Ruiz Blasco, and his colleagues, Antonio Muñoz Degrain and Bernardo Ferrandiz, are also displayed, as well as paintings by Alonso Cano, Ribera, Murillo, Luis de Morales (1510?–86), and Zurbarán.

The Málaga Cathedral has a painting by Cano, a crucifix by Montañes, and sculpture by **Pedro de Mena**, who lived most of his life in Málaga.

MUSIC. The adventurer, sailor, novelist, priest, and choirmaster **Vicente Espinel** of Ronda popularized the five-string Spanish guitar, or *guitarra española*. He also developed the *décima*, sometimes called the *espinela*, a dulcimer type of stringed instrument.

CUSTOMS AND SOCIETY. Flamenco, as played in the province, has produced the *malagueña, rondeña*, and fandango, or *fandanguillo*, fiery southern dances that come from Arab songs (*cartageneras*) and early Spanish folk songs. Their common characteristics are bursts of movement and music.

Ronda's unique fame is as the birthplace of modern Spanish bullfighting. The term *estilo rondeño* is used to describe modern contests that are popularly called *corridas*, or "the running of the bulls." The word "bullfight" is not applicable since it is not a sport so much as a spectacle; the *fiesta brava* is its most accurate name. Legend says that during the late eighteenth century a local noble fell while fighting the bulls from horseback, an old tradition that dated back to the Roman era. Several men saved him in such an exciting fashion that fighting bulls on foot became much more popular.

In a modern *corrida*, the bull is first weakened by a mounted picador, who jabs his pic into the lump of muscle in the bull's neck called the *morillo*. On foot, *banderilleros* then place longer pics in the bull's neck. Both are essential if a matador is to slow the bull so that he can move the animal successfully with his *muleta*, or scarlet wool cape, behind which he hides his sword, used to end the display.

The *fiesta brava* reached the peak of its popularity after World War I. José Gómez Ortega, "Joselito" (d. 1920), Juan Belmonte (1892–1962), and Manuel Rodríguez, "Manolete" (d. 1947), attracted the attention of such writers as Ernest Hemingway. During this period, *mano a mano* (hand-to-hand) contests were extremely popular, in which two (rather than the usual three) matadors vied to outdo one another in skill and daring.

HISTORIC SITES. The cathedral of **Málaga** dates from 1528 to 1783, but one of its towers remains uncompleted. A marble stairway leads to the west façade. The interior, 392 feet long by 160 feet high, is ornate and highly decorated with five adjoining chapels. Near the cathedral is the Museo de Bellas Artes. The Alcazaba, an Arab castle, now contains the provincial archaeology museum, with one of the largest and most interesting collections outside Madrid. Close by is a Roman theatre and the Castillo de Gibralfaro, a Muslim relic whose name means "castle of the lighthouse." It is now a mosque of handsome Middle Eastern construction.

Elsewhere in the province, to the north, **Antequera** has an interesting local museum with a large archaeology section based on underground burial galleries of the surrounding area. Not far away are ruins of a Muslim Alcázar, once the residence of Gonzalo de Córdoba, "El Gran Capitán."

Almost directly west of Málaga, in the mountains, is **Ronda**, a dramatic town located at the edge of a mountain gorge. Several seventeenth- and eighteenth-century bridges link different parts of the town, and a number of Muslim buildings are on the south side of the gorge in the walled old town. The Plaza de Toros, oldest in Spain (built in 1785), created the first *estilo rondeño* rules for fighting bulls on foot. The small cathedral in the town became the model for William Randolph Hearst's composite castle at San Simeon, California.

The southwestern coastal resort strip, the Costa del Sol, contains **Marbella**, which has several sections of the town wall, an old Muslim naval building, and a sixteenth-century town hall. **Torremolinos** is another major resort.

CUISINE. Málaga offers most Andalusian foods. Soups include *ajo blanco* (cold garlic soup), shellfish, or in the winter, fried sardines, or *sopa* *de pescado malagueña* (seafood soup). There are also unusual casual foods, or *tapas* (generally served in bars and bodegas as appetizers) such as *boquerones rellenos de jamón y espinaca* (smelts stuffed with cured ham and spinach) or *cigalas* (crayfish). A bodega generally serves a wide selection of wines and brandies along with *tapas* instead of cocktails. A bar mainly serving cocktails often is called a "Bar Americano."

Wines of the "*Denominación de Origen 'Málaga'* " come from the Antequera plateau, north of the city of Málaga, and from along the shores of the Mediterranean, now more to the east of Málaga than the western Costa del Sol because of rising land costs. No true vintage is used here. Young wines are blended with older ones, or *arrope*, a wine-base syrup, is mixed with alcohol to limit fermentation. The result is the sweet "Málaga," a dessert wine.

SEVILLE (Sevilla)

VITAL STATISTICS. Pop., 1,477,428. Area, 14,036 sq. km. Capital and diocesan see: Seville. Much of the province lies in the valley of the Guadalquivir River, with Huelva to the southwest, Badajoz to the northwest, Córdoba to the east, and Málaga and Cádiz to the southeast and south. The University of Seville is the largest in Andalusia.

ECONOMY. Once a region of large estates, Seville is still dominated by large-scale agriculture and large wheat farms. Table olives, sugar beets, cotton (40 percent of the national total), and food preparation (third highest in Spain) are crucial economic activities. A large wheat crop facilitates flour production and baking, and the sizeable tobacco harvest is purchased by the state tobacco manufacturing monopoly, Compañia Arrendataria Tabacalera. Mining is small, but there are reserves of iron, copper, and zinc at Aznalcóllar, and natural gas reserves exist in the lower Guadalquivir Valley. Manufacturing, until now the least developed sector, has grown and includes the assembly of automobile transmissions.

HISTORY. (Hispalis [Celtiberian, root word for Hispanic], Ichbilija [Arabic]). The original settlement centered around a small Celtiberian town called Matres Aufaniae. In 206 B.C., the Roman victory over the Carthaginians in the battle of Ilipa led to the founding of towns such as Hispalis, which served as Spain's only inland river port and later became walled and fortified to govern Andalusia as the administrative and judicial center of Baetica province.

Several figures born in the area rose to distinguish themselves in Rome. The first, Emperor Trajan (A.D. 53–117), held several important military and political posts until he received the rank of Caesar (assistant emperor) from the Emperor Nerva (r. 96–98) and shared political power. Trajan became sole ruler in 98 and excelled in administration, reducing taxes and sponsoring subsidies for the poor, creating a massive building program, and admitting those born in Spain to prominent positions. He expanded the empire north of the Danube and defeated the Parthians near the Persian Gulf.

Hadrian (75–138), Trajan's cousin, rose to the status of a senator during Trajan's era and became his successor in 117. Hadrian followed Trajan's domestic policies but abandoned the Parthian campaign and built Hadrian's Wall in northern Britain to stop the flow of non-Romans into the province of Britannia. He pacified the Greeks and built the temple of Olympian Zeus in Athens, but construction of a Roman temple on the former site of the Great Temple of Jerusalem caused a major Jewish revolt.

In 411, Roman Seville fell to the Vandals, who had sailed up the Guadalquivir River. Another Germanic people, the Visigoths, quickly drove the Vandals from Andalusia and made Seville the capital of Visigothic Spain (ca. 441). The martyrdom in 585 of St. Hermenegild, son of King Leovigild, led to the Christian conversion in 589 of his brother, Recared, through the efforts of St. Isidoro of Murcia (560–636). The Visigothic capital later was moved to Toledo to place it closer to the center of the Church.

The Umayyads, a Syrian aristocratic family of the Sunnite faction in Muhammadanism who favored civil noble rule over the Shiite concept of a strict religious state, ignored Seville for Córdoba. Revival came only after their fall in the eleventh century, when the Abbadid dynasty ruled from Seville. Muhammad (1068–91) allied with Yusef Abd Tashufin (ca. 1086–1106) of the Moroccan Berber Almohads in 1086, causing a fundamentalist Muslim threat that united the quarrelsome northern Christian kingdoms in fear. Fernando III of Castile finally captured Seville in 1248. After expelling the Muslims, he venerated St. Isidoro's early service to Christianity by making Seville his home and beginning a period of Romanesque and Gothic construction, a tradition continued by Alfonso X (1252–84) and Pedro I (1350–69).

Seville reached its zenith in the early sixteenth century as headquarters for the Casa de Contratación (the Castilian board of trade, supervising trade and shipping to the Indies) and as an important center of the Council of the Indies (charged with ruling the new American colonies). Here the Torre de Oro (tower of gold) stored the gold and silver shipped from Mexico and Peru that crossed the Atlantic and came up the Guadalquivir River. During this period, foreign merchants created a wealthy and lively international bazaar, but problems with maintaining river transport weakened Seville's preeminence. By the beginning of the seventeenth century, the final destination of the Atlantic fleets shifted to Cádiz.

Many tried to stem Seville's decline. Don Gaspar de Guzmán, third count of Olivares and duke of San Lucar (1587–1645), a grandee of Miraflores (although raised in Rome) and favorite of Felipe IV, was sympathetic to

Seville's pleas for aid, but he experienced a spectacular failure of his own when his 1624 Union of Arms reform of Spanish taxes and administration provoked later revolts in Portugal and Catalonia and led to his downfall. The decline worsened when half the city died of plague in 1649 and continued into the eighteenth century when the Bourbon dynasty abolished the trade monopoly with America in 1778.

During the War of Independence, Seville briefly led the patriotic junta before being pillaged by the French. The postwar era was equally bleak. Provincial nobles such as the duques de Arcos, Medina Sidonia, and Osuna, the condes de Medinaceli, or the marqués de Peñaflor still controlled 68.2 percent of all arable lands, and the Church owned an additional 4.9 percent. Liberal regimes did little to alleviate peasant poverty, and Seville lived on as a sleepy, religious gentry town, too inert even to celebrate the Columbian quartocentennial of 1892, which was finally staged in 1929 by the dictator, General Primo de Rivera.

Endemic peasant unemployment, which stood at 24.2 percent by 1933, caused more than half of all arable private property to be seized by radical groups during the Popular Front period in early 1936. Yet at the start of the civil war, the garrulous local military commander, General Gonzalo Queipo de Llano (1875–1951), outmaneuvered the rural radicals by allowing Franco to airlift troops from Spanish Morocco directly to Seville before they could act. The province, which later became Franco's chief base, remained a closely controlled nationalist bastion.

After the nationalist victory, religion and traditional society received new support, but the province's poor economy continued to falter despite the economic plan of 1966. The early months of the constitutional monarchy saw the Partido Socialista Obrero Español (PSOE), headed by the *sevillano* Felipe González Márquez (b. 1942), reorganize into a potent force. The maverick nationalism of the Partido Socialista de Andalucia (PSA) of Fernando Abril and Alejandro Rojas Marcos briefly challenged the PSOE, but González managed to respect regional nationalism without becoming its captive. The PSOE's national victory in the 1982 elections made González the premier of Spain after 1982. Regional autonomy became a reality in 1983, and Seville later hosted Expo '92.

LITERATURE. The first major intellectual figure, **St. Isidoro** (560?–636) of Cartagena, Murcia, lived most of his life in Seville as bishop of the city. Through his work, Seville became the creative center of Spanish culture.

After the Reconquest, Elio Antonio Martínez del Cala y Jarava, known as **Antonio de Nebrija** (1480?–1522) of Nebrija, obtained a commission from Isabel the Catholic to write a very modern grammar, *Gramática sobre la lengua castellana*. The work took a Renaissance tone because of Nebrija's interest in language as one of humankind's most distinctive activities.

Seville's strong Renaissance and Golden Age tradition first began when **Lope de Rueda** (1505?–65), a playwright, introduced on the Spanish stage many comedic devices from Italian drama. His innovations included the use of women disguised as men and the genre of *pasos* (short interludes between the acts of a play to introduce a note of reality, change of pace, or observation). He also experimented with *coloquios pastoriles* as an exaggerated pastoral style celebrating rural values.

The Americas figured prominently in Seville's literature because of the city's connection with the colonies. **Bartolomé de las Casas** (1474–1566) of the city was accompanied during his college years in Salamanca by a native American slave Columbus had given to Las Casas's father. His servant's origins so fascinated Las Casas that he joined the Dominican Order and accepted a mission in Hispaniola in 1502 to learn more about indigenous America. As witness to the near extinction of Aztec and Mayan cultures, he protested inhumane policies in a one-man crusade to defend native peoples. *Brevísma relación de la destrucción de las Indias* (1542?) created the black legend (*leyenda negra*) of Spanish cruelty in the New World, while *Historia general de las Indias* (1561), which covered New World history from 1492 to 1520, idealized indigenous American culture by popularizing an early concept of the noble savage.

Other writers defended the Spanish conquest of the New World. **El Inca Garcilaso** (1540–1615), son of a Spaniard by an Inca princess, lived in Peru until he arrived in Seville in 1560 to write histories such as *Florida del Incas, or Historia del adelantado Hernando de Soto* (1595) and *Comentarios reales que tratan del origen de los Incas* (1609). He and other historians or theologians such as **Juan Ginés de Sepúlveda** (1490–1573) and **Antonio de Herrera y Tordesillas** (1549–1625) often disputed Las Casas's arguments. **Pedro de Cieza de León** (1518–54) in *Parte primera de la Crónica del Perú* (1553), and **Juan de Castellanos** (1522–1607) in his epic *Elegías de varones ilustres de Indias* (1605), romanticized the Conquest.

The city's prosperity subsidized many other writers. **Fernando de Herrera** (1534–97), called "El Divino" for his poetic skills, used Petrarchan sonnets in poetry such as *Elegías* that later influenced Góngora. After writing *Canción a la victoria de Lepanto* to celebrate the famous Spanish naval victory of 1571, he received a subsidy from the great-grandson of Columbus, Alvaro Colón y Portugal, the conde de Gelves, to write more patriotic poetry. **Juan de la Cueva** (1550?–1610?) also introduced Spanish history and legend into drama. *Cerco de Zamora* (1579?) focused on Sancho II's siege of Zamora, but he also wrote the creative drama *El infamador* (1581), the story of a thief with don Juan inclinations who is finally executed. *Exemplar poético* (1606) urged the creation of an authentic Spanish drama based on epic traditions and legends of the *crónicas* and *romances*. To a considerable extent, Cueva prepared the way for the later focus of Spanish drama on national epics and the Spanish character.

Juan de Mal Lara (1524–71), founder of the Sevillian school of poetry, introduced everyday speech to poetry and drama in *Filosofía vulgar* (1568), a collection of Renaissance *refranes* (sayings). But **Mateo Alemán** (1547–1615), son of a Jewish prison doctor in Seville, diverged from this tradition in *Guzmán de Alfarache* (1599), the second picaresque novel of importance after the anonymous *Lazarillo de Tormes*. The author's hard life, full of disappointments, led him to create a cautionary novel that describes a man without money confronted by a very harsh world. He finally marries for money, only to be deserted by his wife, and after some misdeeds is sentenced to serve as a galley slave. Gerald Brenan describes the main character as a Charlie Chaplin viewed through the eyes of a sixteenth-century Calvinist minister, although in fact Guzmán remained a devout Catholic and never missed daily mass. Picaresque literature might best be seen as a safety valve that helped Spaniards deal with difficulties through sarcasm and irony.

Other writers of the period include **Guillén Castro y Bellvís** (1569–1631) of Seville, a dramatist of the Lope de Vega school who introduced a new type of theatrical writing by using popular speech in formal drama. Fray **Diego de Hojeda** (1570?–1615?) wrote one of the most powerful religious epics in *La cristiada* (1611), the passion of Christ's last days.

The Golden Century anticipated by these writers climaxed with the work of the Mexican-born **Juan Ruiz de Alarcón y Mendoza** (1581?–1639), employed in Seville by the Council of the Indies. Alarcón, a contemporary of Tirso de Molina, showed signs of Tirso's skepticism. *La verdad sospechosa* is the story of a habitual liar who finds himself obliged to marry a girl he does not love, the moral being that lies negate nobility and honor. Alarcón's other plays include *Las paredes oyen*, an attack on slander; *Los pechos privilegiados*, on the popular topic of royal favorites; and *La prueba de las promesas*, another play about lies.

The decline of Hapsburg Spain caused theatre and poetry to wane until the eighteenth-century Enlightenment, when **Alberto Lista y Aragón** (1775–1848), a pre-romantic poet, established the Sevillian school, Academia de letras humanas. Lista, a supporter of France during the War of Independence, went into exile in 1813. **José Maria Blanco y Crespo** (1775–1841), known as Blanco White in Great Britain, broke with the Church and converted to Protestantism in London. His influence led to the introduction of English sonnets. **José Marchena Ruiz de Cueto** (1768–1821) of Utrera led a similar life. He taught and preached in Seville before abandoning his career to join the French Revolution. His major work, *Cristo crucificado*, typified the enlightened, radical work of the Sevillian school.

In the nineteenth century, **Gustavo Adolfo Bécquer** (1836–70) of Seville was the major Spanish post-romantic poet, famous for his work *Rimas* (1871), a collection of pure love poems that constitute a spiritual autobiography of great intimacy ranging from love of nature to love between the sexes. Bécquer moved from Seville to Madrid and then in 1854 to Novierca in Soria, where he wrote his *Leyendas* (1860–64), but his death at age thirty-four meant that his fame was almost entirely posthumous.

In the early twentieth century, the poet **Antonio Machado y Ruiz** (1875–1939) of Seville was a leading national poet and member of the Generation of 1898. His first major work, *Soledades, galeriás y otros poemas* (1907), explores the poet's great use of symbolism. *Campos de Castilla* (1912) takes a much more realistic tone by combining a pessimistic view of the present with a more hopeful vision of the future. *Nuevas canciones* (1924) won him membership in the Royal Academy. Since he lived much of his life in Madrid or Soria, his poetry deals more with these areas than with Seville or Andalusia. He supported the republican cause during the civil war and fled to France at the end of the war, where he died within days of his arrival.

Joaquín Dicenta Benedicto (1863–1917) wrote *El señor feudal* (1896) about pressing rural problems of the province. **Blas Infante** (1881?–1924?), a lawyer and political essayist, wrote in *Ideal Andaluz* (1915) that a stimulation of regional regeneration would lead to agrarian reform. The chief leader of the *andalucistas* in the early twentieth century, he mingled ideas taken from two nineteenth-century social theorists, the American Henry George (a socialized agrarian sector, a single tax on urban property) and the Spanish federal republican, Francisco Pi y Margall. Blas Infante's support for a *mancomunidad andaluza* (a regional agency to develop education and culture) constituted the main evidence of prior Andalusian regionalist sentiment during the struggle to obtain regional status in the 1977–78 debates of the early constitutional monarchy.

Also in the twentieth century, **Vicente Aleixandre y Merlo** (1898–1984) of Seville grew up in Málaga and lived in Madrid as an adult. Extremely open to Latin American poetry (especially Rubén Dario) and French surrealism, he belonged to the Generation of 1927 and wrote surrealist poetry such as *Espadas como labios* (1932) and *La destrucción o el amor* (1935), which won the National Prize for Literature. Some of his later works such as *Ambito* (1928) constituted pure poetry, while *Historia del corazón* (1954) and *Diálogos del conocimiento* are more natural, spare, and tragic. In 1977, he won the Nobel Prize for Literature, surpassing the accomplishments of many other southerners.

Luis Cernuda (1902–63), also a member of the Generation of 1927 and a friend of Aleixandre, was especially active in the development of democratic and secular educational policies during the Second Republic. As a poet, his *Perfil del aire* (1927) follows a naturalistic style somewhat like that of Bécquer. Cernuda also experimented with surrealism, but *Egloga, elegía, oda* (1929) and other works of this period remain lyric. The difficulties of the Second Republic caused his *Invocaciones a las gracias del mundo* (1935) to be pessimistic about humankind's ability to avoid violence. *La realidad y el deseo* (1936), perhaps his best work, uses a romantic style to examine the torment of religion and daily life. Cernuda lived in exile after Franco's victory in 1939.

Today, **Fernando Quiñones** (b. 1930) is one of the leading contemporary poets.

Seville furnished the setting for many plays and novels. Its prosperity attracted **Miguel de Cervantes Saavedra** (1547–1616) of Madrid, who wrote and produced plays in Seville such as *Los Baños de Argel* (1580) and *El cerco de Numancia* (1585). *Exemplary Novels* (1613) gives a picture of Seville's everyday life. Background on this period may be found in **Nicolás Antonio** (1617–84), the first scholar to write a complete literary history of Spain.

The most famous play about Seville came from the pen of **Tirso de Molina** (Fray Gabriel Téllez) of Soria. *El Burlador de Sevilla y convidado de piedra* (ca. 1630) is the story of a Sevillian nobleman, don Juan Tenorio, whose rakish ways include several seductions and a murder, until his sins and mockery of morality cause him to be pulled down into hell by the stone effigy of one of his victims. This play introduced the don Juan character into literature and drama which later influenced foreign writers and composers such as Molière, Corneille, Mérimée, Dumas, Purcell, Byron, Gluck, Mozart, and Richard Strauss.

Seville also is the setting for the play by Francisco de Rojas Zorrilla, *Del rey abajo, ninguno: el labrador más honrado García del Castañar* (1650). Armando Palacio Valdés of Asturias wrote *La Hermana San Sulpicio* (1889) as a clever spoof of society in Seville. The novel concerns a man who falls in love with and marries a young nun, only to find his life complicated by the consternation and opposition of local society. Lope de Vega also used Seville as a setting on occasion.

Among the institutions for writers in Seville, the Real Academia Sevillana de Buenas Letras organized readings and trained writers and poets, while the Archivo de las Indias, established in 1920, makes records of the American empire available for historical research.

ART. While no one artist brings great change single-handedly, late Gothic painting blossomed with **Alejo Fernández** of Córdoba, whose *Virgin of the Navigators* hangs in the Alcázar. **Alonso Berruguete** (1489–1561) of Valladolid, an Italian-trained painter and sculptor, also became very popular in Seville during the era of Carlos I, along with the Flemish **Pedro de Campaña** (Pieter de Kempener), whose *Descent from the Cross* is in the cathedral and whose massive retablo dominates the altar of the parish church of Santa Ana. Still another sixteenth-century painter, **Luis de Vargas** (1505?–67), painted the *Allegory of the Immaculate Conception* for a chapel of the cathedral. **Luis de Morales** (1509?–85?), called "El Divino," painted a *Pietà* that hangs in the Real Academia de Bellas Artes and is considered to be one of the greatest of Seville's sixteenth-century works.

His competitor, **Francisco de Herrera** (1530?–97), has four distinguished paintings in the church of San Buenaventura.

From about 1590 to 1625, a new sense of naturalism stressing human beauty more than religious symbolism was introduced by a Portuguese, **Vasco Pereira** (1535–1609), and developed by **Pablo de Céspedes** (1538–70). Céspedes trained in Italy, and his frescoes in the chapter room of the cathedral won great acclaim. **Francisco Pacheco** (1564–1644) brought Sevillian art into the Renaissance and also created a sophisticated theological image of the Virgin Mary in his *Arte de la Pintura*, inspired by the Portuguese mystic Beatrice de Solva (d. 1490). Art dealing with Mary, he wrote, should emphasize the spotlessness of the Virgin and present her as a "great wonder," always standing for the victory of Christ over Satan and, if possible, including the sun and moon in paintings to symbolize her cosmic importance. Pacheco was the teacher of **Diego Rodríguez de Silva y Velázquez** (1599–1660), his son-in-law. Velázquez remained in Seville only until 1623, when he left for the court of Felipe IV in Madrid.

A new period in the art of Seville began in 1625 with **Francisco de Zurbarán y Salazar** (1598–1644), originally from Badajoz, who spent much of his career in Seville or Madrid and is well known for his work at the Franciscan Colegio de San Buenaventura and his *St. Gregory* at the Museo de Bellas Artes in Seville. *Christ on the Cross* (Chicago Institute of Art, 1626) made Zurbarán famous, and *St. Peter Nolasco's Vision of Christ* (Prado, 1628), *St. Bonaventure at the Council of Lyon* (Louvre, 1630), *Hercules and Antaeus* (Prado, 1635), and the altarpiece of St. Peter in the cathedral at Seville increased his prestige. Zurbarán dressed the Virgin Mary in silks, brocades, and the full costume of the period. A series of these works can be found in the Museo de Bellas Artes. His portrayal of the Virgin had special impact on Latin American art.

After Zurbarán's death in 1644, the fame of **Bartolomé Estéban Murillo** (1617–82), a native of Seville, rose very quickly. His works include *San Diego de Alcalá Feeding the Poor* (Madrid, Real Academia de San Fernando, 1646), *Angels' Kitchen* (Louvre, 1646), *Vision of St. Anthony of Padua* (Seville Cathedral, 1656), *Birth of the Virgin* (Louvre, 1660), and all of his female saints. He also did major works for the churches of Santa María la Blanca (1665), Capuchinos (1666), and the Mission of Caridad (1668) in Seville. One of these, *Return of the Prodigal Son*, is in the National Gallery of Art in Washington, D.C. All are an essential part of the era's mystical, militant phase of Spanish Catholicism. Particularly important is the tradition begun by Murillo of painting the Virgin as a fiery figure to give her a powerful type of holiness.

Other artists of this period include **Juan de Valdés Leal** (1622–90), whose works *In Ictu Oculi* (1672), *Finis Gloriae Mundi* (1672), and the famous *Exaltation of the Cross* (1685) hang in La Caridad. **Francisco de Herrera the Younger** (1622–85), a native, remained in Seville until 1660, competing with Murillo and founding an academy of art, but as Spain's economic difficulties made commissions more difficult to obtain, art in Seville declined after 1700. The only sculptors of note are a father and daughter, **Pedro Roldán** (1624?–79?), who did the retablo at the Hospital of Charity, and **Luisa Roldán** (1656–1704), noted for the costume details she included in her works.

MUSIC. The choirmaster of Seville Cathedral, **Cristóbal Morales** (1500?–1553), wrote masses, magnificats, lamentations, and motets with a deep religious passion that was the chief Andalusian contribution to religious music. **Francisco Guerrero** (1528–99), one of Morales's successors, wrote Christmas music to popular tunes and is called the Murillo of Spanish music because his compositions honored the Virgin.

Manuel del Popolo Vicente Garcia (1775–1832) of Seville, a singer, actor, composer, conductor, and father of a musical family, achieved fame first in France and Italy and then in North and South America as a singer of popular songs, *tonadillas*, and Spanish folk music. His daughter, **María Felicidad García** (1805–36), used the name of her elderly French husband, Malibran, to attain popularity as a singer. **Pauline García** (1821–1910) was an operatic mezzo-soprano, while her brother, **Manuel Patricio Rodriguez García** (1805–1904), originally an operatic basso, became a noted voice teacher in Paris and London and was the inventor of the laryngoscope.

The most prominent modern composer of Seville, **Joaquín Turina** (1867–1949), a contemporary of Manuel de Falla and a fellow student in Paris, carried out a musical love affair with his native city. His three major works, *Canto a Sevilla, Saeta en forma de Salve*, and *Poema en forma de canciones*, use guitars and flamenco melodies in a romantic classical context. **Jerónimo Giménez** (1854–1923) of Seville was the first to conduct *Carmen* in Spain. His compositions, largely orchestral works, include *La Boda de Luis Alfonso*.

The two famous operas written about Seville are both by non-Spanish composers. The Italian **Gioacchino Rossini** (1792–1868) wrote *Il Barbiere di Siviglia* (1816), based on the earlier play by the Frenchman Pierre Augustin Caron de Beaumarchais. Its libretto is a love story between the young count Almaviva and the lovely Rosina and the comedy provided by their go-between, the barber Figaro. The French composer **Georges Bizet** (1838–75) wrote his acclaimed opera, *Carmen* (1875), at the very end of his life. He utilized the flavor of southern Spanish music and social types to immortalize Carmen, the girl from the cigarette factory whose looks and smoldering passion drove the men around her to madness.

Folk music in Seville specializes in the *saeta*, which are requests or vows sung by spectators as the image of the Virgin is carried through the streets during Holy Week.

CUSTOMS AND SOCIETY. Semana Santa (Holy Week) is the largest festival in Spain. Processions of brotherhoods (penitential religious fraternities known as *cofradías*) such as the Apósteles de Cristo, Hermandad de Gloria de Nuestra Señora de Los Angeles, or the Hermandad de La Paz originated between the fourteenth and sixteenth centuries. They dress as *penitentes* (pilgrim worshippers) and carry huge altarpieces of the saints. The Good Friday procession is particularly passionate, and more than fifty images of the Virgin Mary are displayed in parades from Thursday night to Saturday morning when copies of the *Virgen del Rocío, Señora de los Reyes, Virgen de la Macarena*, and the *Virgen de Triana* pass by on huge *pasos* (floats). After Easter, there is a weeklong Feria de Sevilla to celebrate the end of the season. Songs classified as *sevillanas* (the origin of Mexican *ranchero* music) are featured, along with all-night flamenco dancing, bullfights, horseback riding, flower-decked wagons, numerous concerts and exhibitions of art, and the building of *casetas* (small huts) on the streets by various groups.

The Romeria del Rocio passes through the province bound for Almonte in Huelva province as a pilgrimage in honor of *Nuestra Señora de Rocio*.

A unique custom is the opening of Fernando III's tomb twice a year to celebrate the reconquest of Seville in 1248. The mummified king, dressed in robes and wearing his crown, can be viewed in his coffin, sometimes in a semi-raised position. Some natives feel duty-bound to observe this custom.

Dances of the province include the famous *sevillanas*, done by couples who use as a basic step the *pas de Basque*, an alternating step, with one foot always on the floor, that produces a swaying movement. The pace can become so rapid that it sometimes takes on a dervish-like quality, probably revealing its Middle Eastern origins.

Traditional dress for women included long red, yellow, or blue silk skirts trimmed with black or white lace, and a short, tight-fitting jacket decorated with tassels of silk. The high-heeled satin shoes worn by Seville's women created a craze at one time that spread to the rest of Europe. Elaborate mantillas of filmy lace were lifted from the forehead by large combs. Males wore close-fitting silk breeches, white stockings, and low slippers. Their jackets were usually very short and covered with braid and silver buttons, worn over a frilled shirt.

HISTORIC SITES. The city of **Seville** is dominated by the cathedral of Santa María, a huge structure in the center of the city built between 1402 and 1506, the third largest cathedral after St. Peter's in Rome and St. Paul's in London. A Visigothic church and a mosque built by the Almohads preceded it. The mosque's prayer tower, the Giralda (a word that means weathervane) is 305 feet high. Originally built as a minaret in 1184–96, it became a bell tower in 1568. There is an unusual interior ramp that can be used by visitors.

The grandeur, size, and mosquelike plan of the cathedral are notable. Nine main portals are decorated with terra cotta or stone reliefs. The Puerta del Perdón encloses the Patio de los Naranjos, next to the Giralda. The Patio de las Naranjos leads to a portal of the same name that brings visitors inside the cathedral. The interior is 384 feet long, 249 feet wide, and 131 feet high, with a nave, four aisles, and fourteen chapels on the north and south sides. There are three enclosures along the axis of the cathedral, all handsomely furnished, as are the lavish chapels. Some horseshoe arches still remain from the cathedral's origin as a mosque. The library left by the Columbus family as the Biblioteca Colombina is also a part of the cathedral. Fernando Columbus, Alfonso X, and Pedro the Cruel are buried here. Other important features inside include the Capilla Real and the great Gothic retablo (ca. 1482–1564).

Next to the cathedral is the Plaza del Triunfo, where the Archive of the Indies and the Museum of Contemporary Art are located. Slightly northeast lies the Barrio de Santa Cruz, a beautiful remnant of the medieval city with narrow, twisting streets and whitewashed houses, some with petite but graceful courtyards. All the houses have red tile roofs. They are the stereotype of Hispanic architecture carried to the New World.

The other chief structure of Seville is the Alcázar, originally a Muslim fortress begun by the Almohads and later the residence of Christian monarchs. The Patio de las Doncellas (maids of honor) has marble columns. The Salón de Carlos I, state apartments, dining room, Hall of the Ambassadors, Felipe II's bedchamber, Court of the Dolls, inner courtyards, Queen's bedchamber, and the bedchamber of the Moorish Kings can all be visited. The beautiful gardens of the Alcázar surround the buildings. In the surrounding neighborhood, there are many sixteenth- and seventeenth-century churches and convents.

Among the other sights of Seville are the Expo '92 grounds on an island in the middle of the Guadalquivir River. Elsewhere in the city are found a folk costume museum, the Museo de Bellas Artes, and an archaeological museum. The Plaza de España, site of a 1929 exposition, is a park, and the walk along the Guadalquivir River can be pleasant in the evening.

Elsewhere in the province, **Carmona,** east of Seville, is a Romano-Muslim town with its walls intact. The church of Santa María la Mayor occupies a former mosque site with a Muslim patio at one end of the church. It is reputed to be the oldest Christian church that can be accurately dated from inscriptions in the building. A Roman cemetery on the west side of Carmona is in good repair, and the Alcázar and a number of parish churches are worth seeing. Further east, halfway between Seville and Córdoba, **Ecija,** originally settled by Romans, is one of the oldest centers of Christianity in Spain. The church of Santiago el Mayor suffered damage in the earthquake of 1755, but the remodeled church of Santa Cruz has Greek, Roman, Visigothic, and Muslim artifacts, as well as Byzantine reliefs on the altar. In addition, the town's Plaza Mayor has traditional arcades, the town hall has a Roman mosaic floor, and the Peñaflor Palace is an exemplar of Sevillian fashion and style.

In the southeast, **Osuna** received the patronage of the dukes of Osuna, who founded a sixteenth-century university there with a large collegiate church. **Alcalá de Guadaira** is the site of a Romano-Muslim castle used by Castilian monarchs as an early center of government and military power, and also has Roman and Arab flour mills that have been restored.

CUISINE. Restaurants in Seville have reworked Andalusian food into an international cuisine. Among the most popular dishes are *ensalada sevillana* (rice, red peppers, tomatoes, and olives), *huevos a la flamenca* (eggs with onions, ham, tomatoes, shrimp, *chorizos*, and green vegetables), and *salmorejo con huevos* (bread, olive oil, garlic, eggs, and tomatoes). *Mantecados*, a small cookie sold throughout Spain during the Christmas season, is made at Estepa.

Gazpacho (iced vegetable soup) to serve four can be made as follows:

GAZPACHO

¼ green pepper	6 Tbs. olive oil
1 clove garlic, peeled	2 Tbs. wine vinegar
2 large ripe tomatoes	cold water
¼ cucumber	salt and pepper to taste
½ onion	

Cut the pepper into strips, crush the garlic, mash the tomatoes and cucumber, and dice the onion. Combine in deep bowl, stir in the olive oil and vinegar slowly, and add water to desired consistency. Add salt and pepper. For garnish, add:

2 Tbs. croutons or bread crumbs	2 cloves garlic, crushed
2 Tbs. wine vinegar	2 Tbs. olive oil
1 tomato, chopped	1 cucumber, chopped
1 hard-boiled egg, chopped	6 oz. almonds, chopped

Chill the entire mixture for an hour before serving.

The following egg recipe serves four:

HUEVOS A LA FLAMENCA

¾ cup olive oil

4 oz. cooked ham

8 slices *chorizos* or pepperoni

2 potatoes, peeled and chopped

2 Tbs. cooked peas

2 Tbs. cooked green beans

2 Tbs. asparagus tips

2 peeled tomatoes, chopped

sherry, chicken bouillon, and salt
   to taste

8 eggs

In half the olive oil, warm the ham and *chorizos*, or pepperoni.
Set aside the ham and *chorizo* mix. Add potatoes, peas, beans,
asparagus, and the tomatoes last in remaining olive oil, cooking
just long enough to make tender. Flavor with sherry and bouillon, add salt to taste, then put into a flat baking dish with *chorizo* or pepperoni slices on top. Poach or fry eggs and mound
over the meat layer, then bake entire mixture for 15 minutes at
350°F.

Local red wines are used in sangria, the famous Andalusian wine punch
typically made of tonic, fruit juices, and chunks of fruit over ice.

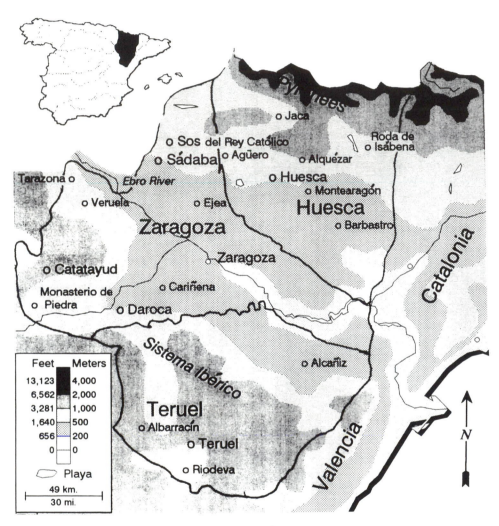

ARAGÓN

Chapter 2

ARAGÓN

REGIONAL CHARACTERISTICS. Pop., 1,213,099. Area, 47,669 sq. km., 9.5 percent of Spain. Regional capital: Zaragoza. The region of Aragón lies between the border of France on the north and Valencia, Cuenca, and Guadalajara on the south, Lleida (Lérida) and Tarragona in Catalonia on the east, and the regions of Navarre and La Rioja and the province of Soria (New Castile) on the west. Aragón occupies the area north and south of the Ebro River, named Eberus by the Celtiberians from the Celtic word *aber*, or river. The northern section of Aragón above Zaragoza is dominated by upland valleys and the Pyrenees Mountains. The southern region is arid, and the southeastern zone around Teruel is broken by the Montes Universales.

The three Aragonese provinces, Spanish-speaking and linked by a millennium of history, voted in the referendum of 1978 to continue centralism and reject limited autonomy by a 13 percent margin, the largest no vote next to León. This result was somewhat surprising since Aragón had remained independent of Castile until the sixteenth century, kept its local liberties until the early eighteenth century, and experienced several regional movements during the nineteenth century. What tempered enthusiasm for regional status was fear of losing central industrial subsidies and memories of Aragón's searing experience in the Spanish Civil War with labor and the left, now again on the rise in the constitutional monarchy. Only after passage of the LOAPA legislation did Aragón approve limited autonomy in 1982.

The flag of Aragón has four red stripes on a field of yellow with its shield in the center topped by a crown.

Aragón ranks sixth in income among the regions.

HUESCA

VITAL STATISTICS. Also called Alto Aragón. Pop., 414,492. Area, 10,128 sq. km. Capital: Huesca. Diocesan sees: Jaca, Barbastro, Huesca. Huesca is the most mountainous section of Aragón, bounded by France on the north, Lleida (Lérida) in Catalonia on the east, Zaragoza and Pamplona (Navarre) on the west, and Zaragoza on the south. The national park of Ordesa lies close to the northern border of the province.

ECONOMY. Huesca produces large wheat and alfalfa crops, but recently energy production has outstripped other economic activities. The Serrablo natural gas field near the Pyrenees began production in 1982 and pumped 12.7 million cubic meters in 1989, representing 99 percent of all domestic production. It is linked by pipeline as far south as Seville.

HISTORY. (Osca [Visigothic and Roman], Vechca [Arabic]). The fertile plain of Huesca, watered by the Pyrenees, attracted the Celtiberians, who built the first walled town on the peninsula. After the area became Roman, the forces of Sartorius and Sulla clashed in a small civil war (77 B.C.) during the crisis of the Roman Republic. An early Roman institution of higher education on the peninsula, Sartorius University, later was established in Huesca. Christianity appeared by A.D. 250, strengthened by the legend of St. Lorenzo of Huesca (ca. 304?), which recalls a martyr who, though starved and roasted on a grill, never recanted. Muslims captured the town in 723 and fortified the walls with ninety-three towers strong enough to withstand a later siege by troops of Charlemagne.

Higher in the Pyrenees than Huesca, the town of Jaca (Jacca [Roman]) remained a Christian stronghold through several centuries of sporadic warfare with the Muslims. When the county of Aragón was founded by Navarre in 824, Jaca became its center, but after the Muslims were driven out of Huesca in 1096, the capital of Aragón moved there and then later to Zaragoza in 1119, when the full Kingdom of Aragón was created.

The area prospered as farming and grazing expanded. The city of Huesca reestablished the university, now called Sartorius, in 1354, and Carlos I endowed the Colegio Mayor de Santiago in 1534. In the early eighteenth century, the province sided with Karl of Austria in the War of Spanish Succession and experienced a brief Castilian occupation. A century later, despite intense resistance, the French seized the area in 1810 during the

Napoleonic War. In 1822, when the former Kingdom of Aragón was divided into three provinces, the city of Huesca was made a provincial capital. During the First Carlist War, defeat of government troops on May 24, 1837, left the area Carlist until 1839.

Anticentralist opposition never entirely died out. Joaquín Costa of Graus, a leading critic of late nineteenth-century politics, stressed the need for populist control of government. His message, supported by small farmers impoverished by the cold climate and thin, stony soil that made the land suitable mainly for grazing, stigmatized the few Aragonese magnates whose large estates dominated sheep herding. By putting the two groups at odds with each other, Costa badly divided provincial politics.

As political tension increased, radical peasants organized by the Confederación Nacional del Trabajo demanded land reform in December 1930 and rioted in Jaca. The Second Republic led reform efforts in 1932 and 1933 that unfortunately confiscated land not only of the magnates but also of medium-sized farmers. Resistance from both sides made land reform even more complicated in Huesca than elsewhere. When the left took power in early 1936, the millenarian behavior of poor peasants caused Barbastro, Alcalá de Gurrea, Alcampel, Albalate de Cinca, Villanueva de Sigena, and most of eastern Huesca to reject Franco's subsequent revolt against the Republic to join the anarchist-led Barcelona Anti-Fascist Militia Committee and collectivize into communes administered by the Council of Aragón. The cities of Huesca and Zaragoza, however, remained in nationalist hands, besieged by the militia army but never falling into its hands. Franco's forces recaptured the eastern republican zone during February and March 1938.

The peasantry was closely watched in the post–civil war period for having sided with the left. The spiritual leader of Franco's Spain, Josémaria Escrivá de Balaguer y Albás (1902–75) of Barbastro, founded the modern Catholic movement Opus Dei, as a devout new order that did not confine its members to monasteries or convents but rather sought to train them in the professions so that they might have a more powerful impact on lay society. Escrivá's Opus was active in the area and later established several retreats. Nonetheless, familiar problems of depopulation and inability to make a living in the countryside plagued the area, and between 1939 and 1950 an exodus of peasants sought work in the cities. New jobs created by the expansion of hydroelectric plants in the valleys of Bielsa and Xistau (Gistaín) were not nearly enough.

Today, however, the encouragement of crop husbandry rather than grazing has brought a new prosperity even to small-scale agriculture. As in the rest of Spain, local agriculturalists are better integrated into the national economy. Spain's unprecedented rate of economic growth has improved living conditions in the province, and local culture is more homogeneous with national life.

LITERATURE. The *converso* **Pedro Alfonso** (Rabbi Moisés Sefardí, 1062–1140) of Huesca wrote *Disciplina clericalis* (ca. 1140) as a manual for priests that made interesting comparisons between Judaism and Catholicism. As an apostate, he strongly protested the high status of Jews in Christian Spain. **Juan Cristóbal Calvete de Estrella** (1526?–93), a graduate of Alcala de Henares, chronicled Felipe II's court. **Lupercio Leonardo de Argensola** (1559–1613) of Barbastro, leader of the Aragonese school of literature, reacted to the baroque style of Góngora by simplifying Spanish verse and adopting a classic Renaissance style. He taught for a time in Huesca, which became the main literary center of Aragón. **José Mor de Fuentes** (1762–1848), poet and novelist, wrote an autobiography, *Bosquejillo de la vida y escritos de don José Mor de Fuentes*, useful for the history of the region and period.

In the nineteenth century, **Braulio Foz** (1791–1865), a novelist, historian, and classicist, taught at Salamanca. His *Vida de Pedro Saputo* (1836?) won praise as the portrait of a rational man. Later, **Joaquín Costa y Martínez** (1846–1911) of Graus, a well-known lawyer, essayist, and reformer who lived in Madrid, anticipated the Generation of 1898 by demanding increased modernization of Spain through development of better local government and land reform. Particularly in *Colectivismo agrario en España* (1898), *Reconstitución y europeización de España* (1900), and *Oligarquía y caciquismo como la forma de gobierno de España* (1902), Costa called for an "iron surgeon" to remove traditionalism and put a "double lock on the grave of the Cid" to make sure Spain followed a course of national renovation and modernization. While a radical force at the time, his ideas carried seeds of authoritarianism that germinated several decades later in the regimes of the generals José María Primo de Rivera and Francisco Franco.

During the Second Republic, **Ramón Sender** (1902–81) of Chalamera left the staff of the Madrid newspaper *El Sol* to write fiction. *Imán* (1931) won acclaim as a story that deals frankly with the life of soldiers during the Moroccan war. *Orden público* (1932) criticizes the violence of Primo de Rivera's military dictatorship. *Siete domingos rojos* (1932) dramatizes the growth of sectarian militancy at the very start of the Second Republic. *Mister Witt en el cantón* (1935), winner of the National Prize for Literature, examines the First Republic (1873–74) as an attempt to establish popular government, and *Contrataque* (1937) describes the military struggles early in the civil war. The murder of Sender's wife, Amparo, in Zamora during the early days of the war forced him to smuggle his two children out of Spain, and he later went into exile himself, teaching in the United States. His last novels covered Mexico as well as Spain. *Crónica del Alba* (1942) and *Before Noon* (1957) examine the life of an Aragonese villager by contrasting the happiness of his childhood with the misery he faced in the civil war.

Of all the writers, a foreigner, the Englishman **George Orwell** (1903–50), is best known for his description of the civil war in Aragón through his book *Homage to Catalonia* (1938). The title refers to his hospitalization in Barcelona just as the Popular Front disintegrated in May 1937, but the early chapters give a sense of what life was like on the Aragón front. Above all, the novel is an important early expression of disillusionment with communism.

ART. Jaca is important as an early point of the diffusion of the Romanesque into Spain. The cathedral of Jaca has a unity of style derived from the so-called **Master of Jaca,** who carved the tympanum of the west portal and the capital, some with nude figures of great naturalism and beauty that suggest a classic style in touch with Italian sources. Tourist authorities have created Romanesque and Roman routes to guide travelers through the best of these remains.

CUSTOMS AND SOCIETY. The *jota* is the traditional dance of Aragón, done in triple time accompanied by a harmony that alternates between the dominant and tonic, usually four measures of each. Various-sized guitars and *bandurrias* (mandolins) accompany the singers and dancers using strummed chords of *rasgueado* guitar style. Danced by one or two couples, the *jota* expresses courtship. The man sometimes pirouettes around the seated woman, or the man and woman kneel on one knee opposite each other and alternately bump the ground with their left and right knees. One arm is usually held above the head, the other across the body.

The important fiestas of this province include San Lorenzo (August 9–15), Santa Oracío (June), and the Concurso Provincial de Viños de Huesca at Barbastro (late September), the latter a celebration marking the harvest season's end. But almost all towns and villages have a profusion of festivals and fairs throughout the summer and fall. Banners of great weight and size advertise the event or the groups involved in the celebration, which may include *cofradías*, or religious fraternities, who use popular religious art on their banners. Sword and stick dances of Celtic origin are popular, and pageants maintain local traditions.

The historic dress of the Jaca area also shows Celtic influence and differs greatly from the rest of Spain. Men have always worn a white shirt and wide, short linen pants called *zaraguelles*, over which breeches made of dark cloth come to the knees, where they are tied by cords with tassels. Blue cotton stockings and leather sandals are worn on the legs and feet. The waist is wrapped by a violet-colored *faja*, or sash, of many folds, topped by a loose jacket, a bright cloth around the forehead, and a small round hat. Women wore two skirts of green serge, the top one lined with red material and caught up and hooked to the back of the waist. Over their blouses, a long linen robe or duster with loose sleeves, banded at the elbow, and with a high linen collar pleated and starched to frame the neck and head completed the ensemble.

In the Ansó Valley, women wore a very heavy pleated full-length dress of thick green cloth with blue or black oversleeves embroidered in jet, pressed so the sleeves formed a crescent over the shoulders.

HISTORIC SITES. The provincial capital of **Huesca** is dwarfed by the cathedral, built between 1273 and 1515. Its best features are the stained-glass windows and the large treasury of valuable artifacts. The town has a number of Romanesque parish churches and Spain's oldest university, Sartorius. The twelfth-century palace of the Kings of Aragón contains a provincial museum. The rebuilt version of a twelfth-century monastery, Nuestra Señora de Salas, is on the southern outskirts of the city.

Elsewhere in the province, northwest of the provincial capital, the castles of Loarre and Navascues are well-preserved Romanesque fortresses, the former with ten large semicircular towers. The church of San Jaime in **Agüero** exemplifies twelfth-century ecclesiastical architecture.

Directly north of the capital, **Jaca** has an important cathedral, perhaps the earliest Romanesque design in Spain, and a twelfth-century Benedictine monastery from the early medieval period when the town was an entry point to Spain on the route to Santiago de Compostela.

In the northeast, the walled town of **Aínsa**, once capital of the tiny early medieval kingdom of Sobrarbe that ruled over the Pyrenees, is a national monument. In **Alquézar**, the early Gothic church of Santa María, consecrated in 1099, has a number of frescoes and a treasury containing several valuable gold altars. Further east in the province, the former Roman village of **Barbastro** has a cathedral in the Renaissance style with churrigueresque chapels. The term derives from the extremely ornate Spanish baroque style named after its original designer, José Churriguera (1665–1725) of Madrid. The archbishop's palace, the handsome Plaza Mayor, and several city palaces also contain elements of the baroque. On the border with Lleida (Lérida), **Roda de Isábena** has a cathedral dating from 1067, although it was badly damaged in the Spanish Civil War. The chapter house is a museum.

CUISINE. Huesca specializes in serving a mixed grill of lamb, *chorizo* (spiced sausage), and *longaniza* (pork sausage). Other dishes are *truchas con jamón* (trout with ham), *revuelto de trigueros con gambas* (eggs scrambled with fresh asparagus and prawns), various bean dishes, and fowl (pigeon and partridge).

Wine of the Somontano demarcation from the foothills of the Pyrenees is a dark red, characteristic of Aragonese wines in general.

TERUEL

VITAL STATISTICS. Pop., 150,900. Area, 14,810 sq. km. Capital and diocesan see: Teruel. At ten persons per square kilometer, Teruel has one of the lowest population densities in Spain. The terrain is rough and encompasses the Sistema Ibérico, five different mountain ranges that provide the headwaters for the west-flowing Tagus River, which enters the Atlantic at Lisbon. The province is bounded by Castellón de la Plana (Valencia) and Tarragona (Catalonia) on the east, Zaragoza and Tarragona on the north, Valencia and Cuenca on the south, and Zaragoza and Guadalajara on the west.

ECONOMY. The economy has declined with iron-mine closures in the Ojós Negros/Setiles area (partly in Guadalajara province), although large reserves remain in the Sierra Albarracín. Sulphur deposits are located at Riodeva, south of Teruel. The province is the fourth-largest coal producer of Spain and has major reserves of lignite, used for electrical generation. Manufacturing is almost nil since the closure of several beet sugar refineries.

HISTORY. (Turba [Iberian], Tugur [Arabic]). An area of major prehistoric settlement in the Mesolithic and Paleolithic ages, Teruel was protected by rough terrain not far from the eastern Mediterranean coast. Ruins have been found of the indigenous Celtic god Lug (or Lugh) as well as traces of the third century B.C. Greek acropolis of Azaila, with its motif of bulls decorated by astral signs. Romans attacked Hannibal here in 218 B.C., destroying the village and making the area part of Tarraconensis. Muslims later created a military frontier district ruled first from Zaragoza, then in A.D. 1012–1104 by the Muslim district of Sahla, centered around Albarracín.

Christian reconquest began with the campaign of Alfonso I the Battler of Aragón in 1120. Ramón Berenguer IV of Barcelona captured Alcañiz in 1157, and Alfonso II and Pedro II of Aragón conquered the remainder of the area in 1171. The Muslim population, driven from the mountains, faced confinement in towns such as Teruel, where over the next several hundred years their Mudéjar artisan tradition fused with European styles and became very popular throughout northern Spain.

With a small population and slight importance as a wool weaving and arms manufacture center, Teruel remained a backwater, but strong resistance to occupation by Napoleonic troops in 1809 won the area provincial status in 1822. In the later liberal era, secularization alienated 80 percent of ecclesiastical properties, and private ownership forced thousands of peasants off the land altogether. Peasant poverty increased to become the major problem of the twentieth century.

Anarchist uprisings took place in January 1933, and during the early civil war Teruel formed a part of the Second Republic under control of Valencia. In October 1937, Franco's forces, seeking to divide loyalist territory, captured the city of Teruel. A republican army counterattacked on December 15 and forced Colonel Rey d'Harcourt to surrender on January 8, 1938, but a nationalist relief column reached the beleaguered town and on February 21 retook it. Thirty thousand died during the three-month-long battle, and the number of wounded, assassinated, and captured was four times higher. The battle of Teruel turned the tide of the civil war in favor of the rebels.

LITERATURE. The output of creative work by those born in Teruel is larger than the small population might indicate. **Miguel de Molinos** (1628–96) of Muniesa pursued a career of religious writing as a priest and founder of Spanish quietism. **Andrés Piquer** (1711–72), a philosopher/scientist of Fórnoles, became the first Spaniard to write a physics text, *Física moderna, racional y experimental* (1745). **Francisco Mariano Nifo** (1719–1803) of Alcañoz, an early professional journalist, founded fifteen newspapers, including *Diario* (1758) and *El Correo General* (1767).

In the twentieth century, **Pedro Laín Entralgo** (1908–82) of Urrea de Gaén, a philosopher and psychiatrist who taught in Madrid and later became rector of the University of Madrid, wrote *España como problema* (1949), which discusses the Spanish struggle to develop a political philosophy matching political and social reality. *Palabras menores* (1952) is a speculation on the role of Catholic intellectuals in the modern world.

In the history of Spanish cinema, **Luis Buñuel** (1900–1983) of Calanda became one of Spain's most famous film directors. With the artistic aid of Salvador Dalí, he made two important early surrealist films, *Un chien andalous* (1928) and *L'âge d'or* (1930). Radical works such as *Las Hurdas/ Tierra sin pan* (1932) and *Don Quintín el amargao* (1935) forced Buñuel into exile after the civil war, and he directed three of his greatest films, *Los Olvidados*, *Nazarín*, and *The Discreet Charm of the Bourgeoisie*, in Mexico, the United States, and France. He did not film again in Spain until *Viridiana* (1961).

ART. Along with Soria and Zaragoza, Teruel is a center of Mudéjar art and architecture. The cathedral of Teruel (1259) and the churches of El Salvador and San Martín are particularly fine examples of Mudéjar tower construction. Muslims faced forcible conversion to Christianity in 1502 (Castile) and 1526 (Aragón), but their value as artisans protected them for several centuries. They numbered in their traditional carpentry, cabinet-making, wainscoting, and wooden ceiling construction. Mudéjar pottery is imaginatively decorated by stamping motifs such as floral displays into the wet clay, which is then glazed in blue and gold. Metalwork is another specialty that includes gates, weapons, lamps, candlesticks, and censers. Many of the later Spanish wrought-iron patterns originated from Mudéjar designs.

In addition, the Mudéjar tradition led in part to the plateresque style, which **Alonso de Covarrubias** (1488–1566) of Torrijas used to strong effect in Toledo.

CUSTOMS AND SOCIETY. One story set in Teruel is of literary significance. It is not clear whether the thirteenth-century affair between Diego de Marsilla and Isabella de Segura, *Los amantes de Teruel* (The Lovers of Teruel), is fact or fiction, but the Italian writer Giovanni Boccaccio (1313–75) alleged that his story about lovers separated by mischance was taken from real life. The plot and title also occur in works by Rey de Artieda (1581) of Valencia, Tirso de Molina (1627) of Soria, Juan Pérez de Montalbán (1638) of Valencia, and Juan Eugenio Hartzenbusch (1835) of Madrid.

The tale is one of the most enduring and popular of all folk love stories. Marsilla, too poor to marry Isabel, is given six years to make his fortune or lose her hand. After obtaining an income, he is captured by the Moors. In some versions, he manages to free himself, only to arrive just as Isabel marries another suitor. In others, complicated subplots involve a Moorish princess or queen and many issues of honor, with both the hero and heroine finally committing suicide at the end of the drama. Folk plays with the same title and theme are sometimes performed in towns throughout the province.

Teruel later figured heavily in the campaigns of Burgos's El Cid, particularly at Alcañiz, and his memory is occasionally honored in village fiestas.

HISTORIC SITES. A good collection of Mudéjar crafts is on display at the Museo Arqueológico Provincial in **Teruel.** The cathedral, Santa María de Mediavilla, is decorated with Mudéjar ceramics, complex vaulting, and a plateresque altar. The church of San Pedro and the Torre de San Martín also have very elaborate Mudéjar designs.

Elsewhere in the province, the northeastern ancient town of **Alcañiz**, of Roman and Muslim origin on the Guadalupe River, was captured by Alfonso I in 1119. The castle of Calatravos became Jaime I's residence for a time, and a variety of buildings, chapels, and towers still remain, including the church of Santa María la Mayor, built in 1737. The Aragonese have a patriotic feeling about Alcañiz arising from heavy fighting in the area during the War of Independence and the Carlist Wars. Nearby, the Charco Cave has prehistoric wall paintings of numerous animals.

Another town of interest, **Albarracín**, west of the provincial capital, was a Muslim principality controlled by the Banu Razin dynasty of Navarre from 1009 to 1102 until captured by a noble from Navarre, Pedro Ruíz de Azagra. He fortified Albarracín so well that it remained independent until 1284, and the town is virtually unchanged today. **Montalbán** has several plateresque churches such as the Iglesia Soledad, with frescoes by local and national artists. The castle of the condes de la Puebla contains Mudéjar, Gothic, and plateresque details.

CUISINE. Jamón serrano (mountain ham, or cured ham), processed naturally in the sun, is used in many dishes. Local plums, apricots, apples, cherries, strawberries, and peaches are available in season.

ZARAGOZA

VITAL STATISTICS. Pop., 842,386. Area, 17, 274 sq. km. Capital: Zaragoza, also the regional capital. Diocesan sees: Tarazona, Zaragoza. The province is bounded by Lleida (Lérida) on the east, Huesca on the north, Navarre and Soria on the west, and Guadalajara on the south. The University of Zaragoza was established in 1474.

ECONOMY. The urban area of Zaragoza is industrial. An automobile assembly plant built by General Motors in suburban Figueruelas represents a major manufacturing investment, but traditional industries such as leather, silk, and textiles have declined in recent years and the industrial plant of the area generally is old. The countryside beyond the Ebro Valley is dry and not very fertile, useful only for grazing where no well irrigation or larger projects are found. The river valley is used for sugar beet cultivation, producing about half of all Spanish sugar.

HISTORY. (Salduie or Salduba [Iberian], Caesar Augusta [Roman], Sarakosta [Arabic]). Zaragoza, founded in 23 B.C. as a Roman base to protect agriculture and silver mining in the vicinity, became famous as the site (ca. A.D. 40) of the legendary miracle of the Virgin Mary of the Pillar.

The Christian community survived destruction of Roman power by two Germanic tribes, the Suevi in 452 and the Visigoths in 476. St. Braulio, seventh-century archbishop of Zaragoza and friend of St. Isidoro, used the legend of the Virgin Mary of the Pillar to keep the power of Christianity alive, but during the Muslim era from 716 to 1119 Christians faced forcible conversion to Muhammadanism. The term *muladíes* used to describe them is best translated as persons of Christian culture ruled by Muslims.

Zaragoza quickly rose as an important Muslim outpost. In the late eighth century, the Franks under Charlemagne created counties to the north and east from which to attack Zaragoza with the help of the papacy. To develop a military society to defeat the Muslims, early Aragonese kings such as Ramiro I (1035–63) and Sancho Ramírez (1063–94) created *ricohombres* (high nobles), *caballeros villanos* (titles and land grants for military service), and *hidalgos* (petty nobility) with hereditary seignorial domain, getting land in exchange for military service. Under this system, the fledgling Kingdom of Aragón managed to expand. King Alfonso I (the Battler, 1104–34) captured the city of Zaragoza and the Ebro Valley in 1119, nearly doubling the size of his realm. But Castile soon threatened to absorb the new monarchy until the daughter of Ramiro II (1134–37), Petronila, married the count of Barcelona, Ramón Berenguer IV (1131–62). By federating, Aragón and Catalonia achieved nearly equal footing with Castile for three centuries. While the pact kept the administrative and social arrangements of Aragón and Catalonia separate, Aragón received new economic and intellectual stimuli and Catalonia obtained important military backing. As a result, Aragón/Catalonia became a major medieval power in the Mediterranean basin.

Institution-building reached completion when King Pere el Gran (1276–85) granted the Privileges of Union creating the Justicia as a noble law court, independent of the monarchy, designed to protect traditional laws (*fueros*). Separate branches (*brazos*) of the legislature for higher and lower nobility offset the addition in 1301 of urban and clerical representatives. The Cortes of Aragón, unlike that of Castile, retained its right to approve all royal laws. As a result, Aragón long remained the most feudal of the major Spanish states.

The unity of this tightly organized feudal society allowed further empire-building. The Kingdom of Majorca was reintegrated and Sardinia captured during the era from Pere III el Gran (1276–85) to Pere IV el Ceremoniós (1336–87), but the plague weakened military expansion after 1347. In the early fifteenth century, when the dynasty died out after two childless monarchs, a commission of judges and theologians wrote the Compromise of Caspe in 1412, recognizing a collateral branch of the royal family, the Trastámaras, as new rulers.

Fernando I (more properly, Fernando de Antequera, a distant relative of Pere IV) ruled only four years, but his Castilian concept of a strong monarchy encouraged his son, Alfonso V (1416–58), to conquer Corsica (1420), Marseilles (1423), and Naples (1442). Alfonso grew so enchanted with the Renaissance culture of Naples that he never returned to Zaragoza, and his younger brother Juan II (1458–85), King of Navarre, acted as regent until Alfonso's death. During his own reign, Juan had the bad luck to encounter poor harvests and a commercial depression. The Remença uprising in Catalonia almost toppled his monarchy until an abrasive intervention by the French salvaged the royal cause.

In 1469, Juan's younger son Fernando the Catholic married Isabel, half-sister of the Castilian king, Enrique II, forming the marriage partnership that would eventually create the future united Spanish monarchy. Fernando II was a good ruler of Aragón (1485–1516), but behind his success lurked the new, previously unthinkable possibility of union with Castile, four times larger than Aragón. In fact, Fernando was Aragón's last independent king.

Loss of Aragón's independence began when the daughter of Fernando and Isabel, Juana, married a Hapsburg prince, Philip the Fair, and bore him one child, the future Carlos I, the only male heir of Fernando and Isabel. After Isabel died in 1504, Fernando clashed with Philip, who died mysteriously in 1506. In an attempt to maintain Spain's independence from Hapsburg control, Fernando banished the infant Carlos to live with relatives in Brussels and imprisoned Juana. Fernando spent his late reign in wars and diplomacy, seeking to thwart the Austrians in Italy in order to block Carlos's inheritance of Spain. In 1509, he married Germaine de Foix, niece of Louis XII of France, but his second marriage remained childless and Carlos succeeded him in 1517, ushering in two centuries of Hapsburg dynastic rule.

Carlos respected the federated monarchy of Catalonia, Valencia, Majorca, Sardinia, and Aragón, but his son, Felipe II (1556–98), tried to destroy the Justicia when an influential former court official, Antonio Pérez, put himself under its protection after being charged with murder. The citizens of Zaragoza rioted at this breach of royal etiquette, and while Pérez managed to escape abroad, more than eighty Aragonese were killed or later executed. The Justicia became a royal institution, non-Aragonese viceroys governed Aragón, and Castilian troops began to be stationed in the region for the first time.

During the reign of Felipe IV (1621–65), the estrangement grew even greater. In 1624, the royal favorite, don Gaspar de Guzmán, the conde-duque de Olivares of Seville, established uniform tax contributions for all regions of Spain in his Union of Arms proposal. The Cortes of Aragón rejected the idea two years later and continued to quarrel with Castile until 1640–41, when Catalonia revolted. An invasion of Catalonia by France then caused Castile to use Aragón as a battleground. The war destroyed the unity of Aragón and Catalonia without repairing Aragonese–Castilian relations.

The final rupture in this long struggle had an odd twist. When the Bourbon Felipe V inherited the Spanish throne in 1700, his absolutism trampled corporate aspects of Aragonese government by billeting troops and collecting taxes in Zaragoza without regard to the *fueros*. In 1705, the Aragonese, preferring old to new enemies, backed Karl of Austria, who promised to restore the old liberties if he was victorious in the War of Spanish Succession. Felipe retaliated by issuing the Nueva Planta decree in 1707, destroying Aragón's federated union with Catalonia, Valencia, and the Balearics. After he defeated Karl, the new Bourbon king created an *audiencia* to replace traditional government and ended Aragón's customs barrier and issuance of currency. Its crown ceased to exist in all but a symbolic sense.

Later in the eighteenth century, the Bourbons repaired relations by adding talented Aragonese to national government. Pedro Pablo Abraca de Bolea, the conde de Aranda (1719–98), was descended from the Jiménez de Urreas family, one of the most powerful Aragonese feudal clans. He served the court as field marshal, ambassador, president of the Council of Castile under Carlos III, and secretary of state for Carlos IV. As both an enlightened reformer and an autocratic elitist, he headed a substantial Aragonese party in Madrid that tried to mediate absolutism by creating an aristocracy of merit. Among their domestic projects, the construction of the Imperial Canal launched the industrialization of Aragón.

During the Napoleonic era, Zaragoza lived under siege from June to

August 1808 and again from November 1808 to February 1809. Despite brilliant leadership by the conservative patriot José Palafox, who swore devotion to the Virgin of the Pillar, the city suffered terrible destruction at the hands of the French. Carlism grew popular until industrial growth and railroad building led Juan Faustin Bruil (1810–78) to form regional groups such as the Liga Regional Aragonesa and Acción Regionalista de Aragón in pursuit of purely local economic interests. Socialism and anarchism grew in the early twentieth century, but bitter sectarian quarrels during the Second Republic limited their political effectiveness.

Shortly after the outbreak of civil war in 1936, Carlists from Pamplona occupied Zaragoza before anarchists from Barcelona could reach the city. The republican army remained at bay under the city's eastern heights, and although the communists reorganized the militia in 1937 in a final effort to take Zaragoza in the Belchite campaign (August 24–September 6), the militia army fell back and lost eastern Aragón by autumn 1938.

During the postwar era, Zaragoza received aid as one of six poles of development for the Franco regime. By 1979, state programs together with private investment had improved the economy, but competition from Valencia and Catalonia has challenged Zaragoza's industrial markets.

LITERATURE. Abd Bajja (d. 1138), known as **Avempace,** a philosopher and author of *The Rule of the Solitary*, asked how an intelligent individual can be free to live and express truth in a world controlled by the ignorant and fanatical. The highest level of humanity is to be found in thought and intellect, but intellect comes from God, who always inspires the thoughts of a good person. Solomon Ben Judah ibn Gabirol, called **Avicebron** or **Avicebrol** (1021?–57), lived most of his life in Zaragoza teaching a composite theology of rationalist philosophy and Neoplatonism. His major work, the philosophical *Fons Vita* (in Hebrew *Mekor Hayyim*), discusses the absolute forms of truth, beauty, and justice. **Juan Fernández de Heredia** (1310?–96) of Munébrega, a historian, soldier, and diplomat who served Pedro IV of Aragón, wrote the *Gran Crónica de España*, one of the earliest major histories of the Middle Ages by a Spaniard.

In the Golden Age, **Jerónimo Zurita y Castro** (1512–80) became another contributor to Spanish historiography. His many volumes of the *Anales de la Corona de Aragón* (1562–80), covering the period from Arab invasion until 1516, avoid biblical images and make careful use of documents. Another important intellectual, **Baltasar Gracián y Morales** (1601–58) of Belmonte de Calatayud, a Jesuit educated at Huesca and Zaragoza and rector of the College of Tarragona, is the major writer of Aragón, but as a person he had capricious and eccentric ways and a deep pessimism. His moral studies took an allegorical rather than a picaresque turn. *El heroe* (1637) praises the use of intellect, while *El político don Fernando el Católico* (1640) provides a brilliant biography of Aragón's greatest monarch. *El discreto* (1646) calls for educational improvements that might create well-balanced individuals to solve Spain's many problems. *Aguadeza y arte de ingenio* (1648) is an anthology of *conceptismo*, a baroque style stressing obscurity and dazzling language. *Oráculo manual y arte de prudencia* (1647) collects clever but cynical maxims. His major work, *El criticón* (1647), is a vast novel that outwardly resembles *Don Quixote* in its chronicle of the travels of Critilo and Andrenio, two very mismatched personalities, one guided by reason and the other by instinct, who live in a world of absurdity. Gracián's writing expresses bitterness about the ruined economy and low political fortunes of seventeenth-century Spain.

Joaquín Dicenta Benedicto (1863–1917) of Calatayud, a liberal playwright and novelist, wrote extensively about the class struggle of rural Aragón in *Juan José* (1896) 6and *El señor feudal* (1896).

Among the nonnatives who have written about Aragón, **Gustavo Adolfo Bécquer** (1836–1870) of Seville composed *Letters from My Cell* (1864–67) while living at the monastery in Vera de Moncayo. The work makes a poetic journey through the landscape of Aragón.

ART. The area around Zaragoza is a noted center of Mudéjar art and architecture from Teruel. The style began about 1200 in towns such as Daroca, particularly in construction of church towers either square, octagonal, or transitional (from a square to an eight-sided plan).

The province's greatest painter, **Francisco de Goya y Lucientes** (1746–1828) of Fuendetodos, spent two years in Italy before painting frescoes for the cathedral and the palace of the archbishop in Zaragoza. He established himself in Madrid as court painter to Carlos IV in 1789 and as director of the Royal Academy in 1795. In 1793 his deafness profoundly changed his interior vision, and he began painting unflattering portraits of the royal family, making Carlos look like the corner baker. Goya's role as a social critic gave his works remarkable emotional depth.

The eighty prints of his *Los Caprichos* (1799) concentrate on human imperfection, skeptical not only of the religious view of a good individual but also of the Enlightenment's faith and optimism in human progress. One of the most striking prints is *El de la rollona* (Nanny's Boy). Similar qualities can be found in his *corrida* series, *La tauromaquía*, and became even more graphic in *Los desastre de la guerra* (1808–13), a set of fifty-six prints documenting atrocities committed during the Napoleonic period. Of these, *No se pueda mirar* (One Can't Look) and *¿Por que?* (Why?) are among the most powerful. Finally, the series *Los disparates*, eighteen prints in all, is composed of his so-called black paintings. The grotesque Saturn chewing off the heads of his own children remains one of Goya's most memorable works.

While a deep personal pessimism caused Goya to portray grotesque abstractions, his fascination with the many layers of society caused him to leave a very clear picture of the times. This included his two extremely well-known works of the clothed and nude *Majas*, graphically exploring exotic passion. He died in exile at Bordeaux in 1828.

The cathedral in Zaragoza contains a rich profusion of Spanish art. Francisco de Herrera the younger (1622–85), son of the Escorial's builder, and Ventura Rodríguez (1717–85) made major additions to it in 1753. Other works of importance include Antonio González Velázquez's Santa Capilla and Goya's decorations of the choir vault. Many of the side chapels contain important works such as *St. Lawrence* by Jusepe de Ribera.

MUSIC. The *juglar*, or public entertainer, greatly developed medieval secular music in Spain. The court of Pedro IV (the Ceremonious, 1335–87) employed singers and instrumentalists from all over Europe and North Africa in an effort to expand Spanish music. Troubadour poetry, much of it from Catalonia and Galicia, was set to simple melodies played on lutes and other stringed instruments. There is evidence of Italian mandolins being used in the small orchestras, and it is not unreasonable to speculate that more sophisticated Spanish guitars were adapted by the court musicians of the era during this period.

In the seventeenth century, **Gaspar Sanz** of Calanda wrote *Instrucción de música sobre la guitarra española* (1674) expounding the *rasqueado* style of guitar playing, which emphasizes a strumming technique and gives guitar music a very dramatic sound.

In 1853, the Italian opera composer Giuseppe Verdi (1814–1901) used a prison cell in La Aliaberia as the setting for the first act of *Il Trovatore*, taken from an important romantic play, *El Trovador*, by Antonio García Gutiérrez of Madrid. The complicated libretto, filled with hidden identities and witchcraft, was loosely based on fifteenth-century events in Aragón and in the life of Fernando de Antequera.

CUSTOMS AND SOCIETY. The most enduring aspect of religious belief and folklore in Zaragoza is the Virgin of the Pillar. According to legend, she appeared to Santiago (St. James the Apostle) on a bank of the Ebro River, standing on a burning pillar. The Virgin commanded St. James to convert Spain to Christianity and to build a church in her honor. While it is disputed that St. James ever visited Spain, medieval Spain embraced the legend of Santiago as the Reconquest's patron saint, the apostle who helped bring Christianity to Spain. The Virgin Mary became the special symbol of Spanish Catholicism, imbuing it with a passionate character.

The Virgin is the major attraction of the cathedral in Zaragoza and presents an incredible sight. She is said to be adorned with 8,000 diamonds, 145 pearls, 74 emeralds, 62 rubies, and 46 sapphires. Two bomb casings once hung near the Virgin. They had been dropped on the cathedral during the civil war, but their failure to explode was considered a miracle that caused the Virgin to be appointed the Captain-General of Zaragoza by the Franco government.

The Fiesta de la Virgen del Pilar takes place in Zaragoza on October 12.

The central event is the Rosario de Cristal procession of *gigantes y cabe-zudos* (cardboard giants and dwarfs), but there are also bullfights and *jota* dancing.

HISTORIC SITES. The most important structure in **Zaragoza** is the cathedral of Nuestra Señora del Pilar, dedicated to St. James's encounter with the Virgin. The cathedral, built on the site of the encounter, is a huge building with four towers in each corner and ten domes. The interior is dominated by the shrine to the Virgin.

A second cathedral in Zaragoza, La Seo or San Salvador, is the archbishop's church, but it has been rebuilt so often that it is a jumble of styles, particularly in the chapels. La Aljafería, the old Muslim palace begun in 864, has arches, carvings, cornices, capitals, and other decorative elements that make it a prime architectural example of the Muslim period. The Audiencia is a former palace of the condes de Luna, begun in 1551. The Museo de Bellas Artes has a large collection of antiquities, and its paintings illustrate the Spanish Middle Ages and the Golden Age.

Elsewhere in the province, **Cariñena**, almost directly south of the provincial capital, has a large baroque church, La Asunción. **Fuendetodos**, east of Cariñena, is Goya's birthplace. His family house is a museum, and the local church has some of his early frescoes and paintings. Close to the Castilian border in the southeast, the ruins of a Roman village, Bilbilis, are just outside the modern town of **Calatayud**, itself once an important Muslim center, as reflected in its architecture. The church of Santa María la Mayor, originally a mosque, has an octagonal Mudéjar tower and a plateresque interior. **Daroca** (Caesaraugusta [Roman], Kalat-Daruca [Arabic]), directly south of Calatayud, is surrounded by a long wall with the original watchtowers. Daroca has a number of churches, the most important being Santa María. There is a parish museum and the Casa de don Juan de Austria, which originally belonged to the Luna family. The Monasterio de Piedra outside Daroca is a twelfth-century Cistercian monastery, now part of a national park.

In the northern part of the province, **Ejea de los Caballeros** is the site of El Salvador Church, built in 1222 and today a national monument. The church building is Romanesque with five towers and two portals, and once served as a fortress. **Sádaba** has a Gothic church of the late Middle Ages, Roman ruins, an ancient synagogue, and a castle. Fernando the Catholic was born in 1452 at the Palacio de los Sada in **Sos del Rey Católico**. The Palacio has been restored and is a national monument and parador.

Almost directly west of the capital, south of the Ebro River, **Tarazona**, an ancient Roman mining town and later briefly a capital of Aragón, has a cathedral of Mudéjar architecture with portal reliefs by Juan de Talavera, several alabaster tombs of early religious leaders, and an altarpiece painted by the Sephardic artist Yojanan Levi, a Christian convert. The Bishop's Palace once served as the palace of the Aragonese kings. The poet Gustavo

Adolfo Bécquer lived and wrote at the monastery of Veruela in **Vera de Moncayo.**

CUISINE. An important Aragonese specialty is *pollo en chilindrón* (chicken in a special sauce made with garlic, tomatoes, onions, and peppers, also used on lamb). *Bocalao ajoarriero* (creamy cod), *menestra de verduras* (mixed vegetables), *jamón serrano* (sun-dried ham), *sopa de ajo* (garlic soup), and *lomo de cerdo a la zaragozana* (pork loin in sauce) are other popular dishes. Calatayud makes a specialty of *tapas* such as *lomo de orza* (marinated pork loin).

The following recipe for chicken in a special sauce serves six.

POLLO EN CHILINDRÓN

2–3 young chickens, cut into pieces

salt and pepper to taste

3 Tbs. olive oil

3 cloves garlic, minced

1 onion, chopped

3 oz. ham

1 can tomatoes

6 red peppers

1 Tbs. paprika

pinch of saffron

After the chicken is seasoned with salt and pepper, warm the olive oil and add the garlic and chicken, but remove both before they become too brown. Cook the onion, ham, tomatoes, and peppers, adding paprika and saffron, and then add the chicken and garlic and cook about 30–40 minutes until the chicken is tender. *Cordero en chilindrón* can be prepared according to this same recipe, using 1½ lb. of lamb in place of the chicken.

The following recipe can be used to prepare mixed vegetables.

MENESTRA DE VERDURAS

½ lb. cooked chicken

¼ cup stock

4 white potatoes, peeled and chopped

½ lb. green peppers

1 cup whole tomatoes

½ lb. green beans

½ cup artichoke hearts

¼ lb. shelled peas

2 carrots, chopped

2 cloves garlic, crushed

1 onion, chopped

2 Tbs. olive oil

2 cups tomato sauce

2 cups white wine or dry sherry

salt, pepper, and nutmeg to taste

Tear the chicken into strips and cook in stock with the potatoes, peppers, tomatoes, and other vegetables. Sauté garlic and onions in olive oil before adding to this mixture. After the vegetables are tender, add tomato sauce and wine. Stir, season with salt, pepper, and nutmeg, and let simmer for 1 hour.

Wine comes from Cariñena, south of Zaragoza and east of Calatayud. The three most important wineries are San Valero, López Pelayo, and the smaller Suso y Pérez, all known for robust red wine, although some rosé is produced.

Chapter 3

ASTURIAS

REGIONAL CHARACTERISTICS. Pop., 1,127,007. Area, 10,565 sq. km. Regional capital: Oviedo. The region lies between the Bay of Biscay on the north, León on the south, Santander on the east, and Lugo (Galicia) on the west. The dominant physical feature is the Cordillera Cantábrica, a western extension of the Pyrenees. Two important natural areas, the Picos de Europa (highest mountains in Spain) and the Muniellos Forest Reserve between Moal and San Antolin, a twenty-three-square-mile tract of virgin forest, are among the few spots of the Cordillera Cantábrica preserved in almost pristine condition.

Regionalist sentiment appeared in the late nineteenth century with the neo-Carlism of Juan Vásquez de Mella y Fanjul. He based this in part on the odd dialect called *bable* spoken by some rural people of the area. An organized movement appeared in 1918–19 when a Junta Regionalista del Principado sought greater regional control for Asturias. Although unsuccessful, the Junta led a backlash against the large number of Castilian or Basque miners employed in the province who were sympathetic to the left. During the Second Republic, the radicalism of the miners overwhelmed Asturian regionalism and conservatism. Not surprisingly, the area was treated with great harshness by Franco for having supported labor and radical political parties.

Voters in the referendum of 1978, wary of continued authoritarian cen-

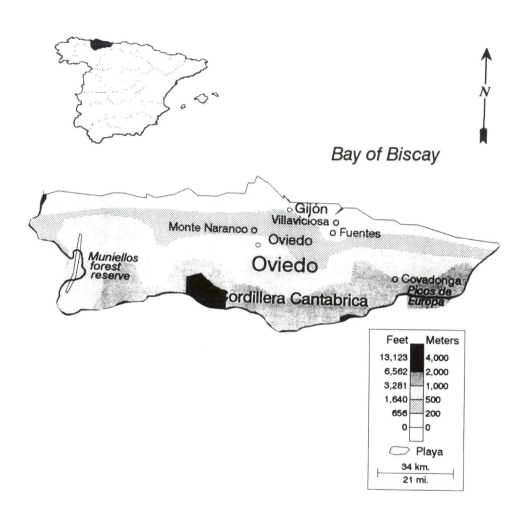

Bay of Biscay

o Gijón
Villaviciosa o
Monte Naranco o   o Fuentes
            o Oviedo

Oviedo

Muniellos
forest
reserve

Cordillera Cantabrica

o Covadonga
Picos de
Europa

Feet	Meters
13,123	4,000
6,562	2,000
3,281	1,000
1,640	500
656	200
0	0

Playa

34 km.
21 mi.

ASTURIAS

tralism, supported limited autonomy by 55 percent. Autonomous status gained final approval on December 30, 1981.

Asturias is called a *principado* (principality) in honor of its early medieval monarchy. The flag of Asturias is solid blue with a yellow cross imposed upon it.

Asturias ranks tenth in income among the regions of Spain and is eighth highest in terms of foreign emigration.

OVIEDO

VITAL STATISTICS. Pop., area, and location: see Regional Characteristics, above. Capital and diocesan see: Oviedo. The University of Oviedo is a state-run institution of higher education in the city.

ECONOMY. Asturias, an important area of industrial employment, is best known for its coal production. The basins of El Bierzo–Villablino (partly in León) and the valleys of the Nalón (Langreo, San Martín del Rey Aurelio), Caudal (Mieres), and Camocha produce 50 percent of all Spanish coal and contain approximately 360 million tons in reserve; but while Asturias is among the top four provinces of Spain in terms of the total amount of coal mined, no Asturian mine ranks within the top twenty in Spain because of small-scale operations, low profitability, and lack of investment by foreign owners. Zinc is also important, with large reserves owned by Asturiana de Zinc, which operates a large smelter at Veriña, near Gijón.

Agriculture is dominated by dairying.

HISTORY. (Astures [Celtiberian]). Asturias, settled by Celtiberians, worshipped such gods as Canamus, similar to the Greco-Roman Jupiter. Roman conquest under Augustus came during the Cantabrian War in 27 B.C. Mining activity grew until the advent of the Suevis and Vandals, and Visigothic supremacy after A.D. 520 relied heavily upon grazing and textile production.

In 722, as Muslim raids imperiled the area, a Visigothic prince by the name of Pelayo fled to Covadonga, where he and his men hid in the cave of Auseva and prepared to do battle. Pelayo was killed (the most dependable date is May 28, 722), but the victory of his men over the Muslims was the legendary beginning of the Reconquest. A dynasty emerged soon afterward under the leadership of Pelayo's son-in-law, Alfonso I (739–57). His raids on the Duero Valley created a buffer zone protecting Galicia, Cantabria, and the Basque region. When the Benedictine monastery of San Vicente moved from Toledo to Cangas de Onís in 761 to proselytize, Christianity spread widely.

Discovery of the sepulcher of Santiago (St. James) in Galicia soon caused Asturian rulers to identify themselves as heirs of the Visigoths, with a mission to reconquer Spain from the Muslims. Alfonso II (791–842) helped Bishop Teodomiro build the first church in honor of St. James at Santiago de Compostela. The king made Oviedo into an imperial capital, building a palace modeled on Charlemagne's castle in Aachen, the church of San Tirso, the treasury-like Cámera Santa, and a martyr's chapel.

Warrior bands led by Alfonso II and Ordoño I (850–66) pressed the attack on Muslim communities in León and Extramadura. Alfonso III el Magno (866–910) began calling himself emperor after seizing Zamora and Coimbra (northern Portugal), but his will divided Galicia, León, and Asturias among his sons, fragmenting his possessions. Ordoño II (910–25) of León ruled the strongest of these successor states, with vast new lands such as Castile on the edge of the slowly retreating Muslim empire. Before long, León surpassed Asturias, just as Navarre was later submerged by León and Castile, or León itself was later incorporated by Castile.

In this way, Castile peacefully absorbed Asturias (and Galicia) into its orbit, swearing that its eldest male heir presumptive to the throne would always carry the title *Principe de Asturias*, a promise it has kept. But Castilian control in the later Middle Ages tightly bound Asturian society. The most powerful Asturian noble family, the Vegas, controlled the office of *adelantado mayor* (governor's office, predecessor to later viceroys) until the murder of Garcilaso de la Vega (d. 1351) by Pedro the Cruel. Even so, later marriages with the Mendozas of Guadalajara raised the Vegas to the highest rank of *caballero* status. Peasants of La Montaña suffered under excessive seignorial power and crushing feudal dues for centuries.

Formal relations with Castile at the governmental level came through the Junta General del Principado (ca. 1388), the Real Audiencia of Felipe V (1717), and finally by the Diputación Provincial (1834–1939). While special local laws (*fueros*) protected local society, they did not become as elaborate as in the Basque Provinces or Navarre, largely because Asturias experienced greater direct economic integration with Castile. The city of Oviedo, for example, survived a destructive fire in 1521 to trade with England and France and to serve Seville in the American trade. Pedro Menéndez de Avilés (1519–74), governor of Cuba who fortified the coast of Florida, was typical of many high-ranking Asturians who served in the Indies.

Colonial riches allowed Bishop Fernando de Valdés y Salas to create the University of Oviedo in 1608. Within a century, the university became one of Spain's most important centers of higher education. Fray Benito Feijóo y Montenegro, the early Spanish social critic who popularized French rationalism, taught at Oviedo and attracted students who went on to become national leaders and reformers.

The work of these graduates was impressive. In 1765, one of them, the conde de Campomanes, denounced mortmain, feudal contracts, price ceilings on grain, and the privileges of the Honrado Compañía de la Mesta, the collective Castilian sheepherding organization, demanding that peasants receive the right to enclose land as their own property. He also castigated the Church for usurping land belonging to the laity. In 1794, another Oviedo graduate, Gaspar Melchor de Jovellanos, argued that liberty and private property should be the proper ends of a well-run state and that mortmain, entail, and the Mesta conspired to keep land from the peasants.

Still a third, the conde de Toreno, leader of the Supreme Junta of Asturias when Napoleon invaded Spain and occupied Asturias, obtained British aid and also helped write the Constitution of 1812 in Cádiz. Other prominent Asturians of the period included Agustín Argüelles (1766–1844) of Ribadesella, one of the writers of the Constitution of 1837, and Colonel Rafael Riego y Florez Valdes (1784–1823) of Tuña, a member of the Masonic Grand Orient Lodge and leader of the revolt against Fernando VII on January 1, 1820, that created the liberal Triennium. This regime's fall in 1823 was accompanied by Riego's execution as a political radical.

Asturias gained little advantage from liberalism once it came to power. Two politicians, Pedro Pidal, the marqués de Pidal (1800–1865), and José Posada Herrera (1814–85) of Llanes, represented the old landed elite and new coal and iron industries. Both manipulated land titles, illegally purchased Church properties, and defrauded the electoral process for their wealthy constituents, making a mockery of liberalism. Antiliberal hostility became so widespread that Juan Vásquez de Mella y Fanjul (1861–1928) proposed the reactivization of the Carlist movement to promote regional separation from Madrid.

The new iron and coal industries, which grew very large, particularly benefited from the machinations of Pidal and Posada Herrera. The region led the nation in iron production between 1860 and 1879, and although Basque steel makers of Bizkaia (Vizcaya) eventually surpassed Asturias, Asturian coal continued to be a vital ingredient in heavy industry. Mining towns experienced bitter labor strife as early as 1873, when miners began joining the newly formed socialist Unión General de Trabajadores (UGT) and its Asturian Miners' Union branch, the Sindicato de Obreros Mineros Asturianos, led by Manuel Llaneza (1879–1931). Strike activity grew heavy between 1890 and 1910 and in the 1930s. The Spanish Socialist Party (PSOE) mushroomed in size under the provincial leadership of Ramón González Peña (1888–1952), although communists challenged the PSOE after 1930.

During the Second Republic, Asturias was a left-wing stronghold, and when a conservative cabinet abrogated labor reform in 1934 and moved toward more authoritarian labor policies, the Asturian uprising of October 1934 raised the banner of revolution. The rising, repressed in a fortnight by 26,000 soldiers, at a cost of several hundred killed, pushed the left to form a Popular Front coalition that won a narrow national electoral victory in February 1936, to the miners' great joy. When the army rebelled in mid-

July 1936, Asturias remained loyal to the Republic in the civil war and put down a nationalist uprising in Gijón. The area did not fall to Franco until October 1937.

During the early postwar era, Franco forcefully tried to eradicate memory of the 1934 revolt as a major symbol of the Spanish labor movement. But in 1957, new militancy led to formation of Comisiones Obreras (CCOO), or Workers' Commissions, the product of a failed illegal strike at the Camocha mine near Gijón, for which strikers had been severely punished. The CCOO, although styling itself as a series of informal and independent committees seeking collective bargaining, was in fact communist-backed, supported by the leader of postwar Spanish communism, Santiago Carrillo (1915–92) of Gijón. The movement spread rapidly throughout Asturias until declared illegal in 1968, but the CCOO example revived pro-labor sentiment throughout Spain and sparked revival of the UGT and PSOE, which played major roles in the anti-Franco opposition until his death in 1975.

Since then, the collapse of Spanish communism has been almost as spectacular as that of Soviet communism. With its ideology of social democracy, the PSOE made some of its most important electoral gains in Asturias, particularly during the elections of 1982, when it replaced the communists as the leader of a now democratic left.

LITERATURE. The literary tradition began in the seventeenth century. **Francisco Antonio de Bances Candamo** (1662–1704) of Avilés, a dramatist, played an important role in setting the rules for Spanish composition. **Alonso Carrió de la Vandera** (1715?–78?) of Gijón traveled extensively through Latin America and popularized travel writing in his guidebooks for different parts of the area.

The towering regional figure, Fray **Benito Feijóo y Montenegro** (1676–1764), was the major philosopher of the Spanish Enlightenment. Born in Orense province of Galicia, Feijóo received his education at the University of Oviedo and taught there from 1709 to 1749. He helped make the university a progressive institution, attracting students interested in modernizing Spain's political economy and statecraft.

Among Feijóo's students, Pedro Rodríguez, the **conde de Campomanes** (1723–1803) of Santa Eulalia, nephew of the canon of the cathedral of Oviedo, studied law and published a history, *Historia de los Templarios* (1747), before advocating economic reform in *Tratado de la regalía de amortización* (1765), *Discurso sobre el fomento de la industria popular* (1774), and *Discurso sobre la educación popular de los artesanos y su fomento* (1775–77). Campomanes promoted free market ideas and physiocratic improvement of the economy, particularly stressing the crucial importance of agricultural reform as a precursor of industrialization. He also helped found an academy of history and edited Feijóo's works. As a politician, he was one of the most important ministers of state under Carlos III (1759–88).

Another enlightened reformer, **Gaspar Melchor de Jovellanos y Ramírez** (1744–1811) of Gijón, emerged as a major eighteenth-century philosopher/statesman who wrote many fables, plays, poems, and political tracts. His *El informe dado a la Junta General de Comercio y Moneda* (1785) argued among other things for the right of women to work on an equal basis with men. The important *Informe en el expediente de ley agraria* (1795), advocating land reform, and *Memoria en defensa de la Junta Central* (1810) defended the Spanish rebellion against Napoleonic France and demanded that the Cortes of Cádiz make liberal reforms. Jovellanos became a councilor of state in 1776, fell in 1790, and was sent into internal exile in Asturias, where he busied himself by founding the Institute of Asturias in Gijón, an advanced faculty of higher education. He returned to political life briefly in 1798, but conflict with Manuel Godoy led to exile in Majorca until 1808.

José Maria Queipo de Llano, the **conde de Toreno** (1786–1843) of Oviedo, after his efforts in the War of Independence, faced exile by Fernando VII in 1814–20 and again in 1823–34 for his liberal ideas. He was a major early figure of Spanish liberalism as minister of finance and president of the government council in 1834–35; his writings, which include *Historia del levantamiento contra los franceses* (1837) and *Discursos parlamentarios* (1840), provided important early history and philosophy for the liberal movement.

In imaginative literature, a wealthy post-romantic poet, **Ramón de Campoamor** (1817–1901) of Navia, a civil governor in several provinces, wrote short, ironic, skeptical poems that achieved great popularity, although critics accused him of writing doggerel.

Leopoldo Alas Ureña (pseud. **Clarín**; 1852–1901), a native Asturian, became nationally important as a caustic literary critic. A student of Francisco Giner de los Ríos, Clarín was interested in social change and modern philosophy. His novel *La Regenta* (1885) constituted a diatribe against the polite society in Oviedo (called Vetusta in the book) who, Clarín claimed, did nothing but play cards, gossip, and have sexual fantasies. Clarín won particular fame for his short stories collected as *Pipa* (1886), *El Señor y lo demás son cuentos* (1893), and *El gallo de Socrates* (1901).

Another Asturian novelist, **Armando Palacio Valdés** (1853–1938), achieved great success with his novel *Marta y María* (1883) by providing a contrast between mysticism and worldliness. *La espuma* (1890) is a protest novel on exploitation of miners, while *La fe* (1892) is a very strong anticlerical work, and *José* (1885) concerns a fisherman who must struggle with the sea. The last work described Asturian coastal society with true local color and flavor. In general, he observed modern social behavior from a naturalistic perspective.

Juan Vásquez de Mella y Fanjul (1861–1928) of Cangas de Onís, a journalist for a number of newspapers and editor of his own *El pensamiento Galaico*, was an important later philosopher of Carlism, revitalizing the neo-Scholastic ideas of Donoso Cortés in order to reformulate corporative concepts of society's supremacy over the state.

Ramón Pérez de Ayala (1880–1962) of Oviedo, a well-known novelist, essayist, poet, and diplomat, grew so troubled by Spanish decadence after 1898 that he used novels such as *Tinieblas en las cumbres* (1907), *La pata de la raposa* (1912), and *Troteras y danzaderas* (1913) to discuss a society that had lost its way. He took a slice-of-life approach, and many figures of the day appeared in his pages only thinly disguised. His later novels included *Prometeo* (1916) attacking caciquismo. *Belarmino y Apolonio* (1921) is a complicated story of men meeting and overcoming their destinies, hailed as a modern *Don Quixote* at the time. *Luna de miel, luna de hiel* (1923) took on the problems of Spanish education, while *Tigre Juan* (1926) is a humorous updating of the don Juan theme attacking Spanish concepts of honor. Particularly acute descriptions of Oviedo can be found in *Belarmino y Apolonio* and *Tigre Juan*.

In the twentieth century, **Alejandro Núñez Alonso** (b. 1905) of Gijón, a novelist and journalist, lived in Mexico from 1929 to 1949 before returning to write popular and historical novels, generally of a conservative nature. **José García Nieto** (b. 1914) of Oviedo spent much of his life in Madrid as an editor and poet. His collection, *Tregua* (1951), won the Garcilaso Prize. **Dolores Medio** (b. 1920) is a novelist whose first work, *Nosotros los Rivero* (1953), tells the autobiographical story of her family in Asturias. She also wrote *Funcionario público* (1956) about the misadventures of a low-ranking state employee in Madrid.

Carlos Bousoño (b. 1923) taught literature at the University of Madrid. A student of Aleixandre, he wrote poetry that is both mystical and existential. **Angel González** (b. 1925), a contemporary poet who worked as an editor in Barcelona, a government employee in Madrid, and a professor in the United States, shows the influences of Juan Ramón Jiménez. González's first work of poetry, *Aspero mundo*, appeared in 1956. *Grado elemental* (1962) won the Antonio Machado Award, and the eight volumes of poetry he wrote between 1965 and 1985 led to the Príncipe de Asturias Prize in 1985.

ART. In the early Reconquest, Asturias became one of the earliest centers of Christian art due to the strong influence of Carolingian France. The Naranco Palace and San Miguel de Lillo are decorated with sculpture and mural paintings in a style influenced by northern and eastern Europe. Other motifs include ornamental representations of buildings and draperies in the Pompeian tradition derived from late Roman work.

MUSIC. Colonel Riego is the heroic subject of *Himno de Riego*, the Spanish anthem of revolution written by another Asturian, **Evaristo Fernández**

San Miguel (1785–1862) of Gijón. Like Riego, San Miguel was a rebellious military officer and lived in exile in England until returning to fight against the Carlists in 1834, later becoming minister of war in various liberal cabinets.

CUSTOMS AND SOCIETY. *Giraldilla* dances and songs in Asturias are similar to traditional northern circle dances. The songs used for these dances are called *estribillos*, or refrain songs, in which the melody is repeated over and over. The *danza prima* (also danced in the Basque Provinces) is a communal round dance accompanied by ballads sung by a man and a woman, with each line beginning with the exclamation "Ay!" and ending with a religious motto. Some of these folk dances date from the pre-Christian era.

Popular traditional sports include contests of strength such as the competitive throwing of the *barra*, a metal shotput, or foot racing and the old sport of ninepin bowling. Traditional female dress includes short woolen skirts ornamented with bright bands, embroidered red or blue stockings, and white blouses worn with a flowered cotton vest, kerchiefs, and black capes. Male dress is similar to that of the Galicians. Folk superstition involves the *jana*, a ghostlike figure much less frightening than the witches and sorcerers of neighboring Galicia.

The Vaqueros of rural Asturias are cattle herders with such a different way of life that they have been traditionally considered Muslim or Jewish, although in fact they are Spanish.

HISTORIC SITES. The oldest structure in **Oviedo** is the basilica of San Julián de los Prados (popularly called Santullano), Spain's largest pre-Romanesque church, built in the first half of the ninth century. The basilica has three aisles, a continuous transept, and a tripartite sanctuary. The buildings of Alfonso II add to Oviedo's medieval heritage. The city's large Gothic cathedral, Sancta Ovetensis, has a 270-foot western tower and several baroque chapels with many historical artifacts from the region. The university is important, and a provincial museum is housed in the ancient monastery of San Vicente, founded in 781.

Elsewhere in the province, north of Oviedo on the coast of the Bay of Biscay, **Gijón** is the second city of the region and a resort, seaport, and site of the Universidad Laboral, a large technical school. The city suffered great damage during the Spanish Civil War. The Instituto Jovellanos, which serves as both a library and museum, is located in Jovellanos's small former palace.

The countryside east of Gijón is a historic and bucolic area. **Villaviciosa**, a village since the Roman period, has a very nice Romanesque church, Santa María. In the countryside around Villaviciosa, stone or wood granaries called *hórreos* are distinctive for their conical tile roofs and floors elevated on stilts. Just a few miles south of Cangas de Onís is the battle site of **Covadonga** and the monumental sanctuary celebrating its importance.

CUISINE. Oviedo is famous for its good food, especially for stews using vegetable broth and blood pudding. *Fabada a la asturiana* (Asturian bean stew) is made with butter beans and blood sausage (*morcilla*).

FABADA A LA ASTURIANA

1½ pints vegetable broth   1 red pepper, chopped

1 lb. butter beans   1 clove garlic, minced

½ lb. chopped ham   3 bay leaves

¼ lb. *chorizo* (or *morcilla*)

Boil the beans in the broth and simmer until tender. Cook the ham, *chorizo*, pepper, and garlic together. Drain the beans and add the meat, pepper, garlic, and bay leaves, cooking over very low heat until the beans are flavored by the mixture.

Fabes con almejas (beans with clams) can be prepared according to the same recipe by using 1 lb. of canned clams and cutting down on the amount of ham and *chorizos*. Since Asturias is a maritime region, fish is often served. *Rape con almejas* (monkfish and clams in fennel vinaigrette), *ventesco de bonito con tomate* (tuna cooked with tomatoes), *pixin con salsa verde* (monkfish in a green sauce), and *crema de andaricas* (cream of crayfish soup) are popular.

Cabrales (blue cheese) is a type of blue roquefort. *Gamonedo* (soft cheese) and *queso de los bellos* (hard goat cheese) are also popular. *Arroz requemada asturiana* (rice pudding) is often served for dessert. While wines are not produced locally, cider is pressed in great quantities.

Chapter 4

BALEARIC ISLANDS

REGIONAL CHARACTERISTICS. Pop., 685,088. Area, 5,014 sq. km. Capital: Palma, Majorca. Diocesan sees: Majorca, Minorca, Ibiza. The Balearic Island region is from 75 to 190 miles off the east coast of Spain and lies south of France and west of Italy. The archipelago, approximately 135 miles long, is composed, in order of size, of Majorca (Mallorca), Minorca (Menorca), Ibiza (Iviza or Aviza), and thirteen other smaller islands. Only two of these, Cabrera and Formentera, are inhabited.

In the debate over autonomy in 1978, 62 percent voted for regionalism. For some, this vote simply acknowledged their oddly accented combination of Spanish and Català (Catalan) called Macorquin or, in Ibiza, Obicenco. Some favored joining Catalonia to acknowledge its long ties with the islands, but a majority probably sought greater control of regional decision-making simply to ensure continuation of economic boom times. Autonomy went into effect on February 25, 1983, vesting power in a "government of the Balearic community."

The region's flag is four red stripes on a field of yellow with a purple field in the upper left-hand corner that bears the outline of a white castle.

The Balearic Islands rank first in per capita income for all of Spain.

PALMA

VITAL STATISTICS. Pop. and area: see Regional Characteristics, above. Palma, pop. 304,422, site of the only university. Maó (Mahón), Minorca,

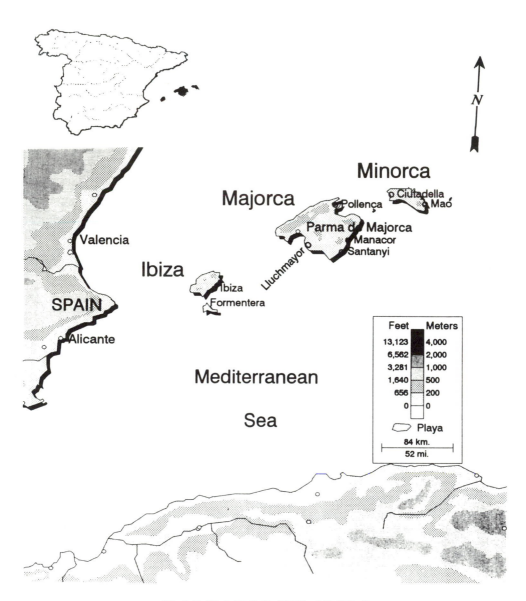

BALEARIC ISLANDS

pop. 22,924. Calviá, Inca, and Manacor also have populations over 20,000. The Tramuntana Mountains run southwest to northeast on Majorca and protect the southern parts of the islands from northern winter winds.

ECONOMY. The Balearics are a tourist haven, attracting about a fifth of all foreign visits to Spain. More than half the tourists are British or German, mostly on commercial tours. The resorts utilize beautiful beaches, particularly on Ibiza or the tropical southern part of Majorca, where orchids, hibiscus, and palms grow. One of the largest Spanish hotel companies, Hoteles Mallorquines Agrupados, operates more than 120 hotels in the Balearic and Canary Islands. Dependence on tourist income (10 percent of total Spanish gross national product) is three or four times higher in the Balearics. As a result, the islands have the highest per capita income of any Spanish region. This high income is derived from land sales for tourism and from the large demand for goods and services.

To a lesser extent, income is earned by fishing, naval services, and horticulture. Almond cultivation is the largest among the four areas of Spain that raise this crop. Light industries include cotton textile spinning, raw silk production, and the shoe factories of Inca, Majorca. So-called Majorcan pearls are manufactured at Manacor by coating glass beads into a very realistic type of artificial pearl solution.

HISTORY. (Gymnesiae [Greek], Major and Minor [Roman]). The Cyclopean or Talayot period of Balearic Neolithic culture, perhaps influenced by Minoan settlements from Crete, anticipated the bull's ritual importance in Hispanic culture with the famous bovine heads at Costig. The extensive colonies of the Phoenicians and Greeks, consolidated by the Carthaginians after the seventh century B.C., fell to Rome during the Punic Wars. The last battle on Minorca in the ancient period took place at Zarma in 202 B.C., although Ibiza (Ebusus or Ibusim [Carthaginian], Iviza [Spanish]) remained Carthaginian for almost a century afterwards.

The town of Palma, chief Roman administrative center and stop from Italy to Iberia, also attracted many Jews in the diaspora after A.D. 69. Judaism merged into Balearic society to a greater extent than elsewhere in Spain, but society grew unstable when the Vandals replaced the Romans in 425, only to fall to the Byzantine Greeks in 533. Muslim raiders from the Barbary Coast dispossessed the Greeks by 798 and the islands became part of the Islamic world, with Arab technology supporting a larger population through expanded agriculture and fishing. In 982, the emirate of Córdoba incorporated the Balearics for the first time with mainland Spain.

Ramón Berenguer III of Catalonia briefly invaded the islands in the early eleventh century, and in 1114 Pisa led an unsuccessful crusade to clear the islands of Muslim pirates. In 1229, the region's wealth attracted the attention of Aragón, recently merged with Catalonia. Jaume the Conqueror successfully invaded the islands between 1229 and 1235 and expelled as many as 100,000 Muslims from Majorca. Catalan merchants and farmers were brought in, and feudal lords from Catalan districts north of the Pyrenees established manors. Ibiza's Muslim community was enslaved, and Catalan peasants (*payeses*) were settled throughout Minorca in 1287.

When Jaume died in 1276, the Balearics briefly joined the northern Pyrenees districts of Roussillon and Cerdaña (in French, Cerdagne) as a separate kingdom until being returned to the Kingdom of Aragón in 1349. With the archipelago under stable control, the economy flourished. The Consell of Palma, representing the three major social estates, prospered from seaborne trade with distant Mediterranean ports. As a part of the Aragonese-Catalan empire of the eastern Mediterranean, the Balearics helped to create Spanish maritime tradition and imperial expertise.

In time, a number of problems clouded this success and prosperity. Defense of the islands remained a problem, particularly against Genoese and Castilian corsairs. The mid-fourteenth-century Black Death struck hard and caused labor shortages and agricultural decline. In its wake, the Jews, blamed for the calamity, faced demands by the Inquisition in 1435 to convert. Bad harvests and the unpopularity of the Palma oligarchy led to a bloody peasant revolt called the Foráneos in Majorca (1450–53) and Minorca (1462–66) along the same lines as the Remença crisis in Catalonia. The royal governor, Miguel de Gurrea, had to flee to Ibiza, which remained loyal to the monarchy. After the government regained control, the Jews were again blamed. Their community was expelled in 1492 by the Catholic Kings, despite the harm to trade. Carlos I put a rigorous set of religious controls over the islands in the hands of the Council of Aragón and the Inquisition.

During the Hapsburg dynasty, Spanish-Turkish rivalry made life in the Balearics even more precarious. When the Muslim community was expelled in 1609, agriculture, fishing, and artisan crafts declined badly. As the Turkish crisis decreased, Britain, France, and Austria saw the islands as strategic naval outposts and vied for control of the archipelago in order to dominate the Mediterranean. In 1706, an Anglo-Dutch bombardment in the War of Spanish Succession allowed British occupation of Minorca from 1708 to 1756 under terms of the Treaty of Utrecht (1713). The French replaced the British between 1756 and 1763, but returned the islands to Britain by the Treaty of Paris (1763) in exchange for the Caribbean Antilles and several trading bases in India. London fortified the island and created George Town as a series of defensive positions to protect Port Mahón, but France and Spain allied in 1782 to foment an internal mutiny that finally expelled the British from Minorca. Admiral Nelson tried unsuccessfully to reestablish British rule in 1798, but Spain resumed full sovereignty in March 1802 by exchanging Trinidad for Minorca.

During this turbulent period, a few islanders achieved prominence in the Americas. The best known, Fray Junípero Serra (1713–84) of Petra, Majorca, founded the California missions. American migration declined when the islands experienced a strong renewal of Catalan influence in the early nineteenth century and thousands of island immigrants were drawn to Barcelona. The national government in Madrid controlled the archipelago by such a corrupt, oligarchical administration that when the Majorcan Antonio Maura y Montaner (1853–1925) twice won the national premiership in the early twentieth century, he sought nationwide local government reform. He failed in 1909 and fell from power, but Maura is remembered as the foremost Balearic politician of the modern era.

Of the few other Majorcans who rose so high, General Valeriano Weyler (1838–1930), son of a German émigré who had settled in the Balearics, was accused of committing atrocities while commander-in-chief of the Spanish army during the colonial war with Cuba in 1895–96.

Organized tourism made its appearance in 1909 when the Grand Hotel opened as a holiday resort, but at first only the wealthy could afford an island vacation, and poverty in the Balearics remained high. Smuggling was the fastest way to make large sums of money. The well-known Juan March (1880–1962), "the last pirate of the Mediterranean," as his enemies called him, eventually became Spain's richest tycoon and Francisco Franco's personal banker.

During the Second Republic, the islands generally supported left-wing and regional nationalist parties. At the start of the Spanish Civil War, the rebel general Manuel Goded seized Majorca on July 18, 1936. Fighting intensified when the republicans took Minorca on July 20 and Ibiza on August 9, but their efforts to free Majorca failed because Franco's ally, Benito Mussolini, sent Italian forces to reinforce the nationalist garrison. Ibiza fell to the Italians in December 1936, while Minorca remained republican and played a key role in badly damaging the German battleship *Deutschland* on May 18, 1937. In retaliation, a blockade kept food shipments from reaching Minorca until starvation forced its surrender in February 1939.

Postwar activity saw the islands struggle to overcome their perennial poverty and isolation, and not until the advent of long-range commercial aviation in 1956 did the Balearics become a mass tourist destination as one of Europe's favorite warm-weather resorts. Along with the Costa Brava in Catalonia, the Balearics were an early focal point of Spanish tourist development. More than 6 million now annually vacation in the islands.

LITERATURE. The greatest Catalan intellectual, **Ramón Llull** (Lull, or Raimundo Lulio; 1235?–1315) of Palma de Majorca, lived in Palma from age twenty-two to forty-five and again from age sixty to eighty. Llull's early education absorbed Arabic culture and Greco-Roman philosophy, but recurring dreams of Christ's crucifixion and of a beautiful woman with cancer haunted his early emotional life, perhaps the product of religious agony. His personality changed after a pilgrimage to Santiago de Compostela, and he joined the Franciscan Order, achieving a brilliant career by middle life as a writer and philosopher in Barcelona, and writing an estimated 276 works.

Llull's writings include *Llibre de Contemplació de Déu*, or *Book of the Contemplation of God* (1282), which contains a story similar to St. Augustine's *Confessions*. Another of his works, *Llibre del orde del la Cavalyeria* (1286?), created the Spanish tradition of chivalric literature, and *Blanquerna* is a long romance that tried to explain the psychology of chivalry.

His masterpiece, *Ars Magna*, or *Ars Compendiosa Inveniendi Veritatem* (The Great Art, or The Complete Art of Discovering the Truth), first published in 1275, tried to encourage missionary activity after the failure of the Crusades. It is filled with tables and strange discs to serve as concordances for general knowledge. Above all, the book sought to isolate the premises of thought accepted by all "civilized" human beings in order to demonstrate everything necessary to convert other religions to Christianity. Theologians attacked the work, but Giordano Bruno later hailed Llull as one of the earliest researchers into the theory of general knowledge. Llull exuded a conviction that Jews and Muslims could be converted to Christianity through an appeal to their sense of reason and belief in the mystery of the Virgin as the central supernatural aspect of Catholicism.

Beyond his religious writings, Llull collected information, ideas, and concepts and may have been the first to advocate an international association of states. He also worked on the astrolabe, a device used by mariners to measure the altitude of celestial bodies.

In the late Middle Ages, an odd figure in Mediterranean intellectual history, **Anselm Turmeda** (1352?–1423) of Palma, entered the Franciscan Order, studied in Spain, and showed promise as a theologian, but then mysteriously turned up in Algiers, where he converted to Muhammadanism and wrote several well-known works defending his newfound faith.

Cultural life declined until the nineteenth century, when **Josep María Quadrado y Nieto** (1819–96) of Ciudadela, Minorca, an archaeologist and archivist, began exhaustive research on the Balearics that culminated with his social history, *Fortenses y ciudadanos: historia de las discusiones civiles de Mallorca en el siglo XV* (1847). Other writers of the modern period include **Mariano Aguiló y Fúster** (1825–97), a poet and historian of the Catalan Renaissance; **Joan Alcover i Maspons** (1854–1926), a poet who wrote in Català; **Miguel Costa i Llobera** (1854–1922) of Pollença (Pollensa), Majorca, a neoclassic poet; and **Gabriel Alomar** (1873–1940), a futurist poet who also wrote in Català and rose to the rank of ambassador during the Second Republic.

Among foreigners who have written about the Balearics, the French intellectual and writer **George Sand** (pseud. of Amandine Lucile Aurore Dupin, the Baronne Dudevant, 1804–76) arrived in the Balearics in the winter of 1838 with her lover, the Polish pianist and composer **Frédéric Chopin**

(1810–49), who was ill at the time and trying to recuperate in a warm climate. *Un hiver à Majorque* (1841), Sand's nonfiction work on Majorca, discusses the poverty and traditionalism of the Balearics and provides an early example of modern ideas in conflict with Spanish traditionalism. Sand and Chopin lived in an abandoned monastery at Valldomossa during their stay, where Chopin composed many of his *Preludes*.

The natural beauty of the Balearics also proved to be an irresistible attraction for other Europeans seeking peace and quiet. One of the first promoters, Archduke **Louis Salvador** of Austria (1847–1915), built a summer home at Son Marroig on Majorca and set about describing the area in his *Balearen in Wort und Bild* (1878). The Valencian novelist **Vicente Blasco Ibáñez** (1867–1928), famous for his *Four Horsemen of the Apocalypse*, lived for brief periods on Ibiza and Formentera and wrote *Los muertos mandan* on the *chuetas*, descendants of Balearic Jews. During the Spanish Civil War, foreign residents drawn into the struggle included the French writer **Georges Bernanos**, author of *Grands Cimetieres sous la Lune* (1938), and the American **Elliot Paul**, who wrote *The Life and Death of a Spanish Town* (1937) about Ibiza. Each produced a best seller by taking a passionate view of the struggle from the republican side. For Bernanos, a noted Catholic writer, this was a particularly painful step.

ART. Cyclopean structures (so-called for their prehistoric era and their size and shape) known as Talayots formed part of the defenses of Bronze Age settlements in the Balearic culture. The Tudons and Gaumes sites on Minorca are two of the most significant settings for these prehistoric artifacts.

One of the most important early Balearic works of art is the so-called *Catalan Atlas*, drawn by a Majorcan cartographer, probably **Abraham Cresques**, ca. 1375. The *Catalan Atlas* achieved significance by combining traditional *portolan* sea charts (star sightings for sea areas) with approximate land masses. The atlas presents an interesting picture of the world as the Europeans knew it immediately prior to the age of world exploration.

In the mid-fourteenth century, a Majorcan school of painting emerged under the influence of the Burgundian Gothic school of Barcelona. The miniaturist and painter known as the **Master of Privileges** (ca. 1334) illuminated manuscripts and created the retablo of St. Eulalia in the cathedral of Palma. By 1400, the **Master of Santa Eulalia** and the **Master of Montesión** began to produce Italian-influenced paintings.

In the early twentieth century, a restoration by the famous Barcelona architect **Antoni Gaudí** of the royal chapel in the Palma Cathedral erected a large marble canopy resembling a crown of thorns over the altar. In 1956, the famous Catalan abstractionist **Joan Miró** (1893–1981) occupied the home on Cala Major in Palma, Majorca, of his late maternal grandparents. Among his Majorcan works are the graphic and simple paintings of 1959 and 1960 such as *Red Disc* and *Women and Birds in the Night*. Miró's work created a universe of forms.

CUSTOMS AND SOCIETY. The region's Menorquín dialect, based on Catalan, varies from island to island. There is considerable ethnic diversity on the islands, including the *chuetas*, or *xuetas*, of Palma de Majorca, whose origins come from medieval Jewish *conversos*.

St. Antonio's Day on January 17 is celebrated by costumes, dancing, and bonfires on Majorca. Men wear long tapered white linen trousers and a white shirt with embroidered collar and cuffs, a red silk sash or, on some occasions, an oriental-looking striped sash, and a *barretina* (a floppy beret). The costume of women is a long narrow skirt of green or red serge, trimmed with an edging of a different color, and an unusual apron heavily embroidered from the hips upward. A large silk kerchief embroidered or stamped in a flower design and trimmed with a fringe is worn around the shoulders.

In the summer, the island also holds the Pillença (Pollensa) Music Festival. At Port de Sóller each May, a celebration called Es Firó commemorates victory of the town's women over invading Muslim troops. According to legend, the women locked up their men and went alone to face the Muslims, knowing that the Islamic soldiers would not fight females.

The songs of Majorcan field laborers, somewhat like slave chants, dominate the folk music of the islands.

HISTORIC SITES. The Consulado del Mar in **Palma, Majorca,** a medieval institution that regulated maritime activity, built as its headquarters a magnificent building that is a good example of indigenous Balearic medieval architecture. It now contains an interesting maritime museum. In the same vicinity, the Almudaina Palace is the major Muslim edifice of the region; it also served as the seat of Christian government for four centuries after 1235. La Seo Cathedral, begun in the thirteenth century, contains the remodeled royal chapel of Antoni Gaudí and the sarcophagi of Kings Jaume II and III. The cathedral's 144 foot high interior is well illuminated by seven rose windows. Jaume II's Bellver Castle, above Palma, now contains an archaeological museum. Elsewhere on Majorca, the Juan March estate is on the beautiful Formentor Peninsula near **Pollença** (**Pollensa**). Near Puig Major, the monastery of **Lluc,** established in honor of the Virgin Mary in 1238, is a major religious center.

Elsewhere on the archipelago, on the island of **Ibiza,** the town incorporates the much older village of Dalt Vila, fortified during the reigns of Carlos I and Felipe II in the shape of a huge irregular heptagon, with seven bastions. The original Gothic cathedral, built in the fourteenth century and redesigned between 1710 and 1728 by two Valencians, Pedro Ferro and Jaime Espinosa, has as its interior a nave without aisles or transepts that is plain but airy. The Puig des Molins Museum in Ibiza specializes on the early history of the Balearics.

Formentera (Ofiusa [Greek], Frumentaria [Roman], *forment* or wheat [Catalan]) is 38 square miles in area, with a population under 4,000. Its administrative center is San Francisco Javier. Formentera is still rural and wild; production of salt is an important part of the economy. It was the favorite island of the Valencian novelist Vicente Blasco Ibáñez.

On **Minorca,** Maó (Mahón, derived from the Semitic word *Maghen,* meaning shield) is surrounded by fortifications, particularly of Fort St. Felipe, a fine (if ruined) example of early modern military architecture. The island rises to the peak of Monte Toro, 1,206 feet high, halfway between Ciudadela and Maó. On the west side of the island, Ciudadela retains the atmosphere of a medieval seaport. More than 1,600 Neolithic sites called Talayotic monuments are scattered around Minorca (and also on the other islands). They are megaliths of odd shapes and heights, thought to be related to burial and maritime activities, though they may have served as clan bastions or watchtowers. The beaches, of course, remain the islands' chief attraction.

CUISINE. Seafood is flavored with garlic-flavored *alioli,* but also popular is *salsa mahonesa,* a mayonnaise-like sauce. (The word *mayonnaise* is reputedly derived from Mahones, or Mahón, where it may have been invented, although the etymology is disputed.) These sauces are put on meat and vegetables; eggplant and zucchini are eaten more often here than elsewhere in Spain. Other dishes include *sopas mallorquina* (a spicy vegetable soup), *ensaïmadas* (a breakfast sweet roll that is shaped like a Moorish turban), *coca mallorquina* (a pizza made from pasta), and *tumbet* (an egg and vegetable pie).

ALIOLI

5 cloves of garlic, minced	2 cups of crumbled bread
1 cup olive oil	½ cup cold water

Combine garlic and olive oil and cook over medium heat. Reduce heat to low, add bread, and brown. Then add water to liquify the consistency. Stir, adding more bread pieces or cold water if mixture is too thick. It is served with fish or chicken.

Salsa mahonesa requires the use of a warm bowl, into which two egg yolks are separated and a cup of olive oil is slowly added. After stirring with a wooden spoon, the juice of a lemon or a tablespoon or two of vinegar and a pinch of salt are added to the mixture.

Local wines, an industry started by the Romans, are good. Reds of the Manto Negro variety produce a slightly sweet wine. *Pomada* (a gin drink mixed with lemonade) may have English origins.

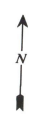

N

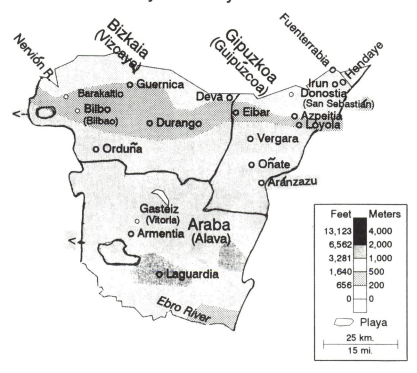

Bay of Biscay

Bizkaia
(Vizcaya)

Gipuzkoa
(Guipúzcoa)

Fuenterrabia

Hendaye

Nervión R.

Guernica

Deva o

Irun o o

Barakaltio

Donostia
(San Sebastián)

Bilbo
(Bilbao)

o Eibar

o Azpeitia

o Durango

o Loyola

o Orduña

o Vergara

o Oñate

o Aránzazu

Gasteiz
o (Vitoria)

Araba
(Alava)

o Armentia

o Laguardia

Ebro River

Feet		Meters
13,123	■	4,000
6,562		2,000
3,281		1,000
1,640		500
656		200
0		0

⬠ Playa

25 km.

15 mi.

BASQUE PROVINCES

Chapter 5

BASQUE PROVINCES
(Euskadi, País Vasco)

REGIONAL CHARACTERISTICS. (Euskadi [Basque], Vascones [Roman], Vasco [Spanish]). Pop., 2,134,967. Area, 7,234 sq. km. Regional capital: Gasteiz (Vitoria). The region is south of the Bay of Biscay, north of La Rioja, east of Santander and Burgos (Castile), and west of Navarre. It is composed of the provinces of Araba (Alava), Gipuzkoa (Guipúzcoa), and Bizkaia (Vizcaya).

The perennial Basque struggle for the preservation of liberties guaranteeing local autonomy is expressed by the Basque word *foruak*, which can be anglicized to mean foral laws. In Spanish, the word is *fuero* and comes from the Latin word *forum*, meaning civic. After a long history devoted to preserving foral law, new demands for local autonomy reached a peak in 1894 when Sabino de Arana y Goiri of Bizkaia created the Basque Nationalist Party (Eusko Alderdi Jeltzalea, PNV in Spanish, or EAJ in Euskara, the Basque language (sometimes spelled Euskera). The party was supported by professionals, intellectuals, the Catholic peasantry, and the clergy, but until late in the Second Republic the PNV could not equal the success of Catalan regionalism (autonomous in 1932). The Basques were forced to wait an additional four years before receiving autonomy because neighboring Navarre, in part ethnically Basque, and Araba (Alava), one of the three main Basque provinces, rejected the Second Republic out of fear of the new ultraradical central government and its anti-Catholicism, preferring to support traditional Catholic opposition to Madrid. In July 1936, they backed General Francisco Franco, who annulled the Basque statute of autonomy a year later. Some of the most bitter fighting of the civil war took place in Bizkaia.

The postwar period witnessed reimposition of centralism and attacks on Basque culture that went much further in unifying the region. The PNV continued to support autonomy, but the Basque Homeland and Freedom Party (Euskadi Ta Askatasuna, or ETA) was founded as a radical terrorist organization seeking complete independence from Spain. In the first elections under the constitutional monarchy for the constituent Cortes, however, the Spanish Socialist Party (PSOE) achieved greater success by organizing industrial workers and thus winning a majority of the region's seats in the first elections. Again in 1982 and later elections, the PSOE's victories have created a pattern of cooperation with premier Felipe González (which now may be in jeopardy because of the PSOE's election defeat on June 13, 1994, in the European parliamentary elections).

When the draft constitution came to a vote in 1978, 14 percent of the Basques favored strong autonomy and 45 percent favored a more limited type. Altogether, almost 60 percent supported diminished ties with the central government. Opinion coalesced around a common theme that Spain was less a nation than a state containing a group of nations, of which the Basque Provinces was one of the most important. To achieve nationhood, the Basque foral privileges (see history of each province) abolished in 1841, 1876, and 1937 had to be restored before cooperation with the constitutional monarchy could begin. Strong feelings also existed that the province (now region) of Navarre was Basque and should be included in the future Basque state. This did not occur.

After this first vote, the moderate PNV urged voters to abstain on the constitutional referendum but to vote yes on the statute of autonomy, arguing that the constitution did not go far enough in recognizing Basque historic rights. This recommendation created a real anomaly: since the constitution empowered the autonomy statute, radical nationalists could claim that neither had legitimacy in the Basque Provinces. The revolutionary ETA insisted upon immediate unilateral independence, dreaming of what they call *zazpiak bat*, the union of the three Spanish Basque Provinces and Navarre with the French Pays Basque provinces of Lapurdi (Labourd), Nafarroa Beherea (Basse Navarre), and Zuberoa (Soule), which as a geographical unit would complete the formation of *Euskalerria* (the Basque Country). According to this argument, once these expatriate Basques unified with the Spanish Basque Provinces, an independent state would emerge. To do so, of course, would mean a struggle of national liberation against two Western European powers, France and Spain. The current odds of this happening are prohibitive unless the process of devolution accelerates throughout Europe and the world.

In the end, the grouping of Araba, Gipuzkoa, and Bizkaia as the region of Euskadi, or the País Vasco, was approved on December 18, 1979, along with the return of local governmental controls. The Comunidad Autónoma del País Vasco, or CAPV, began operating in 1980. Since that time, the PSOE has gained a political majority in the region's national elections.

Basque unity comes from the language, Euskara, a non–Indo-European language spoken by close to a half-million people in the western Pyrenees. Its origins are in dispute: a few scholars argue that Euskara has Afro-Asiatic roots, while others claim a tie with the Kartvelian languages of the Caucasus in distant Asia Minor. The once popular idea that Euskara is a close relative of ancient Iberian is no longer as strongly supported, although it has not been totally abandoned.

Of the various Euskara dialects, which change from village to village, four have appeared in literature: Gipuzkoan, Bizkaian, Navarro-Labourdin, and Souletin. Other large spoken dialects are Roncal, Labourdin, and Eastern and Western Basse-Navarrese. In 1968, the linguist Luis Mitxelena (1915–87) edited a modern version of these dialects for the Eskaltzaindia, or Basque Language Academy, of which he was a member. His compilation, known as *Euskara batua*, created the modern standard Basque literary language.

In general, since Euskaran dialects have few written accents, the oral stress varies from dialect to dialect. It is usually transferred from one syllable to another according to the structure of the phrase and the requirements of emphasis. When a word is cited separately, accentuation tends to come on the final syllable. Linguists also have purged the language of the letters c, *ç*, *q*, *v*, *w*, and the combinations *ch* and *ll*. Nouns have no gender and are declined by means of suffixes or suffixlike words. Adjectives and pronouns are particularly complex.

Another unique aspect of the Basque people is that they have the lowest frequency of blood type B and the highest frequencies of types O and Rh-negative of any European population, a fact that has been used in the past to demonstrate the linkage and difference of the Basque community from surrounding peoples.

The Basque flag, called the *Ikurriña*, has a scarlet field with an upright white cross running from top to bottom and side to side and a green X from corner to corner. The regional capital is Gasteiz (Vitoria).

The region ranks sixth in income among the autonomous areas of Spain.

ARABA (Alava)

VITAL STATISTICS. Pop., 260,580. Area, 3,037 sq. km. Capital and diocesan see: Gasteiz (Vitoria). Araba (Alava) has a Basque majority and significant non-Basque minorities from Navarre, Castile, and La Rioja, all

of which border the province. It is located at the western end of the Ebro
River and extends north into the southern slopes of the Pyrenees and south
into the *meseta* plateau lands. Araba is physically the largest of the three
Basque provinces and constitutes 41 percent of the region's area but holds
only a seventh of the population. The province has been virtually non-
Euskara-speaking. A branch of the Universidad del País Vasco (UPC) is
located in Gasteiz.

ECONOMY. The total industrial work force in Gasteiz is one of the two
largest by percentage in Spain, mainly composed of metallurgical and automobile workers. The Nevosa plant in Gasteiz, owned by Daimler Benz,
builds vans and trucks. Agriculture is difficult because of the rocky, upland
nature of the topography, although dairy farming is of some importance.

HISTORY. (Veleia [Roman]). Araba developed a settled population dur-
ing the Cro-Magnon (10,000 B.C.) and Neolithic periods (4000–2000 B.C.).
The Romans first encountered the Basques (Vascones) in this area, and
Caesar's conquest of Gaul penetrated the region through the Huarte and
Araquil valleys to reach Roman territories north of the Pyrenees. So many
served in the Roman legions that the area became the only Latin-speaking
Basque region. Christianization occurred ca. A.D. 335–400.

The Visigoth Leovigild (568–87) made Vitoria-Gasteiz his northern capital, but the region slipped in and out of his successors' control. With the
arrival of the Muslims, Araba allied with Tudela in 843. Muslim bands
from neighboring La Rioja caused Christians to live a clandestine existence
in cave churches and hermitages, particularly at Laño. Numerous small
monasteries appeared in the tenth century as armed Christian camps.

With Christianity came the Kingdom of Navarre, which for the next
several centuries included Araba in its territory. The Navarrese recognized
the Basque Monnio Vigilaz in 920 as conde de Alava (hence the origin of
its official Spanish name, which will be used in place of Araba until the
contemporary era). Sancho the Great of Navarre (1032–35) unified the
three Basque regions for the first time, but as Navarre's power receded,
medieval rural Basque society grew turbulent, dominated by *parientes mayores*, who were heads of powerful families. Navarre conferred local *fueros*,
or rights of self-government, in 1181, but after Castile's capture of Vitoria
(the modern-day Gasteiz) in 1200, Alava slowly accepted Castile's protection in return for local autonomy to guard against excesses by the *parientes
mayores*. The province recognized Castilian sovereignty while remaining
virtually independent, with local privileges and aristocratic influence intact.

As a tax-free quasi-independent republic, Alava's link with Castile came
through the *corregimiento*, run by a *corregidor* appointed by the Council
of Castile who presided over the Junta General, or general council (more
powerful in the rural areas than in the towns), which met every two years.
The *corregimiento* allowed considerable coordination between Madrid and

Alava, and even when the eighteenth-century Bourbon monarchy destroyed the foral independence of Aragón, Catalonia, and Valencia this arrangement managed to survive in Alava and the other Basque Provinces.

Difficulties arose in the late eighteenth century, when overpopulation and lack of commercial development caused the area to enter a long period of increasing emigration. Trouble increased during the period between the Napoleonic invasion in 1808 and the battle of Vitoria (February–June 21, 1813), and in the wake of the Carlist War of 1833–39 the *corregimiento* and internal tariff barriers were abolished in 1841 by the central government. The new, limited *concierto económico*, or economic agreement, collected national taxes through regressive sales taxes and heavy property taxes on farmland and livestock. As the most agricultural of the Basque Provinces, Alava was hit especially hard.

But while the other Basque areas turned to ethnic nationalism in the twentieth century, Alava's 400 parishes supported conservative Catholic political movements. As a result, the province voted for several small conservative parties in the elections of 1931 and for the Confederación Española de Derechas Autónomas (CEDA) in 1933 rather than the Basque Nationalist Party. At the start of the civil war, Alava enthusiastically supported the military revolt and joined in the nationalist attack on the other Basque provinces in 1936–37. As a reward, the postwar nationalist regime reinstated favorable local controls, the only province other than Navarre to be so favored by Franco. The provincial government used these funds to attract automobile and machine tool manufacturers. Another sign of favor was the decision by the new, conservative Catholic lay organization Opus Dei to make Vitoria (now called Gasteiz) the site of its private university.

In 1979, Araba (Alava) cautiously welcomed autonomy as a way of sustaining traditional governance. Industrialization has somewhat diminished its differences with the other two Basque areas, but conservative Catholicism is still more popular than Basque nationalism.

LITERATURE. The first recorded writer in Alava, the Christian poet **Prudentius** (348?–405?) of Armentia (today a wholly separate part of Burgos), became famous for his poetry. Save for a single trip to Rome, he remained uniquely Spanish. His Latin poetry criticized Roman paganism and praised Christian martyrs. Gerald Brenan finds in Prudentius's *Peristephanon* and *Psychomachia* new rhythms and incantations anticipating the emergence of the Spanish language, a quickness of pace not typically Latin, and a psychology that accepted violence and pain and even celebrated physical and mental discomfort.

Pero López de Ayala, the marqués de Lozoya (1332–1407), has been called Spain's first humanist. Deeply involved in national politics and diplomacy during the wars of Pedro the Cruel, he was captured by the Portuguese and began writing *Rimado de Palacio* while still a prisoner. The

Rimado is a satire and summary of Christian doctrine that excoriates social behavior in the Middle Ages. López de Ayala created a precedent for Spanish literature to speak out in denunciation of social and spiritual ills that gave so many later Spanish works liveliness and social value. He also created a consciousness of history by writing the *Crónicas* for the period 1350–96, a time of civil and foreign wars. Having read Livy, he brought life and drama to the pages of his history without sacrificing accuracy. Finally, his translations from Latin and Italian began to interest Spaniards in history and sparked a revival of literacy.

Fernán Pérez de Guzmán (1376–1460), nephew of López de Ayala and uncle of the marqués de Santillana (famous in Guadalajara), wrote *Generaciones y semblanzas* as a superb prose portrait of major fourteenth-century figures.

The Dominican **Francisco de Vitoria** (1486–1546), a Basque of Vitoria, obtained his education at the universities of Paris and Alcalá de Henares and later taught at Valladolid and Salamanca. While he never published any of his own work because of ecclesiastical constraints, his lecture notes, published posthumously by students, showed a personal tendency to turn all speculative moral matters into a moral standard for politics and imperial affairs. This approach led him to attack the atrocities committed against native people in the colonies, and he had an enlightened influence on the New Laws of the Indies in 1542. He also opposed stringent Italian demands for censorship by the Index at the Council of Trent, but he died before the council concluded its work, and his absence weakened Catholic freedom of thought. In many respects, Vitoria and Las Casas provided a conscience for the sixteenth century.

Other than López de Ayala and Vitoria, Alava's intellectual history is imperfectly known. According to surveys of Basque writing, 102 books in forms of Euskara appeared between 1545 and 1879, but few can be cited reliably. In recent times, **Ignacio Aldecoa** (1925–69) of Gasteiz wrote a best-selling trilogy, *La España Inmóvil*, celebrating local life in Araba and Basque society in general.

ART. The cathedral of Santa María in Gasteiz (Vitoria) contains a painting by Peter Paul Rubens (1577–1640) and a Cellini cross. The hospital of the same name is early Renaissance with Isabeline touches. Other examples of Isabeline decor, with their graphic religious messages and avoidance of Mudéjar design, can be found in Oyón, Navaridas, and Leza.

The major artist of the province, **Julio Beobide** (1891–1969), was born in Zumaia, Gipuzkoa, but spent much of his life in Gasteiz, where he became a sculptor of abstract and figurative religious motifs who creatively reinterpreted Christian images.

CUSTOMS AND SOCIETY. The principal Basque dance is the *aurresku*, an outdoor line dance led by two dancers at each end who compete with one another in daring solos. The line circles the plaza in a large circle before the solo dances begin. The dance is sometimes also called the *zorzico*. Its music consists of eight measures played in a repetitive fashion.

Traditional dress for townsmen included short black trousers tied with ribbons around the knees, a dark undercoat, and a bright waistcoat. Farmers and other workers wore long cloth trousers and jackets with a broad-brimmed hat or the *boina*, the floppy predecessor of the beret. A silk scarf at the neck and on Sundays a high crowned hat with the brim turned up in back completed their costume. Married women preferred dark woolen skirts (often pleated in Araba), a black jacket on Sundays, and a mantilla (a scarf of lace). Custom dictated that women had their hair cut very short on the day they married, with the head covered by a white woolen veil with tassels over the forehead. Unmarried women did not cover their heads, even during mass.

HISTORIC SITES. The old cathedral of Santa María in **Gasteiz (Vitoria)** has several beautiful chapels, but there is also a new neo-Gothic cathedral, María Inmaculada, built in the twentieth century. Two museums of archaeology and history have large collections. Campillo, the old town of Vitoria built in the twelfth century, provides a good introduction to the architecture of the Middle Ages.

Elsewhere in the province, directly south of Gasteiz, **Armentia** is an ancient Christian center and former site of a bishopric (ca. 880–1085). The basilica of San Andrés has lavish carvings. Further south, **Laguardia,** founded by Navarre to guard the Castilian border, has two churches of importance, Santa María de los Reyes and San Juan Bautista. The surrounding area is dotted with numerous prehistoric Celtic tombs and Roman remains, and there is an archaeological museum.

CUISINE. *Chorizo* (sausage), mushroom dishes, wild boar, and *menestra* (vegetable soup) are important in Basque cuisine. Food shortages plagued the region during the late medieval and early modern period, and the mountainous terrain limited access to sources of food and drink. Even wines from nearby La Rioja could not always reach the Basque Provinces because of difficulty in transportation, and overpopulation forced the Basques into fishing activities for survival. This historical deprivation created today's hearty cuisine. Basque lunches and dinners have soup, salad, rice or pasta, and mutton or lamb courses. Wine comes from the Alavesa wine district of Laguardia, near La Rioja, and is similar in quality.

The old dish *habas de Vitoria* (broad beans with *chorizo*) is prepared by boiling the beans for forty minutes. Small amounts of ham, bacon, and *chorizo* are added after twenty minutes. The liquid is poured off and the meat is cut into small pieces and put on top of the beans.

GIPUZKOA (Guipúzcoa)

VITAL STATISTICS. Pop., 692,986. Area, 1,980 sq. km. Capital and diocesan see: Donostiá (San Sebastián). The province is dominated by the Pyrenees, the French border, and the Bay of Biscay. Bizkaia (Viscaya) is to the west, Navarre to the east, and Araba (Alava) and Navarre to the south. The Goierri area is a mountainous zone south and east of the coast dominated by valley towns and the traditional Basque farmsteads known as *baserrias*. A branch of the Universidad del País Vasco (UPV) is located in Donostiá.

ECONOMY. Nearly 40 percent of employment is industrial. Azkoitia manufactures *alpargatas* (espadrilles), a canvas shoe with twisted hemp soles very popular throughout the Mediterranean. Numerous specialty metallurgical firms have created a substantial industrial base. Commercial fishing is another large source of employment.

HISTORY. (Vardulia [prehistoric]). Since Euskara does not have an Indo-European basis, anthropological origins of the Basques involve pre-Celtic theories such as the migration of the Caucasians or Gheg tribes of northern Albania, whose Code of Lek Dukaghin is similar to the Basque *fueros* (see below). Survival of wall-and-ball games such as *pelota*, circle dances, and primitive bagpipes, however, are usually thought to be Celtic.

The Tardesoian site of Deva (Dena) in Guipúzcoa (as Gipuzkoa was called officially until modern times) became a large, active town by 800 B.C. and later fell to Pompey in 75 B.C. The area did not become a part of Rome, and Christianity emerged only ca. A.D. 650 because absence of monasteries minimized influence of early Christian leaders such as Prudentius of Alava/Araba. Visigoths did little more than establish a town or two within the southern Basque area, and Guipúzcoa remained independent until Basque incursions into Frankish areas brought conflict with Gascony and Aquitaine. The latter controlled San Sebastián (used in place of Donostiá until modern times) for three centuries, and the bishopric of Bayonne made Guipúzcoa a part of its see. Fishing rose to become a major industry, utilizing the location on the Bay of Biscay between Río Urumea and Concha Bay, sheltered by the island of Santa Clara.

Both Sancho III of Navarre in the early eleventh century and Alfonso VIII of Castile in the twelfth century set about issuing town charters to contest French control. The church of Santa Euphemia in San Juan de la Peña and the monastery of San Telmo in French-influenced San Sebastián constituted the only major religious centers. The interior's rough topography caused pilgrims going to Santiago de Compostela in Galicia to travel southeast from Bayonne to Roncesvalles and Pamplona. Not until the fourteenth century did Castilian influence grow when the Bay of Biscay emerged as a crucial route for export of wool. Castile subsidized Guipúzcoan commercial maritime activities of ship-building, woodworking, and iron forging, mostly for maritime purposes. The export trade attracted northern Europeans in the fifteenth century, but feuding among rural groups limited penetration to the coastal areas.

France retook San Sebastián in 1476 and again in 1522, but Felipe II restored a degree of Castilian control by instituting the *corregimiento*, a local council of state working with a representative of the throne (later shifted to the *concierto económico*, with greater economic power) based on the *foruak*, or foral laws. Under the Spanish Hapsburgs, San Sebastián grew as a great fishing port and a wool-exporting center. The conde de Peñaflorida established the Real Compañia Guipúzcocana de Caracas in 1728 to promote development of Venezuela from San Sebastián, and his son Javier María Munibe y Idiáquez created the physiocratic Real Sociedad Vascongada de Amigos del País in 1766 to pursue further growth.

In the eighteenth century, the liberal, centralist philosophy of the new Bourbon regime in Spain attacked Basque foral privileges. The French Revolution alienated Basques of Soule, Labourd, and Basse Navarre, who told the French Estates-General in their *cahier* (list) of grievances in 1789 that they felt as foreign in France as if they were citizens of Turkey. Throughout the area, the Napoleonic regime ignored foral law and gave the Basques an unhappy taste of centralization. San Sebastián was badly damaged in the French retreat of 1813.

In subsequent decades, Carlism grew more popular in Guipúzcoa than in Alava or Vizcaya. The province, ravaged by war and social disruption, provided many volunteers for the Carlist army, whose leading general, Tomás Zumalacárregui (1788–1835), came from the province. The Carlist assembly sometimes met in San Sebastián, while volunteers from the province ranged across Aragón, Catalonia, and Valencia, once even reaching as far south as Córdoba.

The Carlists finally had to sue for peace when their supplies were cut off by the British and French and losses took a heavy toll on their manpower. After the Truce of Vergara in 1839, the queen regent, María Cristina, made a special effort to include Guipúzcoa within the orbit of national affairs by establishing her summer residence in San Sebastián. The city's beauty, seaside climate, sandy beaches, and scallop-shaped bay, fronted by promenades, attracted Castilians escaping the heat of the central plateau and gentrified San Sebastián into a resort town, noted for its cobbled streets and pleasant old town. Among Basques of the province, these changes only contributed to a revival of Carlism in Oñate, Bidebieta, and Tolosa. The Second Carlist War (1873–76) again defended Guipúzcoa's pastoral and patriarchal qualities, but within three years the central government crushed Carlism as a military force and reduced the area's freedom.

The late nineteenth century, marked by the introduction of industrial society, changed Guipúzcoa into a manufacturing center of arms, textile, paper, and metal fabrication. After 1892, the middle class joined neighboring Vizcaya's Basque Nationalist Party (PNV), shifting their protest from Carlism to ethnic Basque nationalism. The movement divided in 1920 into a moderate main party and a more radical Aberri (Homeland) faction, but the factions reunited in 1930 and won over 30 percent of the vote during the Second Republic.

In 1936, the PNV remained loyalist in the civil war, but the fall of Irún on September 2 and San Sebastián on September 13 to the nationalist General Emilio Mola put all of Guipúzcoa under the rebellious military even before the Basque autonomy statute could go into effect. Franco called Guipúzcoa a "traitor province" in 1937 and destroyed its foral self-governance, bringing a heavy military occupation, which the Basques say was due to Franco's need to have an occupying force on their territory. In 1940, the eyes of the world momentarily focused on the province when Franco met Hitler at Hendaye, the only face-to-face meeting between the two dictators.

After harsh postwar difficulties, the first wave of labor disturbances began in 1951 and rose in frequency in the 1960s and early 1970s. The assassination of a provincial head of the political police by ultranationalists in August 1968 brought martial law. Consideration was given to reestablishing the old *concierto económico*, but Franco's death led to more radical change. The province backed strong autonomy in 1979 and was a stronghold for both the Euskadiko Ezkerra, an openly Marxist-Leninist party with strong ties to the ETA, and the radical Herri Batasuna party.

LITERATURE. The famous leader of Counter-Reformation Spanish Catholicism, **St. Ignacio Loyola** (Iñigo Beltran y Saenz, 1491–1556), came from an estate in the northern part of the province near Azkoitia (Azcoitia), the son of don Beltran, marqués of Oñaz and Loyola. As a young soldier, he sustained a serious wound in the French siege of Pamplona. While convalescing, he studied the life of Christ while at Manresa, near the famous abbey of Montserrat, in Catalonia. His prayers and penance led to the writing of Ignacio's famed *Spiritual Exercises* (1522). The exercises sought to suppress desire for worldly experience and to purify the soul by using a type of meditation involving memory, understanding, and will.

Loyola later studied at the University of Alcalá de Henares and formed a small group ready to live an ascetic life and endure poverty. The fledgling Society of Jesus attracted the Inquisition's attention, and Loyola left Spain in 1528 to study at the University of Paris. His group attracted few disciples at first, but after ordination Loyola moved to Rome. In 1540, his Jesuit Order became soldiers of the pope, dedicated to teaching and missionary activities. The Jesuits attracted many devoted Catholics during the Counter-Reformation, and Loyola served as the Jesuits' first general until his death in 1556. Canonization came in 1621.

In other religious writing, a French Basque, **Joannes Leizarraga** (1506–1601?), probably a Huguenot from La Rochelle, translated the New Testament into Euskara. In secular works, the major sixteenth-century writer in Guipúzcoa, **Esteban de Garibay** (ca. 1565), provided an early history of the region in *Compendio historial de las Crónicas y Universal Historia de todos los reynos de España* (1565). **Joanes Etcheberri de Sara** (1668–1749), a French Basque who taught in the province, used Euskara as the principal language of instruction and wrote a Latin-Euskara grammar, *Eskuarazko hatapenak latin ikhasteko*.

In the eighteenth century, **Manuel de Larramendi** (1690–1766) pioneered the linguistic creation of the Basque language, Euskara. He compiled an advanced grammar, *Diccionario Trilingüe del euskera, latín y castellano*, but his claim that Euskara was the prehistoric Spanish language caused endless later controversies. He also popularized the idea that Euskara had been one of the languages spoken in the Tower of Babel. In addition to linguistics, Larramendi also wrote moral lessons disguised as fables in *Fábulas morales* (1784) and belonged to the best-known eighteenth-century *tertulia* (a regular meeting of like-minded friends), the Fonda de San Sebastián, made up of authors such as Cadalso, Nicolás de Moratín, Iriarte, and **Félix María Samaniego** (1745–1801), nephew of the count of Peñaflorida and teacher at the seminary of Vergara. Another eighteenth-century figure, **Javier de Munibe** (1723–85), wrote *El Borracho burlado* (1764) with song verses in Euskara. About the same time, **Pedro Ignacio de Barrutia** (1668?–1759) wrote a play, *Nochebuena*, translated into Euskara as *Gabonetako Ikuskizuna*.

During the nineteenth century, **Juan Ignacio Iztueta** ("Txuri"; 1767–1845) collected folklore and folk history in *Guipúzcoaco dantza gogangarrien condaira edo historia* (1824) and *Guipúzcoaco provinciaren con daira edo historia* (1847). **Eugenio de Ochoa** (1815–72) of Lezo, an editor, critic, and translator who spent long periods of exile abroad in England and France, became a good friend of the leading romantic writer, José de Espronceda, and promoted romanticism through collections and histories of Spanish fiction. The major figure of provincial literature, **José María Aguirre** ("Lixardi"; 1864–1903) of Zarautz, wrote lyrics that have been called the most haunting and original in the Euskara language. His efforts in *Biotz-Begietan* and *Umerzurtz-Olerkiak* began the revival of Euskara as a serious literary language. He also did a major orthography of the language.

Nicolás Ormaetxea (1888–1961) continued this poetic tradition in the post–civil war period. At the same time, **Julio de Urquijo** (1871–1950) of Donostía (San Sebastián) created the periodical *Revista Internacional de Estudios Vascos* in order to study Basque culture more thoroughly.

In the Spanish language, **Pío Baroja y Nessi** (1872–1956) of Donostía (San Sebastián) believed in a philosophy of freeing oneself from property and leading a life of adventure. Although trained as a doctor, he traveled extensively before he settled down in Madrid. His first major novel, *Camino de perfección* (1902), set in Madrid and Toledo, concerns a character's struggle to find meaning in his existence and the confusion that arises when his instincts and ethical beliefs conflict. Baroja concludes that civilization is evil because religious morality's stress on individual salvation makes humankind uncomfortable with natural processes and unfeeling toward social problems. Baroja also wrote three novels about the poor of Madrid and the hypocritical attitudes of society toward them: *La busca* (1904), *Mala hierba* (1904), and *Aurora roja* (1904). His prolific output continued until the civil war, and he is probably best remembered for the series *Memorias de un hombre de acción*, not unlike the *Episodios nacionales* of Pérez Galdós. This series of more than twenty novels set against a nineteenth-century background portrayed social outcasts as victims of a cruel society. *Paradox Rey* (1906) particularly expresses Baroja's utopian and personal ideals in a story of a good society destroyed by civilization, a metaphor for the Basque Provinces.

During recent times, **José María Bellido Cormenzana** (b. 1922) of Donostiá has become a symbolist playwright in such works as *El día sencillo* and *Los relojes de cera*.

The province figures in writings by others from outside the region. **Ricardo Baroja y Nessi** (1871–1953), Pío Baroja's brother of Río Tinto, Huelva, wrote *La nao 'Capitana': cuento español del mar antiguo* about Basque seafarers. His nephew, **Julio Caro Baroja** (b. 1914) of Madrid, has written extensively about the Basque area in such nonfiction works as *La vida rural vasca en Vera de Bidasoa* (1944), *Los vascos* (1949), and *Vasconia* (1957), as well as many other volumes of Basque studies. In addition, his well-known *Las brujas y su mundo* (1961), concerned with supernatural practices and witchcraft, has been translated into English as *The World of Witches* (1961).

ART. Excellent Gothic design can be found at the parish church in Fuenterrabía, at the church of San Vicente in Donostiá (San Sebastián), and in Azkoitia at the chapel of don Martín de Azpeitia. Perhaps the finest example of Gothic architecture, however, is at the ancient former university at Oñate.

One of the early Basque sculptors, **Juan de Anchieta** (1540–88) of Azkoitia, worked in Valladolid and Pamplona. Anchieta brought a grandeur of form to the creation of heroic and monumental pieces and trained many other Basque artists of the period.

In the contemporary era, **Eduardo Chillida** (b. 1924) of Donostiá has developed an international reputation for his iron and wood forms and torsos. He moved to Paris in 1947, winning a sculpture prize at Venice in 1958, a Carnegie in 1964, and Germany's Lembruck Prize in 1966. Iron is identified with the Basque people, and Chillida has emphasized it for that reason. **Jorge Oteiza** (b. 1908) won a reputation as a leading abstract sculptor, winning a major prize at the São Paulo Biennial in 1958 for his chunky, squared-off, nearly cubist works, probably best expressed by his so-called *Metaphysical Boxes*. Much of his later career has been spent in teaching and promoting art.

CUSTOMS AND SOCIETY. The *foru* (plural, *foruak*), particularly important in Guipúzcoan law, was codified in 1514, incorporating ancient customary laws of compensation for homicide, injury, exemption from taxation, property rights, and all manner of family law. In this way, ethnic identity survived and found political expression.

Folkloric activity in Guipúzcoa includes the old tradition, sometimes seen at fairs, of competitive log cutting by individual participants. While older practices such as ram fights are no longer popular, the contemporary San Sebastián festival, Semana Grande, is held annually in August to celebrate Assumption Day. There are also film and popular music festivals, and the Tamborrada Festival on January 20 celebrates nineteenth-century folklore.

Dances tend to differ according to village tradition. In the *ezpata-dantza*, or sword dance, one dancer represents a corpse and the others express a desire to avenge his death in choreographic pantomime. Some solo dances are accompanied by simple bagpipes and resemble dance in the Highlands of Scotland. Circle dances are also popular.

HISTORIC SITES. The summer capital of Spain, **Donostiá/San Sebastián**, has the Museo de San Telmo, a Basque historical and ethnographic museum occupying a sixteenth-century monastery. There is also an oceanographic museum at the Palacio del Mar. The city has always been the most Castilian of the Basque urban areas, and the old Miramar Royal Palace and the new Palacio de Ayete are outposts of Madrid. Near the harbor, the Parte Vieja is the picturesque old town that has become a restaurant district.

Elsewhere in the province, on the French border, **Fuenterrabía** possesses a variety of late medieval and Renaissance structures such as the national parador El Emperador, once a palace of Carlos I. Close by is **Irún,** the modern border crossing point to France. The Ayuntamiento (city building) is seventeenth century, and the large church of Nuestra Señora del Juncal is thirteenth century.

Further west and somewhat in from the coast, an estate near **Azkoitia** was the birthplace of Ignacio Loyola, founder of the Society of Jesus. The Hapsburg dynasty donated the property to the Jesuits, who established a large college on the grounds. The Santuario de San Ignacio de Loyola, a pantheon of famous Jesuits, also contains Loyola's home. He was baptized in the parish church of San Sebastián in Azkoitia.

Midway between Donestiá and Bilbo, the western town of **Eibar** witnessed the proclamation of the Second Republic on April 14, 1931. Some distance south is the isolated mountain village of **Onati** (Oñate). During the Middle Ages, Onati remained strongly autonomous and had a university, Sancti Spiritus. In the First Carlist War, the town became a major center of Carlism. Neighboring **Vergara** hosted the negotiations leading to the Truce of Vergara, which ended the First Carlist War in 1839.

CUISINE. Donostiá (San Sebastián) is a major gastronomic center, since Basques are considered to be Spain's best cooks. The maritime influence is quite strong. Traditional dishes include *atún o bonito a la pelotari* or *marmitako de currito* (tuna stews), as well as *mero a la donostiarra* (sea bass Donostiá or San Sebastián style). *Pinchos de ajo arriero* (canapes of dried cod and potatoes) are also popular. Crayfish are sometimes served with a bitter almond puree that is a wonderful contrast to the shellfish. Salt fish, known as Bacalao al Pil-Pil, is made as follows:

BACALAO AL PIL-PIL

3 lbs. salt cod	4 cloves garlic
3 Tbs. olive oil	1 red pepper, cut into rings

The cod must be soaked in water three times to remove the salt. Heat the olive oil in a skillet and brown the garlic, then remove the garlic and part of the oil. In the remainder, brown the cod on low heat and add the remaining olive oil again slowly as the fish breaks up until it reaches a saucelike consistency. Garnish with pepper rings before serving.

Local wines include the very good white Txakoli and some robust reds locally known as Rioja Alta. Sargadoz is the generic name of a lemony apple brandy comparable to the French Calvados. A fizzy local cider is also popular.

——— *BIZKAIA (Vizcaya, Biscaya)* ———

VITAL STATISTICS. Pop., 1,181,401 (second-highest population density in Spain at 532 persons per sq. km.). Area, 2,217 sq. km. Capital and diocesan see: Bilbo (Bilbao). The province is traversed south to north by the Río Nervión and lies south of the Bay of Biscay, west of Gipuzkoa (Guipúzcoa), east of Santander, and north of Araba (Alava) and Burgos. The major university is the branch of the Universidad del País Vasco (UPV) at Lejona (near Bilbo), largest in the system. The Jesuit-run Deusto University is located in Bilbo.

ECONOMY. Iron mining by the Metalquímica de Nervión and Ercosa has declined during the last several decades, although metal fabrication remains a specialty of the province. Ship-building, manufacture of railway cars, and production of other metal products are still very important. More than 10 percent of the fifty largest Spanish companies are headquartered in Bilbo.

Banking is another large industry. Bilbo is home of the Banco de Bilbao (now Banco Banesto), one of the major banks in Spain and one of the hundred largest banks in the world. The Madrid stock exchange has a branch in the city.

Energy has become a new industry. The minor natural gas field of Gaviota, offshore near Bermeo, opened in 1986, but of greater importance is the supertanker anchorage near Bilbo, one of the few ports in Europe where the continental shelf does not preclude their docking. Bilbo also is a large refining center for the former government oil monopoly, CAMPSA, and for Repsosol, a new oil company formed in 1987, which has built a refinery at Somorrostro.

Dairy farming and sheep raising are the most important agricultural activities. Bizkaia is one of the top five provinces of Spain for milk and cheese production. The fishing industry is somewhat smaller than those of Galicia or Cantabria.

HISTORY. (Vascones [Roman]). The caves of Santimamiñe contain remnants of a society at least 20,000 years old. Livy mentions Vascones in his description of the Sertorian War (77–74 B.C.), although it is not clear whether the Vascones were Basque or Gascon since the region adjoined Gaul. Romans dominated the coastal regions of the area but failed to penetrate the mountainous interior, and local Basque society there had minimal contact with either Romans or Christians. Three clerics suffered martyrdom for protesting pagan ceremonies in A.D. 397, and Armandus asserted in *Vita Sancti Amandi* that paganism still existed in the eighth century, although St. Amandus (630?–84), a noble of Aquitaine and an itinerant missionary, proselytized in Vizcaya (as Bizkaia officially was called until the modern era) a century earlier. Political control remained cursory despite claims that the Visigoth Sisebut (612–21) had subdued Cantabria and part of Vizcaya.

Duke Eudo (d. 735) established a short-lived Gascon state in the early eighth century, but both the Asturian and Navarrese monarchies soon claimed Vizcaya. Sancho García I of Navarre chartered some villages in the first document ever written in Euskara, but the López de Haro family brought the area into association with Castile after 1076. These ties and the struggle between powerful landowners (*parientes mayores*) began to alter personal power after 1379 in the conferral of *foruak* (see Customs and Society, below) to villages and rural areas. The Ordenanza of 1394 between the Castilian monarchy and local authorities permitted representatives of towns and rural districts to attend an annual general junta "under the Tree of Guernica" to make laws and organize public order, administration, and tariffs for their areas. Local control was so important that the *foruak* of 1526 limited all outside interference in legal, political, and financial affairs under the *corregimiento* system. Corporal punishment, imprisonment without trial, and debtor's prison were prohibited, and civil rights granted by the *foruak* included the sacrosanct nature of private property and guarantees of freedom to former serfs. The province also obtained a promise that Castilian troops could not enter without permission and that customs and taxes would remain subject to local control.

Vizcaya negotiated these local privileges from a position of economic importance. Several natives of the province sailed with Columbus, and maritime expertise increased when the carrying trade in wool to northern textile centers in England and the Low Countries became profitable. By the sixteenth century, plentiful supplies of iron and wood made the shipyards of Bilbao the largest in Spain, and Vizcaya prospered indirectly from colonial trade through ship construction. Late in the century, Bilbao's role in building part of the Spanish Armada brought English and Dutch retaliation, and in the next several centuries the French also ravaged the Vizcayan coast, capturing Bilbao during the Napoleonic invasion of 1808–13.

Eighteenth-century domestic politics, already made tumultuous by the destruction of ancient privileges elsewhere on the peninsula, centered around Madrid's accusations that Basques sought to enlarge their liberties and engaged in excessive ethnic solidarity. Abolition of customs posts, use of *corregidores*, and demands made on Vizcaya to provide draft recruits in the period between 1790 and 1833 culminated during the liberal Triennium of 1820–23 when *foruak* liberties were disregarded in the battle against widespread smuggling. Government garrisons increased in size without permission after 1830, and government troops held the city of Bilbao against a major Carlist siege five years later. The two Carlist Wars diminished Vizcaya's privileges in much the same way that Alava's and Guipúzcoa's were diminished.

By the end of the nineteenth century, these political problems contrasted vividly with dynamic economic growth. National land reform laws enacted by liberals against the Church and aristocracy allowed the Ibarra and Chávarri families to obtain lands rich in iron deposits. The two families formed Altos Hornos de Bilbao and La Viscaya, the two largest Spanish mining corporations, which collectively controlled about half the iron mines and approximately 60 percent of the Spanish cast iron industry.

Large-scale industry produced inevitable radical labor and nationalist movements. The socialist Unión General de Trabajadores dominated working-class politics through its Metal Workers' Union, while middle-class voters favored the blunt Basque nationalism of the PNV, founded in 1895 by Sabino de Arana y Goiri (1865–1903) of Bilbao, who objected to the influx of non-Basque laborers in the province. A lawyer by profession, he came from a conservative Carlist family. During his studies in Barcelona, he watched the Catalans begin their own brand of regional revitalization. While the Catalans sought an efficient state (or at least an honest one), Arana interpreted the dilemma of the Basque Provinces as a moral crisis: plunder of the area by Spain, which had expanded its power from delegated authority to a tyranny by the Spanish central government. Arana's tactics incorporated the militancy of Carlism into the PNV's defense of the *foruak*, which he and the PNV interpreted as liberties, not privileges. In his view, the Basques had the sovereignty to revoke Madrid's control over their region.

After the death of Arana y Goiri, the PNV came under the leadership of José Antonio Aguirre (1904–60), who raised controversy during the Second Republic by promoting an autonomy statute in cooperation with Madrid, whose radical religious and economic values in this period particularly offended many Basques. The statute, nearly completed when the civil war began, finally went into effect in October 1936.

The civil war pushed several other Vizcayans to positions of importance. The wife of a miner, Dolores Ibarruri Gómez, "La Pasionaria" (1895–1989), led the Spanish Communist Party, while a socialist journalist and newspaper editor of Bilbao, Indalecio Prieto y Tuero (1883–1962), was republican defense minister in 1937–38. Vizcaya represented an anomaly: while remaining very religious and conservative, it would not join Franco's cause, since to do so would mean losing the new autonomy statute. In 1936 and early 1937, the province remained a bulwark of republican efforts.

On April 26, 1939, the town of Guernica, ceremonial center of *foruak* democracy thirty kilometers east of Bilbao, was firebombed by the German Condor Legion in punishment for Basque disobedience. Hundreds died and thousands were injured at Guernica, one of the civil war's great tragedies. The attack on Bilbao's "iron ring" of defenses killed 10,000 more. After intense and massive fighting, the city fell on June 16, 1937, as thousands fled. In the ensuing occupation, abrogation of the regional statute and loss of all foral rights came as a matter of course.

In the postwar period, industry and finance recovered and prospered. By 1975, Banco Banesto had become one of the largest banks in Spain, owning the largest insurance group (Unión y Fénix), the largest construction company (Agroman), and the largest mining company (Asturias de Zinc). In other sectors, the situation was not as good. The Basque Catholic Church lost its regional character and could not use its unique Euskara-language masses. Euskara, in fact, was totally forbidden, and Castilian culture supplanted Basque local customs, at least officially. Many Bizkaianos bitterly opposed Franco, and in 1959 a new ultranationalist group, the Basque Homeland and Freedom Party (Euzkadi Ta Askatasuna, or ETA), emerged as a secret terrorist organization. By 1968, their assassination of a political police commander led to thousands of arrests and a controversial military trial in Burgos that attracted worldwide attention.

After Franco's death, the constitutional monarchy spurred Basque politicians to regain autonomy, supported by a majority vote approving regionalism. Today, while the ETA, crippled by joint French and Spanish security measures, still pursues occasional anti-Spanish acts, the contemporary Bizkaiano crisis is now more focused on the economic decline of the extractive industry's "rust valleys" and the poor ecological condition of the countryside, or international crises like the OPEC-caused energy crisis in the late 1970s.

LITERATURE. One of the first authors identified with Vizcaya (Bizkaia) is **Lope García de Salazar** (ca. 1471), whose chronicle of social struggle in the late fourteenth century, *Las Bienandanças e Fortunas*, is a valuable early history. **Gonzalo Arredondo** (ca. 1490) compiled the first major discussion of Basque liberties in the *Libro de la Recopilación*. The sixteenth-century writer **Tomás de Goicola** (ca. 1528) wrote *Relación de cómo se entienden los Nobles, Hidalgos y los Labradores públicos del Señorío de Vizcaya*, a commentary on the codification of Vizcayan foral law under the Hapsburg dynasty.

Other authors (often difficult to identify precisely as to date or origin) include Fray **Miguel de Alonsótegui** (ca. 1577), *Crónicas de Vizcaya*; **Juan Iñiguez de Ibargüen** (ca. 1588), *Crónica general española y sumaria de la Casa vizcáina*; and **Francisco de Mendieta** (ca. 1588), *Quarta parte de los Annales de Vizcaya*. Fray **Martín de Coscojales's** *Antigüedades de Vizcaya* (ca. 1600) tried to establish an argument legitimizing the orthodoxy of local society. The large number of nobles remained controversial, and **Juan García** (ca. 1588) in *De hispanorum nobilitate exemptione sive ad pragmaticam cordunbensem* attacked the spread of *caballero* status.

Most of the province's literature has emerged during the past two centuries. Fray **Mateo Zabala** (1777–1840) collected folk tales from the countryside. **José Antonio Uriarte** (1812–69) translated the Bible into Euskara in *Biblia edo Testamentu zar eta berria*, and **Jean Martín Hiribarren** (1810–66) and **Indalecio Bizcarrondo** (1831–76) wrote poetry in the vernacular.

The turning point for Euskara as a revived language came in 1879 with the organization of poetry contests. The first journal written in the language, *Euskal-Erria*, appeared the same year. The first Euskaran novel was **Juan Bautista Elissamburu's** (1828–91) *Piarres Adame sarratarraren zenhiat historio* (published posthumously in 1899). **Felipe Arese y Beitia** (1814–1906) produced the first modern poetry collection, *Ama Euskeriaren liburo kantaria* (1900). **Resurrección María de Azkue** (1864–1951), Arana's friend and contemporary from Gipuzkoa, compiled the *Diccionario Vasco-Español-Francés* as a continuation of Larramendi's work. He also created a major study of Euskaran grammar in *La Morfología*, collected Euskaran poetry in *El Cancionero*, and wrote stories gathered in *Literatura Popular del País Vasco*.

The culmination of this early surge came with the publication by **Sabino** de Arana y Goiri (1854–1903) of *Gramática elemental del Euskera Biz-kaino* (1888). Since he was not a native speaker of Euskara, the book really constituted his basic effort to learn the language. His pamphlet *Bizcaya por su independencia* (1892) created a historical context for Basque national-ism, arguing that the Basques had always managed to fight victoriously for liberty until the present moment, when desire for luxury and wealth had allowed Spain to crush local liberties. Spain had become liberal and anti-clerical; the Basques, on the other hand, were a God-fearing race who de-served their own *patria*, their own country. In many respects, Arana wrote as a strict moralist who believed in a powerful brand of ethnic nationalism.

Antonio de Trueba (1919–89), a writer of popular short stories based on Catholic themes, also stressed the moral righteousness of the Basque nation in seeking independence from a less-than-admirable Spain. He too became a crucial figure in the creation of Basque nationalism, along with Azkue and Arana of Bizkaia, Larramendi and Aguirre of Gipuzkoa, Joseph Augustín Chaho of the French Basque region, and Arturo Campión of Navarre.

Not all writers or philosophers moved in this direction. A poet and dip-lomat, **Ramón de Basterra** (1888–1928) of Bilbao, ran against the norm by defending Spanish culture against Protestant and northern European ideas and regionalism at home. **Juan Antonio de Zunzunegui** (b. 1902), a practitioner of nineteenth-century realism, wrote often of Bilbao in such novels as *El chiplichandle* (1939); *Ay estos hijos* (1943), about a disturbed youth; *El barco de la muerte* (1945), in which a man's greed leads to his death; and *La úlcera* (1949), about a hypochondriac who devotes his life to an ulcer until the shock of having found a cure kills him.

The best-known Vizcayan of the time, **Miguel de Unamuno y Jugo** (1869–1936), wrote in Spanish and attracted enormous attention as an educator, philosopher, and writer with a large Spanish and European au-dience. As the leading member of the Generation of 1898 and a longtime professor at Salamanca as well as its rector from 1900 to 1936, Unamuno identified strongly with Castile.

Unamuno's major philosophic works include *En torno al casticismo* (1902), a plea for modernization not by blind imitation but by revitaliza-tion of eternal Spanish qualities and adapting selective aspects of modern-ism. The book has been summarized as how to be European without losing the qualities of Hispanic culture. *Vida de don Quijote y Sancho, según Miguel de Cervantes Saavedra* (1905) made Quijote and Sancho into spir-itual symbols of hope and redemption for the Spanish soul. *Del sentimiento trágico de la vida en los hombres y en los pueblos* (1913) argued that faith can be irrational and could create a tragic sense of life unfeeling toward problems that may have human, nonreligious solutions.

Unamuno's most sensitive work, *La agonía del cristianismo* (1925), is an existential contemplation of reason and faith. Unamuno's god was not a god of reason but a humane god reached only through faith and love.

We are always uncertain about the afterlife and salvation, but if nothingness is our fate, Unamuno wrote, let us live in a way that makes nothingness seem like an injustice. The implication is that faith and love can go beyond religious faith and devotion into committed service for community and humankind. As a philosopher, he went through several crises but finally arrived at a belief in "man as an end in himself rather than as an instrument of God; belief in the immortality of the soul; and denial of the validity of any inflexible philosophical system."

Unamuno wrote poetry in *Poesías* (1907), *El Cristo de Velázquez* (1920), and the posthumously published *Cancionero* (1953). As a novelist, he developed the style called *nivola*, an exploration of epistemological reality in which characters exist only by virtue of what they say, without description of scenery, setting, or physical appearance. *Niebla* (1914) is a story of fictional characters who become independent of their creator. *Abel Sánchez* (1917) is a Cain and Abel story about hate and envy, and *San Manuel Bueno, mártir* (1930) concerns the struggle of a priest to keep his faith. *La tía Tula* (1921), interesting as a product of Unamuno's disillusionment after World War I, is his proposal to support a society based not on the concept of *patria* (the universal brotherhood of man), but on *matria* (a society based on maternal love), an abstract avowal of feminism. He also wrote plays such as *El otro* (1926), which ventured into psychiatric theory.

He participated as a deputy in the Cortes of the Second Republic, but became discouraged by the violence caused by national deadlock and withdrew from politics. On October 12, 1936, he was placed under house arrest after his blistering condemnation of a nationalist general as a man wedded to death. He died a natural death in December of the same year.

Another Vizcayan, **Ramiro de Maeztu** (1874–1936) of Bilbao, wrote philosophy and social essays. His father, a Basque born in Cuba, had Ramiro educated in Paris. He worked in Cuba until 1894 before returning to Bilbao and then later to Madrid, where he propagandized in favor of a liberal Spain.

Close to Azorín and Baroja, Maeztu seemed initially enthusiastic about national reform in *Hacia otra España* (1899), but while serving as a war correspondent on the Western Front he grew cynical about humankind's efforts to improve social life through the modern state. He began to contradict his earlier liberal views in *Don Quijote, Don Juan y La Celestina* (1929), arguing that symbolically Cervantes had killed the spirit of Spain by being too willing to accept change.

Maeztu became the only major writer of the period to support the dictatorship of General José María Primo de Rivera, and he was appointed ambassador to Argentina in 1928. Recalled at the start of the Second Republic, he threw himself into journalism and essay-writing. *La defensa de la hispanidad* (1934) completed his conversion to the traditional perspective by drawing upon sixteenth-century Catholicism and corporative ideologies as the eternal symbols of Spain, which should be used as the basis of a new

Catholic Empire. During the Second Republic, he helped to organize a traditionalist, quasi-fascist youth group, Acción Española, but at the start of the civil war he fell into republican hands and was executed. At the time, his execution was compared to that of Federico García Lorca in Granada, but García Lorca never was as actively engaged in politics as Maeztu.

In recent times, **Blas de Otero** (1916–1978?) of Bilbo was a poet who lived for long periods in Madrid and Barcelona. His *Cántico espiritual* (1942) focused on the uprooted postwar society, while *Pido la paz y la palabra* (1955) concentrated on the lack of freedom. **Gabriel Aresti Segurola** (1933–75), poet and dramatist, attained considerable importance in the early 1960s for his political poetry in *Maldan behera=Pendiente abajo. Herri eta herri=Piedra y pueblo* (1960), which marked a new stage of the Basque struggle. What made Aresti so important was his abandonment of a deeply conservative Catholic faith to take a revolutionary and nationalist position on the Basque question. At the same time, **Federico Krutwig Sagredo** (b. 1938?) of Bilbo, who remains active today, wrote *Vasconia* (1963), triggering the radical claims of the Basque Homeland and Freedom group (ETA). Among outsiders who have written on the province, **Juan Arce de Otalora** (ca. 1570) of Valladolid wrote *Summa nobilitatis hispaniae*, which included valuable material on the aristocracy of the region. **Louis Lucien Bonaparte** (1813–93), nephew of Napoleon Bonaparte and a cousin of Napoleon III, did philological research and created an early linguistic study of Euskara. With **Antonio d'Abbadie** (1810–97) and **Joseph Augustin Chaho** (1810–58), he published *Estudios Gramaticales sobre la lengua euskera* in 1836. Chaho, a French Basque, continued to work on redeveloping Euskara and also sought a nationalistic revival. He can be considered one of the first major figures of the Basque Renaissance.

ART. A ceramicist in Paris and an acquaintance of Apollinaire and Picasso, **Francisco Durrio** (1868–1927?) of Bilbao had some influence on the latter's ceramic experiments. **Nemesio Mogrovejo** (1875–1910) of Bilbao died young of tuberculosis at the start of a brilliant career as a sculptor. **Quintín de Torre** (1879–1935?) sculpted busts, while **Fructuoso Orduña** (1893–1974?) did neoclassical and heroic statues. **Néstor Basterrechea** (b. 1924) has done constructivist works based on Basque legend and myth. His versatility spills over into film-making, photography, painting, and design.

MUSIC. The composer, critic, and scholar **Antón Larrauri** (b. 1932) is best known for his adaptation of Basque folk songs to avant-garde music in works such as *Espatadantza.*

CUSTOMS AND SOCIETY. Rural life is extremely important in the history of Basque society. During the fourteenth and fifteenth centuries, *parientes mayores*, as heads of powerful families, sought political prestige by creating armed bands of followers in order to control the countryside. This struggle, known as the *luchas de bandos* (struggle of the clans), created instability and led to the establishment of the Castilian *corregidores* in Vizcaya. The Castilian kings of the time used the *foruak* to put the countryside under the jurisdiction of the *juntas generales* (general assemblies). To a great extent, towns remained totally under royal jurisdiction.

Under the *foruak*, the *baserritarra*, or peasants, lived on farmsteads, the *baserritarrak* (singular, *baserria*) usually named for the founding family. In matters of inheritance, the *baserria* was transmitted intact to a sole heir, the *etxekojaun*. This person was obliged to compensate both male and female disinherited siblings with dowries (*dotes*) and portions of the estate (*legitimas*, usually paid in cash). Wealth came to be determined by the number of cows or by the *fanegos* (a unit of measure, about 45 kilos of wheat) that the *baserria* produced.

Farmsteads were linked in a voluntary neighborhood association called the *auzoa*, each with its own chapel and patron saint. Member families of the *auzoa* attended the important rituals of their neighbors' lives, participating in gift exchanges and collective labor at planting and harvesting time and engaging in local projects such as road or chapel maintenance.

This society flourished ca. 1450–1770, after which rural indebtedness began to force the sale of land, disrupting the agrarian pattern of life. Sometimes all of the *baserria* except the ancestral home had to be sold. The families became heavily encumbered with debt, forcing younger male members to seek their fortunes in North or South America for the sake of the farmstead. The political impact of this crisis over time created a gulf between rural-dwellers and urban-dwellers (*kalet-arrak*), who tended to see the *baserritarrak* as the idealized symbol of Basque nationalism. Much of the passion in the twentieth-century Basque struggle comes from the conviction that rural society was a paradise compared to the urban, industrial contemporary era, although history indicates that this probably was not the case. In recent decades, migration and low agricultural incomes have continued to cause the *baserritarrak* sector to decline.

Among the various folk activities, *pelota* is a series of wall-and-ball games played by the Basques. *Blaid* is a simple form of handball; jai alai uses the *chistera*, or long-curved basket, to add great velocity to the ball. Betting is common at all levels of *pelota*, and parimutuel betting is a part of professional jai alai, played on indoor courts called frontons. *Pelota* began as a village game and is the center of local social life in the main squares of smaller Basque towns. The provincial dance is the *zortzico*, with a curious 5/8 rhythm.

Mythology centers around the role of the Mari, the queen of the underworld, who has the power to destroy individuals and entire communities by ruining harvests. Lamiñak, a half-fish, half-human female supernatural being who tests human qualities by punishing those who are greedy or in some other way violate rural solidarity, is a lesser folkloric figure.

Leather work is an old provincial custom. *Pellejas* are whole goatskin receptacles sewn together to keep the shape of the pig or goat. They can hold about 120 liters of wine and are often seen hanging from ceilings in bars and country inns. *Botas* are smaller crescent-shaped leather wine bags used by holding the bag above the head and squeezing the liquid into the mouth. Both are commonplace throughout Spain.

HISTORIC SITES. The largest Basque city, **Bilbo/Bilbao,** has been an industrial center since the late medieval period. The cathedral of Santiago, completed in 1379, suffered too much damage from fire and revolution to retain its original beauty. The cultural center of the Parque de Doña Casilda de Iturriza includes the Museo de Bellas Artes and the Museo de Arte Moderno, which both contain fine collections, and an archaeological museum. In addition, the Getty Museum of Los Angeles is currently building a new branch in Bilbo.

Elsewhere in the province, **Guernica** (Guernica y Luno), east of Bilbo near the Bay of Biscay, is the site of the Oak of Guernica, where ancient Basque assemblies (*batzarrak*) met to reaffirm local foral liberties. In the nineteenth century, these assemblies met in the Casa de Juntas Forales, the Basque parliament building. Guernica suffered a severe bombing on April 26, 1937, immortalized by Pablo Picasso in his painting by the same name.

Just to the southeast, the namesake of several towns in the Americas, **Durango** is an old mining center with three large churches: the baroque Santa Ana, the Gothic Santa María de Uribarri, and the Romanesque San Pedro de Tavira. **Orduña** housed the headquarters of the Carlist pretender during the First Carlist War.

CUISINE. The rural side of Basque cuisine consists of meat dishes such as *buzkantzak* (blood sausage), *bacalao a la Vizcaína* (salt cod in red pepper sauce), *merluza koskera* (hake in green sauce), and *menestra a la Bilbo* (mutton stew). In urban areas, this cuisine is one of the best and most sophisticated in Spain.

Here is the recipe for one popular dish, *marmitako* (fresh tuna fish).

MARMITAKO

1 cup olive oil	2 lbs. tuna
1 onion, chopped	salt and cayenne pepper to taste
3 potatoes, peeled and chopped	2–3 cups water
2 cloves garlic, minced	

Heat the olive oil in an earthenware casserole and fry the onion, potatoes, and garlic briefly. Add the tuna; mix and season with salt and cayenne pepper. The dish is covered with water and simmered until the fish is done and the potatoes are tender.

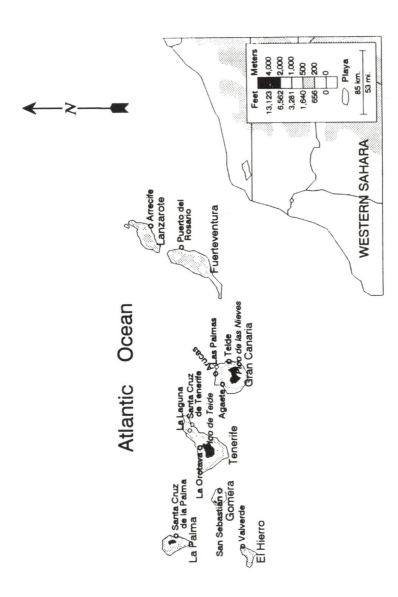

Atlantic Ocean

Santa Cruz
de la Palma
La Palma

San Sebastián
Gomera

Valverde
El Hierro

La Laguna
Santa Cruz
de Tenerife
La Orotava
Pico de Teide
Tenerife

Añaza
Las Palmas
Agaete
Teide
Pico de las Nieves
Gran Canaria

Arrecife
Lanzarote

Puerto del
Rosario
Fuerteventura

WESTERN SAHARA

Feet	Meters
13,123	4,000
6,562	2,000
3,281	1,000
1,640	500
656	200
0	0

Playa

85 km.
53 mi.

CANARY ISLANDS

Chapter 6

CANARY ISLANDS
(Canarias)

REGIONAL CHARACTERISTICS. Pop., 1,444,626. Area, 7,447 sq. km. Capital: Las Palmas, Gran Canaria. The seven main and six smaller islands of the Canaries are located approximately 680 miles south of Cádiz in the Atlantic Ocean and 65 miles west of Cape Yubi on the far southern coast of Morocco. The people of the islands are called *isleños*.

Unlike the rest of Spain, the Canary Islands do not belong to the European Community. Even the Spanish state petroleum and tobacco monopolies share markets competitively in the region. Free trade in the Canaries, begun in the nineteenth century, increased in 1976 when the Portuguese empire collapsed in Africa. Spain became vulnerable to attack in the Western Sahara, sought by both the Kingdom of Morocco and the Algerian-aided Saharan Frente Polisario. As part of this struggle, the Movimiento para la Autodeterminación y Independencia del Archipiélago Canario (MPAIAC) used national liberation tactics to stage a brief rising in the Canary Islands.

The new constitutional monarchy of Juan Carlos I could ill afford to lose territory less than a year after coming into power. Thus the king granted far-reaching free trade concessions to the islands not long before the debate on the Constitution of 1978 began, greatly increasing the importance of autonomy in the national political consciousness.

The December 1978 plebiscite in the Canary Islands supported limited autonomy by a 64 percent rate. The autonomous government began its life in January 1983. The Canary Islands have a yellow, blue, and white vertically striped flag.

The region ranks seventh in personal income.

LAS PALMAS (Gran Canaria)

VITAL STATISTICS. Pop., 756,353, one of the youngest and fastest growing populations in Spain. Area, 4,066 sq. km. Capital and diocesan see: Las Palmas. The eastern part of the Canary Islands (Gran Canaria, Fuerteventura, Lanzarote) forms the province of Las Palmas, usually called Gran Canaria.

ECONOMY. Tourism is the biggest industry, but agriculture is also important. Winter vegetables such as cucumbers, tomatoes, and potatoes are exported to Europe from Lanzarote, whose volcanic soil is particularly rich. Fields must be lowered below the terrain for protection against the wind since the treeless island is in the path of the trade winds. Black volcanic ash called *picón* is spread on the fields to nurture special crops such as bananas, orchilla weed (used to make purple dye), tropical nuts, sugar, and tobacco.

Las Palmas is the third-largest fishing port in Spain and the largest local port to fish in South Atlantic waters.

HISTORY. (Islas Canis [Roman], named not for birds, as many suppose, but for the wild dogs [in Latin *canis*] originally found in the islands). The Greeks first discovered the islands; Ptolemy called them the Fortunate Isles. The Romans, who considered colonizing the archipelago, noted the presence of indigenous inhabitants, the Guanches, a tall, fair-skinned people related to the Berber tribes of the Atlas Mountains in Morocco. The Guanches, who mummified their dead, were once thought to have had Egyptian origins, an idea now disproved.

When Europeans began to sail westward in the early fourteenth century, an expedition in A.D. 1312 named the island of Lanzarote after the voyage's leader, the Genoese Lancelot Malocello. Organization of Spanish settlements did not come until the founding of Las Palmas in 1404–8 by a Majorcan Norman clan, the Betencourts, who in driving away the Guanches began the destruction of the first indigenous culture in the Spanish imperial period. Exactly when the Guanches entirely disappeared or were completely assimilated is not clear.

Portugal and Spain clashed over possession of the archipelago early in the fifteenth century. Prince Henry (1395–1460) of Portugal lost several naval engagements between 1420 and 1425. Portugal finally acknowledged Spain's possession of the islands in 1479 by the Treaty of Alcaçovas, Castile's initial step in acquiring a trans-Atlantic empire.

A Catalan captain, Juan de Réjon, founded the city of Las Palmas in 1478. Christopher Columbus stopped on his inaugural voyage to the New World and again on his return and on his second voyage. The early sixteenth century saw construction of the cathedral and the harbor castle of Nuestra Señora de la Luz, but pirate attacks continued, and raids by the French pirate François Leclerq, sometimes known as "Pegleg," caused even more elaborate fortifications to be built in 1553. Trade, shipping, and agriculture made these Atlantic isles among the most agriculturally stable and innovative in the Spanish Empire. Sugar exports to mainland Spain earned great profits but suffered a setback in 1730 when a five-year-long series of volcanic explosions on Lanzarote destroyed a third of the island and created a lunar landscape of 130 volcanos or volcanic cones.

Up to 1823, captains-general ruled the islands to ensure that the anchorages remained peaceful as a last stop for provisions and naval repairs before the long ocean crossing on the voyage to the Indies. Their job was often difficult. In 1611, the *consulado* of Seville prohibited islanders from any further trading with the Indies after island pirates diverted American silver from Spanish convoys. In the seventeenth and eighteenth centuries, the islands became a contraband center for British, French, and Dutch merchants. During the reign of Carlos III, strong mainland Spanish protectionism increased this illegal trade. Piratical behavior protected the islands against British capture, since the contraband damaged the Spanish economy much more than occupation could possibly benefit London.

The era of Latin American independence caused Madrid to end Canary colonial status and make the islands into a single Spanish province in 1823 before they too were lost. Against the wishes of Gran Canaria, Lanzarote, and Fuerteventura, Santa Cruz de Tenerife was made capital of the entire archipelago. Collapse of colonial trade, which minimized the islands' strategic location, created new problems of poverty and loss of settlers to Cuba and Venezuela. In 1852, Madrid granted free trade concessions, but endemic lawlessness, a dead economy, and tax avoidance made the region difficult for Spanish bureaucrats to administer.

In 1927, the islands were divided into two provinces; Las Palmas incorporated Gran Canaria, Fuerteventura, and Lanzarote, while Santa Cruz de Tenerife administered the southwestern part of the archipelago. Both temporarily housed political exiles from metropolitan Spain during the stormy dictatorship of General Miguel Primo de Rivera, among them the Basque intellectual, Miguel de Unamuno, who served a brief term on Fuerteventura. Juan Negrín López (1892–1956), a medical professor of Madrid whose family owned large properties on Las Palmas, led the protests against such practices at the start of his political career. In time, Negrín was the last premier of the Second Republic (1937–39).

After the republicans returned to power in February 1936, Premier Manuel Azaña imitated Primo by forcing the leading Spanish general, Francisco Franco, to begin a near exile of his own as military governor of Santa Cruz de Tenerife. The appointment put the popular, conservative general as far away from mainland Spain as possible in case of a military conspiracy. When confrontation between left and right began leading to civil war in mid-July 1936, Franco's supporters rented a plane in London. It arrived in Las Palmas on July 14 and secretly took Franco, who was on the island to attend the funeral of General Amadeo Balmes, military governor of Las Palmas, to Morocco on July 18, where he took command of the rebellious Spanish army, soon to invade republican Spain.

Naval and military personnel remained loyal to Franco during the civil war and guaranteed the islands' support of the nationalist cause. Uncertain strategic fortunes during World War II increased the military presence, which lasted until the postwar era's tourist boom began in the late 1950s.

LITERATURE. The Canary Islands form an isolated pocket of Spanish culture. In the early period, only **Bartolomé Cariasco de Figueroa** [1540–?] of Gran Canaria, canon of the cathedral of Las Palmas, wrote poetry and plays. During the Enlightenment, **José Clavijo y Fajardo** (1730–1806) of Lanzarote wrote satires, did translations, and occupied a number of official diplomatic posts. After meeting Voltaire and Buffon in Paris, he became an enthusiastic supporter of the Enlightenment and in 1767 founded *El Pensador*, a satirical weekly in Madrid that attacked tradition and superstition. His romance with the sister of Pierre Beaumarchais (1732–99, author of *The Barber of Seville* and *The Marriage of Figaro*), became the subject of Goethe's romantic tragedy *Clavijo* (1802).

In the nineteenth century, the birth in Las Palmas of the prolific **Benito Pérez Galdós** (1843–1920), who lived in the islands his first twenty years, single-handedly remedied this lack of literature. Pérez Galdós is a writer ranked with Dickens, Balzac, and Dostoyevski. He spent his adult life in Madrid and wrote almost nothing about the islands, but his *Episodios Nacionales* (composed of two parts, *Novelas de la primera época* [1873–79], 20 vols., and *Novelas españolas contemporáneas* [1898–1912], 26 vols.) shows the cravings he must have felt as a provincial outsider to understand national history and come to terms with his Spanish heritage. The middle period of his career produced *Doña Perfecta* (1876), *La desheredada* (1881), *Fortunata y Jacinta* (1887), *Misericordia* (1897), and thirty-one other novels as well as twenty-four plays.

Pérez Galdós personified the modern outlook of a late nineteenth-century Spaniard's desire to assimilate Western European aesthetic, social, and political tendencies. He debated the religious and political conflicts of his day in his narrative works and wrote polemics against traditional society. Novels such as *Torquemada en la hoguera* (1889), *Angel Guerra* (1891), and *Nazarín* (1895) showed the influence of Leo Tolstoy's neo-Christian teachings, and the plays *Electra* (1901) and *El abuelo* (1905) reflected skepticism regarding the ability of political institutions to solve mounting social problems. He became such a national Spanish novelist that he completely transcended his Canary origins.

While no one of Pérez Galdós's stature has appeared in the twentieth century, literary production has been relatively large. **Rafael Romero** (1886–1925) sympathized with the Generation of 1898, and his novel *Crónicas de la ciudad y de la noche* (1919) included some material from the region. **Carmen Laforet Díaz** (b. 1921) of Las Palmas grew up here before moving to Barcelona, where she wrote extensively about the islands. *Nada* (1944; the first Nadal Prize winner, now one of the leading literary prizes) told the story of a young girl from the Canaries who seeks a new life in Spain, only to be confronted by great difficulties when she moves to the mainland. Her *La isla y los demonios* (1952) examined the impact of religion in the islands. **Justo Jorge Padrón** (b. 1943), educated and employed in Barcelona, is an award-winning poet, whose works include *Los oscuros fuegos* (1970), *Mar de la noche* (1974), and *Los circulos del infierno* (1976).

CUSTOMS AND SOCIETY. Traditional dress in the islands was always slightly different from the rest of Spain. Peasant women wore fine striped woolen skirts and black sleeveless bodices over a white camisole, with a silk handkerchief around the neck and a mantilla or cape of flannel edged with ribbons. Both men and women wore small straw hats in hot weather. In the mild winters, males frequently wore *serapes*, a form of outerwear adapted from the American colonies.

Sand paintings of religious scenes are common in Arrecife, the capital of Lanzarote, and elsewhere on the island. *Romerias*, or pilgrimages celebrating local saints' days, take place in many villages.

The music of the islands is very distinctive. Folk songs and dances of the original inhabitants mix with Spanish and Latin American music to create a special slow and rhythmic dance, far removed from passionate gypsy flamenco.

The addition of Gran Canaria to the crown of Castile is celebrated during the last week of April and the first week of May by the Fiesta de San Pedro de Verona.

HISTORIC SITES. On the island of **Gran Canaria**, the cathedral of Santa Ana in **Las Palmas** is made out of basalt. Begun in 1497 and completed in 1570, it was renovated between 1781 and 1820 to create a classic Gothic style with rib vaulting, a chapter house, and cloister. The Casa de Colón, the late fifteenth-century house where Columbus lived during several periods, is now the Columbus Museum. Not far away, the Museo Canario contains many archaeological items. The Pueblo Canario in the Parque Doramas is an outdoor cultural exhibit of local architecture and society, and the Casa Museo de Pérez Galdós honors the great writer. At **Telde**, the second largest town on Gran Canaria, San Juan Bautista is a church built of lava stone. The interior contains various indigenous homages to Christ, including one by the Tarasco Indians of Mexico. In **Teror**, the Casa Manrique de Lara is an informal local museum and art collection.

On **Fuerteventura**, a long and thin island ninety miles long and fifteen miles wide, the climate is very arid, with only six inches of rain a year. The main town, **Puerto del Rosario**, is 110 miles by sea from Las Palmas. A quiet provincial place, it is typical of the island itself, one of the least developed in the archipelago and less mountainous than the others. Beaches on the southern part of the island are unspoiled, and **Las Dunas National Park** is in the north. The most interesting town on the island is **Betancuria**, a former administrative center, which has an old fifteenth-century cathedral rebuilt in an eighteenth-century baroque style.

The island of **Lanzarote**, 111 miles from Las Palmas, is an island of volcanos covered with lava and cinders but rich in plant life due to its incredibly fertile soil. The administrative center of **Arrecife** is also the main port and has an archaeological museum in the San Gabriel Castle and a fine museum of contemporary art in the harbor castle. Directly across the island from Arrecife is the **Montanas del Fuego Timanfaya National Park**, adjacent to the volcanos, with an excellent museum of volcanology and a restaurant that cooks with volcanic heat. There are camel rides around the lunar landscape and a tour through the park that takes visitors close to the volcanos and their streams of molten lava. South of the volcanos, the pretty village of **Yaiza** has a good view of the whole panorama of volcanic activity. At the northern end of the island, the former capital of **Teguise** operates a folk craft market and attracts visitors to the church of St. Miguel, constructed from lava stone and wood. Nearby is the Guanapay Volcano, and to the northeast the **Cueva de los Verdes** is a volcanic tube leading to an underground lake. The Jameos del Agua Lagoon is another local tourist center.

CUISINE. *Mojo*, a very hot red dipping sauce, is a Canary specialty used on fish and potatoes. *Mojo colorado* is made of paprika, cumin, garlic, oil, and vinegar; *mojo picón* is a mixture of red peppers, sweet peppers, vinegar, oil, herbs, and garlic. *Mojo verde* uses cilantro. Coriander leaves are often used on fish dishes.

Garbanzos are popular in a variety of dishes, and fish is cheap and widely available. *Calamares rellenos* (stuffed squid), *choco* (squid in sauce), *sama* (sea bream), and *mero* (grouper) are frequent entrées. The villagers also eat a traditional gruel called *gofio*, made of wheat and flour. It is much like the Italian dish polenta.

Wine is produced on Lanzarote, but vines must be planted in pits for protection against the wind. The volcanic soil makes the grape crop very productive.

SANTA CRUZ DE TENERIFE

VITAL STATISTICS. Pop., 688,273. Area, 3,381 sq. km. Capital: Santa Cruz de Tenerife (152 miles west of Las Palmas, Gran Canaria). Diocesan see: Las Palmas. The province is the most westerly of the two Canary administrative units and is made up of Tenerife, La Palma, Gómera, and Hierro. The largest university in the islands is in La Laguna.

Mount Teide ("white mountain," a Guanche word) is a dormant volcano 12,200 feet high on the interior of Tenerife. One of the largest volcanic cones in the world, it last erupted in 1825.

The southern part of Santa Cruz de Tenerife, largest of the Canary Islands, has an extremely mild climate. There is a rainy period between November and February on the northern side.

ECONOMY. The Canary wine trade with Great Britain produced Canary Sack and Malmsey until cheaper wines and rising transportation costs undercut profits in the nineteenth century. New plantations of subtropical flowers and bananas from the Orotava Valley only partly replaced wine as export commodities.

Tourism began at the end of the nineteenth century with the construction of the Grand Hotel, and air travel has greatly increased the volume of this new industry. At one time, the Melía hotel chain had a near monopoly over Canary tourism and heavily promoted Tenerife, but today there is a wide range of accommodations.

Tenerife also has an important oil refinery that imports Venezuelan crude in order to export gasoline, butane, and propane to the African market.

HISTORY. (Tenerife [Spanish adaptation of a Guanche place name]). Catalan exploration began in 1342 with the voyage of Francesc dez Valers. The Majorcan Jaume Ferrer sailed from Tenerife to Río de Oro on the coast of Senegal in 1346 to trade for ivory and slaves. Direct colonization from Spain began in 1464, and Columbus spent three months at the island of Gomera before leaving on September 6, 1492, to sail west on his fateful first voyage to the Indies. The indigenous Guanche people fought the new Spanish colonists until about 1494, when extermination and assimilation destroyed their culture.

Early economic activity included the slave trade from Africa, Tenerife, and the Americas, recognized in a royal patent of 1509, and export of wine to Spain and Latin America, although illicit traffic in contraband was the most lucrative pursuit. Tenerife, 52 miles east of the capital of Las Palmas de Gran Canaria, remained almost ungovernable, and until approval of free trade with the colonies on October 12, 1778, considered itself a freebooter's paradise. The crown invested very little except for Carlos III's creation of a royal botanical garden at Orotava in 1788.

La Laguna, the first administrative center of Tenerife, suffered English naval attacks by Sir Francis Drake in 1595, Admiral Blake on April 30, 1657, and Admiral Jennings on November 6, 1706. The capital was moved to Santa Cruz de Tenerife in 1723, but Tenerife itself was attacked by the English admiral Horatio Nelson, who lost an arm in the battle of July 27, 1797. The city increased in size when it replaced Las Palmas as capital of the region in 1823, but severe economic collapse followed Latin American independence and bred a corrupt form of liberalism that completely secularized religious properties between 1837 and 1870.

The attack on the Church, designed to stimulate the economy, was led by General Leopoldo O'Donnell y Joris, duke of Tetuán (1809–67), the unrivaled Canary politician of the mid-nineteenth century. As a part-Irish military officer who had earned a heroic Carlist War reputation on the side of the central government, he became premier of Spain three times, most prominently as head of a coalition Unión Liberal cabinet from 1858 to 1863. To alleviate the growing poverty of his home province, he also lobbied hard to obtain the Treaty of Free Ports in 1852, hoping that the islands' proximity to international shipping routes would attract greater commerce if tariffs were reduced. Little improvement actually occurred, and rising costs of transporting Tenerife wines to market caused trade to fall even further.

By 1927, Tenerife lost power when the archipelago's territory was divided into two provinces, largely to better supervise the large number of political prisoners transported to the islands during the military dictatorship of the twenties. General Franco was appointed military governor of Tenerife on February 20, 1936, several days after the Popular Front elections; hostile crowds met him on his arrival a few weeks later, but over the next few months he won considerable support. When he departed on July 17 for Las Palmas, Morocco, and Spain, the islands remained tied to his cause during the civil war.

This legacy caused difficulties during World War II. In June 1940, Franco asked Germany for aid in the Canary Islands should the British attack Spain. On the other side, rumors that Franco planned to put the islands entirely under German control caused the British army to begin planning Operation Puma to seize the Canary Islands in April 1941. Allied planners, however, could never justify the time and cost necessary to subdue Spain, and so the operation never was undertaken.

The postwar world saw the islands begin their role as a mass tourist destination, but social change and population growth caused some serious problems. The brief MPAIAC episode in 1976 grew out of student rebellion and national liberation ideology. Many young Canary Islanders, influenced by the end of imperialism in Africa and the era of national independence, briefly supported a radical bid for separation until the economic benefits of free trade persuaded other islanders that association with Spain under such circumstances represented a saner policy.

Since that time, tourism and the development of the islands as an off-shore source of goods and products purchased by the African states have brought prosperity, but the Canary Islands still lag behind the Balearic Islands in wealth because of their greater distance from Europe.

LITERATURE. The earliest intellectual of Tenerife, **Antonio de Viana** (1578?–1650) of La Laguna, wrote epic poems about the Canary Islands. His major work, *Antiqüedades de las Islas Afortunadas de la Gran Canaria, conquista de Tenerife y aparecimiento de la Imagen de la Candelaria*, provided Lope de Vega with the background for his play *Los guanches de Tenerife y conquista de Canarias*, which sounded a slight note of sympathy for the fate of indigenous peoples in contact with the Spanish Empire.

The eighteenth century saw the spread of education and creativity. **José Viera y Clavijo** (1731–1813) of Los Realejo, a Dominican priest who spent much of his life in Madrid, wrote *Noticias de la Historia general de las Islas de Canarias* (1772–83), which is a relatively good source on the area. **Tomás de Iriarte y Oropesa** (1750–91) of La Orotava studied in Madrid and wrote satires inspired by the Enlightenment. He also composed neo-classical verse and wrote a number of plays, but he is best remembered as a kind of Spanish La Fontaine, a fabulist whose *Fábulas literarias* appeared in 1782.

In the nineteenth century, **Angel Guimerà** (1849–1924) grew up in Santa Cruz de Tenerife, but his later life in Barcelona led to a career as the editor of the daily Catalan-language newspaper *La Renaixença*.

CUSTOMS AND SOCIETY. Corpus Christi is celebrated in Tenerife by the building of flower-covered floats. The Mardi Gras–like festival, similar to that of New Orleans or Río de Janeiro, is one of the biggest in Spain and features elaborate costumes and nightly parades for two weeks. Another festival, called Guimar, is held in honor of St. Peter on June 29.

Guanche-ascribed folklore includes the *luchas canaria*, wrestling matches in which competitors struggle to stay on their feet (hence the origin of the wrestling term "fall"), as in North Africa and Egypt. *Juego del palo* is a jousting game, a type of fencing using long poles.

Traditional dress is similar to Las Palmas, but in La Laguna women once wore two long black skirts, the top one of which was turned up to cover the head and arms entirely. Fine embroidery of linen, aprons, handkerchiefs, and towels is still produced, and the lace work of the islands is popular.

HISTORIC SITES. On the island of **Tenerife**, the Iglesia de la Concepción is the largest church of **Santa Cruz de Tenerife**, built in 1502 and rebuilt after a fire in 1562. The church of San Francisco, begun in 1680, has an interesting colonial baroque style. There is a municipal museum with works by Ribera, Jordaens, and Reni; an archaeological museum that examines

Guanche culture; and a military museum in the Castillo de Paso Alto. Six miles away is **La Laguna,** the islands' university town. In the town, the Concepción Church has a pretty tower. The cathedral, which has been under construction for centuries, still is not complete.

Much of Tenerife's interior is verdant with unusual species. The dragon tree has dark red sap and is unusually long-lived; one in **Icod de los Viñas** is claimed to be thousands of years old. Another attraction is the volcano of **Mount Teide National Park.** Several roads and a cable car lead to the top of its huge caldera.

The island of **Gómera** is fourteen miles west of Tenerife. The chief town and port, **San Sebastián de la Gomera,** is dominated by the memory of Columbus, who spent part of the summer of 1492 here laying in final provisions and waiting for the trade winds. The house he lived in, now called the Casa de Colón, is a small museum. Elsewhere on the island, **Garajonay National Park,** 10,000 acres of forest land, contains one of the world's largest stands of laurel trees, many rare bird species, and subtropical plants.

The island of **La Palma,** a hundred miles west of Santa Cruz de Tenerife, is a lush 280 square mile island dominated by the Roque de los Muchachos, a peak of 7,950 feet. There is an important astrophysical observatory on the summit, and bananas grow in the valleys at the bottom. The administrative center of **Santa Cruz de La Palma** is a charming colonial town.

Finally, the island of **Hierro,** 111 miles from Santa Cruz de Tenerife, is the smallest island of the province (107 sq. mi.) and the least involved in tourism.

CUISINE. Several surviving native Guanche dishes include a round loaf of bread called *gofio* (not to be confused with the gruel by the same name served elsewhere in the islands), made from dried chickpea flour. Influence of the spice trade can be found in *papas arrugadas,* potatoes boiled in seawater before baking and served with a spicy combination of garlic, olive oil, cayenne pepper, and cumin seeds.

Otherwise, the cuisine is eclectic but generally Spanish, with an eye to the tourist trade in such dishes as baked Alaska shaped like the crater of the famous Teide Volcano. Another dessert is *platanos fritos* (fried bananas), green bananas cut lengthwise and fried in oil. Served hot or cold, they are sprinkled with sugar, lemon juice, and brandy. A thick soup known as *potaje canariense* is made as follows:

POTAJE CANARIENSE

½ lb. chickpeas	1 onion, chopped
2 cups water	½ tsp. olive oil
4 potatoes	1 tsp. paprika
4 carrots	1 Tbs. crushed cumin
4 tomatoes	pinch of saffron
¼ lb. green beans	salt and pepper to taste
1 cup diced pumpkin	¼ loaf bread, crumbled
2 cloves garlic, minced	

Soak the chickpeas overnight, then boil and simmer them for 2 hours. In the meantime, the potatoes, carrots, tomatoes, and green beans are chopped and mixed with the pumpkin. When the chickpeas are soft, the vegetables are added and cooked over low heat. Sauté the garlic and onion in olive oil. Add to soup, then season with paprika, cumin, saffron, salt, and pepper. Finally, crumble bread or *gofio* (see above) into soup.

While the islands are no longer a thriving center of viticulture, red and white wines are still produced. The bulk of the wine consumed, however, comes from the Spanish mainland.

BAY OF BISCAY

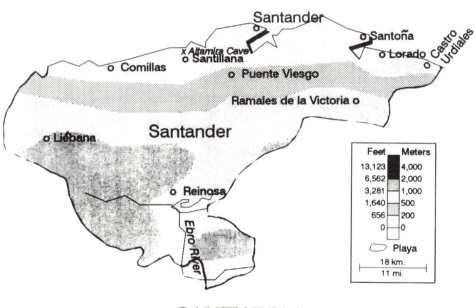

Santander

x *Altamira Cave*
o Santillana
o Comillas
o Santoña
o Lorado
Castro Urdiales
o Puente Viesgo
Ramales de la Victoria o
o Liébana
Santander
o Reinosa
Ebro River

Feet	Meters
13,123	4,000
6,562	2,000
3,281	1,000
1,640	500
656	200
0	0

Playa

18 km.
11 mi.

CANTABRIA

Chapter 7

CANTABRIA

REGIONAL CHARACTERISTICS. Pop., 510,816. Area, 5,321 sq. km. Capital: Santander. Cantabria is a one-province, Spanish-speaking region located between the Basque Provinces on the east, Asturias on the west, and León and Burgos to the south.

The name Cantabria, familiar as a geographic term for the lands bordering the Bay of Biscay, has little political connotation. In the ancient past, it was dominated by Asturias, Navarre, and finally in the twelfth century by Castile, serving to a limited degree as an outlet for trade between central Castile and Europe via the Bay of Biscay and the Atlantic Ocean. Only a few signs of regionalism existed, such as the odd dialects of Spanish spoken in the mountainous interior, a strong hostility to the neighboring Basques, and maintenance of a Cantabrian community in the American colonies. A nineteenth-century writer, José María Pereda, finally did make a case for greater autonomy, but no lobbying group formed until 1976. In the debate on the Constitution of 1978, the geographic separation of Cantabria from surrounding areas emerged as its only qualification for autonomy.

The first referendum recorded a low vote for such a step, revealing great indecision. Some drafters of the constitution argued that leaving Santander as a northern branch of Castile would hinder development of the other autonomous regions, but Cantabrians showed little interest in joining the neighboring and more industrial Basque Provinces or Asturias. An option to the constitution was eventually added, allowing Cantabria to rejoin Old

Castile voluntarily if so desired at a later date. Autonomy was thus approved on December 30, 1981.

The Cantabrian flag is a simple two-color design, the upper half white, the bottom half red.

The region ranks eighth in personal income.

SANTANDER

VITAL STATISTICS. Pop. and area: see above. Capital and diocesan see: Santander. The area borders the Bay of Biscay on the north and rises southward into the high western Pyrenees. Santander is connected with central Spain by the passes of Puerto de Tajahierro and Palombera or the Hoces de Bárcena gorge. Two of the most important urban areas are Santander and Torrelavega. The former houses the University of Cantabria, the International University of Menéndez Pelayo, and the Catholic Pontificia Comillas University.

ECONOMY. Much of the region is either upland pasture or timber land. Cantabria and Galicia are the only two areas of Spain with extensive woodlands and a forest-products industry. Dairy farming is an important agricultural occupation, and fishing provided a catch valued at 29.4 billion pesetas in 1989. Salt and zinc at Reocín are major extractive operations, and automobile parts and guns are important industrial products. Finance and banking conducted by the large Banco de Santander provide employment in the service area. Tourism comes from summer domestic visitors.

HISTORY. (Puerto de San Emeterio [Roman]). Cantabria was the site of early Cantabro-Pyrenean culture during the Paleolithic period. The cave paintings of Altamira produced during this period are world famous. Prehistoric society gravitated to the area because of the presence of game and fish. Some of the earliest cultivation of fields and domestication of animals in Iberia took place in the area.

Roman conquest of the coast and the Cantabrian tribes was accomplished over twelve years during Augustus's reign (ca. 25 B.C.), pacifying northeastern Iberia and the Atlantic coast in the Cantabrian War as far south as Braga, although another two centuries passed before the interior was conquered. The late Roman imperial period conducted extensive trade with Britannia and Gaul from the coast here and created a vigorous village life which continued under the Visigoths, ca. A.D. 574.

Cantabria's early medieval political contacts came from León, Asturias, and Navarre. In his will, Sancho el Mayor of Navarre left Santander in his will to his son, García III (1035–54), the king of Castile. The Castilian-Cantabrian relationship created *fueros* for self-government, extensive grants of common lands to each village, and local control of customs duties.

Cantabrian ships served Fernando III by sailing up the Guadalquivir River to help take Seville from the Muslims in 1248. Permission was granted in 1296 to create a powerful brotherhood (*hermandad*) linking Santander with a series of other towns (some outside the present borders of Cantabria) in a quasi-provincial governmental and economic unit.

The agricultural economy of Santander remained poor, but wool trade with Bayonne and Bordeaux created a thriving exchange economy. As the Mesta grew, Santander shipped Castilian wool in competition with Bilbao. Both sought the favor of Burgos, the Castilian wool center that monopolized foreign trade on the Cantabrian Sea, but Basque shipping won out decisively, becoming eight times larger by 1564.

To supplement the wool trade, the Cantabrian towns negotiated with the *consulado* of Seville to provide ships for colonial commerce with the Indies. The *hermandad* played an important role in the Castilian navy, and in 1622 the conde-duque Olivares built cannon and munitions factories on the Cantabrian coast to better arm its ships. But the commercial collapse of Castile hurt the northern coast badly, and by the end of the seventeenth century Santander's urban population fell to less than 2,000.

The new Bourbon monarchy granted Santander a fishing monopoly and invested in blast-furnace technology and drop forges, allowing Cantabrian iron production briefly to challenge Vizcaya. Internal trade rose with the construction of the first highway across the mountains to the south, a project of the marqués de Ensenada, but unfortunately this new route of commerce did not markedly improve the economy after the advent of free trade in 1778, since Cantabria preferred to maintain the foral right of levying tariffs on interior trade. In 1785, Carlos III granted a *consulado de mar y tierra* to further stimulate economic activity, but French seizure of Santander in 1808 weakened the metal trades industry and placed major restrictions on Cantabrian fishing rights.

In the nineteenth century, liberals privatized 70 percent of the municipal common lands, seeking to generate greater local wealth. The confiscations in Cantabria, among the largest in Spain, destroyed the dairy industry, promoted deforestation and erosion by hastily clearing and plowing the land, and dispossessed peasants, who were forced to search for jobs as miners or industrial workers in other provinces. The economy became dependent on milling wheat for flour export (particularly to Cuba) or subcontracting metallurgical specialties for Asturias or the Basque Provinces. A tourist industry grew up when Castilians began summering in the area by the thousands.

Republicanism manifested itself as early as 1883, and the socialist PSOE grew strong among the poor in provincial politics during the Second Republic. After the neighboring Asturian revolt and the Popular Front election intensified political sectarianism between 1934 and 1936, more than 200 rightist prisoners on board a prison ship in the harbor of Santander were secretly executed. Cantabria remained loyalist in the civil war and came under heavy nationalist bombing attacks in April 1937. When the Basque Provinces fell in July, the campaign to conquer Santander began on August 14. The city, new home of the Basque government-in-exile and crowded with tens of thousands of refugees embarking for exile, experienced continuous bombing until its fall on August 28, 1937.

The postwar period, made worse in Santander by a large fire in 1941, was slow to revive general trade and economic development until growth of the Bank of Santander and the specialty metallurgical industry. In the 1970s, a downturn of metal prices and the energy crisis slowed the economy, although Spain's membership in the European Community has recently attracted new French and German enterprises.

LITERATURE. At the monastery of Santo Toribio, the monk **Beato** or **Beatus** (ca. 785) wrote *De Apocalypsi Commentarius* (Commentary to the Apocalypse) to argue in favor of separating northern Catholicism from the control of the archbishop of Toledo. His ideas received renewed attention during the nineteenth-century Carlist crisis when northerners sought ways to protect their religious institutions from the central government of Madrid.

The bishop of Cantabria, **Dulcidio** (ca. 825), played an important role in formulating and popularizing the story of St. James. Some scholars have argued that he made the legend understandable by incorporating familiar Roman legends to explain the symbolism of St. James's life.

During the late Middle Ages, **Antonio de Guevara** (1480?–1545), a Franciscan friar educated at the court of the Catholic Kings and later an aide to Carlos I, wrote the classical *Reloj de príncipes* (1529) to provide the king with a model of a perfect ruler, based upon the Roman emperor Marcus Aurelius. As part of an effort to help the Hapsburg court emulate the universal Roman Empire, Guevara published many other classical discussions during his lifetime.

During the Golden Age, **Antonio Hurtado de Mendoza y Larrea** (1586–1644) of Castro Urdiales was a minor poet and dramatist at the court of Felipe IV, but intellectual productivity remained practically nil until the nineteenth century, when **Amós de Escalante y Prieto** (1831–1902), a novelist and poet born in Santander, wrote historical novels and travel literature. **José María de Pereda** (1833–1906) of Polanco produced the outstanding *costumbrismo* work *Escenas Monañesas*. Pereda, who was a Carlist, also wrote the realistic novel *Pedro Sánchez* (1883) as a diatribe against city life in Madrid. His *Peñas arriba* (1895), one of the best Cantabrian regional novels, focuses on the death in Santander of an old patriarch, don Celso. Pereda loved traditional Spain and hated liberalism and socialism. He praised simple country life and called for regional autonomy.

Ricardo Macías Picavea (1847–99), a teacher and regional novelist of Santoña, is usually considered a radical reformer since he allied with Joaquín Costa just prior to the Generation of 1898, but several of his works, such as *La instrucción pública y sus reformas* (1891?) and *El problema nacional* (1894), argue in favor of strong local educational and economic initiatives to replace the abuses of centralism.

The region's most famed scholar, **Marcelino Menéndez y Pelayo** (1856–1912), taught at the University of Madrid from 1878 to 1898, eventually becoming the national librarian. Menéndez y Pelayo defended arts and letters against modernism in *Historia de los heterodoxos españoles* (1880), *La ciencia española* (1880), *Historia de las ideas estéticas en España* (1883–91), and many other studies. He stood out in the late nineteenth century as the best-known scholarly supporter of Spanish traditionalism and religiosity against the general intellectual tone of radical secular philosophy.

In recent times, **Concha Espina** (1877–1955) of Santander lived for a time in Chile and Argentina before returning to Santander to write. Among her seventeen major works, *La esfinge maragata* (1912) is a novel that seeks to describe the impact of isolation and difficult climate upon Castilian women. Espina also wrote about the repressive nature of local life and the oppressive emotional state of Spanish families and gender relationships, although she also wrote a comedy, *La rosa de los vientos* (1916) about the impact of remarriage on one family. Another popular writer, **José Maria de Cossio** (1893–1979?), became well known for his essays on the *corrida*.

Gerardo Diego Cendova (1896–1988?), a poet, musicologist, member of the Generation of 1927, and teacher of literature and music at a number of Spanish universities, wrote the widely hailed *Diez años de música de España* (1949). As a leading scholar of Góngora, he also edited the special edition of *Revista de Occidente* on the three-hundredth anniversary of the poet's death. Cendova's own prolific poetry showed classical and religious influences, but he sometimes produced other diverse, surrealist works. *Versos humanos* (1925) won a National Prize of Literature for its deeply felt description of love.

Of the contemporary writers, **Elena Quiroga de la Válgoma** (b. 1921) is a novelist who has written extensively about the strange impact of love and passion. She won the 1951 Nadal Prize for *Viento del norte*, the story of a loveless marriage between a Galician nobleman and a young servant girl and the consequences of the relationship for each individual. *La sangre* (1952) covers four generations of a family during its final decline. *La enferma* (1955) is the moody story of a woman who permanently takes to her bed when her lover refuses to marry her, while *La careta* (1955) examines the psychological impact on a young man who saw his parents killed in the civil war.

Finally, **José Hierro** (b. 1922), although born in Madrid, has spent nearly all of his life in Santander. Too young to participate in the civil war, he nevertheless served a jail term between 1939 and 1944. Upon his release, he began writing and publishing poetry and in time coedited the poetry magazine *Proel*, which advocated a poetry of shared experiences and sentiments. His own collection of poems, *Alegría* (1947), won the Adonais Award, and *Antología poética* (1953) won the Premio Nacional. In addition, *Cuanto sé de mí* won both the Premio de la Crítica and the Premio March.

ART. The wall paintings in the Altamira caves are world famous. Life-sized figures of bison, horses, wild boars, and other animals are shown in a variety of natural poses and in distinctly different styles, left as a visual history of the ancient evolution of human expression by a series of primitive artists. The main colors used on the walls are black, red, yellow ocher, and a few mixed pigments.

The Museo Municipal Bellas Artes in Santander has paintings by Zurbarán and Goya, while the Museum of Prehistory contains the *Venus del Pendo* and other remains.

CUSTOMS AND SOCIETY. The Montañés music of Cantabria is based on melodies of Gregorian origin that have passed through *tonadilla* and *zarzuela* formats. Their verses are full of local commentary, and the music is somewhat reminiscent of the bluegrass sound.

Traditions of the Montes de Pas area center around cattle-raising. The Pasiegos, a tribelike herding people, lead migratory lives dominated by transhumance from pasture to pasture, their lives centering around cattle and other pastoral pursuits. Because their life style differed so much from that of other Spaniards, they were once considered to be Moorish or Jewish, like other small, isolated, and marginal rural groups in León or Cáceres. Their dress is distinctive. Men traditionally wear short pants, a woolen sash, and two waistcoats, the top one of black velvet or heavy cloth. The women wear thick green skirts, a black bodice, and a frilled vest, and cover their heads with a kerchief stretched across the forehead and tied around the neck, leaving their hair in tresses on either side.

During the month of August, the Santander International Festival of Music and Dance is a good opportunity to hear classical and chamber music or to see ballet and contemporary theatre.

HISTORIC SITES. The cathedral of **Santander**, originally built in 791 as the church of an abbey, was elevated to the status of a cathedral in 1752 after much construction and expansion. The tomb of the writer Marcelino Menéndez y Pelayo is in one of its chapels. The Museo Municipal de Bellas Artes shares space with the library of Marcelino Menéndez y Pelayo.

The coast west of Santander is the route to the world-famous Altamira cave near **Santillana** and **Torrelavega**, with its Paleolithic cave paintings (particularly of bulls), ca. 14,000–13,000 B.C. A five-year-old girl discovered the cave in 1879, and tourists flocked to the site until the paintings began to fade badly from exposure to the visitors' body chemistry. Today, those who wish to visit the cave must send applications four to six weeks in advance for approval by the Museo de Altamira in Santillana del Mar, since only ten to forty visitors are admitted a day. Elsewhere in this area are the caves of Buxo and Tito Bustillo and a number of resorts. **Comillas** is a small town with some interesting buildings of the seventeenth century.

East of Santander, **Laredo** has some of the region's best ecclesiastical architecture, in particular the church of Nuestra Señora de la Asunción, with many thirteenth- to sixteenth-century details. **Santoña**, also to the east, and **Ramales de la Victoria**, to the southeast, have village churches with Flemish and plateresque touches. The coastal harbor of **Castro-Urdiales**, once an active medieval port, is dominated by the church of Santa María and the ancient castle of Santa Ana, which occupy beautiful sites on one side of the entrance to the harbor.

Finally, to the south of the provincial capital, near **Puente Viesgo**, the caves of Castillo and Pasiega both contain ancient wall paintings.

CUISINE. Santander is a center of seafood. Appetizers might include *calamares a la romana* (fried squid), *percebes* (edible barnacles), or crab soup. Main courses of *merluza* (hake or any white fish) with lemon, *almeas* (clams) with kidney beans, and sea bass are popular. Anchovy sauce is a local specialty. The anchovies are crushed into a mixture of olive oil and lemon juice until they become slightly liquid.

Cantabria does not have large commercial wineries.

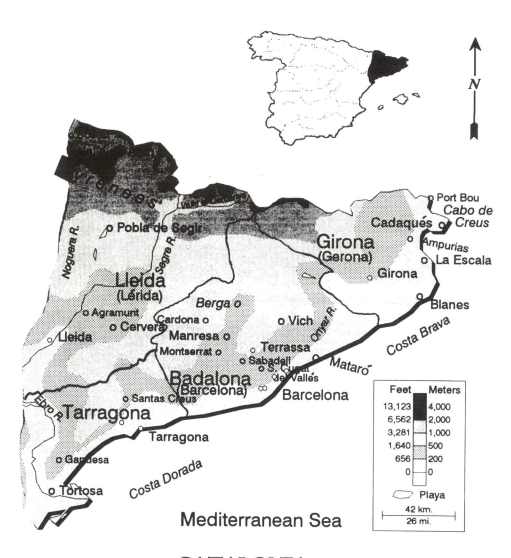

N

Port Bou
Cabo de
Cadaqués o *Creus*
Ampurias
Girona
(Gerona)
o La Escala

Girona

Blanes

Costa Brava

Feet	Meters
13,123	4,000
6,562	2,000
3,281	1,000
1,640	500
656	200
0	0

Playa

42 km.
26 mi.

Pyrenees

Pobla de Segir

Noguera R.

Segre R.

Lleida
(Lérida)

Berga o

o Agramurt

Cardona o

o Cervera

o Vich

Manresa o

Onyar R.

Montserrat o

Terrassa

o Sabadell

Mataró

Lleida

S. Cugat
del Vallés

Badalona
(Barcelona)

Barcelona

Ebro R.

o Santas Creus

Tarragona

Tarragona

o Gandesa

Costa Dorada

o Tortosa

Mediterranean Sea

CATALONIA

Chapter 8

CATALONIA
(Catalunya)

REGIONAL CHARACTERISTICS. Pop., 5,958,208, second largest population of the Spanish regions after Andalusia. Area, 31,932 sq. km., approximately 6.3 percent of Spanish territory. Capital: Barcelona. Catalonia is bounded by the Mediterranean on the east, Aragón on the west, France on the north, and Valencia on the south. The Pyrenees Mountains run east and west along the northern frontier.

Over the past century, Catalonia has actively sought to develop a new federated or autonomous status to accommodate its linguistic and cultural differences. The region speaks Català (Catalan), which is a separate Romance language from Castilian Spanish. It belongs to a branch of Gallo-Romance similar to Provençal, the language of medieval southern France. Poetry, which originated as a spoken art in Provence, came to Catalonia in the fourteenth century when Català began its own evolution. After a relatively short period of development, written Català almost disappeared in favor of Castilian after Castile absorbed Catalonia in the sixteenth century, not reappearing until its late nineteenth-century linguistic revival. Today, about 6 million Català speakers live in the Països Catalans, composed not only of Catalonia but of parts of northern Valencia and eastern Aragón in Spain, Roussillon and the Pyrénées-Orientales in France, and the Balearic Islands.

The modern question of autonomy in Spain has often centered around Catalonia. Abolition of the *furos* (singular, *fur*, the Català term for *fu-*

eros) in 1707 and 1715 led to emergence of regional associations such as the Lliga Regionalista in 1901 or the Esquerra Republicana de Catalunya of Francesc Macià in the twenties. Madrid permitted the creation of a limited Mancomunitat (regional agency) to supervise minor elements of education and culture in 1913. The Second Republic, grateful to Catalonia for its role in overthrowing Alfonso XIII and his military dictatorship, recognized the Generalitat as an autonomous regional government (Spain's first) in 1933. The Generalitat led a checkered existence from 1932 to 1939 until it was destroyed by Franco, but in 1971 an opposition coalition of the left, the Assamblea de Catalunya, demanded its reestablishment.

After Franco's death, King Juan Carlos's commitment to autonomy in the Constitution of 1978 sought to insure survival of a general Spanish community without authoritarian coercion or political extremism. To accomplish this, the first premier of the constitutional monarchy, Adolfo Suárez, persuaded a former president of the Catalan regional government, Josep Tarradellas (1899–1988), to end his thirty-eight-year exile and reestablish a regional government as the guardian of Catalan culture and repository of the ancient *furos*. Tarradellas's leadership of the middle-class Esquerra party stabilized the region's politics and insured overwhelming approval of autonomy in the referendum of 1978, supported by 68 percent of the electorate. The Catalan autonomy measure, ratified again on December 18, 1979, went into effect in 1980. Since that time, the coalition Convergència i Unió, a fusion party led by Jordi Pujol, has dominated the regional elections of 1980, 1984, 1988, and 1992, always seeking to enlarge the scope of Catalan autonomy.

The Catalan flag is the heraldic *Senyera* of four red bars on a field of yellow.

Catalonia ranks third among the regions in personal income.

BARCELONA

VITAL STATISTICS. Pop., 4,618,734. Area, 7,728 sq. km. Capital: Barcelona. Diocesan sees: Barcelona, Vic (Vich). The province, most densely populated in Spain (595 per sq. km.), includes thirty-one urban areas with a population of over 25,000. The province of Barcelona is located between the Mediterranean and Lleida (Lérida) on the east and west, and Girona (Gerona) and Tarragona on the north and south.

Higher education in Barcelona includes the University of Barcelona, the Autónoma, and the Catalan Politécnic.

ECONOMY. The province of Barcelona is the major manufacturing center of the peninsula, representing a quarter of total national industrial employment. About 40 percent of its work force is actively employed in manufacturing. Approximately 85 percent of all manufactured goods from the Catalan region are made in the province, including 90 percent of cotton spinning and 80 percent of cotton weaving. Silk and leather are other major products.

The province produces a fourth of all Spanish textiles, and commercial food preparation accounts for 11 percent of the national total. Spanish automobile production, originally begun by Hispano-Suiza and Elizalde, is continued today by VW/Seat and Nissan, although of late the industry has had to cope with an old physical plant and complicated union rules. Motorcycles, farm equipment (especially tractors), and trucks are also produced in large numbers. The electronics industry is new and growing, and the finance sector is promoted by a stock exchange begun in 1915. The province attracts about 40 percent of all foreign investment in Spain.

The western part of the province is a potash-mining center, with its hub at Manresa, site of the three largest potash mines. Potash is used to make explosives by the government-owned Unión Española de Explosivos. Lignite is produced in the upper Llobregat Valley at Berga, Figols, and La Pobla de Lillet. Dairy farms, truck gardening, wine production in the Penedés area, and fishing also are sizeable.

HISTORY. (Barcino [Roman], Barcinoa [Visigoth], Barshaluna [Arab]). Early Iberian and Celtic society grew rapidly when the Greeks introduced viticulture along the coast. Wine exports, already important by 500 B.C., expanded under Roman rule. The administrative center of Barcino grew to be a sizeable walled city with port facilities. Christianity arrived from Africa with the legendary saints Felix and Cugat and was spread widely by the efforts of Bishop Pacian, ca. A.D. 325.

In A.D. 716, abstemious Arabs of the Muslim conquest eradicated viticulture, causing agricultural decline and popular resistance. While Charlemagne failed in the late eighth century to establish a "Spanish March" south of the Pyrenees, a descendant of Sant Guillem (count of Toulouse and one of Charlemagne's lieutenants), Guifré (or Guilfred) el Pilós (Wilfred the Hairy, 878–97), organized a loose Catalan principality under the suzerainty of Córdoba. This uneasy relationship led to a Muslim sack of Barcelona and destruction of the monasteries of San Pedro de las Puellas and San Cugat del Vallés in 905, but Catalonia's prestige as a newly reclaimed Christian state grew when a monk from Vic, Gerberto de Aurillac, became Pope Silvester II (999–1003).

Independence came under Ramón Berenguer I (1035–76). His dynasty (1076–1162) captured Tarragona, began the conquest of the Balearic Islands, and through the marriage of Ramón Berenguer IV (1131–62) to Petronila, queen of Aragón (1137–62), created the powerful federated monarchy of Aragón and Catalonia. As confirmed by the Act of Union agreement of 1319, Aragón linked Valencia, the Balearic Islands, and Naples

(1162–1516) with Barcelona, which served as the imperial commercial center.

Albigensian refugees from France brought technical expertise in woolen textiles and metallurgy, Italian merchants added new techniques and sophistication in trade, and a large Jewish community provided finance and banking. Barcelona's class structure differed from other feudal Spanish principalities by having, in addition to the usual feudal landed lords, a new stratum of wealthy native traders and a less privileged middle class of merchants and financiers that stood above professionals, artisans, and workers. These classes developed the Corts, perhaps the most effective parliament of high medieval Europe, guardian of the ancient *furos*, or privileges, covering many aspects of public and private life.

Not all change was so positive. Prejudice against Jews came from France, preached by St. Raymond of Peñafort (1175–1275), a descendant of the counts of Barcelona and third master-general of the Dominican Order. Jews were later blamed for the bubonic plague in the mid-fourteenth century and for the Remença revolt (1462–72), a struggle between the craft unions (Busca) of Barcelona and the merchant oligarchy (Biga) for control of city government (Generalitat) and between peasants and feudal lords for dominance of the countryside. The Jewish community was expelled to calm the situation, and Fernando II decreed judicial freedom for the peasants and abolished feudal payments in 1486.

A long period of decline followed the Remença. King Fernando II (the Catholic, 1479–1516), last of the Aragonese dynasty, married Isabel of Castile to obtain aid against the Remença, thus linking Catalonia and Aragón to Castile. Seville's trade monopoly with the New World weakened Barcelona's commercial importance just as Fernando's grandson, the Hapsburg Carlos I, inherited the united Spanish monarchy.

Under Hapsburg rule, absolutism eroded local autonomy, and the conde-duque de Olivares's 1624 Union of Arms proposal calling for larger taxes to pay for continuing religious wars caused the Catalans to revolt. The so-called Reapers' War of 1640 led to invasion by the French, who abandoned Catalonia in 1648 but permanently transferred Roussillon (the area surrounding Perpignan, spelled Rousillón in Castilian, Roselló in Català) and the Cerdaña (or Cerdagne, the valley from the Pyrénées-Orientales area to Gerona and Lérida) to their own rule. In 1652, Castile starved Barcelona into submission.

Relations between Castile and Barcelona improved enough to allow taxation to be normalized and Catalan ships to begin carrying American goods from Cádiz to Italy and France; but in 1700 the last Spanish Hapsburg willed the Spanish crown to a Bourbon prince, reviving memories of the French role in the Reapers' War. Catalonia supported an unsuccessful claimant, Karl of Austria, but the Bourbon Felipe V's victory caused Catalonia to lose its special privileges (*furo*) in the Nueva Planta decree.

Barcelona's old civic structure deteriorated further under Bourbon centralism, and in the Napoleonic era the area was even incorporated into metropolitan France for five years. But exposure to northern European modernism led to a mid-nineteenth-century renovation of the textile industry. This Renaixença, or renaissance, fed Catalan desire for change.

Their first impulse was to make the Spanish state more efficient and progressive, or at least less corrupt. In 1868, when Isabel II abdicated, General Juan Prim y Prats (1814–70) Reus created a constitutional monarchy stressing fundamental freedoms. When disorder destroyed this state (1871–73), the president of the even briefer First Republic, Francesc Pi y Margall (1824–1901) of Barcelona, proposed a new federal structure that incorporated regionalism into the state framework for the first time. It proved to be a spectacular failure, and by 1876 Spain again fell under Castilian leadership and the Bourbon monarchy.

Catalans henceforth abandoned efforts to reform Spain to concentrate upon their own region. The concept of Catalanisme spread by Valentí Almirall i Llozer (1841–1904) and Enrique Prat de la Riba i Sarrá (1870–1917) encouraged a cultural revival to unify Catalonia and provide a foundation for future political separation. During the period 1902–9, Francesc Cambó y Battle (1876–1947), a millionaire political organizer, put together a Catalan regionalist party, but in late July 1909 the *Semana trágica*, a week of violent resistance against the mobilization of Catalan reserves to serve in an unpopular occupation of Morocco, discredited Cambó's movement. When unrest continued, an alarmed central government in 1913 approved the Mancomunitat, a limited regional authority primarily educational and cultural in nature.

During World War I, neutral Spain prospered by supplying war materiel to the Western Powers, providing such enormous profits for Catalonia that new, almost farcical efforts to secede took place in 1917. Labor unrest in the postwar era added to the chaos until General José María Primo de Rivera, bitterly anti-Catalan, imposed military rule over the whole nation from 1923 to early 1930 by tapping conservative fears of Catalonia's eventual independence. In 1930–31, Catalan socialists and progressives campaigned for the creation of a democratic Spanish republic, and when the dictatorship fell the Second Republic gratefully passed a Catalan autonomy statute. In 1933, the autonomy of Catalonia caused Spaniards to support a conservative backlash in the national parliamentary elections of November. The new right-wing government soon suspended the autonomy statute, and Catalonia's president, Lluis Companys (1883–1940), proclaimed secession in 1934, only to see the revolt suppressed by Spanish troops on the streets of Barcelona. Catalans redoubled their efforts by supporting the Popular Front of united left parties that regained national parliamentary control in February 1936.

During the civil war, Barcelona remained loyalist, absorbed in its own intense revolution. The initial victory of the anarchosyndicalist Confederación Nacional de Trabajo (CNT) against rebellious nationalists in Barcelona allowed the CNT-led Anti-Fascist Militia Committee to act as an informal regional government. Its sizeable armed force of militia troops seized the banking system and imposed workers' control over industry, but ten months later the committee fell when communists and middle-class Catalan nationalists, hostile to the CNT reign of terror, which put social revolution before antifascism, rebelled in early May 1937. In Madrid, the Popular Front cabinet of Largo Caballero collapsed in mid-May, and until the end of the war power remained in the hands of Companys and the communist-dominated Partit Socialista Unificat de Catalunya (PSUC), who collaborated with the republican government of Valencia and followed the lead of the Soviet Union on many matters, particularly in persecuting members of the independent leftist Partido Obrero de Unificación Marxista (POUM) and driving the CNT from power.

Republican forces lost the initiative to Franco by mid–1938. Barcelona, bombed for the first time in December 1938, fell to the rebels on January 26, 1939. The Franco regime executed Companys, abolished regional government, prohibited use of Català as an official language, and curtailed regional cultural life. Throughout the postwar era, Barcelona was an occupied city.

In 1975, however, Franco's death reopened the issue of autonomy, which was regained in 1979; only the Basque Provinces acted as quickly. The region is still under national control in matters of foreign policy and currency but follows a distinctly Catalan course in matters of language, culture, education, and local life. In 1992, Barcelona staged the Olympic games to celebrate this new era of revival, but it remains to be seen whether the new arrangements will continue to satisfy aspirations.

LITERATURE. Barcelona became a major Mediterranean intellectual center when Ramón Llull (Lull or Raimundo Lulio, ca. 1233–1315) of the Balearic Islands made Català into a literary language. Another figure of the thirteenth-century renaissance, **Ramón Martí** (1230–86), imitated St. Thomas Aquinas in studying the Koran and Talmud to be better able to convert Muslims and Jews to Christianity. **Bernat Desclot** (ca. 1325) compiled important histories of Ramón Berenguer IV (1131–62) and Pere II (1276–85). **Solomon ben Adret** (1235–1310?), chief rabbi of Spain, wrote the *Responsa*, a discussion of Sephardic life and ritual.

The courtly love lyrics written in Provençal by troubadours, the poet/singers of the Middle Ages, were widely performed. This poetry used the Virgin Mary as the ideal comparison for all women. **Lluís d'Averco** (ca. 1350?) may have been the first to write such lyrics in Català. **Andreu Febrer** (1375?–1444) of Vic, a soldier, wrote some of the finest lyrics of love poetry and translated Dante's *Divine Comedy* into the vernacular language. One of the first books printed with moveable type on the peninsula, the anonymous *Trobes en lahors de la Verge Maria* (1474), is a collection of poems to the Virgin Mary.

Renaissance style, introduced by **Joan Boscà Almugaver** (Juan Boscán Almogáver, 1487?–1542) of Barcelona, a poet, translator, and court tutor for Carlos I, transferred Italian meter and sonnets into Castilian and created a new literary language for Barcelona. The Golden Age largely bypassed the city, although Barcelona did provide the setting for plays such as *El Desdén con el desdén*, a comedy by **Agustín Moreto y Cabaña** (1618–69). In the sixteenth century, Castilian control of Barcelona permitted few works to be published in Català. **Rafael d'Amat de Cortada i de Sentjust,** baron of Maldá (1746–1819), kept the art of writing the vernacular alive by composing his elaborate memoirs. **Antonio de Capmany Suris y Montpalau** (1742–1813), a historian of the era, supported the enlightened despotism of Carlos III and later became a deputy in the Cortes of Cádiz (1810–12).

The Catalan Renaixença of the nineteenth century created a literary explosion. **Jaime Luciano Balmes i Urpiá** (1810–48) of Vic, a radical Catholic polemicist and philosopher, published a periodical, *La Sociedad* (1843), instrumental in developing the anticentralism fundamental to Catalan nationalism. According to his thesis, the monarchy and Madrid were parasites on Catalan industry. Only protectionism could free Catalonia to become the true leader of Spain. **Pere-Felipe Monlau i Roca** (1808–71), a utopian socialist editor of such magazines as *El Vapor* and *El Nuevo Vapor*, supported a federal Catalonia only loosely linked to Madrid. His associate, **Pere Mata i Fontanet** (1811–77), believed in the radical republicanism of the Italian nationalist Giuseppe Mazzini.

Others of this age such as **Manuel Milà i Fortanals** (1818–84) and **Paul Fiferrer i Fàbregas** (1818–48) collected folk stories for poetic use. **Joaquím Rubío i Ors** (1818–99) reworked these collections for publication in his *La Gayter de Llobregat*. He also provided early support for the Renaixença by demanding revival of Català as a written language so that the people could express their political opinions accurately. **Victor Balaguer** (1824–1901), a poet, dramatist, and cultural nationalist, revived the Jocs Florals, a poetry contest, as a way of popularizing the reemergence of the written language. **Manuel de Cabanyes** (1808–33) of Villanueva y Geltrú, an important neo-classic and pre-romantic poet, set an example for aspiring poets with his experimental use of Català. **Francesc Pi y Margall** (1824–1901), president of the First Republic (1873–74) and a historian and essayist whose *Historia de España* (1902) contained anti-Castilian and anticentralist themes, used these early nationalist publications as a forum for his ideas.

The second generation of nationalist and cultural reawakening had considerable talent. **Jacint Verdaguer** (1845–1902), a major Catalan poet, wrote *Atlántida* (1877, first-prize winner at the Jocs Florals), and *Canigó*

(1885), the myth of Atlantis as simile for the disappearance of Catalonia's national identity. **Joan Maragall** (1860–1911), last of the Catalan romantics, wrote at great length about northeastern life in a lyrical format known as *modernisme*, discussed at length in *Següencies* (1911). He also composed poetry such as *Elogi de la paraula* (1905) and discussed literary theory in *Elogi de la poesia* (1907). **Eugenio d'Ors y Rovira** (1882–1954), a rationalist and a nationalist, often wrote in Català. *Glossari* (1906) advocated *noucentisme*, a movement that tried to move beyond romanticism or Art Nouveau but ended by celebrating premodernism. He also wrote fiction, philology, and conservative historical-philosophical essays. **Josep Carner i Puig-Oriol** (1884–1970) continued the revival of Català as a literary language by editing *Le Veu de Catalunya*, a leading periodical.

Not all creative writers of the nineteenth or twentieth century concentrated exclusively on regional culture. **Jacinto Grau Delgado** (1877–1959) of Barcelona, a dramatist, used themes from early Spanish literature for some of his plays such as the *romancero El Conde Alarcos* (1917), the classical *El burlador que no se burla* (1930), or *Don Juan de Carillana* (1913), in which don Juan falls in love with a woman he cannot possess because she is his illegitimate daughter. **Eduardo Marquina** (1879–1946), a poet, novelist, and dramatist, and a Catalan by birth and heritage, preferred to write in Castilian. As a historical dramatist, his *teatro poético* mingled lyricism and epic theatre. He experienced great success with *Las hijas del Cid* (1908), based on the *Cantar de Mio Cid* but with new imaginary details such as the death of one of the Cid's daughters. *En Flandes se ha puesto el sol* (1910) became an equally popular play about the last days of the Spanish Netherlands.

In the twentieth century, **Ignacio Agustí** (b. 1913) of Llissá de Vall, a journalist, wrote a series of novels collectively titled *La Ceniza fue árbol*. The first of these, *Marina Rebull*, while written in Castilian, provides a good discussion of Catalan society between 1865 and 1944. **Juan-Eduard Cirlot** (b. 1916) is a surrealist poet and critic. **Alfonso Cosstafreda** (1926–74) and **Carlos Barral** (1928–89) were leading postmodernist poets in the post–civil war period. **Josep María Espinàs** (b. 1927) writes novels and songs in the vernacular.

Luis Romero (b. 1916) is the author of a very contemporary work, *La noria*, about Barcelona during the Spanish Civil War. He has also written history in *Tres días en julio* (1967) and a novel, *El cacique* (1963), about earlier Spanish political corruption. **José Luis Sampedro** (b. 1917) is an economist, novelist, and playwright who won the national prize for drama with his play *La paloma de cartón* (1952). Another of his plays, *Un sitio para vivir* (1958), has an ecological theme. **Ana Marí Matute** (b. 1926) of Barcelona has written about her vivid memories of childhood during the civil war in more than twenty novels and collections of stories such as *Fiesta* *al Noroeste* (1953), *Los hijos muertos* (1958), *Los soldados lloran de noche* (1964), and *El polizón de Ulises* (1967?).

The best-known modern Catalan author today is **Juan Goytisolo** (b. 1933). After his early writings were banned, he spent a long exile in Paris as an opponent of the Franco regime. *Juegos de manos* (1954), translated as *The Young Assassins*, became a successful film in 1959. *Masks of Identity*, *Forbidden Territory*, and *Landscapes After a Battle* also have appeared in English, and among his other works, *Duelo en el Paraíso* (1955) is a tense drama about refugee children during the civil war. *Las virtudes del pájaro solitario* (1988) and other later works have examined Arab culture sympathetically.

Lidia Falcón (b. 1935), a lawyer who often writes about the legal status of women, founded the first feminist party in Spain and a feminist magazine, *Poder y libertad*. Her several arrests during the Franco era were followed by such acclaimed works as *En el infierno: Ser mujer en las cárceles de España* (1977) and *Viernes y 13 en la Calle del Correro* (1981). **Juan Mersé** (b. 1933) has written a number of realistic novels including *Ultimas tardes con Teresa* (1970) and *Si te dicen que cai* (1973). Four of his books have been made into movies.

Eduardo Mendoza (b. 1943) lived in New York as a Spanish translator for eleven years before publishing *The City of Marvels* (1988), his celebrated and ironic novel about Barcelona in the nineteenth and twentieth centuries, partly based on the life of the Balearic millionaire Juan March. **Manuel Vázquez Montalbán** (b. 1939) writes novels of dark humor such as *Yo maté a Kennedy* (1972). He also has popularized the genre of detective stories and writes poetry.

ART. The church of St. Vicente at Cardona, ca. 1020, is an early example of the Lombard-Catalan style. St. Vincent's vaulted nave, transept, aisles, and dome create a unity of design that continues down the piers.

In the monastery of Sant María de Ripoll, the portal is covered with a series of reliefs, possibly derived from the famous Bible of Ripoll, dominated by the figure of Christ. San Cugat del Vallés has capitals by the sculptor Arnau Gatell (ca. 1200) and a retablo by Pere Serra (ca. 1375).

The Italo-Gothic style made a great impact on Barcelona through the work of **Ferrer Bassa** (d. 1348) in the monastery of Pedralbes. Somewhat like linear painting, the backgrounds of this style are subdued, while foreground figures often are done in gold. The school of Burgundian Gothic painting led by **Bernardo Martorell** (d. 1452) transformed this style by the sensitive use of colors and glazes in the retablo of the Savior that hangs in the cathedral of Barcelona, Sant María del Pí. About the same time, **Jaime Huguet** (1414–92) elaborated Martorell's humanistic themes.

Fernando Yáñez, a student of Leonardo, lived in Barcelona (1513–23) and introduced many themes and styles of Italian Renaissance art. **Joan de**

Burgunya (active 1510?–1525?) did *Virgin and Child with St. John in a Landscape,* which today hangs in the Museo de Arte de Cataluña.

The leading architect of nineteenth- and early twentieth-century Barcelona was **Antoni Gaudí i Cornet** (1852–1926), who became famous for developing an Art Nouveau style based on a belief that right angles should be banished from modern architecture because they do not exist in nature. His masterpiece, the basilica of Sagrada Familia, is a wonderful example of naturalistic Art Nouveau, filled with fascinating details. Other Gaudí projects in the city of Barcelona include the Casa Calvet (1898), Casa Batlló (1904), Parque Güell (1900–1914), and Casa Milá (1906–10). The major nineteenth-century sculptor **José Llimona** (1864–1934) used oversized, natural shapes.

Pablo Picasso and **Joan Miró** started their careers in Barcelona when both studied at the Academy of Fine Arts (La Lonja), where Picasso's father, José Ruiz Blasco, taught. During this period, Picasso began to use his matronymic rather than his patronymic (his mother was doña María Picasso y López) because his Catalan friends found it more picturesque than Ruiz. Picasso's early paintings in the period 1896–1900 immortalized Els Quatre Gats café, a bohemian meeting place of painters, sculptors, poets, and writers. Other early works done in Barcelona include *The Alms* (1896–96), *The Choir Boy, First Communion* (1897), *Science and Charity* (1898), and some of the first Blue Period works. In 1904, Picasso left Barcelona permanently for Paris and found greater fame as his career passed through cubist, neoclassic realist, dada, and surrealist phases. His most spectacular return to Barcelona came on November 10, 1917, when he designed the sets and costumes for choreographer Sergei Diaghilev's avant-garde production of *Parade,* performed by the Ballets Russes.

Miró, who was born in Barcelona, divided his early career between Barcelona and his grandparents' town of Montroig in the province of Tarragona, spending only the decade of the twenties in Paris. He survived the civil war in Palma de Majorca and settled permanently there after 1956. In his art, he explored the world of fantasy by composing pictures characterized by brightly colored shapes and expressive lines that were called childlike and primitive by critics. At the same time, they provided a sensual experience of color, texture, and form. His mature style used large schematized, whimsical figures floating in backgrounds of gray, blue, beige, or brown. His forms are delineated by wiry black lines. Both Miró and Picasso have museums in Barcelona dedicated to their works.

Among other artists and architects, **José Luis Sert** (1874–1934) created the architecture of University City on the edge of Madrid. **Antonio Tàpies** (b. 1923) has become well known for his experimental abstractions. Beginning in 1955, he developed the theory that a painting is above all an object that becomes a site of negotiation between the artist and the viewer. His mixed media canvases, which he calls "walls," incorporate graffiti-like scrawls into abstract expressionism. Using marble dust and varnish, Tàpies creates backgrounds that allow his subjects to float on the surface. Other painters of considerable contemporary reputation include Modesto Cuixart, Juan-José Tharrats, August Puig, and Román Vallés.

MUSIC. Early music at the monastery of Montserrat included pilgrim songs called *cants del romeu*. Many of these are preserved in the *Llibre Vermell*, a codex from the fourteenth century. Most early Catalan songs were in canon form for two or three voices.

Juan Pujol (1573?–1626) bridged the gap from earlier ecclesiastic music to the Italian baroque period. He trained a series of Catalan baroque composers and performers such as Sebastián Aguilera de Heredia (1570?–?), Juan Bautista Comes (1568–1643), and Juan Barahona de Esquivel who made the monastery of Montserrat a musical center. **Francisco Valls** (1665–1747), choirmaster at the cathedral in Barcelona, stirred great controversy when his *Missa Scala Aretina* diverged from conservative counterpoint.

Domingo Terradellas (1713–51) was trained in Italy and later became a choirmaster in Rome. He composed the operas *Mitridate* and *Bellerophon*. **Ramón Carnicer** (1779–1855) directed the Barcelona and Madrid operas and became professor of composition at the new Madrid Conservatory in 1830. His most ambitious work is *Don Giovanni Tenorio, ossia Il convitato di Pietra* (1822).

Cellist **Pau (Pablo) Casals** (1876–1973) gained renown as a soloist after his 1899 debut in Paris. He founded the acclaimed Orquestra Pau Casals of Barcelona in 1919, but in 1938 self-imposed exile took him back to Paris, to Prades (a small town in the French Pyrenees), and later to Puerto Rico. He became particularly known for performing J. S. Bach's unaccompanied cello works.

Another world-famous instrumentalist is pianist **Alicia de Larrocha** (b. 1923), who made her first public appearance when she was six years old. After studying at the academy founded in Barcelona by Enrique Granados of Lleida, she made her first international tour in 1947, with her American debut coming in 1955. She won the Paderewski Prize in 1961, the Medallo d'Oro from the city of Barcelona in 1982, and the same year was recognized by the Spanish government as one of the nation's great artists.

The current operatic careers of sopranos **Victoria de los Angeles** (b. 1923) and **Montserrat Caballé** (b. 1933) or tenor **José Carreras** (b. 1948) indicate Catalan music's great contemporary success. Los Angeles, who is best known for her solo recitals, first sang in the United States at Carnegie Hall in 1950. Caballé, one of the most accomplished practitioners of the bel canto style, played Lucrezia Borgia in Donizetti's opera at the Metropolitan Opera in 1965. Carreras, identified with traditional heroic tenor roles, first appeared with the New York Opera in 1972 as Pinkerton in Puccini's *Madame Butterfly*.

CUSTOMS AND SOCIETY. Music and dance are Catalan cultural pre-occupations. The national dance is a circle dance known as the *sardana*, done in double rows accompanied by *fiscorns* (high, piercing horns), oboes, drums, and cymbals. Other dances include the very old *zarabandas, chaconas, pasacelles*, and *folias*.

Lenten performances of the Passion of Christ are particularly important at Montserrat, where the tradition dates back to 1642. Barcelona celebrates the Verbena de Sant Joan on June 24 with fireworks on Montjuic and dancing in the streets. June is also the month of the prestigious Barcelona international cinema festival. The Setmana Cran of late August stages weeklong *sardana* dances to honor the city's patron saint, the Virgin of Merced. On September 11, the Diada Fiesta celebrates the autonomy of Catalonia.

The rural custom of *rabassa morta* originated as a medieval form of sharecropping. Peasants called *rabassaires* shared their crops with land-owners and received the right to work the land for the life of the vines. When a phylloxera epidemic destroyed vineyards in the late nineteenth century, new stock grafted from American roots shortened the lifetime of the vines and created great controversy until the system's abolition in the 1950s.

HISTORIC SITES. The center of **Barcelona** is the old town, Barri Gòtic (Barrio Gótico), a district that contains the cathedral of Sant María del Pí, the Bishop's Palace, Palacio de la Generalitat, Museu d'Historia de la Ciutat, and Palacio Real Mayor. The ten-block area preserves a medieval atmosphere in the middle of a modern city. The cathedral is especially historic, since remains of a church built in 559 have been found on the site. The earliest standing structure, built between 1045 and 1058, is the Romanesque San Ivo gate and part of the transept. In 1298, Bertrand Riquer added the Chapel of Santa Agueda, but a distinctive redesign was added in 1318 when the famous Majorcan architect, Jaime Febre, created a severe Cistercian style of transverse vaulted aisles and French ribbed vaults, a transformation completed in 1486. The interior is 273 feet long, 122 feet wide, and 84 feet high, with a dome over the nave rather than at the crossing. Small columns rise almost fifty feet to support the nave and aisle vaults. One chapel contains the tomb of Ramón Berenguer I; another is decorated by a flag from the Battle of Lepanto. Other relics can be found in three nearby museums: Museu d'Art de Catalunya, Museu Frederic Marés, and Museu d'Historia.

Barcelona has too many beautiful parish churches to mention in detail, but the church of Sant María del Mar celebrates the capture of the Balearic Islands. The most unusual ecclesiastical structure is the basilica of La Sagrada Familia designed by Antoni Gaudí, begun in 1891 but still uncompleted. The basilica is famous for its naturalistic, almost surrealist Art Nouveau style, inspired by events surrounding the birth of Christ and done with an unusual mixture of materials, such as ceramic chips set in concrete, and unusual topics, such as angelic bassoonists carved in stone. The odd but beautiful shape of Sagrada Familia's four towers is created by interlaced streams of stone designed to look like tree branches or vines. It may be the most unusual building in Europe.

The central spot in Barcelona is Las Ramblas, a tree-lined street with a central promenade with cafés and stalls that leads from the Plaça de Catalunya to the harbor. South of the Plaça is Eixample, a residential area of more than 500 square blocks built between the 1860s and the 1920s from designs by Gaudí, Josep Puig i Cadafalch (1867–1957), and Lluís Domènech i Montaner (1850–1924), the three leading Catalan architects of Barcelona's great era of building.

The new Museum of Modern Art at the monastery of Pedralbes is a branch of Madrid's Thyssen-Bornemisza modern collection, and there are separate Miró and Picasso museums and an open-air architectural museum in Parc Montjuic (literally, "mountain of the Jews," so named because of an old Jewish cemetery located on it), which contains examples of Spanish regional architecture. The park itself, which dominates Barcelona's skyline, today includes the Olympic stadium, the Miró Museum, and many other attractions.

Elsewhere in the province, fine old churches include the beautiful baroque basilica of Sant María in **Mataró,** on the coast northeast of the capital. The neo-Gothic church of San Feliu in **Sabadel,** directly north of Barcelona, is handsome. Much further northeast, **Cardona** contains the eleventh-century church of San Vicente. The Gothic Collegiata Sant María in **Manresa** is filled with medieval art, and Loyola wrote his *Spiritual Exercises* in 1522 at the hermitage of Sant Cuerva. In **Terrassa** (Tarrasa), also due north of Barcelona, the churches of San Miguel, San Pedro, and Sant María are three well-preserved early medieval buildings with Visigothic and Mozarabic details.

Several Benedictine monasteries dominate the province of Barcelona. **Montserrat,** just slightly southwest of Terrassa, more than 2,400 feet high in the coastal hills adjacent to Barcelona, was established in the late ninth century as a spiritual, intellectual, and political center. The famous Black Virgin of Montserrat (so named for its African features) is a statue allegedly found in a nearby cave, ca. A.D. 880. Pilgrims who climb the mountain still receive a special blessing. Montserrat's architecture is a mixture of medieval and modern, reminiscent of Buddhist lamaseries of Tibet. The area, accessible by cable car, highway, or hiking trails, is dotted with parks. The other monastery of importance is on the border of Girona province at **Vic/Vich.** Founded by Count Oliba of Desalu (ca. 925), an emissary from Monte Cassino, Vic was the first reformed Benedictine monastery south of the Pyrenees and the home monastery of Pope Silvester II. The cathedral of the monastery is historic and beautiful, and there is an important museum of church history. Northwest of Vic, the once-independent state of **Bergà** has several early Catalan chapels.

CUISINE. Food in Barcelona bears similarities to that of other Latin countries. The bouillabaisse seafood soups of Provence are *bullabesa* in Catalonia, and the popular winter dish *canalon* is the Italian *cannelloni*. *Canalon* uses ground duck or fish mousse in a blue cheese sauce.

Langosta a la catalana (lobster), *rape a la Costa Brava* (monkfish with vegetables), and *suquet* (fish soup with potatoes) show various uses of seafood. The recipe for *suquet* follows.

SUQUET

1 dozen mussels/clams/shrimp	4 cloves garlic
2 carrots, sliced	2 shallots, whole
½ lb. leeks (or potatoes), sliced	1 oz. cognac
2 lbs. white fish	3–4 chunks bread, crumbled
¼ cup olive oil	2 oz. butter
1 onion, chopped	

Clean the shellfish thoroughly, boil, and set aside when the shells open. Remove the fish from the shells. Boil the carrots and leeks (or potatoes), then brown the white fish in olive oil for 3–5 minutes. Sauté onion, garlic, and shallots. Combine the fish, shellfish meat, and vegetables, covering with water. Boil and stir until mixture thickens. Add cognac and strain mixture into another bowl before adding bits of bread and butter just before serving.

Fowl is also popular, spiced with various sauces. These sauces are the heart of Barcelona cooking. *Alioli* of the Balearic Islands is made of garlic and olive oil. *Picada* uses fifty grams of almonds and hazelnuts, two pinches of saffron, two cloves of garlic, and a half teaspoon of cinnamon, which are pounded and combined into a fine paste diluted by sherry. *Chaufaino* is a combination of peppers, onions, tomatoes, and garlic.

Wine comes from Penedès, south of the city, which produces *cava* sparkling wines by the champagne method of cold fermentation and the addition of sugar. Cheaper types of sparkling wine avoid this cumbersome process by injecting small amounts of carbon dioxide through the cork. A wide range of *cava* from *brut* to *seco* is produced by varying the time of preparation or degree of sweetness. The major producer of Penedès's sparkling wine is Codorníu, at Sant Sadurni d'Anoia, founded by the Reventós family at their estate, which was designed by a leading nineteenth-century Catalan architect, José María Puig i Cadalfalch.

GIRONA (Gerona)

VITAL STATISTICS. Pop., 467,945. Area, 5,910 sq. km. Capital: Girona (Gerona). Diocesan sees: Girona and Vic. The province, much of which is either coastal plain or mountains, touches the Pyrenees and France on the north (connected by the passes of Perthus and Port-Bou), the Costa Brava (Wild Coast) on the Mediterranean to the east, Barcelona on the south, and Lleida (Lérida) and the tiny independent principality of Andorra on the west. It is watered by the Ter, Mug, and Fluviá rivers.

ECONOMY. Girona is a textile-producing area, recently revitalized by Japanese investment in cotton-thread factories. Paper, lumber, and furniture also are manufactured. Cork is the most important agricultural product, and tourism on the Costa Brava has created a large service industry.

HISTORY. (Gerunda [Roman], Jerunda [Arab]). Ancient Celtiberian society attracted Phoenicians who established a colony on the then-island of San Martín just off the coast. The Greeks built Emporion as the first of their colonies, later expanded and renamed Ampurias by the Romans. An early synagogue here and a Greek temple at Ullastret, north of Gerona, served travelers on the Viá Domitia, the Roman road from Italy to Spain across the Pyrenees.

Visigothic rule, Frankish culture, and Christianity flourished by ca. A.D. 650. The Church grew so strong that Christian resistance to the Muslims after 714 attracted Charlemagne to Gerona in 785. The Carolingians departed in the early ninth century, but a petty state with a Provençal culture and close ties to the northern areas of Languedoc (lost during the Albigensian Crusade), Cerdaña (spelled variously as Cerdanya or Cardagne), and Roussillon (in Català Roselló, in Castilian Rousillón) developed by the mid-tenth century until Ramón Berenguer I, count of Barcelona (1035–76), added Gerona as a dynastic possession of the Barcelona state.

After 1235, many settlers followed Jaume I in the Mediterranean conquests made by Aragón and Catalonia. Shipping to the Balearics from Rosas and La Escala on the north coast rose during the later Middle Ages, attracting a large Jewish community that lived in Gerona under special royal privilege. The university was founded in 1446.

The border location led to violence and upheaval each time Spain and France went to war. Over the centuries, the Albigensian Crusade of the early thirteenth century, French invasion during the Remença revolt in 1464, Francis I in 1520–21, and the Reapers' War were destructive interludes. The Peace of the Pyrenees in 1659 stripped away Languedoc, Cerdaña (Cerdagne), and Roussillon, taking the last Catalan territories north of the Pyrenees and sharply reducing Gerona's trade and general importance. The violence of the War of Spanish Succession, the French Revolution (1794–95), and the Napoleonic War (1809, a siege of seven months) prolonged the agony.

Yet despite this chaos, furniture and textile industries created a strong nineteenth-century industrial sector. Cheap electrical power from the mountains helped make Gerona the first Spanish city to install electric lighting. Its large work force, left-wing in its politics, exploded in the general strike of May 1936, leading to the murder of several dozen priests and nuns. Anarchists controlled the province until May 1937, when communists and Catalan regionalists replaced them. The forces of Franco invaded from the west after capturing Lleida (Lérida) in 1938. The line held even after the fall of Barcelona, when refugees by the hundreds of thousands poured through the province during the final weeks of the war, headed for exile in France.

The province, tightly controlled during and after World War II, saw occasional guerrilla outbreaks, but by the late fifties Costa Brava's beaches became one of the first areas to benefit from tourism. This wild and rocky coast, especially popular between 1958 and 1965, spread the concept of mass tourism to the rest of continental Spain.

LITERATURE. The theologian and ambassador **Francesc Eiximenis** (1325?–1409) of Gerona wrote a Christian encyclopedia, *Lo Crestià*, widely used during the Middle Ages. His *Regiment de la Cosa Publica* (1383) praised the commercial middle class as the best guarantee against tyrants and warlords.

In the nineteenth century, **Abdo Terradas i Puli** (1812–56) of Figueres (Figueras), a youthful revolutionary, wrote *El Rei Micomico*, a farce attacking Fernando VII. He fled to France in order to escape arrest and became a utopian socialist. Upon returning to Barcelona in 1840, he founded *El Republicano* as a radical newspaper to support trade unions and agitate for creation of a people's militia to fight for Catalan independence. The idea germinated until 1936 when anarchists seized upon the idea as a model to follow in creating the Anti-Fascist Militia Committee. **Narcis Monturiol i Estarriol** (1819–85) of Figueres became a socialist editor and follower of the French utopian socialist Etíenne Cabet (1785–1856), whose utopian community in Icaria, Louisiana, included a few Catalan members.

In the twentieth century, **Josep Pla y Casadevall** (1897–1964?) of Palafrugell, a journalist, wrote a history of the Second Republic. His use of Català in prose represented something of a departure from its primary use as a poetic language. **Salvador Espriu** (1913–89?) of Santa Coloma de Farnés wrote poetry in the vernacular language.

José María Gironella (1917–92) of Darnius, who wrote in Castilian, received early success when he won the Nadal Prize for *Un hombre* (1946), which described the Spanish virtues of stoicism and devotion. But after his novel *La Marea* (1948) criticized German involvement in the civil war, Gironella found it prudent to leave Spain for several short periods. New controversy occurred when he published the first part of his trilogy on the civil war, *Los cipreses creen en Dios* (Only the Cypresses Believe in God, 1953), an especially controversial best seller. The novelist's slice-of-life technique in chronicling the civil war allowed him to use a daring approach, for the time, of presenting the war as a human tragedy on both sides. The story, set in Girona, took a national perspective by using a broad range of characters and incidents. The trilogy's other two novels, *Un millón de muertos* (A Million Dead, 1961) and *Ha estallado la paz* (Peace Has Broken Out, 1966), did not achieve the same level of success, but their image of a Catholic society haunted by a defeated enemy publicized the degree to which opinion about the civil war had changed by the sixties.

ART. The Greek and Roman colony at Ampurias is the site of the *Sacrifice of Iphigenia*, one of the many important mosaics in Spain. Medieval Girona's close connection with the Provençal areas of Cerdagne and Rousillon north of the Pyrenees brought a Lombard-Catalan style to the monastery and church of St. Martín-du-Canigous, begun in 1001 by Count Guilford of Cerdagne. The lower structure is distinguished by barrel vaults and massive groin vaults on heavy granite columns, while the 84-foot-long upper church has a 20-foot-high barrel-vaulted nave. Italian construction techniques, particularly in the use of masonry in unbroken planes, made their way to Spain through such buildings. Strip buttresses and arched corbels strengthened the walls and supported the additional weight of higher walls. In addition, the church of the village of San Clemente was designed by the **Master of Taüll** (twelfth century). It is a beautiful example of the use of frescoes during the early Romanesque period.

The church of Sant Félix contains a number of ancient tombs with interesting stone designs. The cathedral, begun by **Master Enrique** and substantially enlarged by **Jacobo de Favarán**, builder of the cathedral at Narbonne, is claimed to have the widest nave of any Gothic cathedral in the world. There are retablos by Maestro Bartomeu, Ramón Andreu, and Pedro Bernec (all fourteenth century). The wall hanging known as the *Tapestry of Creation* dates from the eleventh or twelfth century and may be the province's most important art treasure since it is one of the best tapestries in Spain. In addition, **Pedro Fernández** (1480–1521?), an Italian-trained artist of the Leonardo school, created the altarpiece dedicated to St. Helena. The cathedral also exhibits a casket (ca. 970) that a caliph had made for his son.

During the fourteenth century, **Luis Borrassá** (ca. 1383) of Girona brought an international Gothic style to Spanish painting. Borrassá introduced a great sense of realism to his work and used livelier, more realistic topics from daily life. Much of his work, which can be classified as being in the Burgundian style, hangs in the cathedral of Barcelona. The silver altar in the cathedral of Girona by **Master Bartomeu** (ca. 1320) is one of the masterpieces of this genre.

In the twentieth century, **Salvador Dalí** (1904–89) of Figueres, the famous surrealist painter who used delusion and hallucination to turn the real world into a gallery of formerly taboo subjects, lived there during much of his life, although he also traveled widely. Of a politically and culturally progressive family, Dalí was expelled from the Academia de San Fernando in Madrid. Nonetheless, he devoured what he saw in other artists' work and then produced pastiches in the style of each, confusing and outraging his critics. A close friend of Federico García Lorca, he also provided the art direction for Luis Buñuel's two famous surrealist films, *Un chien Andalou* (1929) and *L'âge d'or* (1931). As a painter, the drooping *Persistence of Memory* is his indelible work, but his work ranged very widely in style, medium, and quality. He specialized in the concept of metamorphosis, and his images seem to change before the eyes of the viewer.

MUSIC. The organist, writer, teacher, chapel master, and composer **Antonio Soler** (1729–83) of Olot originally wrote very plain choral church music until he began to experiment with modulation and contrapuntal complexities in his *Sonatas for Clavichord*, which gained him notice and some notoriety as a musical experimenter.

Isaac Albéniz (1860–1909) achieved fame as the first Spanish composer of major international stature to incorporate folk-music elements into his works. A child prodigy as a pianist, he ran away from home at nine and wandered through North and South America before being sent back to Spain. He later studied at the Brussels Conservatory and also with the aged Franz Liszt (1811–86). Upon his return, he worked with Felipe Pedrell (1841–1920), who introduced Albéniz to Spanish folk music. Albéniz, who spent most of his later life in Paris, after a period of unsuccessful operatic composition began to produce memorable works such as *Tango in D*, *Asturias*, and *Ibérica*. The latter is generally regarded as his best composition.

CUSTOMS AND SOCIETY. Musicologists think that Byzantine chants provided the original inspiration for Catalan songs. Chromatism, in which the third step of the scale is constantly altered in major and minor, is one of the most important technical qualities of this music. The development of Catalan song, in any case, came through development of large choruses, which one old source calls *orfeones*.

Revival of *sardana* dancing became the life work of Josep Ventura (1817–75) of Figueres. In his reconstruction of this dance, the first part is short and sad, while the second part becomes festive and very active. The basic movement is two steps to the left and two to the right, with the toes pointed before the steps are taken and with the arms raised to the shoulder. In the second part, the use of four steps in each direction increases the scope and speed of the dance.

HISTORIC SITES. The provincial capital of **Girona (Gerona)** has an old town on the right bank of the Onyar River, the site of a Gothic cathedral built between 1312 and 1500. It is 165 feet long, 75 feet wide, and 112 feet high. An unusual feature is a bishop's throne beyond the high altar called the "throne of Charlemagne." There is also an episcopal palace, several parish churches (San Félix, San Nicolás, San Martín Sacasta), and several monasteries (San Pedro Galligans, St. Daniel). The Centre Isaac el Sec is a center for Jewish studies about Girona's medieval Jewish population.

The Costa Brava dominates the area between **Blanes** on the south and Salvador Dalí's birthplace of **Cadaqués** on the north. The coast is rocky and wild with beautiful stone formations and many inlets. **Figueres** is the main town of the northern region and an important cultural center, home of the Dalí Museum, an archaeological museum, and a number of historic churches. **L'Escala,** near San Martín de Ampurias, is the archaeological site of **Empúries** (Ampurias), the colony founded in the seventh century B.C. Ruins of another early colony, **Ullastet,** are not far away, also near the coast south of Empúries. At the top of the Gulf of Roses, **Castelló de Empúries** grew to prominence as an active trading center during the Middle Ages. The church of Santa María has a stunning Gothic main portal formed by five recessed and pointed arches filled with symmetrical sculptures.

The mountainous north near the French border rises very dramatically. At **Vilajuiga,** the Benedictine monastery of San Pedro de Roda, founded in 948 and looted by the French during the Napoleonic War, is a good example of Catalan Romanesque, a synthesis of Visigothic and Mozarabic styles. **Besalú,** a beautiful village, has a fine medieval bridge, the church of San Pedro, and an old Jewish quarter.

CUISINE. Fish, deliciously flavored with saffron or fruit juices, such as sole in orange sauce, supports the claim that the cuisine of Girona is the best in Catalonia. *Mar i muntanya* dishes combine chicken and prawns; rabbit, snails, monkfish, cuttlefish, and prawns; or rabbit, pork, sole, and mussels. The *zarzuela* is a hearty fish soup.

Viticulture of the Ampurdán district (or Costa Brava, as it is sometimes called) is perhaps the oldest in Spain, begun by Greek colonists who brought the grape and olive culture of the eastern Mediterranean to Iberia. Monasteries replanted the vineyards after the Muslim period, and today there are some beautiful wineries such as Castillo de Perelada that can claim an ancient reputation. Vines in the mountains must be staked to prevent wind damage. Much of the wine produced is of a mild rosé variety.

LLEIDA (Lérida)

VITAL STATISTICS. Pop., 355,451. Area, 12,173 sq. km. Capital: Lleida. Diocesan sees: Lleida, Vic, Urgel, Solsona. Lleida is the only Catalan province not on the Mediterranean coast. Barcelona and Girona are to the east, Zaragoza (Aragón) to the west, and France and Zaragoza to the north and south.

ECONOMY. The Río Segre and two branches of the Noguera River irrigate the province. From the Pyrenees in the north to the Ebro Valley in the south, the province is a fertile and productive agricultural region for meat, cereals, and wine. Forestry also is important in the northern Pyrenees foothills.

HISTORY. (Ilergetes [Iberian], Ilerda or Llerda [Roman], Lareda [Arab]). The area's large population during the early Hispanoafrican Paleolithic culture, ca. 4000 B.C., fought continually, first with the Carthaginians and later with the Romans. The city of Lérida was founded as a military camp from which the armies of Pompey and Caesar clashed for control of Rome in 49 B.C.

Marauding German tribes raided as early as A.D. 375. The Swabian king Requiario claimed the region in 448, but little formal government existed throughout the Gothic period. Muslims reached the area in 714–19 and made Lérida into a frontier district ruled from Zaragoza. The area broke away in the eleventh century into a Muslim principality incorporating part of northern Valencia, but in 1149 Ramón Berenguer IV conquered the area for the Catalan crown.

Medieval rule, often disputed by the Kingdom of Aragón, came through magistrates (pahers) and a consejo general, while the see of Tarragona provided ecclesiastical direction. A university was founded at the start of the fourteenth century, although it was soon eclipsed by Barcelona. Settlers did not stay long, following the religious frontier to the Balearics, Valencia, and Murcia. Apart from the manufacture of canvas and calico, agriculture and grazing provided the only employment. Much of the land as well as political authority was held by the counts of Urgel, who often organized raids on their opponents and social rivals.

The Catalan revolt in 1640–41 left Lérida under Castilian occupation. The area was a combat zone during the War of Spanish Succession and again fell to Castile on November 14, 1707. French occupation during the Napoleonic era, the First Carlist War (1834–39), and a series of later cholera epidemics all disrupted life, but the economy grew and improved. The Amigos del País established an agricultural academy in 1764. Suppression of the *bolla* tax by Carlos III in 1770 (a 15 percent sales tax) stimulated the growth of small industry, and construction of the canal of Urgel in 1860 greatly improved the province's agriculture. Railway transportation enabled viticulture and truck farms to serve Zaragoza and Barcelona.

The intensification of agriculture converted many peasants into field workers, and as sectarian politics of the twentieth century emerged Lérida developed a strong left. One local leader, Joaquín Maurín (1897–1973), a school teacher, attended the 1920 Second Congress of the Communist International in Moscow and later became a prominent leftist. The anarchosyndicalist Confederación Nacional del Trabajo (CNT), strong among railway workers and peasant agriculturalists, stressed ancient grievances over the land, anticentralism previously fostered by Carlism or Catalan nationalism, and anticlericalism. On January 8, 1933, five anarchists and one soldier died in an attack on the army barracks in the city of Lérida. The movement was repressed for several years, but in the early stages of the civil war the CNT achieved complete control of the region. Lérida went through a libertarian social revolution with local collectives, crude revolutionary justice, a total purge of all religious institutions, and control by the Council of Aragón. Anticlericalism caused Buenaventura Durruti of León, anarchist military commander, to burn the cathedral in 1936.

The militia army lost the city of Lérida on April 20, 1938, after its unsuccessful campaign against Zaragoza. Eastern areas of the province remained a battle zone until the general republican collapse of January 1939. The Franco regime prohibited local use of the Catalan language and banned political and cultural radicalism. In time, agricultural modernization transformed the agricultural sector by greatly improving viticulture.

LITERATURE. The province is too rural to have a strong literary tradition. **Pedro Calderón de la Barca** (1600–1681) suffered wounds in the 1641 siege of Lérida during the Reapers' War. In the modern period, **Manuel del Palacio** (1832–1906), a noted poet, dramatist, and journalist, became deeply involved in radical politics. At one time he was deported to Puerto Rico for his political activities, but under the liberals he became a Spanish diplomat in Uruguay. His main published work, *Sonetos filósficos* (1884?), is less important than his articles acquainting Spaniards with Latin American poetry and fiction. **Manuel Peadrolo** (b. 1918) is an existentialist playwright and novelist, author of *Darrera versió, per ara* (1958) and *Técnica de cambra* (1959).

ART. In the Valle de Aràn, the **Master of Aràn** (twelfth century) created polychrome sculptures. The **Master of Maderuelo** used a limited color scale of white, black, and red and yellow ocher to paint narrative cycles depicting the Last Judgment and the torments of the damned in a Mediterranean style of possible Byzantine origin.

The old cathedral in Lleida, called Seu Velle, provides one of the best examples of overlapping French and Italian influences in the Spanish Gothic. The sculpture is Italian, while the tombs of the counts of Urgel are covered with French designs. The new cathedral has paintings by Anton Raphael Mengs (1728–79) and Guido Reni (1575–1642).

MUSIC. The talented composer **Enrique Granados** (1867–1916) of Lérida studied music in Barcelona. Illness prevented him from taking a scholarship he had won to the Paris Conservatoire. He settled in Barcelona, where he composed *Twelve Spanish Dances*, the piano suite *Goyescas* for Goya's sesquicentennial, many romantic and folkloric piano works (including the beautiful *Allego de concierto* and the remarkable *Danza lenta*), as well as a considerable library of orchestral music. He died in 1916 when a German submarine torpedoed the ship bringing him back to Spain from a visit to New York, where his one-act opera adapted from *Goyescas* had just premiered.

Ricardo Viñes (1875–1941?), a piano interpreter of Debussy and Ravel, was a close friend of Manuel de Falla.

CUSTOMS AND SOCIETY. Traditional male dress in the northern Pyrenees districts included the typically Spanish long coat, breeches, red sash at the waist, and white knitted stockings. Female costume was also similar to that of many other northern districts of Spain: long heavy skirts, silk or cotton blouses, and silk aprons. Mantillas were less commonly worn than hair nets decorated with beads and velvet.

St. James' Day is celebrated in July. The fiesta in Lleida has fireworks, religious dramas, popular songs, and regional dances. Much of the province's folklore comes from the northern mountainous area like the Valle de Aràn, one of the finest Alpine areas in Spain; but part of the ballad of El Cid recounts fighting around Lleida against the Moors, and El Cid is a popular figure in village fiestas throughout the province.

HISTORIC SITES. In the capital of **Lleida (Lérida),** there is an old cathedral, Seu Velle, begun in 1203, and a new cathedral begun in 1761. The old cathedral is Romanesque and Gothic with a nave, two aisles, and a transept on a Latin cross plan. Its unusual cloister is in front of the main portal. The new cathedral is one of the relatively small number of churches commissioned by the Spanish Bourbons. Lesser churches such as San Lorenzo and San Martín or the old Hospital de Sant María illustrate a limited architectural heritage. More interesting is the Plaza de la Paeria, a square with arcades and offices for the paer, an official somewhat like the medieval sheriff. Slightly above the town, near where the old cathedral stands, is the Castell La Suda, a twelfth-century stronghold of the kings of Aragón.

Elsewhere in the province, the church of Sant María in northeastern **Agramunt** was begun in 1163. The ancient town of **Bellpuig,** due east of the capital, is very unspoiled. Further east, the former university town of **Cervera** is a fine example of thirteenth-century architecture. Further northeast at **Balaguer,** the Monestir les Franqueses attests to the French influence in the area. The Monestir d'Avellanes and Castell Montero are north of the town.

Several valleys lead into the Pyrenees: **Pobla de Segur** along the Segre above the **La Cerdanya** region between Bellver de Cerdanya and Seo de Urgel, the **Valle de Aràn** to the west, and the **Aigües Tortes National Park** in the Bohí Valley (or Boí in Catalan).

CUISINE. A Muslim word for abundant, *fideos* is a Catalan pasta, shorter and thinner than the Italian variety, something like vermicelli. A recipe for *fideos a la cazuela* (vermicelli with pork ribs) follows.

FIDEOS A LA CAZUELA

2–3 lbs. trimmed pork ribs	1 cup chicken stock
1 lb. pork sausage	pinch of paprika and saffron
1 clove of garlic, peeled	1 lb. *fideos* or vermicelli
1 cup hot salted water	1 can of tomatoes
2 onions, chopped	¼ cup hazelnuts, chopped
1 bell pepper, cut in strips	1 bunch of parsley, chopped

The ribs and sausage may be cooked together with the garlic and salted water. Add the onions, bell pepper, chicken stock, spices, and *fideos* (vermicelli), and simmer for 20 minutes. Add the tomatoes 5 minutes before serving. Hazelnuts and parsley garnish the dish.

Lleida has a variety of smaller wine-making operations, although none are marked as a special district. Many of the vineyards are run with modern irrigation technology to overcome the high elevation and dry climate relatively far from the coast. Cabernet Sauvignon is the most important type of wine produced.

TARRAGONA

VITAL STATISTICS. Pop., 516,078. Area, 6,303 sq. km. Capital and diocesan see: Tarragona. The province occupies the area from the Mediterranean on the east to Lleida (Lérida) and the Aragonese provinces of Zaragoza and Teruel on the west, and from Barcelona on the north to Castellón de la Plana (Valencia) on the south. Its geographic features include the Costa Dorada along the Mediterranean, the mouth of the Ebro River, and the hilly inland districts of Priorat and Alt Camp.

ECONOMY. Tarragona's main source of employment, agriculture, includes commercial food preparation and the bottling of wine. The harbor of the main city is a major fishing center and services offshore oil wells of the Casablanca field. A terminal for gas and oil pipelines connects Tarragona with the national network. Petroleum by-products such as plastics and rubber also are produced.

HISTORY. (Tarraco [Roman]). Prehistoric settlers favored Tarragona's location for its good anchorage and hilly protection near the shore. The native Iberian Cessetani tribe erected the first city walls before their defeat by the Carthaginians in the fourth century B.C. In the second century, the Romans made Tarraco (Tarragona) the capital of Tarraconensis, the northern province of Roman Spain. River boats could travel 928 kilometers west on the Ebro River to administer and supply inland areas and posts from the capital.

Tarraco's population of 27,000, the second-largest Roman settlement on the peninsula after Cádiz and its largest military base, was a classical Mediterranean city with an amphitheater seating 12,000, several temples, theatres, a large *agora*, and a beautiful tree-lined Imperial Way. The emperor Augustus lived in Tarraco in 26–25 B.C. Much later, Christianity made its appearance when St. Fructuoso and two of his deacons were martyred in A.D. 259. Another wave of Christian persecution came under Diocletian in 303–4, but within a generation the town was a Christian bishopric which produced the early pope Damasus (Damaso, 304?–84?). Damasus, born and educated in Tarragona, converted to Christianity while living in Rome, where he became a church leader. Damasus's fourth-century term as pope (366–83) was a period in which Christianity became the Roman state religion, the Arian and Donatist heresies were prosecuted, and Jerome edited the Vulgate Bible.

Attacks on Roman outposts by marauding tribes began as early as 265. The Visigoths seized the area completely by 475, but in the later Muslim period Tarraco's population fell by two-thirds. The Muslim conquest destroyed the bishopric and almost totally depopulated the province of Christians. When Ramón Berenguer IV reconquered the border region in 1149, a similar fate awaited the Muslims. Revival of the wine trade restored growth, and Christian settlers flocked to towns such as Montblanch, Reus, and Tortosa. A new cathedral was built in Tarragona on a site once occupied by the Roman temple of Jupiter, and the reestablished bishopric grew into a see of considerable zealotry. In the early fifteenth century, two Valencians, St. Vicente Ferrer and Pedro de Luna (the future Gregory XIII), chose the town as the site for an emotional discussion of the religious differences between Christians and Jews. The province soon was convulsed by a series of pogroms, and Ferrer and Luna convinced Rome to order the expulsion of the Jews from the province almost eighty years before the general diaspora in 1492.

Peasant problems reminiscent of Barcelona's Remença riots led to the revision of leases (*censo enfiteútivo*) that gave tenants a longer, fairer leasehold, in return for paying a moderate quitrent and dues to the seignorial lord. The reform worked; Tarragona's vineyards became some of the best in Spain, coveted in the nineteenth century by Mediterranean traders and ship captains of the larger-than-usual middle class who purchased large amounts of land taken from ecclesiastical mortmain. An infestation of aphids or plant lice called phylloxera, however, began destroying the vine roots in the late nineteenth century and nearly bankrupted the industry.

Financial survival came through greater commercial development of the vineyards, but during the Second Republic the greater size of these holdings attracted the ire of the Federación Nacional de Agricultores de España (FNAE), which sought unsuccessfully to get the province classified as a latifundist zone in the republican land reform legislation of 1932–33, provoking the left to create a revolutionary regime during the civil war. Churches closed, and while the cathedral was not harmed, the murder of the archbishop led to German naval bombardment of the port. After the fall of Teruel, Franco's forces reached the Mediterranean coast between Castelló de la Plana and Tarragona in April 1938. Fighting centered on Tarragona during the Ebro campaign in the summer of 1938, and Franco's forces occupied the entire province on January 14, 1939.

LITERATURE. The historian and playwright **Antonio de Bofarull y Brocá** (1821–92) of Reus became a contributor to the Catalan cultural revival. **Sebastiá Joan Arbó** (b. 1902), a novelist, has written *Terras del Ebro* and *Sobre las piedras grises* (1949), which won the Nadal Prize for its psychological study of a municipal employee who loses his job but gains the love of his daughter and friends.

ART. Significant Roman remains in Tarragona include the Hellenistic-style statue of Dionysus and the palace of Augustus. The sarcophagus of Leocadius at Tarragona and the unusual domed structure at Centcelles are good examples of early Christian artisan work. The cathedral in Tarragona has a collection of Gothic paintings and a retablo by Jaime Huguet, a Catalan architect and artist.

Mariano Fortuny y Marsal (1838–74) of Tarragona, a famed realist painter, began his art studies in Barcelona, won the Rome Prize in 1857, and spent much of his later career in Italy and France. He married the daughter of the artist Federico de Madrazo and became popular in Madrid for his etchings, done in the tradition of Goya, and his small oils and watercolors.

The paternal grandparents of **Joan Miró** (1893–1981), born in the village of Cornudella, caused his parents to purchase a farmhouse in 1910 at nearby Montroig. Miró's Fauvist-influenced landscapes of Montroig and neighboring villages of Cambrils, Siurana, and Prades in 1916 and 1917 led to his first great success, *Montroig, the Church and Village* (1919). He kept a workshop in Montroig throughout his life.

MUSIC. A popular composer in the early seventeenth century, **Juan Pujol** (1573?–1626), spent his life as a choirmaster of religious music in the province. **Felipe Pedrell** (1841–1922) of Tortosa, one of Spain's leading musicologists and supporters of a national opera, wrote *Por nuestra música* (1891) to establish a purely Spanish musical format. His operas *La Celestina* (1904) and *Comedía de Calisto y Melibea* (1908) achieved considerable critical success.

CUSTOMS AND SOCIETY. The Feast of St. Juan takes place in Valls on June 24 and features *xiquets de valls*, human towers formed by as many as thirty participants, a popular aspect of the province's gymnastic activity.

There is special *xiquet* music performed by a clarinet *(gralla)* and a small drum *(tamboril).*

HISTORIC SITES. The city of **Tarragona** faces the sea from its Balcó del Mediterraní, a terrace with good views of the sea. There are some beautiful streets like the Rambla Nova that lend charm to the town. The cathedral of Tarragona, begun in the late twelfth century on a site formerly occupied by a Roman temple and a Muslim mosque, has Romanesque pillars and doors and Gothic rib vaults and windows. Its most important characteristic is the carved reliefs on columns and pillars throughout the building, including one of a large cat attacking a group of rodents. There is a cathedral museum.

Adjoining the modern city is ancient **Tarraco,** expanded in the Punic Wars by the Scipios, Roman commanders of Hispania against Carthage (250?–200 B.C.). The Museo Arqueológico includes the Greek and Roman periods, while the Museo Paleocristiano deals with early Spanish Christianity. Elsewhere in the province, another excavated Roman town, **Centcelles** (with an aqueduct), also can be visited, and there is a Roman arch at Berà between Tarragona and El Vendrell.

Tortosa, built on the north bank of the Ebro River, is the capital of a former Muslim principality that held out against Aragón and Catalonia until 1148, guarded by an immense Arab fortress on the hill behind the town. Tortosa also became a base for the Christian invasions of northern Valencia. The cathedral, begun in 1347, largely is composed of eighteenth-century details. The Ebro delta is nearby.

CUISINE. Shellfish is a staple item, but sole with almonds is a local specialty. Fish is often grilled, and for dessert there is a confection made of ground almonds, cream, kirsch, and lemon called *menja blanca.*

A unique dish is *calçotada* (green onions blackened over a fire and served with a spicy nut sauce known as *romesco).*

ROMESCO

4 whole tomatoes	1 clove garlic, minced
8 green peppers	2 Tbs. wine vinegar
10 almonds	½ cup dry sherry
10 hazelnuts	parsley, chopped

The tomatoes and peppers are baked at 350°F for 20 minutes. Afterward the almonds and hazelnuts are baked separately for 5 minutes, then pounded together in a large mortar. After the tomatoes are skinned, they are mixed with the nuts, garlic, and peppers into a paste. Wine vinegar is added at intervals and after a few minutes of stirring a small glass of dry sherry and some chopped parsley are also added.

One gastronome calls *romesco* a sauce from antiquity, perhaps of Celt or Phoenician origin. It is often used in a seafood stew called *romesco de peix*. The liqueur Chartreuse is produced by a branch of the monastery of La Grande Chartreuse, originally of Grenoble, France. Production in Tarragona began in the early twentieth century after a tax dispute between the monastery and the French government. Spanish Chartreuse continues to be produced by the same recipe and methods used elsewhere.

The two viticulture areas in the province of Tarragona are Priorato in the northwest and Tarragona in the southern part of the province. Much of Priorato is owned by the Carthusian Order, and its wine has a very high alcohol content caused by high summer temperatures. Tarragona, which has the largest area of demarcated wine in Catalonia, is divided in subzones of Camp de Tarragona, Falset, and Ribera d'Ebre. Here too, the heat makes the red wine very strong and sweet until it borders on being a type of aromatic sherry.

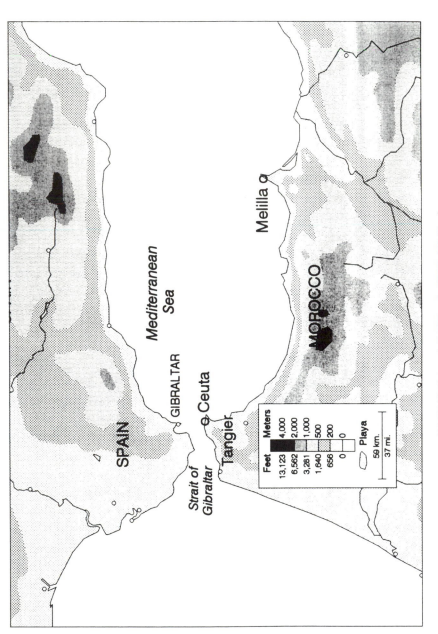

CEUTA AND MELILLA

Chapter 9

CEUTA AND MELILLA

REGIONAL CHARACTERISTICS. Pop., 132,458. Area, 32.4 sq. ki. Both Ceuta and Melilla are urban Spanish enclaves on the Moroccan coast, separated by more than a hundred miles on a straight line across coastal Mediterranean waters and almost twice that distance by a coastal route by land through Moroccan territory. Ceuta is about 12 miles south of the closest tip of Spanish metropolitan territory, but Melilla lies more than 150 miles south of Almería across the Mediterranean.

Thus, like the Balearic and Canary Islands, Ceuta and Melilla are physically separate from Iberia. Ceuta sits on a promontory marking the eastern entrance to the Straits of Gibraltar, while Melilla occupies the tip of a cape on the eastern approaches to the Straits of Gibraltar. But unlike the island archipelagoes, neither possesses an overwhelming Hispanic character or culture, since they are surrounded by the Muslim society of Morocco, an Islamic state.

The incorporation of Ceuta and Melilla into Spain as national communities came without much argument during the constitutional debates in 1977–78. Having evacuated Spanish West Africa (also called Río de Oro or Spanish Sahara) in 1976, the restored monarchy wished to avoid a further loss of overseas territory. The military felt strongly that abandonment would tarnish their sacrifice and effort in Morocco during the past century. In this light, preservation of both enclaves as integral Spanish territories represents the greatest concession made to the military sector of Spanish society by the constitutional monarchy. Despite the Kingdom of Morocco's protests, Ceuta and Melilla gained representation in the Cortes and full constitutional protection. Their two deputies possess full voting rights, a more secure relationship than that of Guam or Puerto Rico with the United States. Nonetheless, their very small physical size and large, rapidly growing non-Spanish population make them something of a precarious liability.

CEUTA AND MELILLA

VITAL STATISTICS. Ceuta: pop., 67,187; area, 19 sq. km. Melilla: pop., 65,271; area, 13.4 sq. km. Ceuta is located on Punta Almina, while Melilla is located on the Cabo Tres Forcas.

ECONOMY. Finance is subsidized by the national government, largely through military expenditures. Trade with the Moroccan interior and fishing provide about 20 percent of the revenues generated by the two towns.

HISTORY. Iberia's involvement in Morocco began with the Portuguese capture of Ceuta (1415). Following the conquest of Granada, Spain seized Melilla (1497), Mazalquivir (1505), Oran (1509), and Bejaia, Tunis, and Tripoli (1510). A complete conquest of North Africa seemed possible after the Spaniards defeated the Ottoman Empire in the famous eastern Mediterranean naval battle of Lepanto (1571), but the defeat and death in battle with the Moroccans of Portugal's Sebastian I in 1578 soon restricted a Spanish presence to the *presidios* (fortresses) of Ceuta (obtained when Felipe II inherited Portugal in 1580), Melilla, Vélez, and Alhucemas.

Relations improved with Morocco during the reign of Carlos III, only to collapse when futile and ill-advised efforts to undermine the Moroccan monarchy were made after the War of Independence. Instead, French imperialism swept through northwestern Africa, colonizing the present-day states of Algeria, Morocco, Mauritania, Senegal, and Mali. To make matters worse, Britain refused a proposed exchange of Ceuta for Gibraltar, deeply wounding Spanish national pride. Spain was able to acquire only Tetuan, south of Ceuta, captured in 1860 when the Anjera tribe unsuccessfully attacked Ceuta.

In the early twentieth century, when Germany's newfound interest in Morocco stimulated intense European Great Power rivalries, the situation changed dramatically. A Hispano-French treaty on October 3, 1904, subsequently confirmed by the Algeciras Conference of 1906, partitioned Morocco between Spain and France. Spain obtained the Mediterranean coast of Morocco (except for Tangier, which was put under international control) and occupied the rough, mountainous northern region of the Rif adjacent to the northern coast, as well as two southern enclaves, Sidi-Ifni (Santa Cruz del la Mar Pequeña) and Río de Oro (Spanish Sahara or West

Africa). Together, they totalled about 12,400 square miles, far poorer and smaller than the French section of Morocco.

Occupying these new acquisitions proved expensive and unpopular, most notably in July 1909 during the "Tragic Week" of Barcelona when mobilization of Catalan reserves to serve in Morocco provoked violence and bitter debate. The Rif proved to be almost impossible to govern after World War I when a local tribal leader, Muhammad ibn abd al-Krim al-Khatabi (1882–1963), put together an effective military force. He decimated a Spanish division in the Battle of Anwal on July 16, 1921, causing 13,192 casualties. The setback almost toppled King Alfonso XIII, who in the popular imagination was seen as one of the Anwal campaign's planners or backers. Finally, in September 1923, the king permitted General José María Primo de Rivera to create a military dictatorship, effectively closing further speculation on his role. For many years, Spaniards referred to Anwal as *el desastre.*

With expansion of the Spanish Foreign Legion, created a few years earlier, the pacification of the Rif began during Primo's dictatorship. The legion's commander, General Francisco Franco, won great popularity when he crushed al-Krim's insurrection in the Battle of Alhucemas in September 1925 and brought peace to the protectorate in May 1926. Franco, of course, went on to become the leader of traditional Spain in the later Spanish Civil War. The Army of Morocco, Franco's bulwark against the forces of the Second Republic, rose to new heights as the core of a revitalized military establishment.

After the civil war, penal battalions of former republicans caused the number of Spaniards in Morocco to increase for a time. With France defeated and occupied by Germany in World War II, Hitler allowed Franco to occupy Tangier in 1940. This control was restricted by the Allied invasion of Morocco in 1943, but in the postwar era it remained one of many divisive Hispano-French issues. Cooperation between the two European nations collapsed, and Moroccan nationalism rose steadily until the French abandoned their protectorate in 1954–55. Faced by a newly independent Moroccan monarchy and pan-Arab hostility, Spain evacuated the northern Rif on April 4, 1956, but kept Ceuta and Melilla. Pressure by the UN organization forced Madrid to relinquish Sidi-Ifni in 1969 and the Spanish Sahara in 1976.

The status of Ceuta and Melilla remained extremely troublesome. Franco had met King Muhammad V of Morocco in 1956 but avoided making any commitment concerning the enclaves' future. Over the following years, sporadic demonstrations culminated with renewed Moroccan claims of sovereignty over the two communities on January 30, 1975. Ceuta's border was closed to Moroccans on June 27, and non-Spaniards were expelled on June 30. Later the same year, Franco's death made Ceuta and Melilla the first order of business facing the new constitutional monarchy of Juan Carlos. Minor concessions relaxed border tensions, and the Constitution of 1978 making Ceuta and Melilla a part of the Spanish national *patria* removed the stigma of colonial status. Yet Spain and Morocco are border states of two vastly different civilizations, and the future of these two communities is particularly difficult to predict.

LITERATURE. The major figure, playwright **Fernando Arrabal** (b. 1932) of Melilla, was raised in Ciudad Real, New Castile. As author of *The Automobile Junkyard* and many other surrealist and existential plays, he has become an international figure of avant-garde theatre as well as a film director and playwright of more than sixteen plays such as *The Red Madonna* (1974) or *A Damsel for a Gorilla* (1986, produced in New York), *Guernica* (1961), and *La Inquisición* (1982). His novel *La torre herida por el rayo* won the 1983 Nadal Prize. Much of his adult life has been spent in Paris.

HISTORIC SITES. Both towns mingle Muslim and Hispanic elements in their architecture. Of special note is the church of Nuestra Señora de Africa and the hermitage of San Antonio in Ceuta, interesting for the combination of Iberian and African decorative elements. The seventeenth-century baroque church of Purísima, also in Ceuta, is more traditionally Spanish.

CUISINE. Spanish and Moroccan cuisine lend their different qualities to one another, as in the Moroccan dish *couscous* (beef or chicken over rice or special wheat grain) flavored with saffron.

Zaragoza: Old ruins overlook main highway from Barcelona.

Church at Santo Domingo de Calzada looks out upon old plaza.

Granada: Generalife Gardens in La Alhambra are a wonderland of flowers, fountains, and foliage.

Girona: With sixteenth-century cathedral in rear, tourist gazes upon city's old historic walls.

Seville: La Giralda tower and sixteenth-century cathedral, one of the largest Gothic edifices ever built.

Villamayor: Navarrese town has ubiquitous castle, church, and fields typical of old Spain.

Castro-Urdiales: Small fishing fleet at anchor in picturesque Cantabrian coastal harbor.

L/erida: Thirteenth-century *Seu Vella* ("Old See") is one of the greatest Catalan monuments.

Burgos: Unusual thirteenth- to fifteenth-century spires of Spain's third largest cathedral rise above city.

Toledo: Spain's second largest cathedral (after Seville) also holds many art treasures.

Madrid: Felipe V's Royal Palace (eighteenth century); one of Europe's largest, now only ceremonial.

Valencia: Central Market (1928), with 1,300 vendor stalls, is one of Europe's largest.

Majorca: Cabo de Formentor is a popular north coast field trip for secondary school students.

Figueras: Dalí Museum is a mecca for students of modern art, especially on sunny days.

Liendo: Basque country west of Bilbao is a pretty coastal mix of farms and forests.

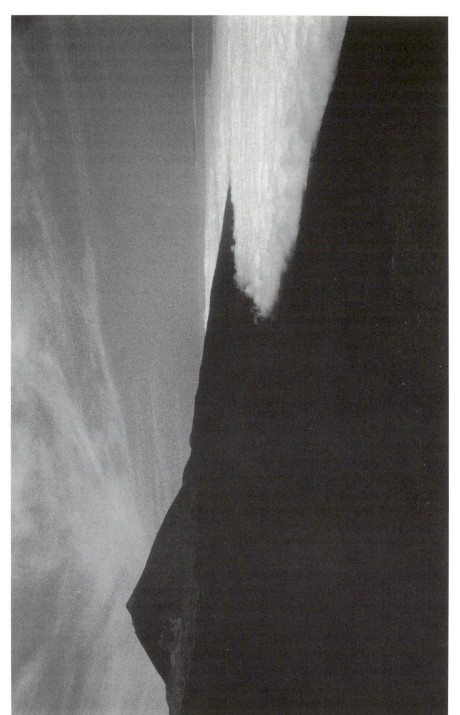

Tenerife: Teide volcano, highest point in all of Spain.

Mérida: Roman theatre was a gift from Emperor Agrippa; excavated and restored just this century.

Castle ruins stand silent guard over La Mancha grape vines.

Felipe V's eighteenth-century palace and gardens at San Ildefonso La Granja imitate Versailles.

Cuenca: Medieval hanging houses date back over 600 years, giving the city a historic presence.

Chapter 10

EXTREMADURA

REGIONAL CHARACTERISTICS. Pop., 1,050,119 (4 percent loss since 1980). Area, 41,634 sq. km. Regional capital: Badajoz. Extremadura is a name which may have come from an early Castilian word, *extremos*, meaning distant winter grazing grounds. The region is bordered by Portugal on the west, Salamanca and Avila (Old Castile) on the north, Avila again as well as Toledo, Ciudad Real (New Castile), Córdoba, and Seville (Andalusia) on the east, and Huelva on the south.

Regionalism was never an acute issue in Extremadura until 1925, when the Diputación Provincial of Badajoz formed the Centro de Estudios Extremeños to consider economic reform. Discussion of a *mancomunidad andaluza* (regional agency) to include Extremadura continued through the Second Republic, but the bitter issue of land reform generated far more controversy. While *extremeños* have no special ethnic or linguistic differences, the region's great poverty has always been a major social problem.

The chief question in 1977–78 during the constitutional debates centered around how regional autonomy might ameliorate Extremadura's poverty. No easy answer presented itself, and in the referendum of December 1978 regional opinion divided evenly between continuing centralism (42 percent) or adopting limited autonomy (44 percent). Those favoring autonomy hoped to join Andalusia, but in 1979 the Andalusians rejected inclusion of Extremadura in their region. Union with New Castile was explored, but little could be gained from the unification of two such poor areas.

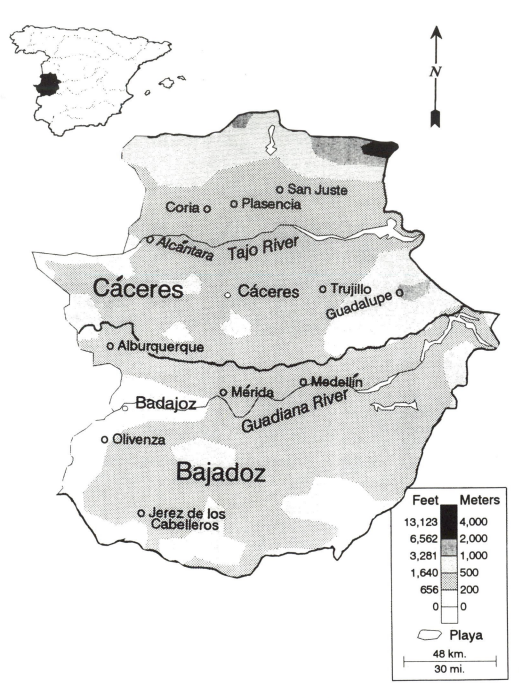

EXTREMADURA

Finally, on February 25, 1983, Badajoz and Cáceres joined together as the Extremaduran autonomous region, creating a regional government called the junta with its capital in Mérida. The flag of Extremadura has green, white, and black stripes.

The region ranks sixteenth in personal income.

BADAJOZ

VITAL STATISTICS. Pop., 635,375. Area, 21,766 sq. km. (largest Spanish province in territory). Capital and diocesan see: Badajoz. The province's neighbors are Portugal on the west (the Guadiana River creates the border southwest of Badajoz); Cáceres and Toledo on the north; Ciudad Real, Córdoba, and Seville on the east; and Huelva (Andalusia) on the south. On the southern rim, the Cordillera Mariánica forms the boundary with Andalusia. The University College of Extremadura is in the city of Badajoz.

ECONOMY. Extremadura has several important products. It is an olive-growing region, producing more than 9 percent of the Spanish crop in Badajoz and Cáceres. Cork and cotton crops also are large, but in Badajoz sheep raising, the most important economic activity, makes the province Spain's largest wool producer. Iron, iron pyrite, and lesser deposits of mercury and uranium are also mined.

HISTORY. (Badalvoz [Arabic]). Roman expansion into Celtiberian territory caused the Lusitanian War (155–138 B.C.), a revolt led by Viriathus (particularly from 147 to 138), whom Livy described as a bandit and a poacher. Together with the campaign in Soria, Scipio Aemilianus's conquest of Badajoz marked a major turning point in the Roman absorption of Iberia. The indigenous population was killed or enslaved, and Mérida (Emerita Augusta [Roman]) was made into an important military post, seat of early bishops, and at one time the capital of Lusitania, now Portugal.

The Suevi brought Gothic society to Extremadura from the west via Galicia and Lusitania. Their Christianity, dominated by Priscillianism, contained a heresy that condoned magic as a means of controlling nature. Its spread caused bitter religious controversy in Mérida, where traditional Christians rallied to a rival legend of St. Eulalia in an effort to stress faith over magic.

After the Muslim conquest of southern Spain, Berbers settled border areas such as Badajoz and created a perennial separatist problem. The principality of Ibn Hafsun (A.D. 879?–917?) harassed richer Muslim settlements of the Guadalquivir Valley until falling in 928, an event celebrated by Abd ar-Rahman III's proclamation of the caliphate in Córdoba. When the caliphate collapsed a century later, another minor principality, this one led by Abu-Muhammad-Abdallah, quickly emerged.

Raids by northern Christians from León began the Reconquest; Alfonso IX of Castile finally seized all of Badajoz in 1229. For a time, the Order of St. James administered much of the province from Medellín, but large landowners such as Gonzalo Yáñez de Mendoza (c. 1300) and his son, Pedro González de Mendoza (d. 1385) of Guadalajara province, also obtained vast estates. Through their efforts, the green pastures of Extremadura became the winter grazing grounds for two *cañadas* (sheep walks) that converged on the area. The Leonese, or western route, ran from the Cantabrian range south through Zamora, Salamanca, and Béjar, where it joined the second, from Segovia and Avila. The Honrada Compañía de la Mesta, formed in 1273, remained an important force in the economy of Badajoz until it was dissolved in 1836.

These lords of the Mesta subleased land to grain farmers in order to obtain feed for the herds. This *yuntero* arrangement (the word means a system of ploughing) limited the amount of land devoted to agriculture and saddled poor grain farmers with onerous dues and obligations. Many poverty-stricken agriculturalists, as well as impecunious young squires, escaped to become early colonists in the New World. Until 1580, Extremadura, with only 7 percent of the national population, supplied 17 percent of the immigrants to the Indies. Some of its more famous native sons include the conqueror of Mexico, Hernán Cortés (1485–1547) of Medellín, and two migrants from Jerez de los Caballeros, Vasco Núñez de Balboa (1475–1517), first European to discover the Pacific Ocean, and Hernando de Soto (1500–1542), the early explorer of western North America.

Other *extremeños* fled the frequent wars between Castile and Portugal in 1385, 1396, and 1542, since Badajoz was an ideal battlefield. When Felipe II inherited Portugal in 1580, he headquartered his army in Badajoz, which possessed the thickest walls of any peninsular city. The Portuguese counterattacked in 1660 in their own War of Independence and also held the town for several years during the early eighteenth-century War of Spanish Succession.

Modest reform began under the new Bourbon dynasty. Carlos III, eager to revive the economy, leased common lands of the towns in 1766 to needy peasants and in 1770 resettled *jornaleros* (poor peasants). But warfare soon returned. The royal favorite of Carlos IV, Manuel Godoy (1767–1821) of Badajoz, used the area as a base from which to attack Portugal in the War of the Oranges, seizing Olivenza in a futile search for his own kingdom, an act that later put hundreds of his supporters from the province at the mercy of the Portuguese and English. Badajoz supported the Bourbons against Napoleon and rebelled in 1808 against French control by murdering a pro-French captain-general at the start of the War of Spanish Independence. With Badajoz as the main field of battle, the irregular campaign lasted four years until the duke of Wellington ended the epic siege of Badajoz by driving Marshal Massena out of the province in 1812.

Liberal disentailment and abolition of mortmain greatly worsened agrarian problems after 1837. The corrupt liberal parties took advantage of rural poverty and the 60 percent illiteracy rate to steal land, reducing the number of landowners until 26.6 percent of the total province (32.5 percent of the cultivated area) was held by fewer than 400 persons. By 1930, 80,000 families of the province were either landless or owned insufficient property to support themselves.

Reaction came in several forms. Conservatives found a hero in Juan Bravo Murillo (1803–73) of Badajoz, who attacked liberalism by equating it with socialism. When his national premiership of 1850–51 ended suddenly after he tried to establish a clerical dictatorship, a group of landowners created the Federación de Propietarios de Fincas Rústicas, which lobbied strongly for the Church and their own property rights.

Peasants also protested liberal political and economic practices and rebelled in 1835, 1859, and 1883. A powerful revolutionary league of peasants, the Federación Nacional de Trabajadores de la Tierra (FNTT), eventually dominated rural politics. The FNTT assassinated four Civil Guards on December 31, 1931, and revolted against a conservative cabinet of the Second Republic in June 1934. At the heart of its protest was a land reform report identifying 46.3 percent of the cultivated land in the province as *latifundia* subject to expropriation, the third largest total of any province. Few properties were ever distributed officially, and peasants simply seized large estates after the Popular Front elections of 1936.

Before this revolutionary momentum could be consolidated, the civil war's outbreak placed the province directly in the path of General Francisco Franco's advancing army. Hundreds of republicans died in a massacre at the Plaza de Toros in Badajoz on August 14–15, 1936; press reports of this incident gave the first indication of the war's true violence. The Badajoz massacre caused rebellion to collapse throughout the province, and the area never again was a theatre of operations. Indeed, it is possible to claim that crushing the peasant revolutionaries of Badajoz made the rebel victory possible.

Franco's regime zealously prevented further protest and returned landed estates to their previous owners. By 1959, more than 70 percent of the land still remained classified as latifundia, and while a "Plan Badajoz" was created to provide model towns and improve housing, only the national rural exodus finally eased this crisis. Peasants simply migrated in search of work. More than a quarter of the former population now lives in Madrid, Barcelona, or Bilbao.

For those who remain, the recent extension of social welfare and decentralization of education and culture have improved rural life, and new agrarian practices have reduced the amount of wasteland and introduced better agrarian husbandry to the region. The decrease of grazing activity has also made crop production more important.

LITERATURE. The earliest contributor to the province's culture, **Shemuel Ha-Levi Ben Yosef Nagrella** (993–1056) of Mérida, a rabbi and statesman who acted as the vizier of Granada for a time, wrote religious poetry that is among the finest in the Hebrew language written in Spain.

An early Golden Age dramatist, **Bartolomé de Torres Naharro** (1485?–1520?), studied at the University of Salamanca. His vocation is not clear; he was either a priest or a soldier, living in Seville and Valencia until his capture by Moorish pirates. After being ransomed, he lived in Italy, where he wrote comedies such as *Ymenea* (1516?). A collection of his work, *Propaladia*, published in Seville, gave a scholarly definition of comedy and examples from the Italian Renaissance comedy that influenced later Spanish drama. As one of the earliest Spanish dramatists to know the Italian theatre, Torres established the five-act, six-to-twelve character rules of the stage.

Another writer of this period, **Diego Sánchez de Badajoz** (active 1533–54), a parish priest in Talavera la Real, became an outstanding writer of religious drama. His collection, *Recopilación en metro* (1554), consisted of plays celebrating Corpus Christi.

In the eighteenth century, **Juan Pablo Forner** (1756–97) of Mérida, a lawyer and writer who became famous in Madrid for his literary feuds and polemics, took an elitist view of culture in *Sátira contra los abusos introducidos en la poesía castellana* (1782) and defended Spanish letters against a growing French influence in *Oración apologética por la España y su mérito literario* (1789). **Juan Meléndez Valdés** (1754–1817) of Badajoz wrote pastoral poetry in Salamanca. **Bartolomé José Gallardo y Blanco** (1776–1852) of Campanario, a bibliographer and scholar, did the first serious study of ancient books in Spain.

During the nineteenth century, the ultraconservative **Juan Donoso Cortés,** the marqués de Valdegamas (1809–53) of Valle de la Serena, a descendant of Hernán Cortés, pursued a long career as a politician and diplomat. His major work, *Ensayo sobre el catolicismo, el liberalismo y el socialismo* (1851), identified liberalism with socialism and expressed a conservative Catholic corporative social philosophy stressing ecclesiastical, institutional, and patriarchal controls over general abstract and individual liberties.

Radicalism also formed currents in the provincial society. **José de Espronceda** (1808–42), the "Spanish Byron," according to Gerald Brenan, was born at the side of the road during his mother's flight from the French at the start of the War of Independence. He grew up to be a rebellious youth who flouted authority, went to jail in 1823 for supporting Colonel Riego, and after his release fell in love with a colonel's daughter, Teresa Mancha, who fled with him to London and Paris in 1827–33. They returned to Madrid, but Teresa died tragically a year later. Espronceda lived on until 1842 and during this period did the bulk of his writing, which included poetry attacking the monarchy's despotism or hailing revolution and anarchy. He scorned the established order and demanded that each person be allowed full individualism and the complete enjoyment of liberty. The *Canción del pirata* (1831) and *El estudiante de Salamanca* (1834) were styled loosely after Lord Byron's work, and *El diablo mundo* (1842) took on qualities of Goethe with its Faust-like character, Adán. His *Canto a Teresa* is one of the greatest Spanish love poems.

ART. The painters **Luis Morales** (1509–1586) of Badajoz and **Francisco Zurbarán y Salazar** (1598–1664) of Fuente de León dominated the early modern period. Morales, called "El Divino," used a painstaking technique inherited from the Flemish masters that elongated forms somewhat like El Greco. He painted numerous versions of the Virgin and Child, but his most popular work is *Ecce Homo* (now at the Hispanic Society of America, New York). Zurbarán, a friend of Diego Velázquez while still an apprentice, produced beautifully tranquil paintings and received many royal commissions to do work in Madrid.

CUSTOMS AND SOCIETY. The basilica of Santa Eulalia in Mérida honors a young girl who in A.D. 304 fled from Barcelona to escape the Edicts of Diocletian, which compelled all citizens to pay homage to the gods of the Roman Empire. Eulalia refused to abandon her belief in Christianity and suffered martyrdom for abandoning the state religion. Her saint's day is December 10.

Traditional life for shepherds in the province centered around a hut (*chozo*) near the sheepfold, occasionally adjacent to the manor house (*cortijo*). The huts resembled thatched cones and usually were small, accommodating only one person, since shepherds seldom married. Earthenware jars and tanned sheepskins held condiments and water, but other furnishings were scant. Male and female dress was usually made of goat- and sheepskin, the men wearing sheepskin overalls (*zahones*), black felt hats, wooden shoes, and an indispensable leather bag (*zamarra*) in which to carry provisions. When shepherds did marry, they tended to play a very patriarchal role. The nineteenth-century English traveler Richard Ford called one he met "St. John of the Wilderness."

The embroidery of the province is particularly famous. Girls applied embroidery to blouses, aprons, skirts, and shirts. Patterns often incorporated green leaves and four-petaled flowers in cut loops of orange, yellow, pink, red, and blue arranged in two overlapped, waved lines. Through the petals ran double lines of a contrasting color, often white.

HISTORIC SITES. The town of **Badajoz** is dominated by its high city walls and a long bridge over the Río Guadiana that has Roman foundations. The Alcazaba is a fortress built during early Christian times and greatly expanded by the Muslims. The cathedral of San Juan, begun in the thirteenth century, is a fortified basilica with twelve chapels and some valuable religious art.

Elsewhere in the province, **Alburquerque**, directly north of Badajoz, has several Gothic churches and historic houses. The castle of Azagala between Alburquerque and Cáceres is early medieval in origin. North of Albuquerque, the Valencia de Alcántara Castle figured in numerous border disputes between Spain and Portugal.

Southwest of Badajoz, **Olivenza** remained a Portuguese possession between 1298 and 1607 and has a number of churches and public buildings that reflect this dual heritage. Much further south, **Jerez de los Caballeros** is a hilltop city with part of its ancient walls still standing. The Knights Templar conquered Jerez in 1229, but a year later, Fernando IV, fearing loss of royal prerogatives, dissolved the order and sparked a rebellion. The Torre Sangrienta, or bleeding tower, still stands as the site where many knights faced execution. The church of Santa María, begun in 556, is the oldest church in Jerez de los Caballeros and all of Extremadura. The town is also the birthplace of Vasco Núñez de Balboa (1475–1519), Spanish discoverer of the Pacific.

To the east of Badajoz, **Mérida** is the most important historical site in the province, with extensive ruins of the Roman capital of Lusitania and the ninth-largest city of the Roman Empire, Augusta Emerita. The ancient city contains a bridge, a theatre built in 18 B.C., a Circus Maximus, an aqueduct (one of three), the Trajan arch, and many lesser buildings. Augusta Emerita had a population of 30,000; the amphitheater alone seats 14,000. The Roman bridge across the Guadiana River is a half-mile long and has eighty-one arches. The modern town of Mérida has an archaeological museum and the Parador Nacional Vía de la Plata. Once the center of Mendoza family power in Badajoz province, their palace is now the Hotel Emperatriz.

Slightly southeast of Mérida, **Medellín** is the birthplace of Hernán Cortés. The Cortés museum occupies his former house, and there is a local museum in the palace of the dukes of Medinaceli.

CUISINE. The region eats country food for a hot climate, such as *gazpacho extremeño* (a cold soup) and *coliflor al estilo de Badajoz* (fried cauliflower served cold). *Cochifrito* (lamb with onions and spices), *frito típico extremeño* (kid), and *riñonada* (sweetbreads) are common. Another popular dish is potato stew.

PATATAS EXTREMEÑAS

1½ lbs. potatoes	1 clove garlic, peeled
2 tomatoes, chopped	1 bay leaf
1 onion	1 bunch parsley, chopped
½ cup green beans	salt and pepper to taste
½ cup olive oil	1 cup water

Peel potatoes and cut into large slices, then chop tomatoes, onion, and beans. Heat olive oil in a casserole and cook the garlic. Add vegetables and cook over moderate heat for 15 minutes before adding the remaining ingredients. Add water as needed. Continue simmering for an additional 45 minutes.

The area around Almendralejo is the region's only large wine-producing area.

CÁCERES

VITAL STATISTICS. Pop., 414,744. Area, 19,868 sq. km., one of the largest provinces in area but lowest in population density. Capital: Cáceres. Diocesan sees: Coria and Plasencia. The Sierra de Gredos lies on the northern border of Cáceres and separates it from Avila. The province is surrounded by Portugal on the west, Salamanca on the north, Avila and Toledo on the east, and Badajoz on the south.

ECONOMY. Cáceres is one of the five provinces of Spain notable for the size of individual properties. So-called *charro* lands are large ranching areas, one of the few districts in Western Europe with unfenced range land. Three-quarters of Spain's tobacco is grown in the province's valleys on approximately 20,000 hectares of land. Olives and cork are other crops of importance.

The region is a tourist destination because of the Guadalupe pilgrimage site. In 1928, the first parador in what is now a major national chain opened as a hunting lodge in the Sierra de Gredos.

HISTORY. (Castra Caecilii [Roman], al-Cazires [Arabic]). The prehistoric Vetones and Lusitanos tribes of the area were defeated in the Viriathian War. After 54 B.C., the Romans turned Alcántara into an administrative center and promoted settled agriculture, but the Visigoths later made grazing more common. Christianity, widespread by A.D. 650, disappeared under the Muslims, whose rule took the form of Berber settlements outside the main currents of Andalusian life.

The main Arab town of al-Cazires (Cáceres) changed hands five times during the Reconquest, being held by Alfonso VII of Castile (1141), the Portuguese adventurer Giraldo Sempavor (1165), the Order of St. James (1170), and Alfonso IX of Castile twice (1213 and 1220). Plasencia, founded as a Christian city in 1189, grew as a crucial forward Castilian base. Alcántara (Norba Casearea [Roman]) originally came under rule by the Portuguese Order of Pereiro in the Reconquest. One of the last towns to fall was Trujillo, which became Christian in 1232. Large rural tracts were taken by the marqués de Torre Orgaz, the conde de Oropesa, the vizsconde de la Torre, and the duque de Alba, all of whom played major roles in local social and political life.

Discovery of the Virgin of Guadalupe in 1325 by a shepherd, Gil Córdero, delighted this newly Christianized society. The wooden statue, claimed to be the work of St. Luke, the painter-physician-evangelist of the island of Patmos in Greece (ca. A.D. 60), had come to Spain when Pope Gregory presented it as a gift to St. Isidoro of Seville. Hidden away from the Muslims for more than 600 years, the Virgin of Guadalupe quickly became the region's most important icon, patron saint of the province and later also of Mexico.

The role of the Virgin in the Americas was considerable. Isabel the Catholic approved Columbus's final grant in 1492 while visiting the monastery of Guadalupe, and Columbus later named Guadalupe Island in the Caribbean after the Virgin. Nicolás de Ovando (1451?–1511), first governor of the Indies, brought a replica of the Virgin to Cuba, and soldiers of Hernán Cortés carried small portraits of her during the original Spanish campaign in Mexico (1519–25). Near Mexico City in 1531, Juan Diego experienced a vision of the Virgin that led to her adoption as the patron saint of a Christian Mexico.

Cáceres furnished thousands of settlers to the colonies. Francisco Pizarro (1475?–1541) of Trujillo conquered Peru, and Francisco Orellana (1511–42?) first explored the Amazon. This depopulation made Cáceres less important in later national events, although the area witnessed violence during the struggle between Juana la Beltaneja and Isabel the Catholic for the Castilian throne in the 1460s. Fernando the Catholic died in Madrigalejo, and Carlos I (Emperor Charles V) in La Vera. Felipe II met Sebastián of Portugal at the monastery of Guadalupe in 1577 but refused to join him in a crusade against Morocco. The Portuguese king died on the battlefield in Morocco on August 4, 1578, and Felipe inherited Portugal through his Portuguese mother in 1580. Later retaliatory invasions by Portugal in 1660, 1705, and 1810 stemmed in part from this episode.

The War of Independence continued an assault on local stability, and social conditions continued to worsen during the nineteenth and early twentieth centuries as illiteracy, landlessness, and agricultural day labor dominated peasant life. But unlike Badajoz, the large religious community around Guadalupe provided a measure of conservative stability. In 1933, its support for the conservative Federación Española de Derechas Autónomas was substantial, and peasant protest never reached the same high level of violence as in Badajoz. A majority welcomed General Franco in mid-August 1936, and the town of Cáceres was headquarters of his campaign against Madrid and site of air bases that kept it under aerial attack throughout the civil war.

In the postwar era, Franco bought an estate for himself in the province and often hunted there, but the pattern of life for many villagers and peasants involved migration in search of work and better opportunities. For those who remained behind, the political orientation has been very traditionalist.

LITERATURE. An early important intellectual figure of the province, **Peter of Alcántara** (1499–1562), a Franciscan priest educated at Salamanca, was guardian of a remote contemplative house in Lapa. His writings on prayer, acclaimed for their extreme devotion, became a major influence on St. Teresa. A new branch of the Franciscan Order, the Alcántarines, was created to honor Peter.

In the sixteenth century, **Francisco Sánchez de las Brozas** (1523–1601), a professor at the University of Salamanca who specialized in literature, used his studies of ancient Greek to improve later Spanish poetry. His philosophical work, influenced by Erasmus, grew critical of Scholasticism and of Aristotle's importance in Christian thought. The Inquisition had him arrested for advocating Church reform, but he died before his trial.

Much later, **José María Valverde** (b. 1926) of Valencia de Alcántara wrote poems of love and mysticism chronicling the changes an individual encounters in relationships throughout a lifetime. His *La espera* (1949) won the Premio Nacional de Poesía for its nostalgic recreation of the past. Cáceres also provided the setting for the novel *La Familia de Pascual Duarte* by **Camilo José Cela** of La Coruña.

ART. The art of the province is largely at the shrine of the Virgin in Guadalupe. The statue of the Virgin is a major attraction. Carvings surround a moveable stage cranked by hand to make the Virgin appear, adorned by gold and jewels and costumed in a variety of rich robes, some of which are on display. The Virgin holds a small infant Jesus.

The shrine has a large collection of paintings, including a series of nine large religious works by the Italian **Luca Giordano** (1632–1705); eight polychrome statues of Old Testament women (anonymous); and eight paintings by **Francisco Zurbarán** of the friars who first headed the monastery. The painting of Father Yáñez is one of Zurbarán's greatest works.

CUSTOMS AND SOCIETY. Much of the province's pageantry involves religious holidays at the shrine to the Virgin of Guadalupe, particularly at pilgrimage time (check annually). Occasional South American programs and celebrations are held in Trujillo and elsewhere in the area due to its close connection with the Americas. Mérida's Roman theatre sometimes stages classical Greek and Latin drama in June.

The area of Las Hurdes (sometimes spelled Jurdes), a barren mountainous zone near Plasencia, has long been considered one of the most poverty-stricken areas of Spain. At one time, the Hurdano people of the area were thought to be Visigothic tribal survivors, but those few left in the contemporary period are more often seen as victims of cultural isolation and nutritional deprivation.

Traditional dress in the province is quite diverse. Women's skirts made of red dyed wool were tucked four or five times just below the hips and embroidered down to the hem in a stylized floral design. Bodices of silk, trimmed with jet and lace at the wrist, and traditional aprons of silk brocade, lace, and net, contrasted with plain woolen shawls (*pañuelo de clavel*) worn at the shoulders and often pulled over the head. Jewelry frequently included gilt horseshoe earrings and large gilt crosses.

HISTORIC SITES. The old town of **Cáceres,** the city of storks (the whole area is a nesting spot), is walled. The Torre de Bujaco (a Roman clock tower) stands out as a particularly handsome structure, but the basilica of Santa María de Mayor, numerous fine homes, and an archaeological museum all are within the walls.

Elsewhere in the province, directly north of Cáceres, the town of **Coria** (Caura [Celtiberian], Vetona [Roman]) has well-preserved Roman walls, four gates, and a cathedral begun in 1108 with particularly fine plateresque and Renaissance decorations. In the northeast, the once-walled city of **Plasencia** (Dulcis Placidea [Roman]) on the Río Jerte has a cathedral begun in the thirteenth century with a Jusepe de Ribera painting and many other Renaissance-period works. Further north, between Plasencia and Béjar, the Cistercian abbey at **Abadía** is of the thirteenth century. Directly east of Plasencia is **La Vera de Plasencia,** the Hieronymite monastery of San Jerónimo de San Yuste where Carlos I, first Hapsburg ruler of Spain, spent his retirement from 1556 to 1558 at what was then called the "court of La Vera." His quarters are preserved and the monastery has several beautiful cloisters.

Northwest of Cáceres, toward Portugal, **Alcántara** preserves a Roman bridge (ca. 100 B.C.), the monastery of San Benito (ca. A.D. 1500), and many sites associated with the Christian military orders of the Reconquest.

A considerable distance to the southeast of Cáceres, located in the Sierra de Guadalupe, **Guadalupe** is the site of an important Hieronymite monastery dedicated to the Virgin Mary, founded in 1340. Alfonso XIII made the Virgin an official symbol of the Spanish state in 1928.

The monastery of Guadalupe is huge and at one time possessed within its walls three hospitals and a school of medicine, together with whole districts of artisans. Both Columbus and Hernán Cortés visited the monastery before they left for the New World. In the early modern period, the pilgrimage to Guadalupe became second only to that of Santiago de Compostela in the north and actually supplanted Santiago for a time.

Directly east of Cáceres, **Trujillo** (Turgalium [Roman], Truxillo [Arabic]) was the birthplace of the conqueror of Peru, Francisco Pizarro. It has four interesting churches: Santa María la Mayor, San Martín, Santiago, and San Francisco, the latter with the Pizarro family tomb. The conquistador Francisco Pizarro is buried in Lima, but his son Hernando and Hernando's wife, Inés Yupanqui, an Inca princess, are buried in Trujillo. The palace of the marqués de la Conquista is the Pizarro family mansion, built with the enormous revenues the family received from Peru. Spaniards who served in Peru built a number of other, smaller palaces in the town as well. The Plaza Mayor of Trujillo, with its arcades, connects many of these noble houses with the palace. A statue of Francisco Pizarro occupies the center of the square.

CUISINE. Country cooking predominates with such dishes as goat or lamb stew.

CALDERATA EXTREMEÑA

4 cloves garlic, peeled	1 sweet red pepper
½ cup olive oil	1 cup water
1½ lbs. kid, including liver	1 cup white wine
¼ cup cayenne pepper	black pepper to taste
salt to taste	1 bay leaf

Cook the garlic in heated oil. Cut the kid into small pieces and brown it in oil. Flavor with cayenne and salt. Chop the sweet red pepper, add to mixture, and cover with 1 cup of water and the wine. Cook for 15 minutes. Meanwhile, chop the liver into tiny pieces, add to the kid, along with black pepper and bay leaf, and cook over a low flame until the meat is tender.

The area around Plasencia produces a light red wine.

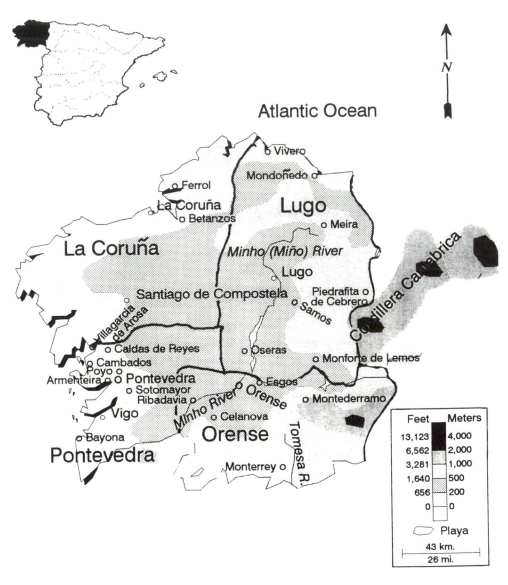

Atlantic Ocean

N

o Vivero

Mondoñedo o

o Ferrol

La Coruña

o Betanzos

Lugo

o Meira

La Coruña

Minho (Miño) River

Lugo

Santiago de Compostela

Piedrafita o
de Cebrero

o Samos

Villagarcia
de Arosa

Cordillera Canabrica

o Caldas de Reyes

o Oseras

o Monforte de Lemos

o Cambados

Poyo o

Armenteira o o Pontevedra

o Esgos

o Sotomayor

Minho River o Orense

Ribadavia o

o Montederramo

Vigo

o Celanova

Tomesa R.

o Bayona

Orense

Pontevedra

Monterrey o

Feet	Meters
13,123	4,000
6,562	2,000
3,281	1,000
1,640	500
656	200
0	0

Playa

43 km.

26 mi.

GALICIA

Chapter 11

GALICIA

REGIONAL CHARACTERISTICS. Pop., 2,753,836. Area, 29,574 sq. km. Regional capital: Santiago de Compostela. The Galician region, Spain's northwest coast, is bordered by the Atlantic on the west and the Bay of Biscay on the north, Portugal on its southern border, and Asturias, León, and Zamora (Old Castile) on the east. The four provinces of La Coruña, Lugo, Orense, and Pontevedra make up the region.

Ancient Galicia's name derives from the Celtiberian Gallaecia. Its long and unhappy inclusion in Asturias and Castile led to great poverty, later emigration of nearly 2 million Galicians between 1860 and 1980, and the rising aspirations of modern nationalism. In the nineteenth century, political and cultural autonomy ideas flourished among such groups as the Asociación Regionalista Galega (1891), Liga Galega (1897), Solidaridad Galega (1907), Irmandades de Fala (1918), and the Partido Galeguista (1931). This latter group was in the process of writing an autonomy statute when the civil war broke out, but not until the Constitution of 1978 were such aspirations recognized. The region was defined as a historic area separated from Spain by geography, lack of economic integration, and the special history of the regional Galego language.

Galego (as it is spelled in Portuguese, although in Castilian it is Gallego) developed in the early Middle Ages, originally as a regional tongue. As the progenitor of Portuguese, its close relative, both Galego and Portuguese are Ibero-Romance in character, closer to early medieval Leonese or Mozarabic

Spanish than to contemporary Castilian. Someone who knows Spanish can read but usually not speak Galego or Portuguese with equal fluency. Later Castilian changes such as *fl-* to *ll-* or *ch-* to *ll-*, *ss-* to *s-*, *ç-* to *s-*, and *x-* to *j-* are not found in Galego or Portuguese, but *l-* and *n-* are reduced between vowels, causing Portuguese words to be joined by the indefinite article *um-* or *uma-*. The vowel sounds in Portuguese became *e- o- eu- ou* and *o-ûo-a*. Portuguese diverged from Galego sometime after 1350. Dozens of changes occurred; *ñ-*, for example, came to be expressed as *ll-* or *un-* in Galego and *lh-* or *nh-* in Portuguese. The vigorous Portuguese national experience added many new words not encountered by the more limited Galician experience. Galego remained a local language divided into three main dialects of the northern, central, and southern parts of the region. Between 80 and 85 percent of Galicia's 3 million inhabitants speak Galego, which is a higher percentage for native speakers than in the Basque Provinces or Catalonia.

Because the regional character of Galicia seemed so well marked, the constitutional monarchy strongly backed regional status for Galicia. In the 1978 referendum, 45 percent of the Galician electorate voted for limited autonomy and 13 percent supported extensive autonomy, while 33 percent voted to maintain the old centralized system of rule. Support for autonomy dropped when the actual constitutional changes were voted on in the elections of April 6, 1981. Voters objected to the terms of the autonomy bill or feared an end to the economic subsidies and special development zones created during the Franco era. The Galician Socialist Party and Adolfo Suárez's Unión de Centro Democrático (with twenty of the twenty-seven Galician parliamentary seats) finally convinced most voters that regional status would give Galicia a greater voice in national affairs. Only the Union of the Galician People, a small party, advocated total separation.

The real problem in the original version of home rule was that while the Statute of Santiago, as it was called, created a regional government, the Xunta (junta, or executive), it received no independent police powers, unlike other autonomous governments. This was largely due to Suárez himself, who tried to limit the degree of autonomy for Galicia to a level below those powers obtained by the Basque and Catalan regions. It took strong support from the other nationalist parties and several rewritten versions of the statute before Galicia received equal treatment correcting most of the problems. Unfortunately, when the statute was ratified in 1981, a 71 percent abstention rate (something of a cultural tradition) marred the elections. Although 77 percent of those who did vote favored limited autonomy, this translated into only a 20 percent support rate for regional autonomy from the total electorate.

Since 1982, the Unión Centro de Democrático has disappeared in favor of the Galician Socialist Party, which dominated power in the regional parliament through its national linkage with the Partido Socialista Obrero

Español (PSOE). In recent elections, however, the more conservative Partido Popular has amassed a considerable following and now dominates the parliament.

The flag of Galicia has a solid field of white with a blue band running from the upper left to the bottom right corner.

Galicia ranks eleventh in personal income among the regions.

LA CORUÑA

VITAL STATISTICS. Pop., 1,083,415. Area, 7,950 sq. km. Capital: La Coruña. Diocesan sees: Mondoñedo and Santiago de Compostela, a religious and university center. The west coast of the province borders the Atlantic Ocean and is indented by *rías*, narrow fjordlike estuaries or bays. La Coruña is west of Lugo and north of Vigo, two of the other Galician provinces. Its climate is the wettest in Spain.

ECONOMY. La Coruña is a large fishing port, usually catching more than half a million tons of seafood annually. For the province as a whole, mining is the most important economic activity, with 84 percent of Spain's brown lignite reserves and large amounts of granite and limestone. As a whole, Galicia also produces 33 percent of Spain's raw lumber. Root crops such as leguminous beans, chickpeas, and lentils are the chief agricultural products. The province ranks second highest in emigration abroad among the Spanish provinces.

HISTORY. (Ardobirum Coronium [Roman]). The northwest was settled by the Celtic Gallaeci tribe, who mined tin and raised grain. La Coruña, founded by Phoenicians, grew to be the chief Roman settlement in Galicia by 137 B.C., dominated by Trajan's 133 foot-high lighthouse, the Torre de Hercules, built in A.D. 105. In the fifth century, migration of the Gothic Suevi tribe into Galicia and northern Portugal was followed by the Visigoths, who defeated the Suevi in 585, reducing their predecessors to subservient rural clans. Two heresies also complicated spiritual life; Arianism treated Christ as a prophet rather than the son of God, while Priscillianism (named after a Galician ecclesiastic [d. 385]) merged magic and religion. St. Martin of Braga converted the region to Roman Catholicism by the two Councils of Braga in 561 and 572.

Muslims invaded the Miño-Douro region in 725, the start of Muslim and Viking raids that created a three-century-long crisis. The Asturian monarchy established a new, if vague, Kingdom of Galicia to shore up defenses as far south as the Miño River, and while Galicians later claimed to have freed themselves, only Portucalense (named for Cale, now Oporto), the area below the Miño, actually became free. North of the Miño, the region remained locally autonomous or, at worst, subject to primitive isolation.

Despite this vacuum, one village of La Coruña province in time achieved tremendous religious importance. Santiago de Compostela (Sant Iago de Campos Stellae, or Saint James of the field of the star) contained a Roman burial ground long rumored to contain the grave of St. James the Apostle (Santiago). According to legend, after the execution of James in Jerusalem by the Romans ca. A.D. 44, Galician fishermen brought his body for burial in the cemetery. After many centuries, the legend of an apostle's burial in Galicia came to be associated with early Christian victories of Covadonga in 737, Clavijo in 844, Simancas, or even the death of Almanzor at Medinaceli in 1002. The legend's key element stressed Santiago's Christlike rise from the grave to lead Spaniards to victory.

Alfonso III of Asturias built a basilica in honor of St. James at Santiago de Compostela in the early tenth century, but Almanzor razed the village and stole the church bells in 997. Construction resumed in 1075, and the main cathedral became the centerpiece of a huge religious center in 1121. Pilgrims from northern Europe followed the *calzada*, route of the pilgrims, across the Pyrenees to worship at one of two spots in Europe (the other was Rome) linked to early Christianity. The pilgrimage started in Paris, with pilgrims wearing the cockleshell as a badge of identity as they passed through Orléans, Tours, and Poitiers, or Vézelay, Nevers, and Limoges. They entered Spain through the Roncesvalles Pass in Navarre and passed through Pamplona, Puente la Reina, Estrella, Logroño, and Santo Domingo de la Calzada before reaching Santiago de Compostela.

The pilgrimage site lessened Galicia's isolation, but when Santiago's churchmen protested the creation of a new archbishopric in Braga, King García of Navarre punished them by annexing all of Galicia to his kingdom in 1073. Castile later inherited Galicia when it absorbed Asturias, and in 1096 made Henry (Enrique) of Burgundy count of Portugal, shattering Galician and Navarrese claims on the entire west coast below the Miño.

As a vassal state, Galicia obtained no rights to organize a Cortes or later to participate in the Mesta organization. Castile ruled Galicia through the Church by a subsidy called the *voto de Santiago*, largely in the form of massive donations of land that gave churchmen a vested interest in Castilian control of Galicia. By the fifteenth century, the violent turmoil of peasant brotherhoods (*irmandades*) against ecclesiastical control led to the crown being petitioned for relief. The Catholic Kings, Fernando and Isabel, created a special royal commission, but its only real reform was to add the Galician towns to the Santa Hermandad of Castile, an association of towns. Peasants could not even freely migrate south to take advantage of the Reconquest.

In the later centuries, La Coruña grew modestly as a port but never obtained the right to carry wool to northern Europe. In 1586 and 1587, England attacked ships of the Armada in the harbor and landed marines, but a woman of the town, María Pita, led a heroic resistance. La Coruña was also the site of the first major engagement in the War of Spanish Independence between Great Britain, now a Spanish ally, and the French army commanded by Marshal Nicolás Soult. General John Moore died in the battle on January 19, 1809, and is buried in San Carlos Park. The British expeditionary army sailed away for Lisbon, leaving La Coruña in ruins.

During the nineteenth century, the complicated *foro* situation, which could be found in all four Galician provinces, created desperate social chaos in La Coruña. Over several centuries, the leasing of Church lands had created several layers of leasers known as *foreros* and *subforeros*, who demanded the greater part of the peasants' crops, leaving them little income from their farming. In the 1830s and 1840s, the liberals abolished mortmain and sold Church lands on the open market. Unprecedented litigiousness developed between *foreros* and *subforeros* over conversion into private property of their leases and subleases. By 1863, middle-class Galician townspeople had managed to assume ownership rights over the former Church lands, converting the leases to their own estates, but it remained for the Civil Code of 1889 to determine that Galician lands no longer could be subject to divided control.

The crisis, similar to the Irish troubles, took a terrible toll. Famine in 1853–54 drove tens of thousands to emigrate. Seasonal farm labor in the south provided an even greater outlet. Galicians became, in Raymond Carr's words, the waiters, water carriers, wet-nurses, and porters of the Spanish cities. Some found their way into radical movements, while the Galician upper classes moved right into the most conservative parties. In the period 1875–1923, Eugenio Montero Ríos (1832–1914) and Eduardo Dato Iradier (1856–1921) took a position of authority as the area's most powerful political bosses, very corrupt in their involvement in the *foro* crisis and quick to use *cacique*-like tactics to dominate local society. Francisco Franco, who was born in 1892 in El Ferrol, developed his distaste for modern politics from this period's political machinations.

Educated Galicians sought to strengthen the society through a cultural renaissance and by adopting the concept of regionalism. The old Galego language was revived to give special distinction to Galician society, and some wished to abandon the Castilian language altogether. The main Galician regionalist party, the Organización Republicana Gallega (ORGA), abandoned its insistence on making Galego the official language in 1929 for a republican political program that sought semi-independence, convinced that the party could gain more by playing a role in Spanish politics than by remaining aloof and linguistically different. During the Second Republic, ORGA designed a regional statute, but a conservative victory in the elections of November 1933 blocked progress until the Left Republican Party won the Popular Front election of 1936, promising to hold a plebiscite on forming a regional government as soon as possible. The outbreak of civil war a few months later made this step impossible.

Those who supported Franco's rebellion included Galician traditionalists, Carlists from Navarre, and naval personnel from El Ferrol. Early efforts to defend republicanism were quickly crushed, and many separatists were executed alongside socialists and anarchists. The right may have hoped to kill off further agitation.

In the postwar period, Franco honored the province of his birth by trying to provide material assistance. Cooperatives introduced new crops, transportation links to national markets improved, and stock breeding grew into an important specialty, but many Galician farms remained too small and inefficient to survive, and emigration continued at very high rates.

LITERATURE. One of the earliest writers, **Pedro of Compostela** (ca. 1175), wrote *De consolatione rationis*, an early collection of pre-Scholastic-influenced sermons.

The first Galician renaissance dominated the twelfth to fourteenth centuries. Verses from the Provençal poets of southern France merged with native Galician folk poetry in troubadours' songs, or *cancioneiros*. The main collections of this music and poetry (Vaticana, Ajuda, Colocci-Brancuti) include satirical songs, love poetry, and love songs. Even the famous Castilian monarch **Alfonso X el Sabio** (1252–84) wrote in Galego, and his *Livro das Cantigas* contained 420 superb compositions. The Galego renaissance made a major contribution to the creation of the Portuguese language and influenced Spaniards to move toward the creation of their own literature.

Last of the troubadours, **Alfonso Alvarez de Villasandino** (ca. 1400) and **Juan Alfonoso de Baena**, who edited the *Cancionero de Baena* (1445), introduced the style of *culteranismo*, a poetic language distinct from ordinary language and influential in Spanish as late as Góngora.

Women played an important role in the nineteenth-century revival of Galician politics and literature. The earliest, **Concepción Arenal** (1820–93), was a pioneering sociologist who spent most of her life in Santander and Madrid where, in order to attend university, she had to dress like a man. Her first book, *Fábulas y romances* (1855), achieved little notice, but her path-finding social study, *El visitador del pobre* (1866), urging greater political attention to the problems of poverty and social dislocation, was very successful. She founded a newspaper, *La Voz de Claridad*, created the Spanish Red Cross, and continued to agitate for equality the rest of her life.

By the mid-nineteenth century, Galician literature began to experience what in Galego is called *rexurdimento*, or renaissance. The most famous writer of this revival, **Rosalía Castro** (1837–1885) of Santiago de Compostela, lived from infancy to age ten with a peasant woman because her father, a priest, would not marry her mother. Castro grew up to be a plain woman, often ill, but possessing a gift for language that exposure to literary society in Madrid stimulated still further. She began to write poetry and novels in Castilian and Galician. *Cantares Gallego* (1863) and *Folhas novas* (1880) both used Galego. *En las orillas del Sar* (1884) is her best collection of Castilian poetry, but even it deeply recalls Galicia. Love that brings joy and sorrow became an important theme in her work, but she pursued the idea of feminism in her later years. Other novelists of Castro's period who wrote in Galego include the doctor **Eduardo Pondal** (1835–1917) of Puenteceso and **Manuel Curros Enríquez** of Orense.

Another woman, **Emilia Pardo Bazán,** countess of Pardo Bazán (1851–1921) of La Coruña, also wrote about Galician life, but only in Castilian. Her first novel, *Viaja de novios* (1879), dealt with the practice of arranged marriages. *La tribuna* (1882) is a study of cigarette workers in La Coruña, in which her heroine, Amparo, becomes a feminist similar to some of Zola's characters. *Los Pazos de Ulloa* (1886), Pardo Bazán's best work, contains a vivid rural and provincial atmosphere and focuses on social unrest and feudal mentality. Her nonfiction *Cuentos de la Tierra* brilliantly described Galicia. At the end of her life, she encountered great prejudice after her appointment as the first female professor of modern literature at the University of Madrid in 1916.

Wenceslao Fernández Flórez (1886–1964) of La Coruña, editor of *Tierra Gallega* and later of *ABC*, wrote more than thirty works, of which *Volvoreta* (1920), a novel about the coastal people living on the rías, or river estuaries, may be his best. Its lyricism celebrates the quiet strength of a peasant girl who finds herself in a difficult romantic situation. **Rafael Dieste** (1899–1978?) of Rianjo, a short-story writer and playwright, was also a professional journalist with *El Pueblo Gallego*. **Salvador de Madariaga** (1886–1976?) of La Coruña, an international diplomat, secretary of the League of Nations in 1921, and ambassador to the League for the Spanish Republic before the civil war, wrote essays, literary criticism, biographies, and novels during his long exile in Great Britain after 1939. He taught at Oxford University and is best known for his biographies of Bolívar, Cortés, and Columbus, popular in the English-speaking world.

Joaquín Calvo Sotelo (b. 1905) of La Coruña is a playwright who uses themes of middle-class life in much of his work. **Ricardo Carballo Calero** (b. 1910), Galician poet and professor of literature, has done much to revive the regional language of Galego. **Gonzalo Torrente Ballester** (b. 1910) of El Ferrol is a novelist who has lived and taught in Madrid, Pontevedra, and Salamanca. The best-known of his works is *El golpe de estado de Guadalupe Limón* (1967), which deals with Latin American politics. He also wrote *El señor llega* (1957), *La saga/fuga de J.B.* (1972), and *Filomeno, a mi pesar* (1982), which won the Miguel de Cervantes Prize in 1985.

The most important contemporary writer is the 1989 Nobel Prize winner for literature, **Camilo José Cela Trulock** (1916–92). He lived most of his life in Madrid, where his reputation as a nonconformist grew. His major work, *La familia de Pascual Duarte* (1941), is the story of a criminal pushed by circumstances into a series of violent acts until he is unable to survive in the civilized world. The novel, filled with the violence and primitivism of the inarticulate and naive main character, became a symbol of the brutality underlying Spain's fratricidal history. *La colmena* (The Hive, 1951) portrayed a seedy café in Madrid and the sad lives of its patrons, presented without compassion or human sentiment in an effort to reflect official sentiment. The Franco government banned the novel in Spain for portraying the misery that Cela felt had followed the civil war. He wrote a number of other novels as well as short stories and nonfiction travel literature ranging across Spain and the Americas, producing more than a hundred books in his lifetime.

The well-known literary scholar **Ramón Menéndez Pidal** (1869–1967) came from La Coruña. A disciple of Marcelino Menéndez y Pelayo, Menéndez Pidal's own two most important works, *El cantar de Mío Cid: Texto, gramática y vocabulario* (1909) and *La España del Cid* (1929), investigate the origins of early medieval Spanish literature. In 1914, he also founded the *Revista de Filología Española*, the most prestigious scholarly journal of Spain during his lifetime.

ART. Among the artisans who contributed to the construction of the cathedral complex in Santiago de Compostela, **Fernando Casas y Nóvoa** (d. 1751?) did the western façade between 1738 and 1750 and the altar of Pilar chapel, and **Maestro Mateo,** a twelfth-century Spaniard (ca. 1160–80) who created the Pórtico de la Gloria (Portal of Glory). Others who contributed their artisan crafts include the Flemish artist Antonio de Arfe (1500?–1543), Juan de Alava (d. 1537), and many other anonymous artists.

Much later, **Pablo Picasso** of Málaga spent part of his adolescence in La Coruña from 1891 to 1895, where he attended the School of Fine Arts from 1892 to 1895. During this period, he broke with his father's academic painting for a much more abstract style, turning out hundreds of works. *Two Old People* is one of his best-known works from this period in his life. In 1895, his father took a job in Barcelona, and the family had no further connection with La Coruña.

MUSIC. The anonymous *Liber Sancti Jacobi* (Codex Calixtinus, ca. 1140) is a collection of the services and music of the cathedral in Santiago de Compostela of the early Middle Ages. It is particularly important in music history for its twenty-one-piece polyphonic repertory of responses, descant style, and a rare early three-voice composition, one of the first known breaks with the monophonic tradition.

CUSTOMS AND SOCIETY. The St. James legend taught that in the seven years between Jesus's crucifixion and James's beheading, the apostle traveled to and preached throughout Spain. After his death, several Galicians brought his body from Jerusalem for burial near what is now Santiago de

Compostela. An inscribed tomb found in A.D. 813 inspired Bishop Teodomiro and Alfonso II of Asturias (791–842) to erect a church on the site,
and other stories insist that ca. 834 St. James appeared as a knight on a
white horse and helped Ramiro I (842–50) of Navarre defeat a band of
Arab invaders. As Santiago Matamoros (St. James the Moor Slayer), he
inspired the Christian struggle against Islam.

Symbolic scallop shells and wooden staffs became the special symbols of
pilgrims venerating St. James. The right to free lodging for a night at the
Seminario Menor de Belvis still can be obtained if a pilgrim walks 100
kilometers by foot or rides 200 by bicycle or horse on the 500-kilometer-
long route of the Camino de Santiago within Spain.

Another custom is of students banging their heads three times against
the Portal of Glory by Maestro Mateo in order to acquire some of the
talent that Mateo put into the 200 extraordinarily beautiful granite religious figures.

St. James's Day is July 25. In years when the date falls on a Sunday
special devotion is paid for the entire year. Spinning wheels of fireworks
are ignited the evening before, and on July 25 a huge religious processional
to the cathedral is led by the swinging of a large *botafumeiro* (censer).
Spain's rulers and the dignitaries of the Catholic world attend a solemn
high mass and the parade of national solidarity that follows.

HISTORIC SITES. In **La Coruña,** a Roman lighthouse, the Tower of Hercules, ca. A.D. 200, is still in use after an eighteenth-century reconstruction.
The major church is the Iglesia de Santiago.

In the south, **Santiago de Compostela** is a major Spanish historic site.
The cathedral of Santiago is one of the great Catholic churches in the
world, "the Jerusalem of the West," as one guidebook calls it. On the west
side of the large and complex pilgrimage center, the Plaza de España (or
Obradoiro) is a huge space surrounded by the university, the *ayuntamiento*
(municipal government) building, the national parador Hostal de los Reyes
Católicos, and the monastery of San Francisco. On the east side of the
plaza, the cathedral begins with a set of steps to the western façade, an
incredibly baroque eighteenth-century wall with two towers (one for bells,
one for the broadcast of prayers across the plaza), divided by the tympanum, a triangular pediment portraying the Adoration of the Magi. Beyond
the façade are the original Romanesque walls of the twelfth-century cathedral and the Portal of Glory with hundreds of biblical statues set into the
wall. According to James Michener, the portal is not only one of the
world's supreme artistic creations, but it is also one of the most human,
alive, and joyous.

The cathedral's interior contains a nave and two aisles and is shaped like
a Latin cross with the transept almost to the top of the nave. A longer nave
leads up to the altar and the substantial thirteenth-century statue of Saint
James above his crypt. Nineteen chapels line the sides. The important ba-

roque Capilla Mayor contains the grave of Saint James, while the Capilla de Reliquias has some of his relics and the Capilla del Pilar celebrates James's encounter in Zaragoza with the Virgin Mary. The Capilla de San Fernando contains the Gothic treasury.

On the south side of the cathedral, a large cloister (100 feet square) built in a late Gothic, early Renaissance style, leads to the museum, library, archive, charter house, and tapestry museum just off the cloister that create a southern plaza. The museum contains considerable Latin American material, while the tapestry museum has designs by Rubens and Goya.

In back of the cloister at the end of the cathedral, the Plaza de la Quintana forms an eastern plaza that is much larger than the Plaza de España, a good spot from which to view the clock tower and royal portico of the cathedral. On the north, the Azabachería Plaza makes the cathedral unique by surrounding it entirely by plazas. The north façade is less spectacular than the west.

In addition to the cathedral complex, the town possesses a half-dozen other major churches, five monasteries, a convent, and two other major structures—the Archbishop's Palace (begun in 1120) and the Hospital Real (a hospice for pilgrims, now converted into a hotel). Two museums worth visiting are the monastery of San Martín Pinario (special exhibitions) and the convent of San Domingo de Bonaval (museum of the Galician people).

CUISINE. Galicia is famous for *mariscos* (shellfish), including *percebes* (edible barnacles), *mécoras* (spider crab), *santiaguiños* (a variety of crayfish whose head is marked by a small cross), and *marisquerías* (lobsters). Scallops marinated in wine appear in a number of dishes, and *pulpo con patatas* (stewed octopus with potatoes) and *merluza a la gallega* (whitefish in garlic, olive oil, and lemon juice) also are popular. Octopus may be the favorite food of Galicia, and there are whole restaurants known as *pulperías* that specialize in it.

Pulpos guisados (stewed octopus) for four people is prepared as follows:

PULPOS GUISADOS

8 small fresh octopus	pinch of cayenne
1 Tbs. olive oil	pinch of fennel
1 red pepper, chopped	2 tsp. chopped parsley
4 large shallots, chopped	½ cup dry white wine
1 Tbs. tomato paste	2 tsp. wine vinegar
2 tsp. paprika	

Remove the ink bags and stomachs from the octopus and clean the rest carefully, cutting into small pieces. Heat the oil in a saucepan and add the red pepper, shallots, tomato paste, paprika, cayenne, fennel, parsley, dry white wine, and vinegar. After stirring this mixture for 5 minutes, add the octopus and simmer for about 1 hour.

LUGO

VITAL STATISTICS. Pop., 399,185. Area, 9,856 sq. km. Capital and diocesan see: Lugo. The relatively short northern border is the coastline of the Bay of Biscay. To the east are Cantabria and Asturias, and to the south Orense, while on the west are La Coruña and Pontevedra. The Cantabrian Mountains limited overland travel south to the interior until the construction of the first major road across them in 1773.

ECONOMY. Zinc and some silver are mined at Piedrafita del Cebrero. Fishing is important, and agriculture produces wheat, beans, and beef cattle. The province ranks sixth highest in foreign emigration among the Spanish provinces.

HISTORY. (Lucas Augusti [Roman]). Lugo, lightly settled by Celtics who worshipped Indo-European gods, developed a confederation of towns known as the Calaici to organize a society based on transhumance of collective cattle and sheep herds. The Romans established Lucas Augusti as a military camp during the Cantabrian War, and by the end of the empire the town of Lugo had become a bishop's see. The Gothic Suevi and Visigoths briefly replaced the Romans, but in 714 Muslims raided and burned the capital. The Norman attack of 969 was the final episode of nomadic violence.

During the reign of Alfonso III el Magno (866–909), Lugo became part of a loose Asturian principality. The rise of Santiago de Compostela hurt Lugo's importance, but its land attracted noble families such as Altamira, Andrade, Amarante, Ribadeo, and Sarria. The conde de Lemos, Pedro Fernández de Castro, built the Franciscan convent of Monforte de Lemos into one of the great defensive structures in Galicia. As Castile's military frontier moved south, however, so did the nobles. Land increasingly fell into possession of the Church, which soon played a considerable role in farming and grazing activities during the Middle Ages.

By the seventeenth century, unfortunately, the Latin American colonial period drained the Church of the manpower or capital to operate its properties capably and caused the *foro* to appear as a new type of primary leasehold. Leasers (*foreros*) gradually obtained hereditary control of their *foros*, obliged to pay only a fixed ground rent, even when rapid population growth in the eighteenth century pushed up commodity prices and made investment in land attractive. *Foreros* profited by creating more *subforeros*, increasing the burden of rents or product shares paid by peasants. The leases could not be broken, and the Church had no way of renegotiating them. In 1763, Carlos III barred religious leaders from doing so, since selling the land to its leasers held out no promise of improved yields or social justice, and no precedent existed for distributing land directly to the peasants.

By 1837, economic circumstances had changed. Liberalism's belief in free enterprise led to abolition of mortmain; *foreros* were permitted to purchase title to their lands and to speculate in land, but peasants found themselves even more destitute than before and during bad years such as 1853 experienced serious famine. The civil code was not revised to prohibit property subleasing until 1889, too late to keep many peasants from being driven off the land and forced to emigrate. Lugo often led Galicia's high rates of emigration and low per capita income. One of those who left in 1899, Angel Castro Argiz, born in the hamlet of Láncara near the city of Lugo, was the father of the Cuban president Fidel Castro, who himself has returned on occasion to visit his father's birthplace.

By the twentieth century, new efforts to remedy the rural crisis created such movements as Antonio Villar Ponte's Irmandade da Falla in 1916, a Christian Democratic movement. The efforts of this organization finally led to the formation of the Partido Galenguista during the Second Republic, but ultra traditional segments of the public supported Franco when the civil war broke out in July 1936.

Franco drew upon fellow Galicians during the postwar era. Manuel Fraga Ibibarne (b. 1922) of Lugo, the chief regional figure in Madrid, became a dynamic cabinet member who from 1962 to 1969 played an important role in the *abertura* (opening) phase of Franco's regime by encouraging tourism and modernizing communications. When he opposed Opus Dei, an angry Franco dismissed Fraga, but the Galician leader remains an important political figure in the present era.

LITERATURE. Brief poems, actually songs called *cantigas*, characterized Gallo-Portuguese literature in the Middle Ages. Many came from Lugo, but little is known of their authors except for **García Ferrandes de Jerena** (ca. 1330), a Galician poet who married a Muslim poetess, migrated to Granada, and renounced Christianity, only to reconvert later. His work marked a high point of the Galician medieval tradition of fantasy.

In the nineteenth century, **Nicomedes Pastor Díaz** (1811–63), poet, author of *Poesías* (1840), and later rector of the University of Madrid, actively encouraged the revival of learning. **Xoan Manuel Pintos Villar** (1811–76) was one of the first regional writers to use the vernacular language in *A gaita gallega* (1853). **Antón Noriega Varela** (1869–1947) of Mondoñedo, a poet who broke with the sentimentalism of Rosalía de Castro, wrote as a social realist about rural ways and customs of Galicia in four books, of which *De ruada* (1895) and *Do ermo* (1920) are the best known.

Among the more recent linguistic nationalists, the doctor and writer **Luis Vázquez Fernández Pimentel** (1895–1958) continued to develop the use of Galego in poetry, while **Alvaro Cunqueiro Mora** (b. 1911) of Mondoñedo is a surrealist poet and collector of Galician ballads.

ART. Perhaps the most significant architectural work in the province is Santa Eulalia de Bóveda, an early Christian subterranean building laid out on a basilica plan.

CUSTOMS AND SOCIETY. Folk music is dominated by the *Muiñeira Gallega*, songs in 6/8 time accompanied by the *gaita gallega* (bagpipes, usually green in color) and the *tamboril*, a small drum. The dances to this music are very old, said to be of Greek, Suevi, or Celtic origin. A single couple dominates the first phase, with the male dancer acting out courtship, then kneeling to his partner before they dance together. Other couples join the dance almost at a gallop, dancing in large sweeping motions until the women form an inner circle and the men an outer one. Several men then stage a mock battle or dance competition before the couples rejoin the dance and finish with a step similar to Scottish Highlanders' flings or reels, with a beat of the foot behind the knee, almost a jump step.

Other Galician dances feature pantomime and round dances. Their themes include spring, love, and the beauty of nature. Maypole ribbon dances still are sometimes seen, and one authority mentions a curious dance (Baile de los Petos) performed in processions celebrating the image of the Virgin Mary where each performer carries a container of vegetables, which they throw in the air and try to catch without losing step.

HISTORIC SITES. The Celtic past of **Lugo** can be found in the ceremonial burial mounds nearby. The area also has Roman ruins of a forum, temple, baths, aqueduct, and city walls from ca. A.D. 200. Many gates and watchtowers from the Middle Ages still survive, and the cathedral of Santa María is a copy of the one at Santiago de Compostela, in this case begun in 1129 but not completed until the late eighteenth century. It has a plateresque altar by Cornelis de Holanda (ca. 1530), a chapel dedicated to the local patron saint (St. Froilan, an early bishop), and an adjoining cloister. The churches of San Francisco and Santo Domingo also are richly appointed.

Elsewhere in the province, directly north of Lugo, **Mondoñedo** has a thirteenth-century cathedral with a baroque façade, Romanesque portal, and medieval rose window. The interior is filled with art, including a carving of the Madonna that originally hung in St. Paul's cathedral in London before the English Reformation. The diocesan museum has paintings by El Greco, Zurbarán, and Tiepolo. In addition, the monastery of San Martín de Mondoñedo is one of the oldest pre-Romanesque buildings in Spain, but its church is pure Romanesque. Further northwest, almost to the coast, the Santa María del Campo, also Romanesque, is in **Vivero**, while the Cistercian convent of Santa María in **Meira**, not far southwest of Lugo, is a mixture of Romanesque and Gothic architectural designs.

Much further south of the provincial capital, the monastery of San Vicente del Pinto in **Monforte de Lemos,** begun in the tenth century, has often been remodeled. El Colegio del Cardinal, a late sixteenth-century church, is a plain Renaissance-era structure. In the southeastern section of the province, **Piedrafita** has the remains of many buildings, all built from the eighth to eleventh centuries. Even more isolated, **Samos** contains the Benedictine monastery of San Julián, typical of large medieval institutions built to house pilgrimage visitors.

CUISINE. The cold and rainy climate favors warm dishes such as *caldereta de pescado* (fish stew), *conchas de peregrino* (fried ham-and-cheese sandwiches with an outer layer of bread shaped like a scallop shell), or *empanadas gallega* (a meat or fish pie with onions, peppers, and tomatoes).

The recipe for fish stew, prepared all over Spain but a staple in Galicia, follows.

CALDERETA DE PESCADO

2–3 lbs. sea bream, sea bass, or hake	1 tsp. paprika
	1 bunch parsley, chopped
1 lb. mussels or clams	1 sweet red pepper
6 prawns	2 pinches grated nutmeg
1 onion, chopped and sautéed	4 whole peppercorns
2 cups water	1 small hot pepper, cut
4 Tbs. olive oil	1 cup sherry

Cut fish into small pieces, scrub shellfish, and add both to onion and water. After the dish comes to a boil, add remainder of the ingredients. The stew should simmer for a half hour or more.

ORENSE (Ourense)

VITAL STATISTICS. Pop., 411,339. Area, 7,273 sq. km. Capital and diocesan see: Orense. The province is the southernmost Galician province between Lugo to the north and Portugal to the south, Pontevedra to the west, and León and Zamora (Old Castile) to the east. The climate is very wet on the west coast, but dry in the south and east. The topography of Orense is primarily that of an inland rough plateau divided by the Miño and Sil rivers.

ECONOMY. The main industrial activity is lignite mining, while a large agricultural sector produces grapes, corn, and other grains. The province ranks fourth highest in foreign emigration.

HISTORY. (Auriense [Roman]). Celtiberians settled the towns of Orense on the Miño River and Ribadavia, while the Romans founded Burgas as a spa. The two cultures clashed often, and disorder continued into the later Suevi and Visigothic periods until the Muslims destroyed Orense in A.D. 725. No lasting occupation occurred because León and Asturias campaigned in 794 and 886 to keep alive a Christian identity, but a Norman/Viking incursion in 970 and a campaign by Almanzor in 987 added to the chaos.

By the eleventh century, Orense was the object of rivalry between Sancho II (1065–72) of Castile and his brother, García of Navarre, who had established a court at Ribadavia. Their struggle proved indecisive, but Orense became a focal point again when Teresa, daughter of Alfonso VI of Castile and wife of the late count Henry of Burgundy, defended her court at Coimbra (Portugal) against the Castilian queen, Urraca I (1109–26). Teresa saw Galego-speaking Orense as a crucial linguistic homeland and a physical bulwark against Castile, but the frontier battle converted Orense's provincial nobility into Castilian military agents against the new Portugal. The Lemos family acquired major properties and a castle at Castro Caldelas, while Sancho López de Ulloa, the conde de Monterrey, rebuilt the town and bestowed the family name on it in the fifteenth century. Ribadavia's domination came from the large nearby estates of the local bishop and the conde de Ribadavia, who built a castle in the town to supervise his properties. Nobles eventually controlled 630 of the 700 benefices in the province, and while their power weakened somewhat when the English invasion of 1386 supported the new Avis dynasty of Portugal, they were always able to negotiate directly with the Castilian monarchy. As a result, Orense never developed a place in the Cortes of Castile and was only indirectly represented by Zamora on occasion, an awkward arrangement that itself ended in 1623. Direct representation did not begin until the liberal era in the nineteenth century.

Without a voice in social life or foral privileges of any type, peasants became increasingly downtrodden. The failure of uprisings by peasant brotherhoods in the mid-fifteenth century caused many peasants to be deported or to emigrate in search of new opportunities. High taxes and the *foro* system, which drove up rents and multiplied masters, blighted the area. Travelers described peasant poverty in Orense as so extreme that life consisted of little more than a crude hut, ragged clothing, and a few potatoes. To add to the misery, when Portugal freed itself from Philip II's inheritance in the seventeenth century, adjacent Orense provided the locale of a lengthy and bloody guerrilla struggle lasting until the Spanish War of Independence.

Little land was secularized during the liberal era in the nineteenth century. In fact, Orense and Lugo had the two lowest totals of property transfer because ecclesiastical lands long ago had fallen into noble possession.

Land scarcity sent rents higher than normal crop returns could cover, and the terrible famine of 1853–54 reached its worst levels here. The province's peasantry once again resorted to migrant labor, and large gangs of Galician reapers (*segadores*) and binders (*rapaces*) were a common sight in the Spanish countryside.

Like most of Galicia, Orense voted moderately left and regionalist during the Second Republic, but elements of the Falange rushed into the area from Old Castile when the civil war broke out and held the province during the first few days until General Mola's army arrived. The province saw no further fighting and in the postwar period followed the common pattern of rural depopulation.

LITERATURE. The major figure in the eighteenth-century Spanish Enlightenment, Padre **Benito Jerónimo Feijóo** (1676–1764), born in Orense, spent his career at the University of Oviedo in Santander. His *Teatro Crítico* (8 vols., 1726–39) and *Cartas Eruditas* (5 vols., 1742–60) triggered major philosophical and political changes. Feijóo's writings can be divided into three groups: (1) articles dealing with science and scientific problems; (2) writings to combat superstition; and (3) philosophical discussions. Feijóo was the first Spaniard to challenge the cherished institutions and superstitions of Spain in a wholesale fashion. While remaining a Catholic, he attacked Scholasticism, false miracles, and the weakness of Catholic education. Having grown up in Orense, he had seen Spanish society at its worst, and he became convinced that changes had to be made if Spain were to survive. In so doing, he became the creator of liberal Spanish scholarship.

The nineteenth-century writer **Manuel Curros Enríquez** (1851–1908) of Celanova, a contemporary of Rosalía de Castro, nearly equalled her as a writer. Obsessed by liberty and critical of political conditions in Galicia, he founded a journal, *Tierra Gallega*, to discuss the region's problems. Two of his best works of poetry, *Aires d'a miña terra* and *O divino Sainete*, utilized the ancient regional language to discuss contemporary problems. **Vicente Martínez Risco Agüero** (1884–1963), a main figure in the Galician linguistic revival of the twentieth century, wrote *Historia de Galicia* (1952) to chronicle the region's crises.

The contemporary **Lauro Olmo** (b. 1922) of El Barco is a writer and dramatist who has protested the poverty and injustice of post–civil war Spain in novels and plays such as *Ayer, 27 de octobre* and *El gran sapo*. *La camisa* (1962) is set in a working-class district and discusses emigration as a reality and a problem of Galician life.

The important Galician regionalist magazine *Nós* was active in Orense from 1920 to 1936. It encouraged Galicians to write in Galego. In the process, the magazine rediscovered many facets of regional culture.

CUSTOMS AND SOCIETY. Traditional dress in Orense was somewhat eccentric. Men wore long dark coats buttoned or laced from the waist to the neck and secured on the outside by a sash of spun wool. The umbrella that all Galicians carry here was replaced in Orense by a light wooden paddle that provided some protection from the rain when held over the head, but also served as a weapon, since the top side had small bladelike projections. Women wore simple shirts with wide, long sleeves, gathered at the wrist. Plain ankle-length wool skirts, bell-shaped aprons, and faded flannel capes completed their wardrobe. The only real color came from large triangular head scarves tied with a bow on the top of the head.

HISTORIC SITES. The cathedral of San Martín in the provincial capital of **Orense** contains an unusual star-shaped dome, beautiful doors, and rich appointments in several of the chapels. There are six other large churches, a Roman bridge over the Miño, a useful archaeological museum, a fountain that taps hot springs, and an extensive old town.

The northern part of the province is the site of the Santa María Convent, built in the twelfth century but so ornately reconstructed in the sixteenth century that guide books call it the "Escorial of Galicia." The southern town of **Celanova** contains the important monastery of San Salvador, built between the sixteenth and eighteenth centuries. Slightly southwest of Orense, the twelfth-century convent of Santa María is in **Montederramo,** and the church of San Pedro de Rocas, also twelfth century, is in **Esgos.**

In the west, **Ribadavia** has the primitive Romanesque churches of San Juan and Santiago, the more elaborate residence of the condes de Ribadavia, and a profusion of churches and monasteries once supported by the condes' charity.

CUISINE. The food is similar to general Galician cuisine, but *empanadas* (pastries) are very popular. These pies may be filled with minced beef and pumpkin, pork and apricot, or tongue and cider.

MINCED BEEF AND PUMPKIN EMPANADA

1 pie crust	⅛ lb. raisins
¼ lb. ground beef	1 Tbs. sugar
½ lb. canned pumpkin	½ tsp. ground cloves
¼ lb. pine nuts or blanched almonds	½ tsp. cinnamon

To make 1 pie, cut pie crust into circles about 4 inches in diameter. Cook ground beef until done. Simmer pumpkin, then put in blender with the other ingredients except pie crust. Do not mix long. Roll into balls and wrap in pie crust; bake for 10–12 minutes at 400°F.

Viticulture is important. Ribeiro produces a good white wine, and *aguardiente* is a grape by-product made from distilling grape pulp to produce a strong brandy.

PONTEVEDRA

VITAL STATISTICS. Pop., 859,897. Area, 4,495 sq. km. Capital: Pontevedra. Diocesan see: Túy. The province, smallest of the Galician region, runs along Portugal's northern border on the south. The Miño River (called Minho in Portuguese) forms the border for forty-seven miles as it flows southwest. Orense and Lugo are on the east, and La Coruña is to the north. The Atlantic coast on the west is punctuated by fjordlike rías.

ECONOMY. Industrial employment comes from the coal mines of León run by the Minero Siderúrgico de Ponferrada. Tin is smelted by Metalúrica de Estano. Fishing remains important, and Vigo is the second-largest Spanish commercial fishing port. Citroen Hispañia's plant in Vigo, owned by Peugeot Citroen, is the central development of a duty-free zone created in 1964 to attract foreign investment. The province ranks number one among all Spanish provinces in foreign emigration.

HISTORY. (Pontis Veteris [Roman]). The original Celtiberian population, touched by Phoenician and Greek traders, fell to the Romans, who settled between the Lérez and Tomeza rivers and at Vigo (Vicus Spacorum) after the Cantabrian War and ruled the district from Braga (now Portugal) until A.D. 212, when Caracalla designated it as Nova Citerior Antoniana of the province of Gallaecia.

Suevis displaced the Romans with the collapse of the empire, but were themselves displaced by the Visigoths, who made Túy the provincial capital and bishopric in 675. Muslim warriors reached Vigo by 716, destroying the Túy bishopric. Asturias did not recapture Túy until Ordoño (850–66), but Almanzor raided Vigo during the late tenth century, Ulfo the Dane led Viking raids in 1032, and Almoravids plundered the area as late as 1115.

Annexation of Pontevedra by Castile in 1137 under Alfonso VIII did not eliminate the last Muslims from the border region until troops from Santiago de Compostela intervened in 1170 and created a military base. The bishopric of Túy was reestablished in 1249. Over the next three centuries, development of maritime trade brought prosperity, but the English ravaged Atlantic commerce in 1585, 1589, 1596, 1702, and 1719. The port, made into a fortified harborage in 1617, experienced severe damage in the battle between English/Dutch and French/Spanish fleets during the War of Spanish Succession in October 1702. In the late eighteenth century, colonial free trade helped revive Vigo.

France occupied Pontevedra during the War of Independence. Once they were driven out, Vigo became an Anglo-Portuguese possession until 1814 and remained a separate province until 1833. The Partido Galenguista was originally founded in Pontevedra. Conservatism remained strong; José Calvo Sotelo (1893–1936) of Vigo, the leading provincial politician of the

modern period, rose to power during the dictatorship of General Primo de
Rivera as a conservative populist modernizer. Calvo Sotelo's assassination
by the left in Madrid on July 13, 1936, was one of the crucial incidents
that triggered the civil war. The province supported General Franco and
remained outside the area of active combat throughout the war. Vigo's
reward came in 1964 when the Franco regime created a heavily subsidized
industrial zone.

LITERATURE. Early culture is indistinct, but Bishop **Lucas** (ca. 1250),
an early historian, wrote the *Cronicón de España*. **Paio Gómez Chariño**
(1225–95), an admiral in the service of Sancho IV, composed twenty-two
canciones of high poetic quality. Bishop **Prudencio de Sandoval** (ca. 1600)
provides one of the earliest histories in his *Antigüedad de la ciudad e iglesia
de Túy y de sus obispos.*

Ramón María del Valle-Inclán (1866–1936) of Villanueva de Arosa is
the major novelist and playwright of the province and an important modernist writer. He attended university in Santiago de Compostela and lived
for a time in Mexico, eventually settling in Madrid, where he lost an arm
in a fight and in 1929 briefly went to jail for criticizing the dictatorship of
General José María Primo de Rivera. His first work, *Femininas* (1894),
exhibited great hostility toward women, whom he blamed for undermining
traditionalism. His conservative inclination continued in the so-called Carlist trilogy of *Los cruzados de la causa* (1908): *El resplandor de la hoguera*
(1909), and *Gerifaltes de antaño* (1909), graphic studies of the Carlist Civil
War that caused Valle-Inclán to abandon the right.

Beginning with the *Comedias bárbaras*, a trilogy about the tragic Montenegro family (1908–22) that included *Cara de plata* (1922), *Aquila de
blasón* (1907), and *Romance de lobos* (1908), Valle-Inclán moved further
to the left. Perhaps the height of his career came with the four *Sonatas*
novels, named for the seasons of the year, which possess a more romantic
and sensual style than his other works and focus more on Galicia. As he
moved further away from conservatism, the radical novel *Los cuernos de
don Friolera* (1921) and two volumes of the uncompleted *El ruedo ibérico*
cycle anticipated many themes of the later civil war.

In the recent past, **Ramón Cabanillas Enríquez** (1873–1959), a contemporary poet, wrote in Galego. **Julio Camba** (1882–1962) of Villanueva de
Arosa became a noted travel writer. Most recently, **Julián Ríos** (b. 1941)
studied law in Madrid and lived abroad in England and France. His unusual experiments with the Spanish language can be found in *Larva: Bable
de una noche de San Juan* (1983) and *Poundemonium* (1986), a study of
Ezra Pound. He has also written *Solo a dos voces* (1970) with Octavio Paz.

ART. Cornelis de Holanda (ca. 1545) did a sculpture and the façade at
the Santa María la Mayor in Pontevedra. The Regional Museum of Galicia
has an important collection of paintings by Pieter Breughel the Elder

(1525?–69), David Teniers (1610–90), Giovanni Battista Tiepolo (1696–1770), Luis de Morales, Jusepe de Ribera, Zurbarán, and Goya.

MUSIC. One of the earliest Galician troubadours, **Martín Codax** (1250?) of Vigo, wrote *Canciones de amigo*, which set poetry to music using the language of Galego. Unlike those of the French troubadours, his words and music remained simple in form and style, more like folk music than chivalric ballads. The format influenced Alfonso X el Sabio to put together his own great collection of medieval music, *Cantigas de Santa María*, which included more than 400 songs from Galicia. The music made a major departure from the chants of the mass.

CUSTOMS AND SOCIETY. According to Julio Caro Baroja, witchcraft still remains a strong element in the folk beliefs of Galicia. A devil with three horns is said to preside over meetings near Cangas on the feasts of St. John, St. Peter, and the Virgin Mary, sometimes replaced by the mysterious St. Comba, a kindred spirit to the German St. Walpurga. Galician witches treated Saturdays as holy, and many households still believe that olive and laurel leaves are the only way to preserve the home from these evil spirits.

Village thought is dominated by many mythological, religious, and supernatural beliefs. After all, Galicians are considered to be the most Celtic of the Spanish ethnic groups, and consequently have been negatively portrayed as introspective, melancholy, and superstitious. A strong belief in druids and the spiritual properties of fire and water once was not uncommon.

On the other hand, there is a great deal of religious piety as well. In earlier times, on Candlemas Day (February 2, in honor of the Virgin Mary), the siblings and godparents of unbaptized stillborn children scattered hyacinths on church floors so that the spirits of the children would come and play and a priest could bless them.

HISTORIC SITES. The provincial capital of **Pontevedra,** on Lapamán Bay (no longer a commercial harbor due to the silted Pontevedra estuary), contains a great deal of ecclesiastical architecture. The basilica of Santa María la Mayor is an old Romanesque structure rebuilt in the early sixteenth century and heavily decorated with sculpture and a famous crucifix, the pilgrim *Virgen Cristo del Buen Viaje*. The churches of San Francisco, La Peregrina, San Bartolomé, Santa Clara, and the ruined Santo Domingo add to Pontevedra's interest. General secular architecture is done in a handsome eighteenth-century style built after the earthquake of 1755. There is a museum with eight statues from Maestro Mateo's Portal of Glory which were removed from the cathedral of Santiago de Compostela for lack of space after completion of the eighteenth-century western façade.

Nearby villages possess many small monasteries, abbeys, and churches. **Cambados** is a town of palaces, of which the Figueroa, Montesacro, and Bazán are the largest. **Villagarcía de Arosa** has Roman ruins, a small port, and several handsome palaces such as Mirador del Monte and Vista Alegre. **Caldas de Reyes** contains a thermal spa, Roman ruins, and a good deal of Romanesque architecture.

Slightly south of Pontevedra, industrial **Vigo**, a major Spanish Atlantic port and the largest city of the area, has few historic remains other than the castles of Castro and San Sebastián overlooking the harbor. Further south, **Bayona** (formerly Erizana) was the landfall for the *Pinta* after Columbus's first voyage to the Indies. The town has a beautiful setting on the ocean, and the castles of Monterreal and Gondomar dominate the port.

CUISINE. While Vigo is known for dishes such as *vieiras estofadas* (scallops with cured ham and saffron) and *percebes* (barnacles), its most famous food is eel. Here is a recipe for oven-baked eel.

ANGUILA AL HORNO

1 conger or moray eel	2 cloves garlic, whole
flour, salt	1 cup white wine
¼ cup olive oil	1 Tbs. chopped parsley
4 tomatoes, peeled	2 Tbs. blanched almonds, crushed
2 onions, chopped	
4 potatoes, sliced	4 lettuce leaves

Skin and chop the eel and discard the head. Roll the pieces in flour and salt and brown in olive oil. Remove eel from oil and cook tomatoes, onions, garlic, and potatoes in the same oil for 10 minutes. Add the eel and the wine. Bake at 350°F for 1 hour. Before serving, place mixture on lettuce leaves and sprinkle oil, parsley, and almonds on top.

Pontevedra is another center of Galician viticulture and produces *vino verde*, an acidic, young white wine that is very popular here and in Portugal.

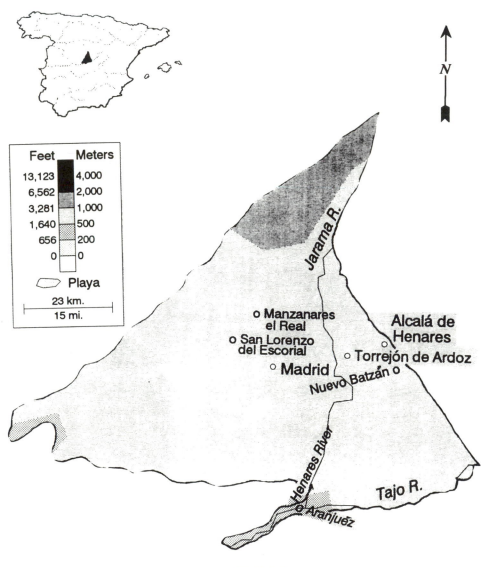

Feet	Meters
13,123	4,000
6,562	2,000
3,281	1,000
1,640	500
656	200
0	0

Playa

23 km.
15 mi.

N

o Manzanares
el Real
o San Lorenzo
del Escorial
o Madrid

Alcalá de
Henares
o
o Torrejón de Ardoz
Nuevo Batzán o

Jarama R.

Henares River

Tajo R.

o Aranjuez

MADRID

Chapter 12

MADRID

REGIONAL CHARACTERISTICS. Pop., 4,726,987. Area, 8,023 sq. km. (606 in the city). Regional capital: Madrid. The region is bordered by Avila and Segovia in Old Castile, and Guadalajara, Cuenca, and Toledo in New Castile.

In the referendum of 1978, Madrid voted 58 to 29 percent for limited autonomy over continued centralism. If Madrid had stayed in Old Castile, the traditional Castilian power base would have remained relatively unchanged. The Partido Socialista Obrero Español (PSOE) was eager to avoid this and used its influence in Madrid to support a more drastic change. A second vote on February 25, 1983, narrowly confirmed the decision to make Madrid an autonomous region.

The regional flag of Madrid is a solid scarlet field with seven white stars set in two rows.

Madrid ranks second among the regions in personal income. It has remained the national capital.

--- *MADRID* ---

VITAL STATISTICS. Pop. and area: see above. Provincial capital and diocesan see: Madrid. As national capital and largest city of Spain, the region of Madrid, while small in physical size, contains fifteen adjacent urban concentrations. Higher education is offered at the huge University of Madrid, the new University of San Pablo, a large technical school, and the University of Alcalá de Henares not far east of Madrid.

ECONOMY. Madrid contains 12.4 percent of Spain's total population. A focal point for foreign investment and headquarters of about 45 percent of all large national companies, the city is a center for the clothing industry, food wholesaling, tobacco manufacturing, and assembly of trucks (Renault) and automobiles (Simca and Dodge by Chrysler-Barrieros Diesel in suburban Villaverde).

Other important sectors include electronics and telecommunications, finance, the arts, and retailing. Telefónica, the government communications monopoly now being privatized, is Madrid-based. So is the cinema industry; the largest studio in Spain is just outside the city. The Spanish central bank, Banco de España, and the state-run Banco de Crédito Agrícola, Banco de Crédito Industrial, Banco de Crédito Local, and Banco Hipotecario de España operate from the capital. Madrid is an insurance center and home of the largest Spanish stock market, established in 1831. National retailers include Galerías Preciados and El Corte Inglés.

HISTORY. (Magerit [Arabic]). Muslims created Magerit about A.D. 900 as a northern defensive outpost for Toledo. It fell into the hands of Alfonso VI of Castile in 1083 and was renamed Madrid. St. Isidro the Farmer, a twelfth-century peasant whose ideal Christian character, liberality toward the poor, and miracles led to his canonization in 1622, is the patron saint of Madrid.

The town's central position attracted trade. It also attracted Enrique III, crowned in 1390, the first Castilian monarch to rule from its precincts. Fernando and Isabel removed the walls in 1474 to expand the town. At about the same time, Cardinal Francisco Ximénez de Cisneros (1436?–1517) established the Universidad Complutense in Alcalá de Henares to provide a cultural center.

Felipe II (1556–98) made Madrid the national capital in 1561 by constructing the Escorial palace on its outskirts as the first fixed residence of the Castilian monarchy. The project did not end until 1584, just as imperial and domestic problems began to overwhelm the Hapsburg dynastic goal of restoring a universal Roman Empire. In the seventeenth century, only the palace of Buen Retiro, built for Felipe IV by his favorite, the conde-duque de Olivares, reached completion.

The Bourbon inheritance of Spain led to a new era of construction: a new royal palace in the city, the Biblioteca Nacional, the Real Academia de Historia, and Real Academia España, all of which possessed a unified architectural style. Distinguished public spaces such as the Plaza de la Independencia, Puerta de Alcalá, Retiro Park, and the Plaza del Sol in the heart of the city opened up the crowded streets. In 1819, inauguration of the famous Prado Museum created one of the world's greatest art galleries.

The Prado area soon saw the construction of the Cortes building, the Ateneo Científico y Literario (a leading intellectual club), and several luxurious hotels.

As Madrid continued to grow, the Paseo de los Recoletos and its extension, the Paseo de la Castellana, took on a more bourgeois appearance and created the Alcalá district, a center of wealth and the first neighborhood to receive gas and electricity. In 1910, the construction of a new shopping street, the Gran Vía, revitalized the San Bernardo district at the center of the city. A decade later, a new national university opened on the northwestern edge of the city, connected by a metropolitan subway system that provided low-cost transportation.

Politics changed more slowly. Francisco Silvela (1845–1905) of Avila, a conservative ally of Antonio Cánovas del Castillo, dominated central Castilian politics and controlled patronage in Madrid, but when he inherited the premiership in 1899 he was dismayed to see his career ruined in the aftermath of the Spanish-American War. The city, once almost exclusively composed of government officeholders, absentee landowners, and the gentry, changed socially into an early twentieth-century industrial metropolis, attracting poor peasants from as far away as Galicia and Andalusia. In 1889, the major Spanish labor organization, the Unión General de Trabajadores (UGT), left its headquarters in Barcelona to relocate in Madrid, and its political counterpart, the Partido Socialista Obrero de España (PSOE), developed a strong constituency in central Castile.

In the 1920s, the impact of the Russian Revolution, inflation, and unemployment caused political protest to sweep the city. Intellectual life became far less traditional during the military dictatorship of General José María Primo de Rivera. The Second Republic (1931–39) put Madrid on center stage in a national drama of change.

Two figures, Manuel Azaña y Díaz (1880–1940) and José Antonio Primo de Rivera (1903–36), dominated opposing sides. Azaña, an essayist and reviewer, became premier in 1931, fell in 1933, but returned as head of the Popular Front in 1936 and manipulated his way into the presidency of the Republic a few months later. Primo, son of the former dictator and founder of the fascist Falange movement, brought cleverness and a genuine desire to modernize Spanish society to the limelight, but he never overcame his father's reputation or suspicions that he represented totalitarian Germany and Italy. Azaña lost control of events and became increasingly unimportant, while Primo, arrested in the spring of 1936 prior to the outbreak of civil war, was executed on November 20, 1936. Francisco Largo Caballero (1869–1946) of Madrid became the first socialist premier of Spain on September 4, 1936.

Madrid remained under siege by the Franco forces from October 1936 until March 1939. Air attacks began on August 28, 1936, but the communist Dolores Ibarruri, "La Pasionaria," declared ¡No Pasaran!—"They shall not pass!"—and a civilian army of workers strengthened the city's defenses. Franco's Army of the South reached the University of Madrid campus on the southwest edge of the city in early November, where it encountered the International Brigades (a volunteer force raised by foreign communist parties), who joined other republican regiments in defending the city. The pitched battle of November 12–20, costly to both sides, was the last major struggle within Madrid itself, although the city's siege made life unbearable during the remainder of the war.

Franco emerged victorious in April 1939. He treated Madrid with suspicion, ringing the city with military bases. Life did not improve until international recognition of the regime in 1953, when the Cold War made accommodation possible. New international credits promoted construction, and the heavy industrial sector, aided by the Instituto Nacional de Industria, made millionaires out of such entrepreneurs as Eduardo Barreiros, who built a large truck-assembly plant near Madrid.

By 1956, economic prosperity led to new demands from students and intellectuals for freedom, culminating in major university closures, which continued periodically for more than a decade. This "bunker" period grew more defensive as protest became a torrent of violence, most spectacularly when Franco's vice president, Admiral Luis Carrero Blanco (1903–73), was assassinated outside a church in central Madrid on December 20, 1973. His successor, Carlos Arias Navarro (1908–89), a *madrileño*, tried tentatively to decrease tension by considering post-corporative reforms and moving away from authoritarianism.

Franco died on November 20, 1975, setting the stage for the constitutional monarchy of Juan Carlos to begin wholesale democratic renovation. In 1979, Madrid elected as mayor an independent socialist, Enrique Tierno Galván (1918–86). The city changed rapidly, particularly developing new museums, and was designated by the European Community as European cultural capital of the year in 1992.

The future, impacted by regional autonomy begun by the Constitution of 1978, may see the role of Madrid deemphasized in education and the arts. Development of regional institutions, such as the regional universities already operating, could result in a revival of local arts and scholarship outside the national capital.

LITERATURE. Medieval poetry in Madrid consisted of the *serranillas*, which used everyday songs of watchmen and shepherds as songs for important occasions. Galician poetry was important at the time when Juan Ruiz (**Archpriest of Hita**) of Alcalá de Henares (1280?–1350?) wrote *Libro de Buen Amor*, the first great medieval poem in Castilian that follows a set of characters from birth to death. Many verses deal with love and passion, but the work also contains a miscellany of other material about periods of Ruiz's own life or incidents he had observed, somewhat like *The Canterbury Tales*. Main characters include the amusing Trotaconventos, a go-between, and don Carnal, "Sir Flesh." Unlike later Spanish literature, the *Libro* has a pagan quality that reflects medieval popular life.

For a time in the early sixteenth century, imaginative literature took second place to serious works of theology and history. Cardinal **Francisco Ximénez de Cisneros** (1436–1517) of Torrelaguna, confessor to Isabel the Catholic, cardinal primate of Toledo, and founder of the university at Alcalá, established the polyglot bible project, the Complutensian Bible, as it was called. The work made careful translations from the various biblical languages of the New Testament. **Gonzalo Fernández de Oviedo y Valdés** (1479–1557), a soldier and chronicler who took part in the reconquest of Granada as well as the Italian wars, traveled six times to the New World and wrote *Sumario de la natural y general historia de las Indias*, his famous early history of the New World. Another poet and soldier of Madrid, **Alfonso de Ercilla y Zuñiga** (1533–94), composed *La Araucana* (1569–90), an epic poem that celebrated the Spanish victory over the Araucanian Indians of Chile, an early work introducing the *indio* theme into Spanish letters. **Francisco de Figueroa** (1536–1617) of Alcalá, poet-friend of Cervantes, used many Italian poetic devices to improve sixteenth-century Spanish poetry.

The Golden Age of Spanish letters centered in Madrid. **Lope de Vega Carpio** (1562–1635) essentially invented Spanish drama. His active and memorable life included several episodes of personal scandal that caused him to be barred from the city for short periods, and he also survived the Spanish Armada.

These tempests provided good drama, because he wrote more than 500 plays and poems on many different themes, including history (*La dragontea* [1598], for instance, about Sir Francis Drake and the Spanish struggle with England); lives of the saints (*El divino africano* [1608?], a biographical drama about St. Augustine); and cloak-and-dagger comedies (*Peribáñez y el comendador de Ocaña* [1613]). In this play, a peasant is ordered into the army by an officer who fancies the peasant's wife. The new recruit finally kills the officer to defend his honor but receives a pardon from the king for being an honorable man.

Lope also wrote romances of chivalry like *El marqués de Mantua* and *La Mocedad de Roldán* (ca. 1615–20); or classics such as *El Caballero de Olmedo* (ca. 1620–25), one of Lope's finest plays, recalling *La Celestina*. He also did satirical epics such as the delightful *La Gatomaquia* (1634) about cats, and social dramas like *Fuente ovejuna* (1613?) about a town's revolt against injustice. Carlos Fuentes believes this last play represents the Spanish discovery of collective action in confrontations between the state and the citizen. Lope's genre of new comedy incorporated a strong knowledge of Spanish history and a great sense of national pride into his work.

Scholars also argue that Lope's poem *Arte nuevo de hacer comedias en este tiempo* (1609) constitutes a manifesto of dramatic principles in the neoclassic tradition. Lyric poetry such as *Romancero general* (1600) and *Rimas* (1602), the prose of the novels *La Arcadia* (1598) and *La Dorotea* (1632), and narrative poetry or epics like *La Filomena* (1621) testify to an incredible productivity, talent, and perspective that made Lope de Vega such a great writer and dramatist.

The Madrid of this era also saw the picaresque novel emerge as a major Spanish contribution to the world of letters. About the anonymous *Lazarillo de Tormes* (1554), John Crow has written that the unknown author made a complete about-face from the pastoral and chivalric novels to draw a portrait of Spanish society seen through the eyes of a shrewd young rogue who goes from job to job finding cruelty, avarice, and opportunism on all sides.

The major contributor to picaresque writing, **Miguel de Cervantes** (1547–1616) of Alcalá de Henares, the son of a poor doctor, studied in Madrid before traveling to Rome to enlist in the Spanish army. Wounded at the Battle of Lepanto on October 7, 1571, he recovered but was captured on the way home and imprisoned for a time. Freed at last, he became a purchasing officer for the Spanish Armada, a tax collector, and finally began writing in Seville.

Cervantes's first novel, *La Galatea* (1585), followed a pastoral style. He also composed plays, of which only two survive: *Los tratos del Argel* (ca. 1580–87), about two lovers captured by Muslim pirates, and *Destrucción de Numantia* (1585), a celebration of Numantia's defenders as the first Spanish heroes. His great masterpiece of a novel, the first volume of *El ingenioso hidalgo don Quijote de la Mancha*, was published in 1605. It describes the various good and bad aspects of Spanish society and burlesques chivalric novels, while at the same time trying to salvage idealism, bravery, loyalty, and a sense of dedication and devotion to high causes in an age when these virtues had all but disappeared. His style expanded upon the picaresque introduced by *Lazarillo de Tormes*.

The word *picaresque* comes from *picante*, a sharp taste or flavor, or *pico*, a sharp tongue, and came to mean tales of crafty, sly, unscrupulous persons who are antiheroes, the antithesis of earlier idealistic, sentimental, and chivalric stories and poems. Even though don Quijote is defeated by the end of the novel, his spiritual idealism lives on.

Cervantes's later works include the twelve *Novelas ejemplares* (1613), divided into short romantic novels and novels of customs told against backgrounds of the Orient, England, and Spain with liberty and honor as their main themes. *Persiles y Sigismunda* (posthumously published in 1617) is a complicated fantasy novel set in northern Europe about lovers whom fate confronts with unusual trials and dangers. In 1614, when a false second volume of *Don Quijote* was published by another author, Cervantes was forced to write his own sequel (1615). In this second volume, Sancho and don Quijote appear less as opposites of idealism and practicality than as having absorbed something of each other in themselves. While Quijote's creative imagination is dead, his Christian ideals persevere. The work can be read as a supremely romantic story of individualism, a philosophic conflict between idealism and realism, a great comic portrait, or a masterpiece of moral and ethical behavior. The diversity of these interpretations gives some indication of the book's greatness.

Cervantes's contemporary, **Francisco de Quevado y Villegas** (1580–1645), became a leading poet/novelist of the seventeenth century and an enemy of Góngora. Quevado began his career in Madrid but spent more time in Salamanca and Alcalá. His literary style of *conceptismo* makes heavy use of paradox and ambiguity. He is perhaps best known for his own picaresque novel, *Historia de la vida del Buscón, llamado Don Pablos, exemplo de Vagamundos, y espejo de Tacaños* (1602). The novel, a bitter social satire, was fueled by Quevado's Stoicism. He worshipped the Roman Stoic Seneca, and an ascetic, moral tone pervades much of his writing, particularly in *Sueños*, a series of five visions (1606–22) of Quevado's contemporaries being punished for their sins in hell. His poetry defends Spanish values and accomplishments in many works against the despotic and corrupt government of Felipe IV.

Pedro Calderón de la Barca (1600–1681) of Madrid was Quevado's great rival. He rose to prominence in Golden Age drama by writing twelve *autos sacramentales* (one-act religious plays). He also did tragedies such as *El pintor de su deshonra* (1641?), and historical dramas like *El príncipe constante* (1629). In addition, he wrote a comedy of manners in *La dama duende* (1628?), and mythological stories such as *Eco y Narciso* (1632?). His masterpiece, *La vida es sueño* (1635), or *Life Is a Dream*, as it is titled in English, concerns a prince, Segismundo, whose mother dies giving birth to him, frightened by an augury that she would produce a monster. Segismundo's father believes his wife's vision and keeps his son imprisoned until guilt causes him to change his mind. Segismundo, once freed, almost fulfills the augury. He is returned to his cell dressed as an animal, symbolizing brutality and human frailty, but in the end, once again free, he begins to reign as an enlightened prince, a wiser man for all of his misfortunes. Calderón also helped to develop the *zarzuela* format of musical comedy, which turned *pasos* and *entremeses* into folk operettas.

Calderón's many competitors included **Juan Pérez de Montalbán** (1602–38), a playwright and novelist in the circle around Lope de Vega. His play *El príncipe don Carlos* speculates about the role played by Felipe II in his son Carlos's death (1568). Felipe also figures in another of Pérez's works, *Comedia famosa del Gran Séneca de España, Felipe II*, which lampooned the king. **Antonio de Solís y Rivadeneira** (1610–86) of Alcalá de Henares, a historian, playwright, and poet, wrote the *Historia de la conquista de México, población y progressos de la América septentrional, conocida por el nombre de Nueva España* (1684), a popular early history of the conquest of the Americas. **Agustín Moreto y Cabaña** (1618–69), born in Madrid of an Italian family, wrote many novels and plays. *El desdén con el desdén* is the clever story of a love affair conducted by psychological means. **Juan Bautista Diamante** (1625–87), a Madrid playwright of Calderón's school, created more than fifty plays, many of them set in Madrid.

The Enlightenment era concentrated on the theatre. **Ramón de la Cruz Cano y Olmedilla** (1731–94) of Madrid developed the *sainetes* genre of theatre, which dramatized parables, a touch of folk culture very popular during a period of French neoclassicism. However, **Nicolás Fernández de Moratín** (1737–80), a neoclassicist, attacked the Golden Age as folklore. His son, **Leandro Fernández de Moratín** (1760–1828), a prolific dramatist who modernized the Spanish stage and received the patronage of Manuel Godoy and Joseph Napoleon, published *La derrota de los pedantes* (1789), an amusing fictitious battle between former great Spanish dramatists, and also wrote a history of the Spanish theatre, *Origenes del teatro español*. **Juan Pablo Forner** (1756–97), another neoclassical playwright, created the plays *La cautiva española* (1784) and *La escuela de la amistad* (1796) and wrote literary essays in *Exequias de la lengua castellana* (1795) and *Sátira contra los abusos introducidos en la poesía castellana* (1796).

In the nineteenth century, **Manuel José Quintana** (1772–1857) completed a biography of Cervantes and wrote some highly praised poetry. **Antonio García Gutiérrez** (1817–93) rose from very humble origins to become a soldier and, later, a dramatist. His most important work, *El trovador* (1836), became the libretto for Verdi's *Il Trovatore*. Manrique, the *trovador* (troubador), and Count Nuño both love Leonor, who poisons herself rather than marry Nuño. The count has Manrique executed for having turned Leonor against him, but a witch reveals that Manrique was really his brother, whereupon Nuño is left with unspeakable grief. The opera very considerably revises the story. García Gutiérrez also wrote *Juan Lorenzo* about the Germania of Valencia.

Gustavo Adolfo Bécquer (1836–70), one of the century's most important poets, lived in Madrid during several periods of his life. So did Spain's first major woman poet, **Rosalía de Castro** (1837–1885). **Mariano José de Larra y Sánchez de Castro** (1809–37) of Madrid, a romantic essayist/satirist, attacked apathy, corruption, and bigotry in Spanish intellectual life. The Generation of 1898 remembered him as a man who believed in freedom, tolerance, and a new Spain. Larra used a *costumbre* style, obtained from social observation, which stressed realistic description of characters, manners, and customs. His work as a journalist allowed him to comment widely on society in Madrid. His major work, *Macías* (1829), is a tragedy that deals with a love triangle ended by murder and suicide. Ironically, in the aftermath of a love affair gone wrong, he took his own life.

Ramón de Mesonero Romanos (1803–82) wrote essays of social observation similar to Larra's. **Juan Eugenio Hartzenbusch** (1806–80), a half-

German dramatist, achieved great success with his *Los amantes de Teruel* (1835). **José Echegaray** (1832–1916), a liberal minister of finance and founder of the Bank of Spain, also was a popular playwright of such works as *El hijo de don Juan*, *Mariana*, and *Mancha que limpia*. When Echegaray won the Nobel Prize for Literature in 1904, Benito Pérez Galdós criticized the selection as tainted by Echegaray's political connections. Another Nobel Prize winner in 1922, **Jacinto Benavente y Martínez** (1866–1954), a prolific playwright of more than 170 plays, also found great success with *El nido ajeno*, *Gente conocida,* and *Lecciones de buen amor* without winning unanimous critical praise.

In the late nineteenth century, **Manuel Tamayo y Baus** (1829–98), a playwright, modernized the Madrid theatre in *Un drama nuevo* (1867) by introducing new themes and seeking a more direct, realistic style. **Juan Bautista Amorós** (1856–1912), a novelist, criticized political corruption in *Ni en la vida, ni en la muerte.* One of the most important writers, **Benito Pérez Galdós** (1843–1920), wrote most of his novels on themes set in Madrid, especially *La desheredada*, *El amigo Manso*, *Tormento*, and *La de Bringas*. Galdós's first novel, *La fontano de oro* (1870), quickly became a best seller. He then began his *Episodios nacionales* (46 vols.), interspersed by *Doña Perfecta* (1876), *Gloria* (1877), *Marianela* (1878), and *La familia de León Roch* (1879), many of them in the manner of Balzac's *Comédie Humaine* or the works of Dickens and Dostoyevski.

Jorge Ruiz "George" Santayana (1863–1952), a philosopher and essayist educated exclusively in Great Britain and the United States, left Spain for the sake of intellectual opportunity. Santayana taught at Harvard and made his reputation by writing in English about philosophical systems. The civil war sent others abroad, most prominently **Arturo Barea** (1897–1957), whose *The Forging of a Rebel* is a well-known memoir of the civil war published in Great Britain. **Américo Castro Quesada** (1885–1972), a scholar and historian, wrote *La realidad histórica de España* and taught extensively in Argentina and the United States. **José Bergamín** (1897–1983?), a neo-Catholic writer close to Jacques Maritain, lived in Mexico and Latin America after 1939; while **Gregorio Marañon** (1887–1960), a historian and biographer of Olivares, Antonio Pérez, and El Greco, lived his later life in London.

The most politically active radical intellectual of Madrid, **Manuel Azaña** (1880–1940) of Alcalá de Henares, a professor, critic, newspaper correspondent, biographer of Juan Valera, politician, writer of the 1931 constitution, and president of the Second Republic, fled Spain in February 1939 at the end of the war and lived briefly in Paris before his death. **Pedro Salinas** (1891–1951) of Madrid taught until 1936 at the University of Seville. A member of the Generation of 1927, he did translations, reviews, plays, and literary studies, but his poetry won him greatest acclaim. *Presagios* (1923), *Fábula y signo* (1931), and *Razón de Amor* (1936) contain interior emotions, mysticism, and a sensuality unusual in modern Spanish poetry. Salinas lived in the United States from 1936 until his death.

Many others stayed in Spain. **Dámaso Alonso** (1898–1968?), a critic, poet, and philologist, did translations, poetry, and scholarly works. His *La lengua poética de Góngora* won a National Prize for literature in 1935, and some of his later work developed existential themes. **Serafín** and **Joaquín Alvarez Quintero** (1871–1938, 1873–1944) wrote popular dramas, and **Enrique Jardiel Poncela** (1901–52) was an author of nearly forty humorous plays such as *La tournée de Dios* (1932).

José Ortega y Gasset (1883–1955) of Madrid may have been the most famous intellectual not to go permanently into exile. As a philosopher and essayist educated in Spain and Germany, a professor of metaphysics (1910–36), and member of the Generation of 1898, Ortega produced a very large and diverse body of work. *España invertebrada* (1921) summed up attitudes of the Generation of 1898 by urging modernization of Spain along northern European lines. *El tema de nuestro tiempo* (1923) is a philosophic work that argues for life above pure thought. *La deshumanización del arte* (1925) approved avant-garde art as demythologizing the mystery of life. *La rebelión de las masas* (1929) focuses on nationalism as the ideology of the masses, arguing in favor of a European community to decrease the intemperance of nationalism.

Ortega's many other books, articles, and reviews made him a leading European intellectual of the period 1920–40. He initially hailed the Second Republic but then rejected its violence. He left Spain for Argentina, where he spent fifteen years before returning to Madrid. During this time, his reputation was greater outside Spain than in it, and although he maintained a political silence about the regime, he was generally ignored.

During the contemporary era, **Leopoldo Panero** (1909–62), although educated abroad, supported Franco and saw the civil war as a religious outrage. His reply in *Canto personal* (1953) to the criticism the Chilean poet Pablo Neruda made of the right's civil war role in *Canto general* (1950) stirred a major debate. A dissenting voice came from **Alfonso Sastre** (b. 1926), a playwright in the tradition of Camus and Sartre who was frequently censored for chronicling postwar bleakness in *Uranio 235*, *Escuadra hacia la muerte*, *La mordaza*, and many other dramas and films.

A new generation began with **José María Carrascal** (b. 1930), a journalist and novelist whose novel *Groovy* (1973) won the Nadal Prize. Carrascal covered the United Nations in New York City as a journalist for eleven years, and he has written about the United States in *USA superstar* (1973) and *La aventura americana* (1982). His recent work, *La revolución del PSOE* (1985), is a study of modern Spanish politics. **Rosa Montero** (b. 1951), a popular journalist, has written eight books, including such novels as *Cronica de desamor* (1979), *La función Delta* (1981), and *Temblor*

(1990). **Francisco Umbral** (b. 1935), columnist for the newspaper *El País*, writes criticism, history, memoirs, observation, and novels.

Literary *tertulias* (literally, a group that frequently meets in some public place) grew in importance and became a very popular form of exchange during the nineteenth century. Romantics congregated at the Café del Príncipe or the Café del Recreo, while conservatives gathered at the Café de la Esmeralda. Some *tertulias* had their own names, such as La Fontana de Oro, later used as the title of a novel by Benito Pérez Galdós. Spanish intellectuals continued this tradition in the early twentieth century by meeting at the Café Gato Negro.

Film has seen great contemporary growth. **Luis García Berlanga** (b. 1921) did a series of comedies, most especially *Bienvenido Mister Marshall* (1952). **Antonio Bardem** (b. 1922), clandestinely communist, made the critical *Calle Mayor* (1954) and *Muerte de un ciclista* (1955). **Carlos Saura** (b. 1932) depicted life in a Madrid slum in *Los golgos* (1959), a film that was not released in Spain until 1963. He also directed *La caza* (1963), an allegory of the civil war, and a gypsy version of *Carmen* (1983).

An actor of distinction, **Fernando Rey** (1918–94) of Madrid, played the drug baron who outwitted Gene Hackman in *The French Connection*. Son of a prominent anti-Franco general, Rey played bit parts until Luis Buñuel cast him as the lead in *Viridiana* (1961) and *The Discreet Charm of the Bourgeoisie* (1972).

ART. Madrid's role in the Spanish art world began with the Catholic monarchs, whose late fifteenth-century court attracted two foreigners, **Michel Sittow** (Melchor Alemán, ca. 1480) and **Juan de Flandes** (John of Flanders, d. 1526), who brought the northern Renaissance to Spain and inspired later Spanish art. Fernando and Isabel's grandson, the Hapsburg Carlos I, increased the amount of foreign art in Castile by his acquaintance with the art of Brussels and Germany, having grown up in the Low Countries. His liking for the Flemish art of Jan van Eyck and Hieronymus Bosch (1450–1516) formed the basis of the later royal bequest to the Prado Museum. Carlos also influenced other nobles to purchase art from the same sources. The condesa de Mendoza's acquisition, Bosch's *Garden of Earthly Delights*, is now one of the Prado's most popular paintings.

Carlos's son, Felipe II (1556–1598), pursued the royal tradition of buying domestic and foreign art. The artists patronized by Felipe include **Alonso Sánchez Coello** (1531?–88), whose portrait of the *Infante Carlos* (Prado) is particularly important as a historical record; **Gaspar Becerra** (1520?–68), creator of the frescoes at the Prado Palace; and **Titian**, whose *Rape of Europa* (now in the Gardner Museum of Boston) and other works came from a commission by Felipe in 1550 after he and Titian met in the German city of Augsburg. Painters who decorated the monastery of El Escorial include **Juan Fernández de Navarrete** (1540–79; *Baptism of Christ* and the *Martyrdom of St. James*), Sánchez Coello, Luis de Carvajal, and a number of minor Italian painters such as Pellegrino Tibaldi (1527–96), painter of the Escorial cloister's frescoes, and Federico Zuccaro (1542/3?–1609). At the same time, the monarchs continued to collect the art of Titian, Antonio Allegri Correggio (1489–1534), Rogier van der Weyden, Tintoretto, Paolo Veronese (1528–88), Raphael, Bosch, and Robert Campin, the Master of Flémalle (1378?–1444).

During the reign of Felipe III (1598–1621), the king's favorite, Francisco de Sandoval y Rojas, the duke of Lerma, continued to collect art. The conservative Lerma disliked the mannerists, but he patronized the Venetian school (Titian, Veronese, Tintoretto) and contemporary artists like Rubens, who in 1603 visited the Spanish court in Valladolid. The Italian **Bartolomé Carducho** (Bartolommeo Carducci, 1560?–1616) spent most of his career in Spain, not only painting but also writing *Diálogos de la pintura* on art theory and lobbying unsuccessfully to create an academy of the fine arts. He also attracted the Tuscan artist Eugenio Cajés (1574–1634).

The art patron during the reign of Felipe IV (1621–65) was the royal favorite, Gaspar de Guzmán, the count-duke of Olivares. Chief among the artists of this era, **Diego Rodríguez de Silva y Velázquez** (1599–1660) became court painter in 1623 and spent much of his career in Madrid. He shared fame with Peter Paul Rubens, who paid a second visit to Spain in 1628–29. As a result, Velázquez entered a second great period of creation beginning with *Forge of Vulcan* (1630) that did not end until his death in 1660. His work of this period encompasses *St. Anthony Abbot and St. Paul the Hermit* (Prado, 1633), *Surrender of Breda* (Prado, 1634–35), *Baltasar Carlos as Hunter* (Prado, 1636), *Francisco Lezcan* (Prado, 1636–40), *Mars* (Prado, 1640), *Philip IV at Fraga* (Frick, 1644), *Venus and Cupid* (National Gallery, London, 1648), and his masterpiece, *Las Meninas* (Prado, 1656).

Velázquez died five years before the reign of Carlos II, when dismal economic conditions weakened Spanish support for art, although the Seville school filled part of the vacuum and **Luca Giordano** (1634–1705) arrived from Italy for a ten-year stay in 1692, painting frescoes at San Antonio de los Portugués, the Buen Retiro palace, and painting the *Triumph of the Spanish Hapsburgs* over the Escorial's imperial staircase.

In many respects, the real decorative masters of the next period are the **Churriguera** brothers: José (1665–1725), Joaquín (1674–1724), and Alberto (1676–1740), creators of the churrigueresco style that dominated the Spanish baroque. José's major works in Madrid are the church of Nuevo Baztán (1709–13) and the convent of St. Basilio (1717), but he also worked in Salamanca, Cuenca, and Segovia. Joaquín's work is entirely outside Madrid in Salamanca, León, Zamora, and Valladolid. Alberto became the true architect of the family and designed the Plaza Mayor of Salamanca, a work whose dome became the hallmark of the Spanish baroque.

Neoclassicism replaced the baroque in the architectural work of **Ventura Rodríguez** (1717–85) and **Juan de Villanueva** (1739–1811). Rodríguez designed the church of San Marcos (1759), while Villanueva designed the Casa de Infantes and other small pleasure palaces before receiving the commission to draw up the plans for the Prado Museum. In painting, no one surpassed **Francisco de Goya y Lucientes** (1746–1828) of Aragón, who spent most of his career in Madrid. One of the largest collections of Goya's work is at the Royal Palace, where his *Holy Trinity, Man with His Hand on His Breast, An Unknown Man, Christ Bearing the Cross, Holy Family, St. John the Evangelist, Resurrection, Portrait of Jeronimo de Cevallos,* and *Descent of the Holy Ghost* are shown. In addition, the palace collection includes Velázquez, El Greco, and, rare for Spain, Jean-Antoine Watteau (1684–1721).

During the nineteenth century, **Federico de Madrazo y Kuntz** (1815–94), son of a Spanish artist trained in Rome, became the court painter of Isabel II and Alfonso XII. Much of his work is composed of neoclassical, highly polished academic paintings. Later, the best modern Madrid-born artist, **Juan Gris** (José Victoriano González, 1887–1927), began his career in 1904 by abandoning his engineering studies at the Escuela de Artes y Manufacturas to begin painting, almost entirely self-taught. He arrived in Paris in 1906, became friendly with Picasso, and soon pioneered the development of cubism, theorizing that it is better to show a subject from various angles than from the one-point perspective traditional since the Renaissance. His work ranged from shattered forms to synthetic, two-dimensional studies created by a series of free forms. Gris spent his entire career in Paris.

In the twentieth century, the many bullfight scenes and literary illustrations of **José Gutierrez Solana** (1886–1945) influenced the development of a School of Madrid style of painting. **Benjamín Palencia** (b. 1902) continued the leadership of this group of painters by doing modernist landscapes, and **Godofredo Ortega Muñoz** (b. 1905) has produced some strikingly subdued landscapes. Younger artists of note include Antonio Saura, Rafael Canogar, and Manolo Millares.

The major cultural institutions of Madrid include the Real Academia Española, the Academia de Buenas Letras, and all of Madrid's museums. The Prado, one of the world's best art museums, was established in 1819 by Fernando VII in a building originally intended by Carlos III to be a natural science museum. The Prado evolved slowly through the strength of its royal collection. Since 1975, two new museums, the Centro de Arte Reina Sofía and the acquisition of the Thyssen-Bornemisza collection for the Palacio de Villahermosa, have made Madrid a center of modern and contemporary art as well.

MUSIC. The first Spanish opera was performed at the court of Felipe when an unknown composer in 1629 provided music for a one-act play by Lope de Vega. The term *zarzuela* arose when Calderón's *El Golfo de las Sirenas* was set to music and performed in 1657 at the Zarzuela Palace.

Ramón de la Cruz (1731–94) adapted opera to the lyric stage for *zar-*

zuelas in *Briseida* (1768). Composition improved when Felipe V's Italian wife, Isabel Farnesio of Parma, sponsored the Italian composer **Domenico Scarlatti** (1685–1757), son of Alessandro. He wrote many works in Madrid, La Granja, and Aranjuez, including *Spanish Dances, Bourée d' Aranjuez* (Sonata No. 263), and *Symphonie espagnole*, as well as adapting the guitar for operatic music.

Other musicians of this era include **Torres Martínez Bravo** (1665–?) of Madrid, a great Spanish organist who wrote a book on the *canto organo*. **José de Nebra** (1681?–1768) of Madrid composed more than a hundred religious works and turned dozens of plays into *zarzuelas*, including Calderón's famous *La Vida es Sueño*. **Federico Moretti**, a naturalized Spaniard of Italian birth, published *Principios para tocar la guitarra de seis ordenes* (1799) to establish fundamental principles for modern guitar technique.

In the nineteenth century, **Francisco Asenjo Barbieri** (1823–94) of Madrid composed *zarzuelas* such as *Pan y Toros* (1864) or *El barberillo de Lavapiés* (1874) and collaborated with Tomás Bretón of Salamanca to develop a Spanish operatic style. **Federico Moreno Torroba** (1891–1990?) of Madrid composed the opera *La Virgen de Mayo* in 1925. Many of his works, like *Sonatina, Fandanguillo, Arada, Concierto de Castilla*, and *Concierto flamenco*, incorporate the guitar into orchestral music. He also wrote such *zarzuelas* as *Luisa Fernando, La chulapona*, and *La Masonera de Tordesillas*.

Of current note, the soprano **Teresa Berganza** (b. 1935), best known for her operatic roles in the works of Mozart and Rossini, made her 1965 Metropolitan Opera debut in Mozart's *The Marriage of Figaro*. The popular tenor **Plácido Domingo** (b. 1941), born in Madrid, grew up in Mexico before returning to live in Madrid and to star throughout Europe in such operas as *Tosca* and *La Bohème*. He made his New York debut with the Metropolitan Opera in 1968 and has done much in recent years to stimulate rediscovery of the *zarzuela* style of Spanish music.

CUSTOMS AND SOCIETY. *Madrileñas* and *madrileños* traditionally possess the reputation for cosmopolitan sophistication. *Majas* (women celebrated for beauty and grace) and their companions, the *chipero* (an urban dandy), made life in Spain's largest city an exception to the sober rural values elsewhere. Younger women, particularly in the eighteenth and nineteenth centuries, copied the silk dresses and shoes of Andalusian women and added bead embroidery, epaulets, and appliquéd designs to the sleeves and bottoms of their dresses. A chenille overskirt was sometimes worn with silk cord or bead embroidery bodices, and white stockings and low black satin slippers became popular. Mantillas of white lace or black tulle commonly were worn to church and in public.

Men during the same period wore knee breeches and short tight-fitting jackets of brightly colored silk with silver buttons, trimmed with bead work for important social occasions. The ubiquitous red waist sash also had its place in Madrid society, while workingmen wore rough jackets of gray or brown cloth, long trousers, and sometimes a *sajones* (a leather apron), which if one worked as a butcher or construction worker was cut extra long to cover the trousers.

Today women favor extremely stylish woolen suits, modishly tailored, during the cooler months, although this has given way lately to more eclecticism in dress. Males wear blue blazers and gray trousers, which are the uniform of successful Spanish businessmen. For both genders, international style is followed as avidly as anywhere else.

The most popular dance in eighteenth-century Madrid was the *seguidilla*. The music, in ¾ time, begins quietly, with the dancers standing in two rows, facing their partners. The step, similar to the *sevillanas*, uses a heel-beat motion, in which the feet move very rapidly according to the music, which suddenly accelerates, while the rest of the body remains relatively stationary. The stress is on quick movement of the feet, although partners do lock arms and swing rapidly during various parts of the dance.

Today, the year is very full of activity. The annual Madrid book fair takes place from mid-April to mid-May along the Paseo del Prado. The Fiesta de San Isidro in May is a ten-day celebration of folkloric events, street parades, bullfights, and other special events. In August, smaller fiestas of Lavapiés and La Paloma celebrate the summer, and in October an autumn festival attracts premier artistic companies for a series of performances.

HISTORIC SITES. The churches of **Madrid** include the cathedral of San Isidro, begun in the seventeenth century, with a dome, a handsome main portal, and a chapel with the remains of the city's patron saint, St. Isidro. Construction began on a new cathedral, Almudena, in the nineteenth century.

Other major churches include Las Calatrava, with an altarpiece by José de Churriguera, and San Antón, which exhibits a painting by Goya. The basilica of San Francisco el Grande contains an extensive collection of religious paintings including works by Zurbarán and Francisco Bayeu y Subias (1734–95). San Ginés has a collection of small El Greco paintings, and the San Antonio de la Florida chapel has frescoes by Goya, who is buried here. At the Convento de las Descalzas Reales (a former royal palace), an extensive collection of ecclesiastical art and objects includes paintings by Breughel, Rubens, and Zurbarán.

Major ceremonial buildings include the Italian-classical royal palace, whose construction began in 1734 after the old Alcázar had burned. The palace, filled with marble and frescoes by Tiepolo and Bayeu, has thirty ceremonial rooms decorated by Flemish tapestries designed by Raphael and others. In the northwest wing, there are museum rooms with many works by Goya. The library is extensive and there is a royal pharmacy and coach museum. The Almudena Cathedral is next door.

Other ceremonial buildings include the Cortes (1843–50); the hospital de San Fernando (1722); the Royal Theatre (1818–50); Palacio de Lira, owned by the Albas, a private art collection with works of Fra Angélico (1400–1455?), Velázquez, Murillo, Rubens, Rembrandt, and Goya; and the palace of Santa Cruz (1629–34). The beautiful outdoor squares of Madrid include the Plaza de la Cibeles (ca. 1623), Plaza Mayor (1617–19), Plaza de Oriente (1810), Puerta del Sol (ca. 1730), and the Puerta de Alcalá (1778)—all handsome and historic examples of good public architecture and planning.

Of the museums, the Prado is one of Europe's best with thousands of works including major collections of Ribera, El Greco, Velázquez, Goya, and Titian. The nucleus of holdings in the royal collection includes Carlos's collection of Titian, Felipe II and Felipe III's mixture of Titian, Rubens, and Hieronymus Bosch, and the Velázquez collection of Felipe IV. There are works by Raphael, Correggio (1494–1534), Paolo Veronese (1528–88), Albrecht Dürer (1471–1528), Gerard David (1450?–1523), Rogier van der Weyden, Bartolomé Murillo, José Ribera, Zurbarán, and El Greco. East of the Prado, an annex of the collection called the Casón de Buen Retiro now contains Picasso's *Guernica* in a specially constructed facility, although it may yet be moved again.

Modern art is covered by two new institutions. The Centro de Arte Reina Sofia in the former Hospital of San Carlos near the Atocha Station covers a broad range of Spanish (Picasso, Dalí, Miró, Gris) and European modern and contemporary art. The Thyssen-Bornemisza Collection at the Palacio de Villahermosa has important European Impressionist and Expressionist sections with more than 700 paintings purchased in 1993 from the Swiss millionaire art collector, Baron Thyssen, to supplement the Prado's medieval, Renaissance, and early modern strengths. Few European cities have invested in art so seriously, and as a result Madrid is a world art center.

The National Library (Biblioteca Nacional) has huge holdings of rare books. Museums of the Army, the Navy, the National Archaeological Museum, and the Royal Factory of Tapestry (founded in 1721) add to the city's history and culture.

On Madrid's eastern outskirts, **Alcalá de Henares** (Complutum [Roman], Al-Kala-en-Nahr [Arabic]) was the site of the Universitas Complutensis founded by Ximénez Cisneros in 1498. After Alcalá declined, the university moved to Madrid in 1836, changing its name to the National University, but of late Alcalá has obtained the Archivo General Nacional and a new University of Alcalá de Henares. Several of the old university buildings are of a mixed Hispano-Flemish-Mudéjar style somewhat like the Palacio del Infantado in Guadalajara. The great hall of the university has a plateresque façade designed by Rodrigo Gil de Hontañon, while the church of San Ildefonso contains the beautiful tomb of Cardinal Cisneros. At the **Oratorio de San Felipe Neri**, there is a collection of paintings by the

Italian Angelo Nardi (1584–1665?), who synthesized Florentine and Venetian art, and a statue of St. Teresa of Avila. The Archbishop's Palace is ornate with Gothic, Mudéjar, and plateresque details. The neighboring village of **Nuevo Baztán** produced glass and ceramics for José de Churriguera in the eighteenth century. **Manzanares el Real** has a lovely fifteenth-century castle built by the duke of the Infantado, Iñigo López de Mendoza, that is a hybrid fortress/palace. One of its main walls has a Gothic-style gallery appended to it.

South of Madrid on the Tagus River, **Aranjuéz**, once a Muslim town, is the site of a palace built by the grand master of the military order of Santiago. The grounds came into royal possession during the era of Felipe II, but the U-shaped palace remained incomplete until 1765. The handsome throne room and royal chapel have art by Anton Rafael Mengs (1728–90), Mariano Salvador de Maella (1739–1819), Andrea Sabatini (1484–1530), Bayeu, and David Teniers the Younger (1610–90), supplemented by a number of copied frescoes and other pieces. The Casita del Labrador, modeled on the Trianon at Versailles, is a three-storied building completed in 1805 with art by Velázquez, Bayeu, and others. Gardens, fountains, and statues surround both buildings as originally planned by Isabel the Catholic, and the Tagus River is set off to good advantage by the French-style landscaping. High-ranking nobles such as Godoy, Medinaceli, and Osuna also built palaces in the area.

To the west, **San Lorenzo del Escorial** was a tiny hamlet until Felipe II built the monastery, cathedral, and royal palace of San Lorenzo del Escorial in 1560–84 to celebrate the victory over the French at St. Quentin in 1557. The huge edifice originally followed a design by Juan Bautista de Toledo (d. 1567), trained by Michelangelo in Rome. Juan de Herrera (1530?–97) continued the project after Bautista de Toledo's death. The geometry of his reductionist treatment of classical architecture is called *estilo desornamentado* (plain style). Herrera's reputation comes from his development of this virtuoso style.

The main façade of the Escorial is 680 feet long and 528 feet wide. Inside the main portal stands a courtyard facing the basilica (the royal chapel) which has a dome nearly 300 feet high. Herrera designed the church's interior, set off by statues by Pompeo Leoni (1465?–1522), Pelligrino Tibaldi (1527–96), and Luca Giordano (1634–1705) and more than forty paintings by sixteenth-century Spanish painters.

Beneath the altar of the basilica is a crypt for the burial of the royal family. This pantheon of kings has tombs placed in tiers with Carlos I, Felipe II, III, and IV on one side and the queens who gave birth to monarchs on the other. Beyond it is the pantheon of the *infantes* (members of the royal family who did not rule). The sacristy is to one side of the basilica with vaulted frescoes and paintings by Ribera, El Greco, and Titian. Between the church and the south end of the Escorial are the cloister and chapter house of the monastery. In front of the monastery is Felipe II's library (perhaps the most beautiful room in the complex) and his quarters. The north side contains the royal palace built for the Bourbons in the eighteenth century.

To the north, another memorial built by a much later ruler, Francisco Franco, Valle de los Caidos (Valley of the Fallen), commemorates Spanish Civil War victims.

CUISINE. All regional cuisines are well represented in Madrid. In season, *reo en salsa de azafrán* (salmon trout in saffron sauce) or *espárragos aliñados en jamón* (asparagus and ham) are served. *Ensalada de bogavante con endivias* (ham, lobster, and endive salad), *tartaletas de atún* (tuna tartlets), *champiñones rellenos de jamón* (ham-filled mushroom caps), *croquetas de pollo* (chicken croquettes), and *merluza en hoja de Grelos* (fish wrapped in Swiss chard leaf) are only a few of the *tapas* served.

Ham and chicken croquettes are made as follows:

CROQUETAS DE POLLO Y JAMÓN

½ lb. ham, shredded	pinch of pepper, salt, cinnamon, nutmeg
½ lb. chicken, shredded	
1 Tbs. shortening	2 eggs, beaten
½ onion, chopped	⅓ cup bread crumbs
1 Tbs. flour	¼ cup olive oil
2 cups chicken stock	

Cook the ham and chicken in shortening, mixed with the onion. Add the flour, chicken stock, pepper, salt, cinnamon, and nutmeg. Remove the mixture from the heat and add half of 1 beaten egg. After the mixture has cooled slightly, roll out into small balls, about 1 inch in diameter. Dip in remaining beaten egg and then in bread crumbs and cook in hot oil until crispy on the outside.

Chapter 13

MURCIA

REGIONAL CHARACTERISTICS. Pop., 957,903. Area, 11,314 sq. km. Regional capital: Murcia. The region is located south of Valencia, north of Almería (Andalusia), and east of Albacete (New Castile), with the Mediterranean as its eastern boundary. The Río Segura runs west to east across the region from the Sierra de la Tabilla to the tourist-filled Mediterranean coastline.

While Murcia is similar to Almería or Albacete in economy and culture, the region was heavily repopulated with Christian peasants after the Reconquest. Cartagena (pop. 172,751) became the center of the Spanish navy and a large port and naval base, while the city of Murcia (pop. 288,631) grew into an agricultural center. This close relationship with Castile became apparent during the referendum of 1978 when the issue of Spanish reorganization caused 51 percent of the electorate to vote in favor of continued centralized rule from Madrid and 43 percent to vote for limited autonomy. *Murcianos* worried about the decline of Cartagena as a Spanish naval center and the lingering rivalry of Murcia and Cartagena for regional control. Extensive talks eased some of these problems, and the region approved autonomy on June 9, 1982.

The Murcian regional flag is deep scarlet or light purple with two rows of four castles in the upper left-hand corner and a diamond shape formed by seven yellow crowns in the bottom right-hand corner.

Murcia ranks thirteenth in personal income among the regions.

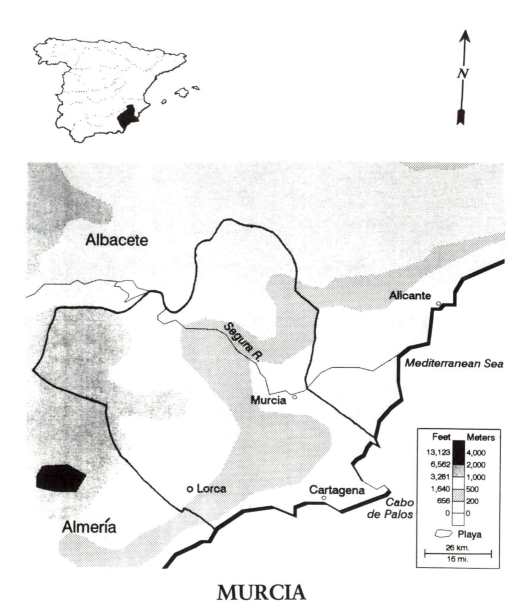

MURCIA

MURCIA

VITAL STATISTICS. Pop. and area: see regional characteristics above. Diocesan sees: Almería, Guadix, and Cartagena. The region's major university is located in the city of Murcia. Much of the coastal area is a fertile *huerta*, or truck gardening area.

ECONOMY. Murcia is one of the three fastest-growing areas in Spain. The climate is mild enough to grow spring vegetables and almonds, the region's leading economic product. Miles of greenhouses (*invernaderos*) or sand-bed fields covered by plastic sheets (*enarenado*) insure protection against occasional frosts. The food industry of Murcia provides 5 percent of the total Spanish food production.

Lead, zinc, silver, and sulphur are mined in medium-sized operations, and there is an oil refinery at Escombreras. The once-important raw silk industry has declined and other industry is minimal, although efforts are being made to attract the electronics industry.

HISTORY. (Medina Mursija [Arabic]). Large prehistoric populations of Turdetani people (Tartessian or Capsienses culture, probably from North Africa) and indigenous Bastetani and Iberians lived a settled agricultural life in the Segura Valley. The Iberians attracted the attention of writers such as Livy and Polybius, who may have named the peninsula for them. The tribes' prosperity also attracted trading colonies of Phoenicians, Greeks (early temple remains can be found at El Cigarralejo), and Carthaginians. Cartagena (Carthago Nova [Carthaginian]) passed to Rome after the Second Punic War, and thousands of settlers surged into Carthaginensis, a Roman province that included Murcia, La Mancha, Valencia, and parts of Old and New Castile. The area, linked by low passes to the Guadalquivir Valley, became a base for Roman expansion west into Andalusia.

The Vandals, a tribe originally from Hungary but dispossessed into North Africa, conquered the southeast in A.D. 427, infiltrating early Christianity with the Arian heresy, a belief that Christ was a prophet rather than the son of God. Byzantium sent soldiers, missionaries, and priests to occupy the area, ca. 550–630. Visigoths replaced the Vandals, but Agila (549–55) and Recared (586–601) did not gain the Byzantine fringe of coastal territory from Cartagena to Cádiz until the mid-seventh century. St. Isidoro, early archbishop of Seville and a major figure of early Spanish Catholicism who came from Carthago Novo, presided over the eradication of Arianism.

Less than a century later, the region fell to the Arabs in 714 and became a semiautonomous Muslim principality, prosperous from agriculture, fishing, and silk production (mulberry trees are still common). Prosperity lasted through the reign of Abd ar-Rahman III, but the subsequent period of petty

Muslim principalities produced instability. The poet Ibn 'Ammar ruled for a few years (ca. 1078), even briefly using Rodrigo Díaz, "El Cid," as a mercenary to defend Murcia against the harsh Berber Almoravid regime. By 1130, another emir, Sayf-al-Dawla (son of Zaragoza's last Muslim ruler), merged Granada and Murcia into a coalition to destroy the Almoravids, but his death in 1146 allowed a Muslim adventurer, Muhammad ibn Mardanish (El Rey Lobo, "King Wolf" to the Christians), to seize Valencia and Murcia briefly and, with Castilian aid, overthrow the Almohads.

Mardanish's death in 1172 led to renewed Castilian and Aragonese raids. In return for aid from Fernando III of Castile, Jaume I of Aragón agreed to stop the Aragonese advance in Valencia at Alicante, but in fact he dismembered Murcia in 1255–56 and settled 10,000 Catalans in the area before allowing Castile to continue the war against Granada. Castile moved the Church's see from Cartagena to the city of Murcia and parcelled out large estates to religious orders or knights such as Pedro Fajardo, the marqués de Los Vélez, whose family controlled Murcia for a time almost like an independent kingdom. Fernando and Isabel, the Catholic Kings, quarreled with another great landowner, the marqués de Villena, and confiscated his property from Cuenca to Almería for the establishment of crown lands. In 1520, nobles of the area protested these acts by joining the unsuccessful Comuneros revolt in Castile.

In 1567, the Muslim revolt of Alpujarras in nearby Granada caused long-term labor shortages in Murcia. After the English sacked Cartagena in 1588, defense needs forced royal investment in fortifying the coast against anticipated raids by the English or Turks. Epidemics also disrupted several periods of the seventeenth century, and the labor shortage became particularly critical after the final Muslim expulsion of 1609.

The next period belonged to Murcia's most important national politician, José Moñino, the conde de Floridablanca (1728–1808). Son of a Murcian mercantile family, he had a brilliant career at Salamanca that led to membership in the Council of Castile in 1764. Two years later, his defense of Carlos III after riots in Madrid caused the expulsion of the Jesuit Order and the curtailment of citizens' rights to bear arms. Floridablanca remained a leading state minister for more than a decade, playing an important role in creating a national banking system, the establishment of free trade, and the development of the Amigos del País as a constituency for national economic change.

The War of Independence left Murcia relatively untouched, and agricultural expansion grew rapidly in the nineteenth century. Liberals secularized more than 40 percent of the region's properties by selling large tracts of crown lands and ecclesiastical estates to urban merchants, whose domination of local politics wavered between modernization and fortune hunting. The most ruthless political boss, Juan de la Cierva (1844–1911), rose to become an unscrupulous minister of the interior under Antonio Cánovas del Castillo in Madrid.

Murcian peasants migrated to Barcelona to find employment, sometimes bringing back schemes of revolution. The peasants supported the Second Republic and the Popular Front and kept Murcia loyalist during the civil war. The republican fleet, after murdering most of its officers, did not leave the harbor of Cartagena despite heavy bombing attacks until it put out to sea to surrender to the French on March 5, 1939.

Immediately after the civil war, the Franco regime carried out many political executions in Cartagena, subjecting the area to military justice. The foreign minister of Franco's early cabinets, his brother-in-law Ramón Serrano Suñer (1901–89), came from Cartagena and was the most important Murcian in the new government. He supported the Axis, but when Franco inclined toward the traditionalist Carlists over the fascist Falange, Serrano left office in 1942. In later years, his politics evolved considerably, and he often opposed his brother-in-law on many issues.

The 1960s brought substantial change to Murcia through tourism and agricultural prosperity. No rural area in Spain has modernized as thoroughly.

LITERATURE. The region has a relatively large body of literature. **St. Isidoro** (560?–636) and his older brother Leandro, born in Cartagena, spent their careers in Seville. Leandro became the archbishop of Seville and fought the Arian heresy during the reign of King Leovigild. Leovigild had executed his own son, Hermenegild, for renouncing Arianism, but Leandro forced Leovigild to beg forgiveness. This demonstration of the Church's power caused Leovigild's successor, Reccared, to convert to Christianity in 587. Isidoro succeeded his brother as archbishop of Seville in 601 and enforced monastic purity and ecclesiastical discipline, putting the Church alongside the state for the first time. He presided over two Councils of Seville in 619 and 633.

Isidoro wrote *Originum seu etymologiarum libri XX*, a vast, sometimes uncritical body of encyclopedic work that recounts ancient history and interprets classical authorities as best he could. The work also includes elements of grammar, rhetoric, history, mathematics, medicine, and theology. Isidoro also wrote *De natura rerum* on natural law and *Chronica majora*, a history of the world from creation to A.D. 615. Hindered by the substandard state of letters and scholarship of the Romano-Gothic age, he nevertheless strengthened the linguistic and legal tradition of post-Roman Spain.

Christian writing later continued with **Pablo de Santa María** (d. 1435), a converted rabbi and bishop of Cartagena who used biblical sources to refute Jewish theology. His son, **Alfonso de Cartagena** (1384–1456), dealt with both historical and religious matters in his own work.

During the Golden Age, **Ginés Pérez de Hita** (1544?–1619?), a historical novelist, wrote *Historia de los bandos de los Zegríes y Abencerrajes, cab-*

alleros moros de Granada, de las civiles guerras que hubo en ella . . . hasta que el rey don Fernando el quinto la ganó (1595), a classic account of Granada's fall to the Christians in 1492. **Francisco de Cascales** (1564–1642) of Fortuna, a historian and literary essayist, wrote the official history of Murcia. **Diego de Saavedra Fajardo** (1584–1648) of Algezares, a political writer and diplomat who lived for a long period in Italy, wrote two studies of statecraft, *Introducciones a la política y razón de Estado del Rey Católico don Fernando* (1631), a discussion of Counter-Reformation political ideas, and *Empresas políticas o Idea de un príncipe político christiano representada en cien empresas* (1640), a reply to Machiavelli.

Modern writers include **Joaquín Arderíus Fortún** (1890–1949?) of Lorca, a novelist and journalist who developed surrealistic techniques for Spanish fiction. **Carmen Conde** (b. 1907) of Cartagena in 1979 became the first woman elected to the Spanish Royal Academy. Married to the poet Antonio Oliver Belmás, she has created poetry, books for children, essays, and memoirs that fill more than fifty volumes, of which *Las oscuras raíces* won the 1953 Elisenda Moncada Prize. *Soy la madre* won the 1979 Ateneo de Sevilla Prize, and *Canciones de nana y desvelos* the 1987 National Prize for Children's Literature.

José Luis Castillo Puche (b. 1919) of Yecla, a novelist, Catholic moralist, and professor at Universidad Complutense of Madrid, wrote the novel *El perro loco* (1965), which relives the civil war from the perspective of a dog. *El vengador* (1956) is the story of a Franco official who returns to the village of relatives murdered in the civil war seeking vengeance only to find his own family's sins too repugnant to avenge.

Other Spanish works written about the area include Ramón Sender's *Mister Witt en el cantón* (1935), a story of the First Republic of 1873 in Cartagena.

ART. The region has produced three artists of some importance. **Pedro Fernández** (ca. 1480–1521?) designed the cathedral in Girona. **Nicolas Villacis** (1616–94), a local artist, was trained by Velázquez. **Francisco Salzillo** (1707–83), the son of an Italian sculptor who had settled in Murcia, specialized in making figures for Holy Week processions, becoming particularly skilled at humanizing sacred personages.

MUSIC. One of the greatest *zarzuelas, Las Labradoras de Murcia* by Antonio Rodríguez de Hita of Palencia, captures Murcian local life for the Spanish imagination. In a scene at the close of the first act, a violent storm is about to strike a silkworm nursery. The women who work at the nursery, believing the superstition that silkworms will die of fright if they hear thunder, block out the noise of the storm by doing a folk dance set to some of the best music ever composed for the *zarzuela*.

The folk songs of Murcia that Rodríguez drew upon are called *murcianas, tarantas,* or *cartageneras.* At one time they were known as *fandango grande* or *jondo grande,* catching the attention of European musicians such as Wolfgang Amadeus Mozart (1756–91), Luigi Boccherini (1743–1805), Rimsky–Korsakov, and Cristobal Halffter (b. 1930). When danced, they are related to the fandango. The tempo of the music and dance is in triple quick time (6/8, but occasionally 3/8 or 3/4). The dance was originally a dance of courtship, but for much of the modern period solo versions, with performers dancing in high-heeled shoes as in flamenco, have taken place in concerts and theatres.

The *paso doble* (sometimes written as one word), a lively form of dance music played in march time, may have originated in Murcia. One theory holds that the *paso doble* originally came from military music of the War of Independence, adapted later in the nineteenth century as music for the *fiesta brava*.

CUSTOMS AND SOCIETY. While Murcia today is typically Spanish, earlier travelers to the region noted an eastern character in its folk life, including dances in which the male had two female partners, and the use of flowers to make all environments gardenlike in appearance. Another example of eastern influence was the *jota murciana* (sometimes called the *parranda*), the local folk dance, almost dervish in its intensity, probably of Middle Eastern origin, accompanied by guitars, mandolins, tambourines, and castanets. But perhaps it is more accurate simply to say that Murcia resembles Andalusia in its music, public life, and fiestas, while being more lush, arable, and prosperous.

Traditional dress was simple. Women wore short but full colorful cotton skirts, white blouses trimmed in lace, and a silk scarf across the shoulders. Urban women used satin as a dress material and wore white linen stockings, elaborate mantillas, and filigree jewelry. Both genders of all classes protected themselves from the summer sun by head coverings that fell to their shoulders. Males wore *zaraguelles*, the white pants that characterize the eastern coast of Spain. Jackets were usually short and tight-fitting, almost like a matador's.

The spring fiesta in Murcia usually begins on Easter Monday in March or April and lasts for five days. The *bando de la huerta* is a mock battle that uses flowers for ammunition, while the *entierro de la sardina*, or burial of the sardine, is held at midnight on the last day of the fiesta as a symbol of spring's arrival.

HISTORIC SITES. The cathedral of Santa María in **Murcia,** built in the late fifteenth century, occupies the site of an earlier mosque. Flood damage during the mid-eighteenth century led to the addition of a baroque façade to the previously Gothic and plateresque structure. The Salzillo is the city's art museum, and there is also a provincial archaeological museum.

Elsewhere in the province, **Lorca,** which is on the road to Almería southwest of the provincial capital, has dozens of churches, one of which, Santa María, is a former mosque. The other major city of the region is **Cartagena,** some distance southeast of Murcia on the Mediterranean coast. It is a major Spanish naval base, with several historic churches and an archaeological museum.

CUISINE. The fruits and vegetables of Murcia, cheap and delicious, include dishes such as stuffed artichokes and *potaje a la murciana*. Here is the recipe for the latter.

POTAJE A LA MURCIANA

½ lb. red beans	½ onion, chopped
1 quart water	3 tomatoes, chopped
1 cup green beans, sliced	2 cloves garlic, crushed
1 cup rice	salt and pepper to taste
2 Tbs. olive oil	

Soak the beans overnight and then boil in a quart of water with sliced green beans until almost done. Add the rice and cook until the rice is partly tender. Meanwhile, sauté onion, tomatoes, and crushed garlic in olive oil. Combine with the rice and beans and cook together for 3 minutes. Add salt and pepper to taste.

Seafood, especially shellfish such as *langostino*, is also available. Prawns in vinaigrette sauce are prepared as follows:

LANGOSTINOS A LA VINAGRETA

¼ onion, chopped	12 large prawns
1 hard-boiled egg, chopped	1 Tbs. wine vinegar
pinch of saffron	1 small glass brandy
½ cup olive oil	

Prepare the sauce by adding onion, hard-boiled egg, and saffron to the olive oil. Cook the prawns in vinegar over a low flame for no more than 10 minutes, adding the brandy at the end. Combine sauce and prawns and let stand for 1 hour before serving.

The wine industry in Murcia clusters around Yecla, where a powerful red wine is produced from Monastrel grapes grown in chalky soil. The Jumilla district is smaller, but San Isidro and La Purísma are two of the largest Spanish wine-making cooperatives.

Chapter 14

NAVARRE
(Navarra, Nafarroa)

REGIONAL CHARACTERISTICS. Pop., 507,367. Area, 10,391 sq. km. Capital: Pamplona. The region is located south of France, north of La Rioja and Zaragoza, east of the Basque Provinces of Gipuzkoa (Guipúzcoa) and Araba (Alava), and west of Zaragoza and Huesca (Aragón). In Euskara, the Basque language, Navarre is called Nafarroa.

Navarre, an ancient northern kingdom with a large Basque population, was loyal to Franco in the Spanish Civil War and rejected Basque nationalism. Its support of Francoism won it back special privileges lost during the nineteenth century. In the post–civil war era, the regional government used its control of fiscal revenues and economic policy to attract foreign industry, thereby diminishing the rural nature of Navarre.

During the debates on the Constitution of 1978, many saw Navarre as a positive example of what regional government could do for other areas if they were given the opportunity to conduct their own affairs. The debate skirted recriminations concerning favoritism shown to Navarre by the Franco regime and ignored the nineteenth-century furor over Carlism. But in the referendum of 1978, the Navarrese themselves voted 49 to 36 percent against becoming an autonomous region. Navarre is a conservative area, and Francoism had remained popular.

Many Basque voters presumably voted no to express their wish to join the rest of their community. In subsequent negotiations, a provision to allow Navarre the future right of voluntarily incorporating with the adja-

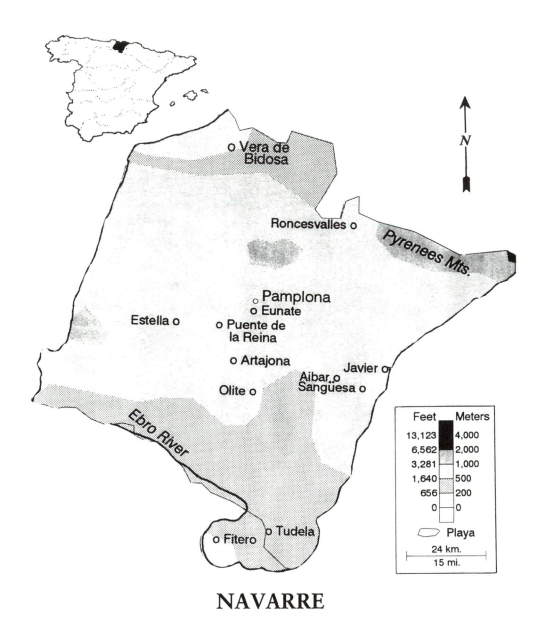

Feet | Meters
13,123 | 4,000
6,562 | 2,000
3,281 | 1,000
1,640 | 500
656 | 200
0 | 0

Playa

24 km.

15 mi.

NAVARRE

cent Basque region won back the Basque bloc, but non-Basque and conservative voters forestalled this eventuality by voting in favor of Navarrese
autonomy. It is fair to say that both groups sought to preserve ancient foral
traditions and economic prerogatives in different ways.

On August 10, 1982, the regional government was created as the Foral
Community of Navarre. The flag of Navarre is red with an elaborate shield
and crown outlined in the center in yellow.

Navarre ranks fourth among the regions in personal income.

PAMPLONA (Iruñea)

VITAL STATISTICS. Pop. and area: see above. Diocesan see: Pamplona,
pop., 183,125. Navarre, whose name has disputed origins, is dominated
physically by a series of upland valleys and heavily forested mountain terrain. The Basque portion of the region's population generally lives north
of Pamplona. The private Catholic University of Navarre, run by the Opus
Dei, an active new order, was established in the postwar era by Josémaría
Escrivá y Balaguer y Albás. A new public university of Navarre also has
been established by the regional authorities.

ECONOMY. By percentage, Pamplona has the largest industrial work
force of any city in Spain. It is the Detroit of the Spanish automobile industry, with the Swedish manufacturer Scandia operating a large truck assembly plant and Seat/VW replacing British Leyland in building automobiles. Potash mining has declined despite the regional government's efforts to support this once-important industry. Dairying is active, but large-
scale agriculture is handicapped by rough topography.

HISTORY. (Nafarroa [Basque]). Vascones, or Basques, living in tribes
such as the Varduli, inhabited the area and created villages like Azilian, ca.
800 B.C. Silver mining attracted the Romans, and Pompey founded Pamplona (Pampelo) in 75 B.C. The Vía de la Plata (silver road) linked Pamplona to the Ebro Valley, and public works such as the aqueduct of
Lodosa-Alcanadre served Calagurris (Calahorra), but social conditions remained primitive, and peasant revolts became common toward the end of
the Roman Empire. Many Basques moved west and north into what is now
Gipuzkoa and Bizkaia.

Pamplona fell to the Visigoths in A.D. 466, the Franks from the north in
542, and the Muslims in 718. Charlemagne passed through the area and
levelled the walls of Pamplona fighting the Muslims, but his Basque allies
rebelled in the battle of Roncesvalles Pass, driving the Franks from northern
Navarre. For a century or more, the Hispano-Roman *muladíes* of lower
Navarre, generally known as the Banu Qasi (family name of the leading
clan), remained dominant.

In the early ninth century, a kingdom of Navarre emerged under the leadership of a Basque noble, Iñigo Iñiguez (Iñigo Arista in Spanish). Iñiguez ruled from 824 to 852, but his dynasty lasted only until the death of his monk grandson in 905 and was replaced by the Jiménez family, relatives who had been powerful warlords. Sancho Garcés, who ruled from 905 to 925, annexed Nájeres (now Logroño, La Rioja) in 923. His son, García Sánchez I (925–70), played a crucial role in the victory over Córdoba at Simancas in 939. The fourth Jiménez ruler, Sancho III el Mayor (1004–35), inherited a realm badly damaged by Almanzor's violent attacks in 999. Unless Navarre expanded, he believed it could not survive, and thus to prevent annihilation he annexed northern Aragón for a time and made the Basque region seigniories.

An even greater opportunity came in 1028 when Sancho el Mayor's nephew, García, the young king of Castile, was murdered. Spurred by imperial ambition, Sancho III claimed Castile and defeated León for its possession in 1034, but his territorial expansion had few long-range benefits because the king's will divided his empire among his different sons. This pivotal mistake allowed the Castile of Fernando I (1037–65), much closer to the military/religious frontier, to replace Navarre as the most important Reconquest principality once Islam began to retreat.

The Jiménez dynasty died out in 1076, and a long period of monarchical instability ensued. Aragón held the crown of Navarre for fifty years. While Alfonso I saved the kingdom from Islamic counterattack by the Almoravids, when he died without an heir in 1134 local nobles chose García Ramírez (1134–50), a great-great-grandson of Sancho III. But once again the native monarchy lasted less than a century until the childless Sancho VIII's death in 1234. Then for the next three hundred years, five French groups of rulers married into the aristocracy of Navarre. In order, they were the Champagne (1234–1305), Capetian (1305–1327), Evreux (1328–1464), Foix (1464–1483), and Labrit (1483–1512) dynasties.

The sudden French appearance on the northern Pyrenees border, provoked by the Albigensian heresy in neighboring Provence, caused the new, powerful national monarchy of Paris to covet Navarre as a border kingdom well worth having. The first product of the French marriages was Teobaldo I (1234–53), the son of Sancho VIII's sister Blanche and a French noble, the count of Champagne.

To guard against royal absolutism and French centralism, nobles and churchmen adapted the Fuero General de Navarra in 1238 from earlier Visigothic laws. Strong local codes controlled tax collection, political representation of the villages, and the justice system. Navarre developed a limited monarchy of contractual kingship that gave the monarch judicial but not absolute power over the noble class. Because of these safeguards, the kings were never able to force the Navarrese nobility to accept full integration into France.

The *fueros* permitted relative peace and prosperity until 1425, when the only surviving daughter of the Evreux dynasty, Blanca, married Juan, younger brother of Alfonso, the Trastámara king of Aragón. Blanca died in 1441, leaving Juan as regent, but in 1458 he inherited the throne of Aragón as Juan II. By Blanca's will, their eldest son, Carlos of Viana, was named heir in Navarre, subject to his father's blessing, which Juan refused to give. Having married again to a Trastámara, Juan had developed an imperial scheme to reincorporate Navarre into Aragón. He imprisoned Carlos of Viana and perhaps had him murdered, while allowing Carlos's sister Leonor, married to the French noble Gaston, count of Foix, to act as regent.

Not until the death of Juan II of Aragón in 1479 did Leonor's son, Francisco (1479–83), occupy the throne of Navarre, but within four years he was dead of tuberculosis. Succeeded by his fifteen-year-old sister, Catherine de Foix, the wife of Jean d'Albret (whose domains north of the Pyrenees included Béarn, Gascony, Perigord, and Limousin); both Catherine and Albret were inattentive to Spanish politics and found themselves challenged in 1512 by Juan II's younger Trastámara son, Fernando II the Catholic, king of Aragón and regent of Castile, who defeated his half-sister's forces and thus realized his father's grand design of incorporating Navarre and Aragón. But already old and ill, he faced intense European diplomatic difficulties that made him grow suddenly unsure of Aragón's ability to hold the area. In 1515, perhaps hoping to create a larger "Spain" to withstand the French and Austrians, Fernando II willed Navarre to Castile.

The Castilians defended Pamplona against French invasion in 1521 but ceded the northern region of Basse Navarre to the Albrets in 1530. France continued to claim Navarre until the next century, when a Spanish offensive against Labourd and Narbonne in 1636 caused the French favorite, Cardinal Richelieu, to besiege Fuenterrabia in nearby Guipúzcoa and contemplate the invasion of Navarre. In 1659, the Peace of the Pyrenees gave Roussillon, part of Cerdaña (or Cerdagne), and other northern Catalan territories to France in exchange for title to Navarre.

During this long crisis, several factors strengthened the Navarrese character and allowed it to endure. Fervent religious belief had been profound ever since missionary activity by the French Cluniac Order had established the faith. Navarrese had participated in the Albigensian crusade, the seventh and eighth crusades in the Holy Land, and in battles with Islam, once holding Athens for a time in the 1380s against the Turks. In the sixteenth century, the founder of the Society of Jesus, Ignacio Loyola of Gipuzkoa, badly wounded at the battle of Pamplona with the French in 1521, incorporated the militant Catholic spirit of Navarre in his *Spiritual Exercises*. One of his original band of seven Jesuits, St. Francis Xavier (1506–52), a Basque from the castle of Javier, near Pamplona, met St. Ignacio while studying at the University of Paris and ultimately became the apostolic nuncio for Asia in 1541, traveling to Goa, Ceylon, Malacca, Kyushu, and Kyoto, Japan, before dying in China.

The other factor that served the Navarrese well, particularly after the shock of Fernando the Catholic's bequest of Navarre to Castile and the Hapsburg inheritance of Spain in 1517, was its foral privileges. Navarre held itself aloof as a separate realm, even numbering the kings "de Castilla y Navarra" differently than in Madrid. The only linkage between Madrid and Pamplona came from creation of a viceroyalty, the first outside the Americas. Viceroys handled interstate matters in conjunction with a Diputación del Reino, the executive committee of the Navarrese Cortes, governing in accordance with the foral laws.

By the eighteenth century, this arrangement proved so durable that not even the Bourbon abolition of traditional laws in Aragón, Valencia, and Catalonia could be extended to Navarre. The Bourbon monarchy sought only to integrate Navarre's elite into national politics. Miguel de Múzquiz y Goyeneche, the marqués de Villar de Ladrón and conde de Guasa (1719–85), who held several important ministries under Carlos III, is a good example of a Navarrese in a national role.

The Diputación del Reino vigorously defended home rule, but in 1792 Carlos IV's royal favorite, Manuel Godoy (1767–1821), committed Navarre without its approval to war against France. Godoy made Navarre a focal point of French military efforts in 1794–95 and again from 1807 to 1813. Navarre formed one of the first guerrilla forces in the War of Independence, but these irregulars evolved into conservative rebels when the Constitution of Cádiz in 1810–12 referred to Navarre as integral Spanish territory and raised fears that the *fueros* might be destroyed and the Church disestablished. Navarre welcomed the return of Fernando VII as king but supported his brother, the traditionalist Carlos María Isidro, when Fernando sought liberal financial assistance in 1827.

Carlos was excluded from succession in 1830. A year later, the birth of Fernando's daughter, Isabel (ultimately Isabel II, who ruled from 1843 to 1868), provided an heir to the throne, bringing to light a confused and secret revision of succession laws more than forty years earlier that had ended Bourbon prohibition of female inheritance. In 1833, Fernando's death brought demands that Isabel step aside in favor of Carlos—hence the term "Carlists." The queen regent, María Cristina, turned to the liberals as the only other force strong enough to uphold Isabel's rights, a situation Navarre saw as a threat to their ecclesiastical and foral liberties. Secretly aided by the anti-liberal Prince Klemens von Metternich of Austria, the army of Tomás de Zumalacárregui supported Carlos in the First Carlist War and staged a brilliant hit-and-run campaign that turned the north of Spain into a guerrilla zone, with Navarre as its heartland. Carlists continued to win even after failing to take Bilbao in 1835, but when Great Britain and France came to the aid of the central government, tipping the balance of power, the Truce of Vergara ended the civil war on August 31, 1839.

Two years later, the region was punished for being on the losing side in the civil war. The Ley Paccionada abolished the realm of Navarre as a special administrative unit and made it into a regular province, without interior customs barriers, led by a civil governor. But only a generation passed before rebellion flared into the Second Carlist War (1873–76), again unsuccessful. In its wake, regular administrative law almost completely replaced the *fueros*, but while violence declined, the Asociación Euskara de Navarra, founded by Arturo Campión and Juan de Iturralde, continued to promote the traditional monarchy and close church-state ties, not even subscribing to the laic politics of Sabino de Arana Goiri's Basque Nationalist Party in neighboring Bizkaia.

In 1932, Carlist leaders such as the conde de Rodezno, Tomás Domínguez Arévalo (1883–1952), refused to accept the Basque Nationalist Party's acceptance of the radical Second Republic as the price of Basque autonomy. In many respects, this division between the Basque Provinces and Navarre created a Basque Ulster: an armed minority in violent disagreement with the revolutionary nationalism of the larger community. Rodezno's paramilitary Requetés, an armed force that had been training for several years, quickly became a major force, playing an important role in Gipuzkoa and Zaragoza shortly after the outbreak of civil war and also marching on Madrid in a campaign led by the Pamplona garrison commander, General Emilio Mola Vidal (1887–1937), Franco's northern commander until his death in a 1937 air crash.

After the war's end, during a time of heightened authoritarian centralism, Franco rewarded Navarre by reinstating the Ley Paccionada of 1841, restoring many of the old foral laws. What had once been unacceptable now was not; local collection of national taxes on a basis favorable to the region aided recovery by promoting a new program of industrialization. Isolation diminished, the economy improved, and Carlism submerged into the conservative Unión del Pueblo Navarro. Debate on the constitution in 1977–78 came as the worldwide oil crisis hurt economic development and the RUMESA banking scandal closed the Banco de Navarra. In the 1980s, the PSOE and Unión Centro de Democrático made political inroads into the formerly ultraconservative constituency.

LITERATURE. Much of Navarre's literature is ancient. The anonymous ballad *Chanson de Roland* chronicled the French defeat at Roncesvalles in 778 by the Basques. As a chivalric epic, it contains great exaggeration: Roland manages to kill 100,000 of his enemies with only 60 men, and Archbishop Turpin slays 400 with his own sword. In fact, the story evolved from a series of chronicles dealing with Charlemagne's attack on the Muslims in defense of Christianity, his apocryphal pilgrimage to Santiago de Compostela, the Moors' sneak attack on the return trip, Roland's behavior as a just knight, and Archbishop Turpin's reputation as a heroic cleric. Over time, the oral tradition that kept the story alive for so long added many legendary details. Despite these inaccuracies, the *Chanson de Roland* is one of Europe's most famous medieval ballads, rivalled in Spain only by the ballad of El Cid.

Judah Ha-Levi (1075?–1140?) of Pamplona, educated in Granada, is remembered as one of the most important poets and authors of Spain who wrote in Hebrew and Arabic. His work *Kitâb al-huyya* justified Judaism on the basis of revelation. **Rodrigo Ximénez de Rada** (1170?–1247) of Puente la Reina, the archbishop of Toledo, compiled the *Historia gothica, vel De rebus Hispaniae*, covering Spanish history from A.D. 400 to 1200. He also did histories of the Romans and the Muslims in Spain. **Benjamin de Tudela** (d. 1185?), a Jew from Tudela, wrote the geography of the twelfth-century Arab world. Like a Jewish Marco Polo, he visited Hebrew communities throughout the Near East in travels that began ca. 1165, but his story was not published until 1543.

The Golden Age was relatively minor in Navarre. **Piarres de Axular** (1556–1640?) was an early prose writer who used the Basque language Euskara, while **Antonio de Eslava** (b. 1570?) of Sangüesa wrote novels in Castilian, including one in which Shakespeare may have found inspiration for *The Tempest*.

In later centuries, **Juan de Palafox y Mendoza** (1601?–69?) of Fitero, a biographer and religious scholar, is best remembered for his life of Santa Teresa de Avila. **Francisco Navarro Villoslada** (1818–95) of Viana, an active Catholic and Carlist, founded *El Pensamiento Español* as a Carlist organ of opinion. His major novel *Amaya, o los vascos en el siglo VIII* tries to imitate the style of Sir Walter Scott in treating the history of Navarre as a romantic epic.

The major figure in Carlist affairs, **Arturo Campión y Jaimabón** (1854–1937) of Pamplona, published his ringing defense of the *fueros, Consideraciones acerca de la cuestión foral y los carlistas en Navarra* (1876), just at the end of the Second Carlist War. He headed the Integrist Party, a neo-Carlist political organization, but found time to do grammars, linguistics, history, and fiction. He also presided over the Academia de la Lengua Vasca and wrote a long series entitled *Euskariana* that solidly linked Carlism and Basque culture, just as his *Gramática de los cuatro dilectos literarios de la lengua euskara* (1884) revitalized the language. His novel *Blancos y Negros* (1898) dramatized the Carlist-liberal struggle, while his important history, *Origenes del pueblo eskaldún* (1892?), defended the *fueros*, Basque identity, and extreme conservatism.

During the twentieth century, **Amado Alonso** (1896–1952), a philologist who studied with Menéndez Pidal, the premier Spanish linguistic expert, did a definitive study of the region's linguistic roots. Also of note, **Santiago Ramón y Cajal** (1852–1934), one of Spain's greatest scientists, was a professor of anatomy and histology in Zaragoza, Valencia, Barcelona, and Madrid. His studies of the human nervous system's morphology led to the cell theory of biology and a share of the Nobel Prize for Science in 1906.

Novels about Navarre by outsiders include *Doña Perfecta* (1876) by **Benito Pérez Galdós**, a portrait of a fanatical Carlist; *Guerra carlista* by **Ramón María del Valle-Inclán** (1866–1936), an early Carlist sympathizer who set most of this work in Navarre; and the international best seller, *The Sun Also Rises* (1926) by **Ernest Hemingway**, which popularized the running of the bulls in the Fiesta de San Fermín and used Pamplona as background for a story about worldly expatriates after World War I.

ART. The first wholly Gothic structure to be built in Spain, the Hospice of Roncesvalles, begun about 1209, followed French ecclesiastical architecture very closely. Good examples of the later French Gothic in Spain are the cathedral of Pamplona and the church of the Holy Sepulcher at Estella, particularly in the design of the portals of the cathedral and chapter house. The carvings surrounding these doors express greater naturalism than the earlier Gothic.

Pamplona also became a center of late medieval linear painting which created schematic backgrounds in monochrome and vividly painted foreground figures of expressive humanity. One of the best linear painters, **Johannes Oliveri** of Navarre, did the murals of the refectory in the cathedral of Pamplona (now in the Museum of Navarre). The important baroque altarpiece of the church in the Trinitarian monastery in Pamplona came from a design by **Juan Rizi** (1614–85) carried out by **Francisco de Herrera** the Younger.

MUSIC. One of Spain's premier violinists, **Pablo Martín Melitón Sarasate y Navascuez** (1844–1908), began as a child virtuoso. After studying at the Paris Conservatoire, he became a specialist in the works of Saint-Saëns as well as writing many works of his own for the violin.

CUSTOMS AND SOCIETY. Early Basque social organization in Navarre was constituted by clans divided into lineages. They intensified in response to the military incursions of Visigoths, Franks, and Muslims by creating the office of *buruzagi*, an official responsible for protection of property and defense of the land. In time, this office evolved to provide Navarre with its monarchy and aristocracy, unlike Vizcaya, where a similar "struggle of the bands" in the fifteenth century ran into royal Castilian interference. The differing outcomes can be explained by a greater outside threat to Navarre and religion's force behind the Navarrese monarchy in aiding clan unification. After the monarchy died out in 1234, the Church and foral law held Navarre together, making both the essential ingredients of Navarrese nationalism.

Religious traditionalism can be felt very strongly at Pentecost, forty-nine days after Easter, when a procession of black-clad penitents wearing hoods makes a pilgrimage up the pass to Roncesvalles in celebration of the battle of 778. A different type of antiquity can be found in the week-long Fiesta de San Fermín, held in early July each year in Pamplona. The running of the bulls through the streets of Pamplona, one of the world's most dangerous public sports, almost pagan in character, begins each morning at 7 A.M. during the week of the fair with a skyrocket marking release of the bulls into the streets. The significance of participating in such an act depends heavily upon explanations based on *machismo* (exaggerated masculinity), Spanish fatalism, or the explosive aftermath of religious festivals. In any case, San Fermín is considered the most exciting Spanish fair and the high point of the *fiesta brava*'s year.

HISTORIC SITES. The ancient capital of Navarre, **Pamplona,** has a large and richly decorated cathedral (1527), one of several religious buildings to occupy this location. The Gothic cloisters and interior with large arches, transept, and high nave contrast with an ugly eighteenth-century Greco-Roman exterior by Ventura Rodríguez (1717–85) that does not match its two Gothic towers. The particularly fine Leyre coffer in the cathedral is an outstanding example of the early Hispano-Moorish period. Another attraction is the Museum of Navarre, which contains historical, archaeological, and art sections. There is a Goya here and also one at the Palacio de la Diputación of Fernando VII.

Elsewhere in the province, north near the French border, **Roncesvalles** provided the site of the historic battle between the French and Basques celebrated in *Song of Roland*. The town church, Real Colegiata, exhibits the Madonna of Roncesvalles, a sacred icon of Navarre. There is also the monastery of San Salvador de Leire built for Sancho III, with many relics of the early Navarrese monarchy.

To the west, near Gipuzkoa, is the commercial center of **Vera de Bidasoa.** Not far southwest of Pamplona, **Puente la Reina** is a small village whose church of Santiago commemorates the Camino de Santiago, which comes from the north at the village to join the main east-west route along the foothills of the Ebro Valley to Santiago de Compostela. Close by, slightly to the south, is **Artajona,** a walled town and home of the hermitage of Nuestra Señora de Jerusalém, a statue of the Virgin Mary supposedly captured by crusaders in the Holy Land. Further west, **Estella,** of Roman origin, was also on the pilgrimage route. Nine churches can be found in the area, including San Piedra de la Rúa (San Piedra of the Route), the twelfth-century San Miguel, and the Santuario de la Virgen del Puy with its treasury of religious articles. Three monasteries and a convent cluster in Estella, and St. Francis Xavier lived at the Casa de los Santos as a child. The house of Carlos VII, pretender during the First Carlist War (1834–39) who made Estella his capital, is now a Carlist museum. Just outside Estella is Nuestra Señora de Irache, an ancient monastic hospice for pilgrims to Santiago de Compostela.

South of Pamplona, **Olite** (the Roman Ologitum, later a busy Visigothic village) briefly was capital of Navarre in 1406, and the large royal castle now is a national parador. Much further southeast on the Ebro River, **Tudela** once possessed a large medieval Jewish and Muslim population. Its architecture shows Mudéjar influence, but the cathedral (1234) is of a mixed Romanesque and Gothic style with strong Reconquest themes. Finally, to the far south below the Ebro River, the Cistercian monastery of Santa María la Real (1147) in **Fitero** was built by St. Raimundo, founder of the military-religious Order of Calatrava.

Some distance east and slightly south, but roughly parallel with Pamplona, is a group of three historic towns. **Aíbar**, a medieval village with streets covered by arcades, is the site of the Romanesque church of San Piedra. **Sangüesa's** church of Santa María la Real is one of the most beautiful in the region. **Javier** was the birthplace of the Jesuit missionary St. Francis Xavier (1506).

CUISINE. The Navarrese make roast lamb with onion, garlic, pepper, parsley, and lemon juice, or *chuletas de cordero a la Navarra* (lamb chops in a ham, onion, and tomato sauce), which can be prepared as follows:

CHULETAS DE CORDERO A LA NAVARRA

2–3 rib lamb chops per person	1 cup white wine
2 Tbs. margarine	1 cup water
2 Tbs. olive oil	12 thin slices *chorizos* or
1 clove garlic	pepperoni
2 onions, chopped	salt and pepper to taste
¼ lb. cured ham, diced	1 bay leaf
3 tomatoes, chopped	

Lightly sauté lamb in a mixture of margarine and oil, then remove and brown the garlic, onions, and ham. Add tomatoes, wine, water, and lamb. Cook gently for 15 minutes, and then add *chorizos* or pepperoni, salt, pepper, and bay leaf, continuing to cook over a low flame until very tender.

Other dishes such as *menestra de habas de Tudela* (broad beans cooked with garlic, saffron, almonds, artichoke hearts, white wine, and seasoning) and *garbure* (thick vegetable soup) are also popular. Tudela is particularly famous for asparagus served in *tortilla de Tudela* (asparagus omelette).

TORTILLA DE TUDELA

4–6 spears of asparagus	2 cups water
2 eggs	3 Tbs. butter
salt and pepper to taste	

Boil asparagus for three minutes and drain. Beat the eggs and add salt and pepper, water, and butter. Cook the egg mixture in a frying pan, adding the asparagus when the eggs begin to thicken.

The whole region is also the source of pimento peppers used in many Spanish dishes.

Local wines share some of neighboring La Rioja's quality. Reds and rosé come from villages south of Pamplona such as Cintruénigo and Cascante along the Ebro, or from Olite and the Valdizarbe, Tierra de Estella, Baja Montaña, and La Ribera Alta.

Chapter 15

NEW CASTILE
(Castilla y La Mancha)

REGIONAL CHARACTERISTICS. Pop., 2,577,105. Area, 79,229 sq. km., 15 percent of Spain's territory. Regional capital: Toledo. The region, irregularly shaped, borders Madrid, Aragón, and Old Castile on the north, Old Castile and Extremadura on the west, and Valencia and Murcia on the east. It also adjoins Andalusia, which is to its south.

Debate on the future form of government was sharp in 1977–78 because the region feared loss of national subsidies that propped up its weak economy. In the referendum of 1978, 52 percent of the voters opted to remain within a centralized national structure, while Ciudad Real briefly considered the possibility of regional status by itself as La Mancha. After a campaign stressing the benefits of economic development that would continue, the various provinces of New Castile approved autonomous status on August 10, 1982.

While the region faces problems of aridity, depopulation, poverty, declining mineral reserves, and meager local resources, the formation of a new decentralized University of Castilla y La Mancha, approved in 1984, has begun to improve educational standards.

The new flag of the region has a purple field and a large yellow castle with three towers in the center.

New Castile ranks fourteenth in personal income.

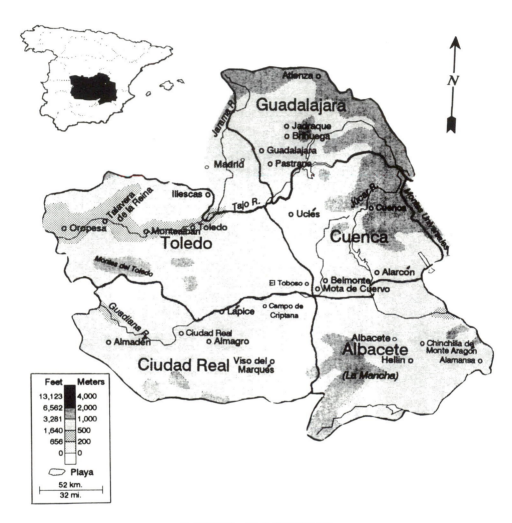

NEW CASTILE

ALBACETE

VITAL STATISTICS. Pop., 334,468. Area, 14,924 sq. km. Capital and diocesan see: Albacete. The province occupies part of the area fictionalized by Cervantes in *Don Quijote* as La Mancha, a plain that is landlocked and outside any major river system. Valencia, Alicante, and Murcia border Albacete to the east, Cuenca and Murcia to the north and south, and Ciudad Real and Jaén to the west.

ECONOMY. Agriculture is almost totally devoted to growing wheat. Industry is light, except for sulphur mined at Hellín and shoe manufacturing in the city of Albacete.

HISTORY. (al-Basiti or al-Baita [Arabic]). Ancient society resembles other southeastern areas such as Murcia, except that population density always has remained much lower. Celtic cave sanctuaries, bull images at Rojales, and an early Greek temple at Cerro de los Santos are prehistoric relics.

The caliphate of Córdoba and Murcia controlled the area until the Castilian conquest of Chinchilla de Monte Aragón by the Order of Santiago in 1241. Isabel the Catholic added Albacete to Castile in 1475, but strong economic ties remained between Murcia and Alicante. The condes de Villena, various nobles of Chinchilla, and the Alba family dominated seignorial life, while the archdiocese of Valencia appointed provincial clergy.

Felipe V rewarded the province's loyalty to the Bourbon cause in the War of Spanish Succession by recognizing Albacete as a province in 1716. Carlos IV began construction of the María Cristina Canal to improve agriculture in 1805. Guerrilla warfare against the Napoleonic regime led to French attacks in 1808 and 1813. When peace returned, the province was enlarged in 1833 and 1851.

The city of Albacete reached a population of 65,000 by 1930, but the province's aridity limited general growth. Low grain yields and large amounts of unused wastelands made Albacete perennially one of the six poorest provinces. Widespread illiteracy inspired the Second Republic to send out pedagogical missions of furloughed university students to teach elementary students in 1932. The socialists promised to include the province in the land reform even though it was not an area of large estates, but the cost of improving abandoned wastelands made reform too expensive to carry out.

At the civil war's start, Falangists seized the province but lost it to republican troops a week later. Albacete remained loyalist throughout the war, serving as a training base for the International Brigades. A whole series of leaders later prominent in European communist politics (Yugoslavia's Tito, France's Maurice Thorez, Italy's Palmiro Togliatti) were stationed here. In late March 1939, the republican decision to surrender was made by military men and politicians who conferred briefly at the Los Llanos Air Base outside the city of Albacete.

LITERATURE. The only creative figure of note, **Huberto Pérez de la Ossa** (1897–1959?), a novelist, director, and biographer, wrote several novels about Barcelona. *Obreros, zánganos y reinas* (1928) and *Los amigos de Claudio* (1931) are interesting because they focus on the plight of southern peasants who sought job opportunities in the north before the civil war.

An account of life in the International Brigades during the Spanish Civil War set mostly in Albacete is found in *Moment of War* (1989) by Laurie Lee, an English volunteer who was also involved in the fighting at Teruel.

CUSTOMS AND SOCIETY. Agricultural activity always has been important in Albacete. Earlier rural social types in Spanish agricultural society, before the changes of the past half century, included *braceros* (landless laborers), *peones* (very small landowners personally farming), *jornaleros* (small landowners occasionally farming), *propietarios* (owner-cultivators using machinery), *prudentes* (well-off farmers), and *ricos* (wealthy noncultivating owners). During the postwar period, a great rural exodus drastically altered this structure, and today modern techniques, specialty crops, mechanization, and larger individual plots have improved rural incomes. In particular, mechanization has removed the need for agricultural day laborers in some types of less intensive agriculture.

HISTORIC SITES. The church of San Juan Bautista in **Albacete** by Diego de Siloé (1495?–1563), later renovated in a baroque style, has Tuscan columns, a churrigueresque altarpiece (1725), and several plateresque chapel altarpieces. Other sites include the Ermita de San Antonio, a sixteenth-century Gothic church, and the provincial archaeological museum, which contains Bronze Age artifacts and many Roman and Muslim pieces.

Southwest of the provincial capital, **Hellín** has three Gothic and Renaissance churches with floors of Valencian ceramic tile. Not far southeast of Albacete, **Chinchilla de Monte-Aragón** is a very old town of Roman origin with a large Plaza Mayor and a ruined castle on a hill behind the town. Its church of Santa María del Salvador is Gothic with plateresque designs on all four exterior walls. Further east, close to the border with Murcia, **Almansa** circles around an Arabic castle built on a rocky hill in the center of the town.

CUISINE. Cooking in this isolated province is rural and hearty. *Setas carmina* (wild mushrooms with brains), *manos de cerdo rebozadas* (cured ham and batter-fried pig's feet), and *pepitoria de gallina* (chicken casserole) are often served.

PEPITORIA DE GALLINA

4 chicken breasts	2 cups chicken or beef stock
4 slices ham	1 cup white wine or cider
1 onion	salt, pepper, nutmeg to taste
1 carrot	handful of pine nuts
2 Tbs. margarine	1 bunch parsley, chopped
1 cup flour	

Slit chicken breasts and insert a slice of ham in each, tying with thread. Chop the onion and carrot. Heat margarine and cook chicken with onion and carrot. When the chicken is partly done, add flour and continue cooking. Add stock, stirring to make a thick sauce. Add wine and boil for 2 minutes. Lower the heat and add salt, pepper, and nutmeg. Simmer for an additional 30 minutes. Add pine nuts and parsley just before serving.

Albacete is a part of the Manchuela wine region adjacent to the Yecla district in Murcia.

CIUDAD REAL

VITAL STATISTICS. Pop., 468,327. Area, 19,813 sq. km., second largest Spanish province in physical size. Capital: Ciudad Real, pop., (1981) 51,118. Diocesan sees: Ciudad Real, Toledo. The province, north of the Guadalquivir River, is located between Albacete and Badajoz to the east and west and Toledo and Jaén to the north and south. Much of the province contains the plain of La Mancha made famous by Cervantes, a very arid, underpopulated border zone with harsh climatic changes. The headwaters of the Guadiana River rise in the province.

ECONOMY. The traditional economy of Ciudad Real, once dominated by the *latifundia* of absentee landowners, is now organized into a more efficient form of corporate agriculture. Incomes have improved somewhat despite difficult climatic and topographical conditions that hinder agricultural production. Valdepeñas has successfully developed specialized vineyard areas, and sheepherders produce the popular *manchego* cheese from ewes' milk. In particular, use of chemical fertilizers has increased crop yields.

The historic mercury mines of Almadén, discovered in the fourth century B.C., produced the essential ingredient that separates precious ore from base metals in the smelting process. The mercury of Almadén was used by Rome,

Muslim Spain, and colonial Mexican and Peruvian miners, but in the six-teenth century foreign bankers such as the Fuggers obtained the mines as a pledge against Spain's foreign debt. In recent years, the new El Entredicho and Las Cuevas mines have increased the supply of mercury but lowered the price just when the extreme environmental dangers of mercury's toxicity have required extensive and costly new waste facilities. Employment and profits have declined as a result.

HISTORY. (Ciudad Real [Spanish]). Various early peoples mined copper and silver in the Almadén area, but mercury became more important during the Roman period. Muslims used slave labor in their mining operations, shipping mercury ore to the Middle East or to Toledo and investing heavily in the region.

In 1218, the town of Almagro became local headquarters of the Order of Calatrava, which used the area as a base from which to continue the attack on Granada. Almagro also serviced the mines at Almadén by storing and shipping mercury; the Fuggers located their warehouses in the town during the sixteenth century. The Knights of Calatrava and Knights Templar founded Ciudad Real in 1255, but Alfonso X el Sabio fortified the town with walls and watchtowers to guard against Muslim attacks and to protect royal officials from the assertive religious orders. As the name indicates, Ciudad Real evolved into the chief royal center of Castile in southern Spain after the religious orders lost their lands and political importance.

When Christian peasants resettled the area, hostility to the old Jewish community grew. The Jews were forced to live as *conversos*, forcibly converted to Christianity, and were often persecuted for celebrating Yom Kippur, Passover, and other religious holidays. Violence in 1449, 1464, 1467, and 1474 eventually drove out most of the Jewish population. The Cortes of Toledo decreed segregation for the rest in 1480, and the expulsion order of 1492 decimated the remaining Jewish community.

The *cancillería* (law chancellery) rewrote the laws to integrate the area more fully between 1494 and 1506, establishing large estates for nobles such as the conde de Cabra, the duques de Infantado, and the marquises of Villena (the largest landowners of La Mancha). Their land use was often inept, and resettlement of smaller farmers also failed to stimulate increased yields. Drought and low productivity caused tax delinquencies to become chronic, population declined after the epidemics of 1596–1602, and subsistence crises grew common.

In the eighteenth century, the Bourbons reorganized the mines at Almadén to again supply mercury to the Mexican silver industry. Mercury production increased by 1760, peaked in 1805, and declined again as invasion by the French during the War of Independence and the Carlists in the royal expedition of 1837 disrupted the area. After 1824, loss of Peru and Mexico forced Spanish mercury production to compete on the open market.

Ecclesiastical lands, stripped of their mortmain restrictions in 1837, often passed into the hands of politicians and their followers. One of the first liberal *caudillos*, Baldomero Espartero (1793–1879) of Granátula, a successful general for the central government during the First Carlist War, became Progressive Party leader and regent for Isabel II, and ruled several times as national premier until he abandoned political life in 1856. Little was gained by the unchallenged liberal control of Ciudad Real. Few agricultural improvements occurred, and failure to use modern fertilizers kept half of the land fallow each year as the only means of renewing it.

By the twentieth century, population growth created an employment crisis among *braceros*. Rural violence broke out in Ciudad Real during the fall of 1931, in 1932–33, and again in the spring of 1936. At the start of the civil war, the assassination of the bishop of Ciudad Real was followed by a mass execution of as many as 800 priests, conservatives, and wealthy persons. With over 50 percent of the land expropriated, the area remained a republican stronghold until its surrender on March 29, 1939.

In the postwar era, the Franco regime executed peasant radicals and restored confiscated lands to private ownership. Few economic initiatives were tried until agronomists developed new types of grains and introduced new irrigation-well technology. While peasant flight has been the fifth-largest exodus of any province, those who have remained benefit from rising levels of income, some of it through European Community subsidy.

LITERATURE. Of all the Spanish works, Cervantes's *Don Quijote* made Ciudad Real and La Mancha its chief locale. According to Carlos Fuentes, Cervantes imagined a world of multiple points of view through an apparently innocent satire on the novels of chivalry. This empty region gave him freedom from constraint to construct multiple meanings for his characters, actions, and reactions. Ciudad Real became a wholly different, fictional world.

Among the other figures who have constituted the intellectual life of this province, Frey **Luis de León** (1527–91), a humanist and poet, studied St. Augustine in order to combine the Christian legacy with a Renaissance heritage. In addition to translating the Book of Job and Song of Songs, he wrote two other works deeply influenced by the Bible: *La perfecta casada* and *Los nombres de Cristo*. As a poet, he used the lyricism of the Salamanca school.

The mystical poet **St. Juan de la Cruz** (1542–91), a discalced Carmelite reformer, lived most of his life in Valladolid or Avila. In 1572, he became the spiritual director of St. Teresa's convent in Avila. Jailed by the Inquisition for nine months in 1577, he wrote his three great poems, *Canciones del alma en la intima comunicación de unión de amor de Dios*, *Canciones entre el alma y el Esposo*, and *Noche oscura*, while in prison. These poems expressed the search for a perfect union with God through active asceticism, a deep purification of the soul by divine grace, and unsought humiliation of the soul by external agents. The soul could achieve a life of pure faith and love of God and eventually attain a deep mystical union. As an *iluminati*, Juan was a religious idealist who made a personal search for God through the mystical illumination of the soul, for which he was often persecuted. His great courage convinced St. Teresa to create a male Carmelite Order.

In the contemporary era, the playwright **Fernando Arrabal** was raised in Ciudad Real after his birth in Ceuta. Of current note, **Pedro Almodovar** (b. 1949) of Calzada de Calatrava has become Spain's leading movie director. His first film, *Laberinto de pasiones* (1980), led to *Dark Habits* (1983), *What Have I Done to Deserve This?* (1985), *Law of Desire* (1987), *Women on the Verge of a Nervous Breakdown* (1988), *Tie Me Up, Tie Me Down* (1990), *High Heels* (1991), and *Kika* (1993). In a new era, Almodovar comes from a postmodern generation of Spanish artists.

CUSTOMS AND SOCIETY. According to anthropologists, the religion of New Castile and Andalusia is a "passional" culture with a penitential ideology; that is, a belief that concentrates on demonstrating its faith with passion, fatalism, and deeply felt reverence. The passional culture is intimately involved with magic-like sacramental rituals such as baptism or penance that reduce anxiety. Lay religious societies known as *cofradías* worship a Mater Dolorosa (a tragic mother-figure), doing penitence by scourging themselves, making long pilgrimages on their knees, or even briefly staging mock crucifixions. Their devotion to the Virgin during Holy Week competes with the image of a risen Christ.

The importance of Marianism, as this focus on the Virgin Mary is called, involves the defense of the Immaculate Conception and of deeply rooted social values of female honor, virginity, and maternity. The passion of Christ is felt through Mary, the grieving Mother of Christ, or Mater Dolorosa.

Courtship and marriage reveal other traditional aspects of life in this province. Until the twentieth century, male-female contacts were rigorously controlled. Only through glances and occasional serenades did relationships grow. Some marriages were arranged by parents, but all suitors had to formally request the permission of the possible bride's mother and father before an engagement could be arranged. Contact between the sexes was severely limited and supervised.

Eventually, the prospective bride and groom would invite their friends to a shower where their engagement was announced. The woman began to prepare living quarters with the gifts from the shower, and the wedding was scheduled as soon as the groom's parents gave her their own presents, usually a silk embroidered shawl and the most expensive lace mantilla they could afford.

In the period between formal recognition of the engagement and the wedding ceremony, the bride, her mother, and their friends put intense labor into the embroidery of linens and clothing and in furnishing the quarters. On the day of the wedding, it was customary for unmarried women to wait at the church while the bride walked from her home accompanied by her mother, mother-in-law, and all her married friends. After the ceremony, dinner and dancing incorporated much of the village into the celebration, with the groom sometimes having to buy the right to retire with his bride. The money would be distributed to the village poor if the couple were well off, or would be returned to the groom later if he could not afford charity.

HISTORIC SITES. The provincial capital, **Ciudad Real**, still has its walls and towers. The cathedral of Santa María del Prado is a small Gothic structure with a single aisle, while the late fourteenth-century church of San Pedro is Gothic with Byzantine touches and a beautiful tomb of the choirmaster who founded the church. The local Diputación building contains a small museum.

The Calatrava la Nueva Fortress in **Almagro**, a short distance southeast of Ciudad Real, is an imposing edifice built by the Order of Calatrava, although it later became a sixteenth-century Dominican monastery. The German banker Jakob Fugger (1459–1525) built the Salvador Chapel and the University of Santo Domingo (1524–1824), now closed. Almagro was the financial center of **Almadén**, where great deposits of mercury were mined, even though it was more than eighty miles west. Almadén is unattractive and dilapidated, like many mining towns. The castle of Santa Cruz in **Viso del Marqués**, a considerable distance southwest of Ciudad Real, is the unlikely, landlocked national archive of the Spanish navy.

Cervantes's *Don Quijote* is celebrated in **Puerto-Lápice**, near where don Quijote supposedly was knighted by an innkeeper, and in **Campo de Criptana**, where Quijote "fought" its windmills in the famous jousting scene. Windmills are still occasionally used in the area to pump water.

CUISINE. *Pisto manchego* is a vegetable dish from La Mancha.

PISTO MANCHEGO

1 onion, chopped

¼ cup olive oil

3 strips bacon, chopped

3 Tbs. chicken or beef stock

4 zucchini, chopped

4 tomatoes, chopped

4 green or red peppers, chopped

Sauté the onion in oil and add the bacon for 5 minutes. Boil the stock and add the zucchini, tomatoes, and peppers. Simmer, using water or white wine to make more liquid.

CUENCA

VITAL STATISTICS. Pop., 210,280. Area, 17,140 sq. km. Capital and diocesan see: Cuenca. The province borders Teruel, Valencia, Albacete, Ciudad Real, Toledo, and Guadalajara. Cuenca's broken topography, dotted by the Montes Universales, the Júcar River, and large *torcas* (sinkholes and depressions), is the center of the Meseta central plateau region of tablelands.

ECONOMY. The provincial economy still centers on the herding and grazing of sheep and goats, but some cereals and olives are grown.

HISTORY. (Cuenca [Spanish]). Little is known of prehistoric Iberian settlements in the area or of its early exploration. Its early history came under the Muslim principalities of Valencia and Seville. The Almoravids established a base during the Valencian campaign, but Alfonso VII of Castile seized Cuenca in September 1177, and Aragón controlled the northern region for more than a century afterwards.

Low population density always has been a serious problem. The bishop of Cuenca appealed to Rome for aid in repopulating the area in 1263, when Christian settlers already had begun moving further south with the Reconquest. Pedro I the Cruel (1350–69) used the open space for a battleground against the Castilian nobility. When his illegitimate half-brother, Enrique II (1369–79, the first of the Trastámaras), came to the throne, estates were distributed in the area to those who helped establish their dynasty.

During the fifteenth century, Alvaro de Luna (1388–1453) of Cañete, a grandnephew of Pope Benedict XIII, led a concerted attack against Aragón, which had been distracted by the Hundred Years' War and was in the midst of an ambitious Mediterranean campaign. As royal favorite (constable of Castile) to Juan II of Castile (1406–54), Alvaro de Luna fought for the personal supremacy of the Castilian monarchy, seeking to free the crown from limitations imposed by the nobility or by the townsmen in the Cortes. Court feuds finally undermined his position, and he was executed as a traitor to the noble cause in 1453.

Some nobles later sided with Isabel of Castile against Juana la Beltraneja to obtain aid for the development of a textile industry, but Cuenca generally remained quiet during the Hapsburg era. During the War of Spanish Succession, Karl of Austria briefly occupied parts of the region in 1706. Napoleonic troops took the town of Cuenca in June 1808 until repulsed by the guerrillas of Juan Martin Díaz (1775–1825). Throughout the remainder of the nineteenth century, failure to modernize the textile industry added to the economic stagnation, so that in the early twentieth century Cuenca was one of the three poorest provinces in Spain. The left flourished during the Second Republic, and electoral corruption against conservative candidates took place in all three elections held in 1931, 1933, and 1936.

At the start of the civil war, arsonists burned 10,000 volumes of the cathedral's library. The situation was so bad that most of the province's religious personnel fled. After local militiamen turned back a force of Carlist irregulars, the province remained loyalist, its manpower so drained by service in the republican army that only 14 percent of the land could be planted in 1938. Surrender came on March 29, 1939.

Postwar life witnessed heavy rural depopulation and continuing agrarian problems, somewhat offset by various initiatives to make Cuenca into a tourist center.

LITERATURE. Despite a small population, Cuenca has contributed some interesting figures to Spanish intellectual history. **Alfonso de Valdés** (1490?–1532), a satirical writer, corresponded with Erasmus. His brother, **Juan de Valdés** (1491–1541), a humanist strongly influenced by the theology of Erasmus, fled from the Inquisition to Italy, where he continued to teach and write, most prominently in *Diálogo de doctrina cristiana* (1529?) and *Diálogo de la lengua* (1534?).

Luis de Molina (1535–1600), educated at Alcalá de Henares, entered the Jesuit Order and taught in Portugal from 1563 to 1591, returning to Cuenca only at the end of his life. Molina, a theologian and lawyer, opposed theological determinism of any kind. God gave humankind sufficient grace to act, but the correctness of human thought can only be divinely judged, a position the Inquisition strenuously criticized. His *Six Books of Justice and Law* was finally printed between 1577 and 1582 after being censored five times. Molina believed in the legality of slavery for prisoners of war, but he denounced the slave trade itself.

Sebastián de Covarrubias Orozco (1539–1613), canon of the cathedral of Cuenca, compiled the *Tesoro de la lengua castellana o española* (1611), an important early Spanish dictionary. Another gifted linguist, **Lorenzo Hervás y Panduro** (1735–1809) of Horcajo de Santiago, was a well-known expert in comparative philology who wrote grammars of the many languages encountered by Spaniards in the Age of Exploration.

Intellectual life declined in the nineteenth and twentieth centuries, although **Luis Astrana Marín** (1889–1960) achieved a national reputation as a leading Spanish authority on Shakespeare and Cervantes.

ART. The cathedral in Cuenca was only the second wholly Gothic structure to be built in Spain, ca. 1225. It has an altar built by Ventura Rodríguez (1717–85), a choir grill by Hernando de Arenas, and paintings by Pedro de Mena y Medrano (1628?–88) and Fernando Yáñez of Valencia. An unusual fourteenth-century Byzantine diptych hangs in a side chapel. The Museo Diocesano exhibits two paintings by El Greco, *Christ on the Cross* and *Prayer in the Garden of Olives*. A new museum of abstract

Spanish painting in Cuenca, the Museo de Arte Abstracto Español, shows works by nineteenth- and twentieth-century artists. Cuenca is a summer art colony, and there are a number of private galleries.

CUSTOMS AND SOCIETY. The society of Cuenca has been infrequently studied by anthropologists, but here as throughout Spain and Latin America the practice of *compadrazgo* is common. In Spanish Catholic thought, since a parent cannot stand as a sponsor to his or her own child at baptism in order to prevent original sin from damaging the preparation of a new soul for salvation, godparents (*compadres*) are vitally necessary to sponsor the child in the Christian community. In the actual ceremony, after the infant has been baptized and given its Christian name, the priest passes the newly blessed infant to the godparent(s) before it is returned to its biological parents.

The godparents usually pay for this ceremony and the celebration that follows. They are also expected to take responsibility for the child's religious education and to pay for the first shoes, Easter dress, and other festive costs. In a broader sense, a powerful compadre's connections may bring economic or political opportunities within reach of the godchild. While it is most common for the father's brother to act as godparent, the assistance of powerful community leaders as *compadres* is popular among ambitious parents and can occasionally figure in local politics and economic life.

HISTORIC SITES. The unusual town of **Cuenca** lies on a rocky hilltop between the Júcar and Huécar rivers. Houses form terraces on the slopes, some of them cantilevered for support, so that the district of Casas Colgadas literally hangs over the edge of the hill. The older upper town is unexcelled for its medieval defensive location above the large plain that surrounds the town. It contains a beautiful medieval square, cobbled streets, and the cathedral, which has Gothic-Norman and Anglo-Norman sections, the latter an unusual style for Spain. There is a museum for abstract Spanish painting and a provincial archaeological museum.

Elsewhere in the province, about a hundred miles directly south of Cuenca, **Alarcón** contains the church of Santa María, which is a composite of various historical periods, and also an old Muslim castle, now a national parador. **Belmonte**, about the same distance southwest of Cuenca, once thrived in the Middle Ages, and its Pacheco Castle is now a national monument. Ten miles south of Belmonte, **Mota del Cuervo** has windmills reminiscent of La Mancha. **Uclés**, a hundred miles west of Cuenca, has a monastery built in the style of the Escorial and the Albar Llana Castle begun in the early Middle Ages.

CUISINE. Local dishes include *aceitunas al tomillo* (thyme-scented green olives), *moje* (tomato, tuna, and egg salad), and *ajo bacalao al estil de Cuenca* (garlic cod and potatoes). Walnuts are served as a snack or dessert.

GUADALAJARA

VITAL STATISTICS. Pop., 143,124, one of the lowest population densities of any province. Area, 12,214 sq. km. Capital: Guadalajara. Diocesan see: Sigüenza. Guadalajara is the northernmost province of New Castile, surrounded by Soria (Old Castile) and Zaragoza (Aragón) to the north, Teruel (Aragón) and Madrid to the east and west, and Cuenca to the southeast.

ECONOMY. The arid, rough, and poor province is largely used for grazing. Iron ore mines of the eastern region no longer operate, but there are unexploited deposits in the Sierra Meneras.

HISTORY. (Wad al-Hajarah [Arabic]). Settled by Celtiberians and Visigoths, the area came into contact with Greeks and Romans at the trade center in what is today the city of Guadalajara. The Romans created a town at Pastrana (Paterniana), which later became a part of the silk-weaving district of El Albaicín, an early tenth-century Muslim area controlled by the Muslim principality of Toledo.

Christian conquest began when Alvar Fañez de Minaya, a relative of El Cid, seized the area with help from the military orders, ca. 1050. The Knights of Calatrava ruled Pastrana until the crown seized their property and Carlos I sold Pastrana to the Mendoza family in 1541 as part of their stewardship of the province.

The Mendozas already were *the* family of the district. Their rise began during the reign of Alfonso XI (1312–50) when a feud drove them from their native Alava to Guadalajara. Gonzalo Yáñez Mendoza married a sister of Iñigo López de Orozco, *alcalde entregador* (chief justice) of the Mesta. In the next generation, Pedro González de Mendoza (d. 1385) provided crucial assistance to Enrique de Trastámara's revolt against Pedro the Cruel. As a reward, Pedro was made *mayordomo mayor* (high steward) of Castile, and his brother-in-law, Pedro López de Ayala, became *canciller mayor* (chief political agent) of Castile. A daughter of Pedro González de Mendoza, Juana, married Diego Gómez Manrique, of a distinguished family from Navarre.

The third generation of Mendozas is best represented by Diego Hurtado de Mendoza (d. 1404). As admiral of Castile, his three defeats of the Portuguese earned him control of the city of Guadalajara in 1395. The leading member of the fourth generation, Diego's son, Iñigo López de Mendoza, the first marqués of Santillana (d. 1458), became the greatest cavalier of the fifteenth century. But the zenith was reached with Diego Hurtado de Mendoza and Pedro González de Mendoza. Diego (d. 1479) received the prestigious title of duque de Infantado, while Pedro (d. 1495) was elevated to the office of cardinal primate of Spain.

The family ruled Guadalajara's Mudéjar peasantry until the seventeenth century, controlling most of the province's villages at one time or another until finally diminished by the rise of Hapsburg royal power and their destruction of the so-called *caballero* renaissance by use of foreign cultural models to supplant indigenous national leadership.

In the eighteenth century, the Bourbons became the leading family of Guadalajara, buying land and establishing a royal cloth factory that operated from 1718 to 1808 without ever making a profit. Their ascendancy, however, proved to be short-lived when the liberal revolution confiscated land titles and sold many of their estates in Guadalajara during the nineteenth century. The Liberal Party leader of the province, the conde de Romanones (1863–1950), amassed huge estates himself. A strong monarchist nevertheless, Romanones proved to be a successful national premier during World War I, but Alfonso XIII's acceptance of military dictatorship from 1923 to 1931 drove the conde from power.

At the start of the Spanish Civil War in July 1936, Guadalajara's proximity to Madrid made it strategically important. Francoists and Carlists invaded from the north in an attempt to encircle Madrid, but republican troops defending Madrid held, and the southern part of the province was recaptured when the International Brigades defeated Italian troops in March 1937. The front remained static but hotly contested throughout the remainder of the war.

Since 1939, minor industrialization of the city of Guadalajara has provided more jobs, but the gigantic growth of adjacent Madrid continues to drain population from the province.

LITERATURE. Early intellectual life had Sephardic content. **Mosé de León** (1240–1305) wrote the largest part of the "Zohar," the main book of the *Kabbalah*. This commentary on the theory of Jewish mysticism and hidden wisdom is part of the kabbalistic tradition in Judaism, which advocates fasting and self-inflicted suffering as a means for the human soul to experience union with the divinity.

The *caballero* renaissance produced a series of Mendoza poets and writers. **Pedro López de Ayala** (d. 1407), educated in Avignon, wrote the first Renaissance history of Castile, *Crónica del rey don Pedro* (1398), and the poetic *Rimaldo del Palacio*, and translated Livy, Boccaccio, and St. Gregory. The first marqués de Santillana, **Iñigo López de Mendoza** (1398–1458), son of Diego Hurtado de Mendoza and the most powerful nobleman of his day, was also a major poet. His beautiful lyric poems such as the *serranillas* (mountain songs) provided Spanish literature with a transition from the Galician school to Italian-inspired poetry. The marqués's forty-two Italian sonnets are among the first in Spanish literature, and he also did literary criticism in *Proemio e carta al Condestable de Portugal* (1449). Several generations later, his grandson, **Diego Hurtado de Mendoza**

(1504–75), a diplomat who has been called the last Renaissance man of Spain, wrote history and poetry.

In the contemporary era, Guadalajara again has become something of a literary center. **Antonio Buero Vallejo** (b. 1916) is a playwright of the post–civil war period who combines qualities of Cervantes, Kafka, and science fiction into plays such as *La tejedora de sueños* (1952); *Historia de una escalera*, winner of the 1949 Lope de Vega Prize; *Un soñador para un pueblo* (1959), a story of a visionary who is betrayed; *Caimán* (1981), a Caribbean play in which a child is eaten by an alligator; and the existentialist *En la ardiente oscuridad* (1985). **Angel María de Lera** (b. 1912) of Baides is a novelist and journalist whose popular *Los olvidados* (1957) about a lost generation of children became a film produced in Mexico. He also wrote a civil war novel, *Las últimas banderas*, published in 1967. **Ramón Hernández** (b. 1935), an engineer and liberal dissenter during the Franco era, is a practitioner of experimental fiction. In his thirteen novels, which began with *Presentimiento de lobos* (1966) and include *Palabras en el muro* (1969), *Eterna memoria* (1974), *Fábula de la ciudad* (1979), *El ayer perdido* (1986), and *Sola en el paraíso* (1987), he deals with the absurdities of modern life and creates characters who invent an imagined reality in which to exist.

The best modern writing about the province of Guadalajara is the so-called vagabond work by Camilo José Cela, *Viaje a la Alcarria* (1948), translated as *Journey to the Alcarria*. The Alcarria occupies the eastern part of the province and is quite rural even today.

ART. Guadalajara is an important center of plateresque architecture. At the cathedral in Sigüenza, **Alonso Covarrubias** did the monumental altar, ca. 1515. The Palacio del duque de Infantado, a late fifteenth-century masterpiece built for Iñigo López de Mendoza, also is plateresque and now houses the Museo de Bellas Artes in Guadalajara, mainly an early modern collection. The cathedral at Sigüenza contains Juan Soreda's sixteenth-century altarpiece of Santa Librada done in a mixed Italo-Flemish style between 1526 and 1528 and also contains paintings by Titian and El Greco. Famous cathedral artisans such as Juan de Sevilla (1643–95) and Domingo de Andrada (1639–1712) contributed retablos or other details of the interior. The church of Santa María in Cogolludo has a painting by Jusepe de Ribera (1591–1652), while the façade of the Medinaceli palace is by Lorenzo Vázquez of Valladolid.

MUSIC. The music director of the cathedral in Las Palmas (Canary Islands) and later of the royal chapel in Madrid, **Sebastián Durán** (1645?–1716?) of Brihuega, used Italian and French music to increase the use of violins in court functions and in Spanish music generally. Durán also wrote *zarzuelas*, of which *Veneno es de Amor la Envidia* (1700) is the best known.

CUSTOMS AND SOCIETY. Until the recent growth of urbanization, village life dominated the basic structure of Spanish society. Anthropological studies of this province stress the importance of membership in the *común de vecinos* (village corporation), a corporate entity crucial for the maintenance of municipal order. The *ayuntamiento* (smallest seat of government within a provincial judicial district, but sometimes made up of more than a single municipality) was run by an *alcalde*, or mayor, responsible for collecting municipal taxes (*arbítrios*) on livestock and real property, and several councilors. The *juez de paz* (justice of the peace) provided rudimentary justice.

The ritual calendar of traditional community life centered around national holidays and local celebrations (*fiestas del pueblo*). Village business tended to be conducted as a prelude to the fiestas or saints' days. Costs of these celebrations were paid by wealthy *vecinos* (citizens) to cover their use of village lands and other grazing facilities. Other important moments of the old village style of life included work on communal properties (*cendera*), baptisms and weddings, and family gatherings.

HISTORIC SITES. In the city of **Guadalajara,** the imposing Palacio del duque de Infantado, built for Iñigo López de Mendoza by the French-born Juan Guas (d. 1495?), has a virtuoso Hispano-Gothic-Mudéjar style. As an expression of family pride, each stone of the dazzling courtyard is inscribed with family crests and emblems of rank, and the interior drips with gilt. The palace later became a jail for Francis I of France in 1525 after his capture on the field of battle in Italy and was the site of Felipe II's marriage to Elizabeth of Valois in 1560. The structure, badly damaged in the civil war, has been restored. Its interior, built from many kinds of rare woods, leads to beautiful patios and courtyards.

Elsewhere in the province, **Alcocer,** to the east, was once controlled by the Mendoza family, who contributed to the building of the church of Santa María, a perfect mixture of Romanesque and Gothic style. Not far northeast of Guadalajara, **Brihuega** is a picturesque relic of Muslim and early medieval times and site of the Peña Bermeja Castle and the Real Fábrica de Paños, the latter a royal cloth factory established by Carlos III in the eighteenth century. Southwest of Guadalajara, **Pastrana** is a historic town associated with St. Teresa and site of her Convento de Concepcionistas and the Franciscan monastery of Pastrana. St. Juan de la Cruz also lived for a time in Pastrana, and mementos of Juan and Teresa can be found in the local museum. Cardinal Pedro González de Mendoza (1428–95), brother of Iñigo López de Mendoza, founded the church of Santa María de la Asunción.

More distant to the north/northeast is **Jadraque,** another Mendoza town. The family built both the crenellated Castle Cid on a high hill overlooking the town and the Jadraque Church, which contains a Zurbarán painting. The Palacio de Medinaceli is in nearby **Cogolludo.** Also in this grouping is

Sigüenza, which has a beautiful cathedral, a fine Plaza Mayor, a Muslim castle (now a parador), and the Renaissance chapel of the Humilladera. Nearby, **Atienza**, encircled by a double outer town wall, possesses five old Romanesque churches: San Bartolomé, La Trinidad, San Gil, Santa María del Rey, and San Juan.

CUISINE. Almond tarts (*bartolillos*) are a popular Spanish confection.

BARTOLILLOS

½ lb. puff pastry	⅛ cup flour
1 oz. toasted almonds	¼ cup water
¼ lb. sugar	2 egg yolks

Roll pastry as thin as possible, cutting round circles 2 inches in diameter. Grease a molded baking tin, then blanch and crush the almonds and mix with sugar, flour, water, and egg yolks. Fill each section of the tray and place a round pastry cover over each section. Bake in the oven at 400°F for 20 minutes, or until brown.

TOLEDO

VITAL STATISTICS. Pop., 471,806. Area, 15,370 sq. km. Regional and provincial capital and diocesan center: Toledo. The province is bounded by Madrid, Cuenca, Ciudad Real, Badajoz, Cáceres, and Avila.

ECONOMY. The city of Toledo is a tourist and ecclesiastical center, while the rural parts of the province are given over to grazing. A number of large estates prized for their game reserves are located within the province.

HISTORY. (Toletum [Roman], Tolaitola [Arabic]). Toledo occupies a spectacular site surrounded on three sides by the Tagus River gorge. No city has a better natural defensive location. The village, founded in very early times, passed through the hands of Celtiberians, Romans (192 B.C.), and Visigoths (A.D. 418). As Toledo grew, it became the political capital of Visigothic Spain during the era of Athanagild (554–67). After Recared's conversion to Christianity in 589, it also became the national center of the Church, the site of twelve national and several provincial councils between 589 and 702. Between 681 and 712, the archbishop of Toledo participated in all episcopal nominations as a deputy of the king and governed by the canon law earlier drawn up by Isidoro of Seville and revised by Julian of Toledo.

During the reign of Receswinth (653–72), canon law influenced the compilation of basic civil and tribal law in the *Liber Judiciorum*, or *Fuero*

Juzgo, source of medieval foral law. The word *fuero* comes from the Latin word *forum* and simply means law of the tribunal. Many *fueros* evolved from simple privileges granted at one point or another in the Reconquest to the northern principalities, whose struggle to preserve their *fueros* became an important aspect of later history.

Despite these legal attainments, by the start of the eighth century the Visigothic state had begun to decline. Rural slavery spread through Hispano-Gothic society, the power of local magnates grew at the expense of the elective Toledo monarchy, urban population declined sharply, and trade, learning, and religion all suffered. Jews faced forcible baptism and accusations of secret worship, until the once prominent community of *conversos* in Toledo fell into deep decline.

The Muslims, attracted to southern Spain by its arable land, were able to take advantage of the endless Visigothic civil wars over monarchical succession to capture Toledo in 712. Within a century, the city's economy soared as the Arabs brought in sophisticated technology and encouraged Jewish commercial participation. Silk or woolen mills and an iron industry producing the Toledo blade (the medieval period's best sword) reestablished trade. The town prospered for 300 years until the Umayyad caliphate's collapse. Toledo then briefly became a minor Muslim state with a Mozarab and Jewish society until Alfonso VI of Castile reconquered the area in 1085.

The Castilian monarchy soon left Burgos to make Toledo the Christian capital of Spain once again. When the archbishop of Toledo became cardinal primate of Spain in 1087, new institutions befitting a major Christian capital emerged, such as the establishment of the School of Translators (ca. 1126–52) by Archbishop Raimundo, for example, which gave medieval scholars access to Greek, Hebrew, and Roman works of science and philosophy. Translations of available Arabic texts adapted famous classical works for use throughout medieval Western Europe.

Many other Toledo institutions involving all aspects of religious life were later added. After religious rioting in 1440 had almost destroyed Toledo's Jewish community, the Council of the Inquisition appeared in 1485. The council was instrumental in the final expulsion of the Jews in 1492 (150,000 expelled, 50,000 converted) and later drew up the ban on the use of Arabic in 1580 and the Muslim expulsion by Felipe III in 1609.

Toledo was ruled, during these years, by the cardinals of the Church. The earliest major figure, Rodrigo Ximénez de Rada (d. 1247), preached hundreds of sermons in France, Germany, and Italy to recruit volunteers against the Almohads, swelling the Christian army's ranks at the battle of Las Navas de Tolosa in 1212 and helping to insure victory. Several centuries later, Pedro González de Mendoza (1428–95), of the famous Guadalajara family, received the royal appointment as cardinal the year after he supported Isabel the Catholic's claim on the throne in 1474. His elevation assured Mendoza-family control of the Church and, in a wider context, introduced Renaissance art to Toledo. He also provided the logistics for the conquest of Granada in 1492 and supported Columbus's proposal to seek a new route to the Indies.

His successor, Cardinal Francisco Ximénez de Cisneros (1436–1517), established the Inquisition as an arm of the state. More important, however, was his contribution to the artistic and political glorification of Toledo. In the world of Machiavelli, he was a churchman with a scholar's mind who amassed power with a prince's touch. Finally, in the seventeenth century, Cardinal Bernardo Sandoval y Rojas (in office 1599–1618) completed the final great art purchases that have given Toledo such character.

After 1519, this great age of growth and power began to crumble when Toledo's city council opposed Carlos I's demands for additional tax revenues and joined the Comuneros revolt. Rioting swept the city in 1520–21, and a *toledaño*, Juan de Padilla, led the Comuneros' forces. The unsuccessful revolt did not entirely destroy the city's privileges, but later Hapsburgs took little interest in Toledo, and Felipe II made Madrid the national capital in 1561. Emigration to the Americas drew away population, the Council of Trent's adoption of a uniform Roman rite weakened the individualism of Spanish ecclesiastical life, and economic decline limited Church funds. Even the Inquisition disappeared in the 1830s.

The city and province of Toledo occupied different worlds by 1931. While the city still possessed ecclesiastical revenues and benefitted from tourism, the rural provincial areas were a part of the southern poverty belt. Agricultural unemployment of nearly 20 percent caused peasant poverty, and during the era of the Second Republic rising expectations caused impatience with moderate reform. When the military revolt occurred in 1936, seventy priests were assassinated or executed. In Toledo proper, only the military garrison in the old Alcázar, with its heavy walls, held out in support of Franco. Its commander, Colonel José Moscardó Ituardi, became an instant Francoist hero by refusing to surrender, not even to save the life of his son, held captive and subsequently executed by the republicans. Franco's forces liberated Toledo on September 27, 1936, trapping in a seminary forty anarchists who took their own lives rather than surrender.

LITERATURE. A priest, **Ildefonso of Toledo** (607–67), wrote *Libellus de virginite perpetua Mariae, adversus tres infidelas* as a defense of Mary's virginity. He later became archbishop of Toledo and led two Councils of Toledo, in 653 and 655. The *converso* **Julián of Toledo** (642?–690) became an important Catholic ecclesiastical writer of his time and ultimately the last great churchman of the Visigothic period.

The Muslim period popularized Arab and Jewish literature and scholarship. **Abebragel** (d. 1040), a mathematician, astronomer, and astrologer, reclaimed Hellenistic science for Western Europe. **Abraham bar Hiyya ha-Nasi** (ca. 1116) wrote *Liber embadorum*, a geometry text, while **Abu Muhammad Jabir ben Aflah** (ca. 1145) wrote *Kitab al-haia*, an astronomy

work critical of Ptolemy. **Abulcasis** (n.d.) and **Avenzoar** (1092–1161) contributed medical texts. When the Reconquest reached Toledo in 1085, the
archbishop of Toledo, Raimundo (1124–51), founded the School of Translators, later used by Western European scholars such as Michael Scotus
and Hermannus Alemannus. An early archbishop, **Rodrigo Ximénez de
Rada** (1170?–1247), wrote *Historia Gothica* as a way of reclaiming Christian history lost to the Muslims.

Local society of the Reconquest initially remained cosmopolitan. **Tudrus
ben Yehuda, Abu 'L-afia** (1247–1303?), a Spanish Hebrew scholar and
friend of Alfonso X, encouraged cross-cultural exchanges. **Juan Manual**
(1282–1384), nephew of Alfonso X of Castile, wrote a book on chivalry,
Libro del caballero, as well as works on falconry and other aspects of
medieval life. Alfonso Martínez de Toledo, the **Archpriest of Talavera**
(1398?–1482?), wrote *El Corvacho*, a Boccaccio-like mixture of Latinized
and colloquial language. This work about moral life, important in the evolution of narrative writing in Castilian, contained vitriolic attacks on
women as the source of all sinfulness and perversity. **Rodrigo de Cota**
(1405?–70?), a converted Jew, wrote *Diálogo entre el amor y un viejo*, a
drama about an old man who falls in love despite his age. His straightfor-
ward storytelling is considered an important dramatic development in the
emergence of modern theatre. **Alfonso de Oropesa** (d. 1478) contributed
sermons and other works of theology for the Hieronymite Order.

As Toledo began the transition toward the Renaissance, the *romanceros*,
or ballads, first appeared. Some were ballads about the Muslim wars composed on the spot; Gerald Brenan calls them instant newspapers. Early
romanceros became popular at the court and then among the people. They
used the meter of a sixteen-syllable line with a strong stress in the middle
that made them rhymed incantations.

This tradition soon produced one of the most famous novels in Spanish
literature. **Fernando de Rojas** (1465?–1541), *converso* mayor of Talavera,
wrote *La Celestina* as a story that concerns the noble youth Calisto, who
falls in love with Melibea and uses the procuress Celestina to cast a spell
over her. Calisto later is killed when Melibea's father discovers the plot,
and after much anguish the despairing Melibea takes her own life to join
him. This strange combination of deceit and loyalty has fascinated readers
for centuries, but what makes *La Celestina* important as a Renaissance
drama is the story of an individual character in a world previously dominated only by an all-powerful God. According to Ramiro de Maeztu, during a period when the state was exploiting religion and ethnicity, the novel
taught Spanish people to live as crafty individuals.

Further Renaissance humanism emerges in the work of **Juan de Vergara**
(1492–1557), a teacher at the University of Alcalá and editor of the Complutensian Bible who fell victim to the Inquisition when his correspondence
with Erasmus led to his imprisonment in 1533–47. Another humanist,

Francisco Cervantes de Salazar (1514?–75), wrote the early history of the conquest of Mexico. **Juan de Mariana** (1535?–1624), a Jesuit historian from the University of Alcalá, taught in many parts of Europe before spending the last part of his life in Toledo. His *Historiae de rebus Hispaniae libri XX* represented a major compilation of the sources and narratives of Spanish history, while his *De rege et regis institutione* attacked the theory of divine right of kings. **Sebastián de Covarrubias Orozco** (1539–1613), a premier Spanish lexicographer, produced an important early dictionary of Spanish.

A new era of Spanish poetry began with **Garcílaso de la Vega** (1501?–36) of Toledo, a noble poet-soldier who later died of his battle wounds. Living at the court in Naples, he produced during his writing career *Écloga primera*, a poem of love and nature, and a series of *Canciónes* and *Coplas*, which are mainly composed of sonnets and elegies. Garcílaso awakened the Spanish literary conscience to the classics and the value of mythology and introduced a new poetic language inspired by the poetry of Latin classics and the Italian Renaissance. He modeled himself on Petrarch by using contrasts to reflect internal conflict and in matters of structure, metrics, and tone.

The Golden Age of drama lightly touched the area. Dramatists with some connection to Toledo included **Tirso de Molina** (Gabriel Téllez, 1581?–1648) of Soria, author of *El Burlador de Sevilla*, who lived in Toledo from 1618 to 1621, and **Pedro Calderón de la Barca** (1600–1681) of Seville, a chaplain at the Hermandad del Refugio.

The seventeenth century saw high culture increase. **Luis Quiñones de Benavente** (1593?–1651), a friend of Lope de Vega, polished the genre of popular short satirical plays called *entremeses*, short scenes of daily life and human shortcomings that were performed between acts of more formal plays. The most important figure was **Francisco de Rojas Zorrilla** (1607–48), who achieved success as a court dramatist for Felipe IV. His prolific career as playwright covered topics such as love, honor, and violence. *Cada cual lo que le toca* (1645?) concerns a bride who proves to be no virgin but nevertheless succeeds in defending her honor. His most serious work, *Del Rey abajo, ninguno* (1650), also dealt in a very Spanish way with personal honor.

Toledo became less important in the later centuries. After a military career in the War of Spanish Succession, **Eugenio Gerardo Lobo** (1679–1750) of Cuerva became a popular poet. Later, one of the best novels by **Benito Pérez Galdós** of Madrid, *Angel Guerra*, used Toledo as a setting.

ART. Visigothic Toledo's material culture is best seen in the so-called Hoard of Guarrazar found near Toledo, a huge mass of semiprecious stones and other jewelry on display at the National Archaeological Museum in Madrid.

Always an important art center, Toledo is a virtual museum of Spanish style. An early architect and designer, **Pedro Berruguete** of Valladolid, established the Hispano-Flemish style in Toledo's cathedral with several now-destroyed altarpieces. His school combined an increasing naturalism with a mannered concept of form and a taste for ornamentation. The plateresque appeared in the early sixteenth century and made Toledo one of its most important centers. The architect and designer **Enrique de Egas** (d. 1534), nephew of Hanequin of Brussels, developed the plateresque style for the ostentatious Hospital of the Holy Cross in Toledo, which mixed some surviving Gothic details with Mudéjar and Renaissance flourishes in pediments, friezes of grotesques, reliefs, scalloped backgrounds, and escutcheons. **Alonso de Covarrubias** of Teruel added to the plateresque tradition by designing the chapel of the New Kings in the cathedral sometime around 1531. The Italian Renaissance influenced **Juan de Borgoña** (John of Burgundy, 1495?–1533) to paint frescoes in the cathedral's chapter house and to do *Descent from the Cross* and a *Pietà* on a commission from Cardinal Francisco Ximénez de Cisneros. He painted many other ecclesiastical works in Toledo during the early sixteenth century with an exacting naturalism.

The Spanish mannerist **Juan Baptista Maino** (1578–1641) also painted in Toledo along with followers of Caravaggio like Carlo Sarceni (1585?–1620) and Vicente Carducho (1578–1638) of Madrid. Their elongated forms set the stylistic stage for Domenicos Theotocopoulos (1548?–1614?), **El Greco**, born in Crete and trained in Italy, who settled in Toledo around the year 1577 and remained until his death. As the greatest artist associated with Toledo, two of his finest paintings are the *Disrobing of Christ* (El Expolio, 1577) at the cathedral and *Burial of Count Orgaz* (1586–87) at the church of Santo Tomé. This last work, based on the legend that when the Toledan Count Orgaz died he was so distinguished for his piety that St. Stephen and St. Augustine personally descended from Heaven to bury him, caused a later writer to comment that the painting epitomizes an alliance between God and the Spanish nobility. The aristocrats looking on in the background seem to represent a class of society that expected miracles as a matter of policy. Other El Greco works are *St. Luke* (at the cathedral), *St. Joseph and the Child, St. Dominic,* and several titled *Assumption of the Virgin* (ca. 1577, one at the Art Institute of Chicago, another at the Museum of San Vicente in Toledo), *St. Bernardino of Siena, The Saviour, View and Plan of Toledo* at the El Greco Museum (and the New York Metropolitan Museum), *Holy Family, Cardinal Tavera,* and the *Baptism of Christ* at the Hospital of San Juan Bautista.

After El Greco, the work of Italians such as Juan Rizi (1608–85) and Juan Carreño de Mirada (1614–85) flourished in Toledo with the decoration of the Sagrario in the cathedral (now destroyed). Luca Giordano (1634–1705), who painted in Spain between 1692 and 1702, did the ceiling frescoes of the cathedral sacristy, but the main period of Toledo's art was drawing to a close.

The cathedral also owns paintings by Cornelis de Holanda (ca. 1495?), Sebastián de Almonacid (ca. 1500), Peti Juan, Alonso Sánchez Coello (1531?–88), Anthony van Dyck (1599–1641), Giovanni Bellini (1430?–1516), Diego Velázquez (1599–1660), Titian (1477?–1576), and Raphael (1483–1576). El Greco's *Spoliation of Christ*, a portrait of Christ just before he was put on the cross, and Goya's *The Arresting of Jesus on the Mount of Olives* are two of the most popular works. Stone work by Alonso de Covarrubias (1488–1570), altars by Narciso Tomé (ca. 1440), and frescoes by Luca Giordano and Claudio Coello also distinguish the cathedral.

The endless line of biblical figures carved in dark wood over the main portal of the cathedral is probably the most important Renaissance work in Spain. Two artisans, the Frenchman **Felipe Vigarní de Borgoña** (1498–1543) and the Spaniard **Alonso Berruguete** (1489–1561), completed the group between 1539 and 1543.

Across the transept facing the choir is the high altar, surrounded by a wrought-iron screen done by Francisco de Villapando (ca. 1548). Above this are fourteen gold-leafed reredos of religious tableaux carved in relief from work done by Enrique de Egas and Pedro Gumiel (ca. 1550?). Workmen cut holes in the wall of the cathedral to allow light to fall on the reredos in the morning and afternoon. This so-called *transparente* leads to further embellishment of the area done by Narciso Tomé and his sons. The whole work is the baroque at its most florid.

The Hospital de Tavera has paintings by El Greco, Titian, Tintoretto, Carreño, Zurburán, and Pedro de Ribera (1683–1742). The Hospital de Santa Cruz, designed by Enrique Egas (1455?–1534?) and Alonso de Covarrubias, has paintings by El Greco and sculpture by Alonso Berruguete.

MUSIC. Mozarab liturgy developed the Hispanic chant as religious music from the eighth to eleventh centuries, although little is known about it. The later composer **Cristobal Morales** (1500?–1553) used contrapuntal technique to become one of the great masters of Spanish-Roman sacred polyphony.

CUSTOMS AND SOCIETY. Toledo and Córdoba are the two cities where the medieval Jewish population of Spain flourished. The term *Sephardim*, applied to the Spanish Jews, originated in 586 B.C. when exiles from Jerusalem arrived in the Asia Minor city of Sepharad after Nebuchadnezzar's attack on Judah. The city name thus came to provide the name Sephardim, denoting those Jews who did not live in traditional Jewish territory. After the rise of Azhkenazi Jewish communities in Germany, Poland, and Russia during the Middle Ages, Sephardic became a general term for Jews of the Mediterranean.

Jews had been living in Spain since the Roman destruction of Jerusalem, but a golden age began during the Muslim period in Córdoba's history when Muslims found the Sephardim useful in running the new Spanish state. Large Jewish communities appeared in Toledo, Córdoba, Burgos, Granada, Tarragona, and Girona, all following ancient Hebrew ritual. By the eleventh century, the less tolerant Almohads forced Spanish Jews to wear clothing that identified their religion. Many Sephardim migrated to León, Aragón-Catalonia, and Navarre.

Sephardic society tended to be very close. Even after expulsion from Spain, the Sephardim sought to keep their own identity, speaking a form of Ibero-Hebrew known as Ladino and rarely intermarrying even with other Jews. Some of the first synagogues in colonial America were created by the Sephardim.

Christian Toledo also has a rich folklore. Many major religious observances and ceremonies concerning the Spanish Church take place in the city, and it has often been visited by the popes of the Church. One of the most passionately religious holidays after Easter is the Feast of Corpus Christi (ascension of Christ), marked by pomp and pageantry in Toledo. Six children, dressed in medieval ceremonial robes, spread flower petals before the sacred Host during the procession, and the walls of the cathedral are covered with flowers.

HISTORIC SITES. The city of **Toledo,** walled to the west and surrounded on its other three sides by the Tagus, was connected to the surrounding territory by the Alcántara bridge, built by the Romans and improved by Muslims in 866. At the center of the city is the Zocodover, the main plaza. The cathedral of Toledo (begun in 1226), second largest Gothic cathedral in Spain after Burgos, occupies the highest point of the city center, a spot where an earlier Visigothic Christian church and a later mosque once stood. Construction of the cathedral lasted from 1226 to 1493.

The cathedral has two tall towers, the northern one a bell tower with the large seventeen-ton bell, Campana Gorda. The interior is dominated by eighty-eight columns and has a large nave, four aisles, fifteen chapels, and a cloister. Above the high altar stands the figure of a mysterious shepherd who, it is claimed, guided the Christians to victory in the battle of Las Navas de Tolosa of 1212. The day was misty, only King Alfonso VIII ever saw the shepherd's face, and the figure was gone when the battle ended. In time, this implication of divine intervention at Las Navas del Tolosa created a story that modestly rivalled the St. James legend.

Most chapels in the cathedral are dedicated to famous Spanish churchmen and nobles such as Alvaro de Luna, Cardinal Albornoz, Enrique II of Castile, and Cardinal Cisneros. The most important chapel is the Capilla de Santiago, past the central choir and altar at the north end of the cathedral. A huge iron grill forms its front wall, and the Lion's door is a design by Hanequin Cueman in a Flemish sculptural style. The ceiling of the main cathedral is composed of complex vaulting, and the outside wall holds a statue of St. James the Moor-Slayer, mounted on a horse and brandishing a huge sword. The chapel's floor contains the tombs of don Alvaro de Luna and his wife, with choir stalls done by a German sculptor, Rodrigo Alemán (active 1489–1512). The nearly unknown Petit Juan sculpted the main altar (*retablo mayor*). Many other ecclesiastical buildings can be found in Toledo. Two of the oldest are the Ermita del Cristo de la Vega, rebuilt from the Visigoth basilica of Santa Leocadia (1166), and the Iglesia del Cristo de la Luz, formerly a Visigothic Christian church and later a mosque. The church of San Andrés and the convents of Santa Isabel de los Reyes and San Juan de los Reyes (designed by Juan Guas, with sculpture by Egas Coeman, both trained in Brussels) are associated with Fernando and Isabel.

Another ecclesiastical style in Toledo is the Mudéjar. San Sebastián and Santiago del Arrabal are particularly well known, but Santo Tomé is famous as the site of El Greco's painting *The Burial of the Count of Orgaz*, which is displayed here because the church was rebuilt in the fourteenth century by Gonzalo Ruiz de Toledo, count of Orgaz.

Two synagogues of the once-vital Sephardic Jewish community are south of the cathedral. Santa María la Blanca (twelfth century), with horseshoe arches, was converted into a Christian church, ca. 1550. Tránsito (1366, funded by Samuel ha-Levi, treasurer of Pedro I of Castile), with a stucco frieze of the psalms in Hebrew, is now a national monument not open for religious services. Also in the old Jewish quarter is the Museo Sefardí, recently remodeled and expanded. It displays aspects of Sephardic life in medieval Spain, including the women's gallery overlooking the prayer room and clothing of the early Middle Ages. There is a 6,000-volume library as well.

The Capilla Mozárabes in the southwest corner of the cathedral celebrates the long and often difficult practice of Christianity in Toledo during the centuries of Muslim occupation. The recapture of Toledo by Christians in 1085 meant that the reformed Roman mass instituted by the Cluniac Order now conflicted with the much more ancient Mozarabic mass. After great controversy, Cardinal Cisneros finally set aside a chapel for maintenance of the old mass. The chapel is decorated with a painted vault by Borgoña.

Other buildings of note include the Palacio Arzobispal; the Alcázar (of civil war fame in August and September 1936, now reconstructed); the beautiful Hospital de Santa Cruz donated by Cardinal Pedro González de Mendoza and designed by Enrique Egas and Alonso de Covarrubias, now a museum and gallery (with eighteen paintings by El Greco); the Casa del Greco and Museo del Greco; the Posada de la Santa Hermandad; and just outside the northern gates to the city, the wonderful Hospital de Tavera, a mixture of courtyards, living quarters, chapels, and a museum (including a good selection of paintings and artifacts of Carlos I and the sixteenth-century Hapsburg Empire).

Elsewhere in the province, the castle of Guadamur a few miles west of

Toledo was built by Pedro López de Ayala in the mid-fifteenth century as a classic Italian-influenced structure. Further west, **Talavera de la Reina,** a Roman town (Casesarobriga), ancient center of silk manufacture and today a ceramics and porcelain center, uses clay that is aged for twenty-five years before use. Its six major churches show strong Mudéjar qualities. Beyond Talavera, **Oropesa** is a heavily fortified town, legacy of the counts of Oropesa, major landowners in this area, who in the fourteenth century built major defensive works to hold the town against the Muslims and later peasant rebellions.

To the north, between Madrid and Toledo, **Illescas** has two interesting churches, Santa María and the church of the Hospital Santuario de la Virgen de la Caridad founded by Cardinal Cisneros in the 1490s. To the southeast of Toledo, the small village of **El Toboso** is where don Quijote found Dulcinea, the love of his life. This imaginary character has a Casa de Dulcinea and a Cervantes center dedicated to her.

CUISINE. Special dishes include partridge in a vinegar sauce.

PERDIZ A LA TOLEDANA

2 whole onions, peeled	4 young partridges
4 cloves garlic, chopped	salt and pepper to taste
10 peeled almonds	3 small tomatoes
¼ cup olive oil	1 Tbs. butter
2 tsp. flour	¼ cup cognac
2 carrots, sliced	2 Tbs. vinegar

Preheat oven to 400°F. Boil onions. Toast the garlic over flame until brown, then peel and mash with the almonds. Stir in the olive oil and flour. Add carrots and onions. Then wash cavities of partridges with vinegar and water, and rub on the outside with olive oil, salt, and pepper. In a roasting pan, add partridges to carrots and tomatoes. Roast at 400°F for 45 minutes, then place in serving dish. Separate the juice and add the garlic-almond paste, butter, cognac, and vinegar, boiling for 5 minutes. Cook the pre-boiled onions in olive oil for several minutes. Spread the paste over the partridges, add the onions, and serve.

Chapter 16

OLD CASTILE
(Castilla y León)

REGIONAL CHARACTERISTICS. (Bardulia [Roman], al-Qila [Arabic], meaning "the castles"). Pop., 2,577,105. Area, 86,173 sq. km., 18.5 percent of Spain's national territory. Regional capital: León. Castilla y León is anglicized as Old Castile to distinguish the northern part of central Iberia from the south. It is "old" in the sense that this region reconquered the "new" (Ciudad Real, Cuenca, Albacete, Guadalajara, Toledo) from the Muslims. The region adjoins Galicia and Portugal on the west; Cantabria, Araba (Basque Provinces), Navarre, and Aragón on the north; Valencia, Murcia, and Aragón on the east; and New Castile and Extremadura on the south.

Old Castile's original unity came from the Castilian language, which emerged out of Visigothic and Mozarabic Latin. Castilian kept the final vowels *a-*, *e-*, and *o-*, dropped *u-* (*-airo* instead of *-aun*, etc.), replaced *-ç* by *-ss*, and made *-t*, *-k*, and *-p* silent. Arab loan words frequently appear in Castilian; approximately 10 percent of the vocabulary comes from Arabic words, many of them technical terms such as fortress, *al-qasr = alcázar*; mayor or justice of the peace, *al-gâdî = alcalde*; shop, *al-maxzan = almacén*; the customs house, *al-dîwâ = aduana*; and technical professions such as architect, *al-arîf = alarife*. Place names sometimes remained Arabic: Guadalquivir (white river), Guadalajara (river of stones), or Guadarrama (river of sand), for example, have *wâdî*, or river, as the root word.

Mozarabs of León began the adaptation of Arabic into Castilian for

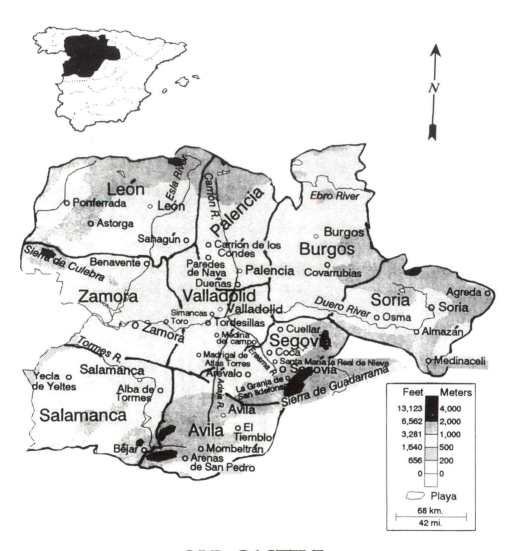

OLD CASTILE

liturgy, general theological vocabulary, and to compete with Visigothic Latin. The Navarro-Aragonese of La Rioja, Navarre, and Aragón introduced early poetry, and Cantabrians introduced dialect changes. Toledo's capture by Castile in A.D. 1085 ended Mozarabic's ecclesiastical use and popularized the Castilian of *Poema del Cid* by 1140. The standard orthography of Old Castilian, beginning about 1275, can still be heard as the Spanish component in Ladino (the Spanish-Hebrew language spoken by Sephardic Jews in the Mediterranean), but Castilian Spanish continued to evolve throughout the Golden Age of the sixteenth and seventeenth centuries as an imperial language, now spoken in the late twentieth century by nearly 350 million throughout the world.

Old Castile contains nine provinces, the largest number of any region in Spain. In the 1978 referendum, 69 percent of the region voted against regional autonomy because the new constitution made such old Castilian provinces as Madrid, La Rioja, Cantabria, and Murcia into separate regions. While some were more organic than others, Castilians found the loss controversial as a punitive act deprecating Castile's former leadership of the union of Spanish principalities.

The stalemate ended on February 25, 1983, when León's inclusion in Old Castile was confirmed, changing the region's name to Castilla y León. The senior principality for 350 years, León possessed a stronger claim on regional independence than other areas such as La Rioja, which had never been a principality. But since all of the areas once colonized by León were already a part of Castile, the Leonese had no alternative but to join the Castilians in forming Castilla y León. The regional capital, located in the city of León, was so placed in honor of the Leonese.

The flag of Castilla y León borrows traditional elements from the old. It is divided into four sections of red and gray; each red panel contains a yellow castle, and each gray panel has a red Castilian lion in an upright position.

The region ranks tenth in personal income.

AVILA

VITAL STATISTICS. Pop., 178,997. Area, 8,050 sq. km. Capital and diocesan see: Avila de los Caballeros (pop. 41,735), highest in elevation of the provincial capitals because of its location near the Guadarrama Mountains. The province borders Madrid on the east, Segovia and Valladolid on the north, Cáceres and Toledo on the south, and Salamanca on the west.

ECONOMY. This lightly populated province is an area of sheep grazing, wheat farming, and tourism.

HISTORY. (Obilia [Celtiberian], Avela [Roman]). Early Celtiberian villages on the cliffs overlooking the Río Adaja or at Guisando on the Toledo border reached a relatively high level of sophistication. The carved granite bulls of Guisando are one of the few large Celtiberian remains. Romans incorporated the area into eastern Lusitania, and during the era of early Christianity Avila was an apostolic diocese and a place of martyrdom during the final Roman persecutions in A.D. 304. Muslim rule lasted for several centuries until raids by Navarre and León encouraged the first resettlement of Christians in 940. Arab and Christian herders and farmers coexisted for a time, but missionary activity by the bishops of Compostela tipped the balance in favor of the Christians.

Collective herding activity by the Honrado Compañía de la Mesta (Honorable Company of the Mesta), founded in the late thirteenth century, provided Avila's first source of prosperity. The Mesta's principal sheepwalk (cañada) from Béjar to Burgos ran through the area, and a woolen textile industry grew up to clothe Toledo and Madrid. The increasing importance of both cities caused court nobles, favorites, and Castilian kings of the later Middle Ages to purchase estates throughout the area. Isabel the Catholic grew up in the province, and she and Fernando later often spent long periods in Avila. Fray Tomás de Torquemada, Isabel's confessor and the first Inquisitor-General, had many facilities built for use by the royal family in Avila de los Caballeros, which as the birthplace of St. Teresa, great mystic and reformer of the Carmelite Order, also became a pilgrimage site.

Agricultural grievances between grain growers and sheep owners caused the province to join the unsuccessful Comuneros protest in 1520. Not everyone, however, was a rebel. Provincial nobles such as the third duke of Alba, Fernando Alvarez de Toledo (1507–82), faithfully served the Hapsburg monarchy, although as governor-general of the Netherlands from 1567 to 1573 Alba's cruelty and arrogance contributed to the loss of the Low Countries. In 1594, rebellion flared again in Avila when the town of Madrigal de las Altas Torres staged an unsuccessful plot against the Portuguese territories inherited by Felipe II fourteen years earlier.

By the eighteenth century, the province showed the ecological ravages of hard use by the Mesta. Erosion and the destruction of timberlands were accompanied by a decline of grain farming and created a class of serranos (hill farmers) who were forced to practice subsistence farming. The Bourbons tried to aid Avila's economy by establishing a royal cotton factory and creating a military academy for infantry, cavalry, and engineers, but Napoleon's forces later destroyed both.

Liberal reforms of the nineteenth century only slightly improved agriculture, since there were few large Church estates to break up in the province. The political boss of Avila and Madrid, Francisco Silvela (1845–1905), tried to use his influence to provide government employment, but many peasants drifted away as the great depopulation of rural Spain began.

Avila became a no-man's-land during the civil war when the struggle for Madrid turned central Castile into a war zone. In the postwar period, the

Franco regime placed great emphasis upon Avila's Catholic heritage. Early in the constitutional monarchy, King Juan Carlos selected as premier the former minister of the national movement, Adolfo Suárez González (b. 1932) of Avila de los Caballeros, to succeed Carlos Arias Navarro on March 26, 1976. Over the next four years, Suárez developed the middle-of-the-road Unión de Centro Democrático party to support the king in the constitutional process that completed the transition from dictatorship to democracy. On January 29, 1980, Suárez resigned over troublesome issues in the autonomy process and the economy.

LITERATURE. The first writer of the province, **Alonso Tostada de Madrigal** (d. 1455), bishop of Avila, furnished prolific commentaries on the scriptures.

The province's most famous writer is **St. Teresa de Jesús** (1515–82). Teresa de Cepeda y Blásquez de Ahumada was one of nine children of a petty noble family; she joined the Carmelite Order at the Convent of the Incarnation in 1533. A serious illness almost caused her death, but she claimed that her survival came from a mystical union with God. This union dominated the rest of her life, and she often experienced direct communion and mystic raptures, visions, and stigmas. At first, Church authorities thought her under the influence of demons, but St. Francisco Borgia, second general of the Jesuits, certified her spirituality. In 1562 she began a campaign to reform the Carmelite Order by restricting outside contact of members to ensure the privacy necessary for the practice of mysticism. She traveled widely to create the Descalzas Carmelitas (Discalced or "barefoot" Carmelites), founding thirty-two convents of the reformed order based on a philosophy of solitude, hardship, manual work, and poverty.

St. Teresa's major works are *Camino de perfección* (1565), a guide to spiritual education; *El libro de las fundaciones* (1573), a history of the Barefoot Carmelites' founding; *El libro de su vida* (1588), her spiritual biography; and *Las moradas* (or *El castillo interior*, 1588), about the relationship between the soul and God. Her concept of the soul contains seven areas, each connected with a series of prayers and experiences leading to greater understanding and mystical experience until union with God could be reached. Teresa expressed a simple, pure, and spontaneous mysticism. Few other persons have ever sacrificed so much for their religion or found such satisfaction in doing so. St. Teresa received beatification in 1614 and canonization in 1622, becoming a doctor of the church in 1967 when Pope Paul VI elevated her as the first woman to reach this highest of all ranks in Catholicism.

Teresa's male counterpart, **St. Juan de la Cruz** (1542–91), a mystical poet and Discalced Carmelite reformer from Ciudad Real, spent part of his career in Avila. The modern writer **Camilo José Cela** of Madrid spent summers at Cebreros from 1947 to 1950, using Avila as a retreat for writing.

ART. Serious painting began with the **Master of Avila** (ca. 1470), but few of his works remain in the province. Juan de Borgoña (John of Burgundy, ca. 1508) greatly enlarged the cathedral of Avila de los Caballeros. It contains paintings by Santa Cruz, Pedro Berruguete, and Borgoña, as well as altars and decorative work by Isidro Villoldo and Juan Frías (1549–53). Berruguete also decorated several lesser altars to St. Peter Martyr and St. Dominic in the Hispano-Flemish manner and did a retablo at the Real Monasterio de Santo Tomás on the life of St. Thomas Aquinas, one of his greatest works.

MUSIC. A major sixteenth-century composer of church music, **Tomás Luis de Victoria** (1548–1611) of Avila, has been compared to Palestrina. His greatest work is *Officium Defunctorum*, a mass for the dead (1603). Victoria was trained in Rome before taking the position of chaplain at the chapel of Felipe II's sister, the Dowager Empress María. He was the first composer to set to music all the hymns of the liturgical year. *O magnum mysterium* (1572), a mass for a four-part choir done in triple time, is another of his great works, typical of Victoria's belief that the mass is something that should be happy and often jubilant.

CUSTOMS AND SOCIETY. Traditional dress for men of the province once centered around the *coleto*, a tunic or smock made of leather or dark brown cloth, laced in the front. Men also wore a black felt hat, its brim turned up at the sides. Women's dress was unexceptional, favoring the long skirts and full blouses, scarves, mantillas, and kerchiefs of other districts.

The most commonly mentioned traditional dance in Avila is the *Dulzania*, *jota*-like and danced by couples. Variations include the woman throwing on the floor a ribbon or a peseta (the basic unit of currency), which her male partner had to pick up without losing a step.

The feast day of St. Teresa, October 15, is the most important celebration in Avila de los Caballeros. *Verbenas* (carnivals), parades, singing, and dancing honor her as the patron saint of the city. The area is rich with the lore of mysticism and often holds religious processions of a penitential character.

HISTORIC SITES. The city of **Avila de los Caballeros** is surrounded by magnificent medieval walls ten feet thick and thirty-five feet high, with eighty-eight watchtowers and nine major gates. This completely walled city is one of Castile's great sights, rising from a considerable elevation to dominate the surrounding area. Inside the walls, cobblestone streets and ecclesiastical architecture continue the medieval illusion. The cathedral of San Salvador is Castile's first major Gothic structure, begun in the early twelfth century by Fruchel, who used red and white stones for the main interior walls. Nine chapels and two exterior façades make the cathedral an unusual and fascinating building.

The basilica de San Vicente, a Romanesque structure on the site where St. Vincent and his sisters, Cristeta and Sabrina, suffered martyrdom, had sandstone walls and extensive statuary somewhat like that of the cathedral of Santiago de Compostela. The churches of San Andrés, San Segundo, San Pedro, Santiago, and San Nicolás are Romanesque. Outside the walls, the church of the Real Monasterio de Santo Tomás, commissioned by the Mendoza conde de Tendilla (1442–1515) and built in the late fifteenth century for Fernando and Isabel, contains the tomb of their only son, Juan (d. 1497), a work done by the Italian sculptor Domenico di Alessandro Fancelli (1469–1519). Another tomb in Santo Tomás, that of the Grand Inquisitor, Tomás de Torquemada, is a replacement for the original, destroyed earlier.

St. Teresa's followers will be interested in the monastery built in the seventeenth century on the site of her childhood home, or the convent of La Encarnación, where she spent twenty-nine years. Her cell is now converted into a chapel, and the convent library has some of her manuscripts.

Outside Avila de los Caballeros, the province is filled with churches built during the late Middle Ages in places such as **Muñopepe** or the Santuario de Nuestra Señora de Cubillo in **Aldavieja.** Remains of fourth century B.C. Iron Age villages can be found near **Cardeñosa** in the Las Cogotas Wilderness Area or near **Solosancho** in the Ulaca Wilderness Area.

In the southern part of the province, the mountain town of **Arenas de San Pedro** in the Sierra de Gredos has the monastery of San Pedro de Alcántara, designed by Ventura Rodríguez during the reign of Carlos III (1759–88). The palace of the *infante* don Luis de Borbón, also here, became his jail after Carlos, his brother, exiled him from Madrid. **El Tiemblo** is the site of the ruined Guisando monastery where Enrique IV of Castile and his sister, Isabel the Catholic, signed the agreement allowing her succession in place of Enrique's daughter Juana. Outside town, the Toros de Guisando are the famed remains of Celtiberian granite bull sculptures.

In the southwest, **Piedrahita** is the chief home of the Albas, one of Spain's richest families. The present castle dates from the eighteenth century. Nearby, the monastery of Santo Domingo, founded in the fourteenth century, now is largely ruined. The cathedral of Asunción is fifteenth century.

In the province's north, legend claims that Hercules founded **Arévalo** and that Saint James once preached in the village. Arévalo was recaptured from the Muslims in 1088 and became an important residence for many noble families. Isabel the Catholic spent part of her youth at the Palacio de Goda, and the Altamirano and Mayorazgo Verdugo palaces and large residences built for the marquises de los Altares, Cárdenas, Villasante, and Arévalo also survive. The walled town of **Madrigal de las Altas Torres** (Madrigal was the name of an early bishop), site of the palace of the Kings of Castile built in the era of Juan II, was the birthplace of Isabel the Catholic in 1451. Carlos I donated the palace to the Augustinian Order for the convent of Madres Agustinas de Nuestra Señora de Gracia, a residence for illegitimate daughters of Castilian monarchs. The town is walled with watchtowers that provide the last part of the town's name. Finally, in the eastern part of the province, the Santuario de Nuestra Señora de Cubilla was designed and built by Juan de Herrera.

CUISINE. *Cocinilla* fireplaces (ceramic ovens) roast the traditional Castilian dish of suckling pig until very tender. Kid is prepared the same way. The dessert *yemas de Santa Teresa*, a beaten confection using eight egg yolks, sugar, cinnamon, and lemon peel, has an obvious connection with Avila de los Caballeros.

BURGOS

VITAL STATISTICS. Pop., 363,474. Area, 14,292 sq. km. Capital and diocesan see: Burgos (pop. 156,449). The northernmost province of Old Castile, Burgos is south of Cantabria and the Basque Provinces; east of Palencia and Valladolid; west of Araba (Alava) of the Basque Provinces, La Rioja, and Soria; and north of Segovia. The Condado de Treviño, a separate county appended to the province of Burgos because the area's ethnicity is overwhelmingly Castilian, is completely surrounded by Araba. The Ebro River traverses the northern part of the province.

ECONOMY. Growth of assorted manufacturing industries has supplemented wool processing industries. Sugar beets are a specialized crop grown in the Ebro Basin, but agriculture has been hurt by minute division of land among farm families.

HISTORY. (Brigaecae [Celtiberian], Clunia Suplicia [Roman]). Evidence of Celtiberian settlement comes from pottery remains and Great Mother cult statues at Brigaecae and Galaice typical of Mediterranean Magna Mater practices. Pompey established a Roman post at Clunia Suplicia, ca. 72 B.C., but the province was relatively uninhabited until A.D. 800, when subjects of the Kingdom of Asturias-León fortified the south bank of the Ebro River. Alfonso III established the town of Burgos in 884, and the castle of the conde Diego Rodríguez Porcelos began to provide military protection for the pass through the Obarenes Mountains where Al-Mundhir was defeated in 882 and 884.

Not long thereafter, the conde Fernán González created an elite cavalry of 600 lesser nobles to fend off further attacks on Castile. Promising land if the knights succeeded in their struggle, Fernán González created the basic Reconquest dynamic of military service for the acquisition of land. Fernando I (1037–65), son of Sancho III el Mayor (1004–35) of Navarre, led Castile (then claimed by both León and Navarre) in campaigns against León as well as the disintegrating Muslim world of southern Spain. These small Muslim principalities, successors of the Umayyads, could not stop Fernando from ranging as far west as Coimbra (Portugal) or as far south as the Guadalquivir River, until Badajoz, Toledo, and Zaragoza were made into Castilian tributaries. Burgos marked these victories by becoming an episcopal seat in 1075.

The era of Rodrigo Díaz de Vivar (1043–1099) introduced the hero of *El Cantar de Mío Cid* as the ideal "captain from Castile" who furnished a paradigm for a true medieval knight, always willing to fight another day for spoils and adventure. His exploits helped confirm the military character of Castile, since the Cid (from the Arabic *sidi*, or lord) or champion (*campeador*) first received notice for valor during the siege of Zamora. In 1091, he conquered Valencia but did not give it to Fernando's successor, Alfonso VI (1065–1109), with whom he had quarreled. Indeed, the Cid quarreled with everyone. His honor was all-important, and by fighting to maintain honor he created a useful mythic standard for Castile as exemplar of the *caudillo* or *conquistador*. His life symbolized the rise of Castile, but his legacy also meant that future rulers had to prove their fitness and could not expect automatic obedience.

Final victory over Islam took centuries to complete, but early cultural nationalism and church-state unity to attain this goal began when the Council of Burgos in 1080 replaced the Mozarabic mass with the Latin rite to purify Castilian Roman Catholicism. Alfonso VI (1158–1214) convoked the first Cortes in 1208 to reward with land those who participated in the crusade-like Reconquest. St. Dominic (Domingo de Guzmán, 1170–1221), a monk from the area who became prior of the monastery of St. Sebastián at Calaruga (now Santo Domingo de Silos), illustrated Castile's rising fervor in 1208 when he helped lead a crusade against heresy in southern France. Dominic created the Dominican Order, a new type of friar preachers who constituted a powerful proselytizing force throughout the later Middle Ages.

The Castilian monarchy suffered a momentary defeat at Alarcos in 1195, but in coalition with other Christian principalities and the military orders of Calatrava, Santiago, and Alcántara they scored a smashing victory in 1212 against the Muslims at Navas de Tolosa. Fernando III (1217–52) used the victory to merge León with Castile (1230) and then complete the conquest of Andalusia by seizing Murcia (1243), Jaén (1246), and Seville (1248). The monarchy obtained so much wealth from these triumphs that it purchased the *patronato real* from the papacy, gaining the right to appoint high ecclesiastical officials throughout Castile.

As the frontier moved south, Castilian monarchs began to spend less time in Burgos. Fernando lived in Seville and was buried there. His successor, the brilliant Alfonso X (1252–84), passed fruitful years in Salamanca and Toledo. Alfonso XI (1312–50) returned to Burgos because of its rising importance in the wool trade, but Pedro the Cruel (1350–69) avoided the town and its restless nobility. When Pedro was defeated by Enrique de Trastámara (eldest son of Alfonso XI's mistress, Leonor de Guzmán, half-brother to Pedro, and first Trastámara), Enrique II (1369–79) renewed the southern campaign and spent all of his time in the field as a military commander. Enrique III (1390–1406), Juan II (1406–54), and Enrique IV (1454–74) rarely appeared in Burgos, but because Isabel the Catholic received financial support from the area during her bid to become queen of Castile, when Granada was conquered in 1492 she gave Burgos the wool *consulado* by the Privilege of 1494.

Long associated with the Mesta, Burgos used its monopoly over Castilian wool to take charge of Spanish wool exports, the largest in Europe. The town quickly grew into a national wholesaler in the marketing, sale, and shipping of wool to textile manufacturers in the Low Countries and Italy, usually via the Cantabrian and Basque regions. Even though Fernando and Isabel (1474–1516) governed more from Avila, Segovia, or Granada than from Burgos, the *consulado* made Burgos into a dynamic economic center and even financed development of the University of Mercaderes.

This exalted position was not without its difficulties. The disputed inheritance of the Hapsburg Carlos I (1517–56) caught Burgos between aggressive nobles, a new foreign monarch, and frustrated citizens in the Comuneros revolt. Its city officials joined those of León, Valladolid, and Zamora to protest fiscal policies in 1517. Burgos originally belonged to the junta of towns in 1520, but dropped out, fearful of losing its royal connections, when populist anger stirred serious violence. Problems continued under Felipe II (1556–98) and later Hapsburgs, who handled the Dutch rebellion (1566–1648) so badly that the wool industry's northern connections were ultimately lost in 1648.

As the wool profits declined, problems with roads, poverty, education, and lack of progress in general grew ever greater. Efforts to expand wheat production during the nineteenth century failed for lack of expert agronomy. Burgos continued to live in the past, its population of 9,000 supporting nine parish churches and at least six monasteries. The popularity of traditional movements was evident from the Carlists on. The democratic Second Republic never achieved popularity or support in the area, and on October 1, 1936, Franco installed his new rebel government in Burgos. The town remained the Francoist capital until Madrid fell in April 1939. During the postwar period, Burgos was rewarded for its loyalty by being made a development zone in the Economic Plan of 1966.

LITERATURE. Burgos is celebrated in the anonymous *El Cantar de Mío Cid*. "El Cid," a Muslim title meaning "My Lord," was an honorific title won by Rodrigo Díaz de Vivar for his exploits in Castile, Aragón, and Valencia. This important epic poem celebrating Spain's Christian Reconquest is filled with motives of personal envy and exaggerated family honor that later became hallmarks of the Spanish personality.

Rodrigo Díaz de Vivar, "El Cid," participated in a series of raid-like victories near Toledo while very young, but when Fernando I died in 1065 Díaz remained loyal to his son Sancho, who was murdered by the traitor

Bellido Dolfos during the siege of Zamora. Although Sancho's brother and successor, Alfonso VI of Castile, swore three times to the Castilian nobles that he had had nothing to do with the plot, Díaz broke with Alfonso in 1073 either over Sancho's murder or because he felt that the new king had slighted him.

The poem begins with El Cid cheating Jewish merchants to put together an army of 300 soldiers. His force defeated the Christian count of Barcelona, served the Muslim king of Zaragoza, and then joined his former lieutenant, Alvar Fáñez, as mercenaries in the struggle between two Muslim kingdoms, Murcia and Valencia. A subplot concerns the marriage of his daughters to the princes of Carrión, their dishonoring, and the revenge El Cid obtained. In the end, he emerged as the Christian conqueror of Valencia, a virtual king in exile, personally victorious and honorable in his long struggle against difficult odds.

The Cid's story was recounted in numerous fragmentary manuscripts, of which the most important are *Carmen Roderici* and other chronicles of Castile and León such as the *Crónica de 1344* and *Rodrigo*, which portray him as a rash young nobleman quite different from the Cid of the primary version, *Cantar de Mío Cid*. There is no question that a real El Cid did exist, since Arab documents found in Middle Eastern archives make considerable mention of him, but the romantic noble version did not fully develop until **Guillén de Castro's** *Las mocedades del Cid*. The Frenchman Pierre Corneille later used Castro's work as source of his own *Le Cid* (1677), which spread the story across the European stage. Other Spaniards who wrote about the Cid include José Zorrilla, *La leyenda del Cid*, and Eduardo Marquina, *Las hijas del Cid*.

During the later Middle Ages, the *converso* **Pablo García de Santa María** (1350–1435) of Burgos, a historian, began recording historical contents of the oral tradition. **Alfonso de Santa María de Cartagena** (1384–1456), another *converso* of Burgos and son of the Great Rabbi of Burgos, Solomon Ha-Levi, made his mark as a humanist poet who as the bishop of Burgos in 1435 encouraged publication of poetry and stories about the Cid. **Alfonso Alvarez de Villasandino** (1345–1425) of Burgos achieved fame as a troubadour who kept alive the story of El Cid, while **Juan Alfonso de Baena** collected many of these ballads in *Cancionero de Baena* (c. 1445).

The Golden Age produced only **Francisco de Enzinas** (1520–52) of Burgos, a humanist who studied at Louvain, taught in England, became a disciple of Luther, and translated the New Testament into Spanish.

In the twentieth century, **Victoriano Crémer Alonso** (b. 1910), an editor and publisher in León, composed poetry such as *Nuevos cantos de vida y esperanza* (1952), reflecting a fear of the human condition and a new belief in God.

ART. Construction of the cathedral of Burgos, the largest Gothic structure in Spain, began in 1222 and turned the town into an art center. By the late fifteenth century, the Burgos school encompassed the Colonia (German) and Siloé (Flemish) families. There is little biographical information about either clan, but **Juan de Colonia** was hired by Archbishop Alonso de Cartagena in 1436 to design and build the cathedral towers. He married a Spanish woman, and his son **Simón de Colonia** finished his father's work after Juan's death in 1480. Simón designed the Condestable Chapel financed by Pedro Fernández de Velasco, constable of Castile and husband of María de Mendoza, daughter of the marqués de Santillana. **Gil de Siloé** did the acclaimed monastery of Miraflores outside Burgos and the altar of the chapel of Santa Ana in Burgos Cathedral as well as a second altar in the Condestable Chapel. His son, **Diego Gil de Siloé**, made the plateresque into an important Burgos style. He is first mentioned in 1517 as a student working in Naples, but by 1521 he had designed the so-called Golden Staircase in the cathedral of Burgos, sometimes considered to be the most beautiful creation of plateresque art. His later work included the central chapel of the cathedral in Granada.

Other foreigners contributing to the art of Burgos include the Frenchman **Felipe Vigarny**, who arrived in 1498 to do the alabaster reliefs in the ambulatory of the cathedral and the great retablo in the cathedral of Toledo. The neo-Flemish painter of the Neapolitan school, **Girolamo Imperato**, did several important works for Santa María de la Vid in Burgos. Fray **Juan Rizi** (1600–1662?), the Spanish-born son of an Italian painter (Antonio Ricci of Ancona), painted the *Stigmatization of St. Francis* for the Burgos Cathedral, while Diego Guillén and Pedro López de Gámiz decorated the monastery of Santa Clara in Brivienca. The churches of Medina de Pomar contain work by Diego de Siloé, Gregorio Fernández, and Cristóbal de Andino. The museum in Medina de Pomar has religious relics of don Juan of Austria. Ecclesiastical art in Covarrubias includes the *Adoration of the Magi* by Gil de Siloé and a diocesan museum with works by El Greco, Zurbarán, Ribera, and Berruguete.

MUSIC. A court organist during the reign of Felipe II, **Antonio de Cabezón** (1510–66) of Castrojeriz, developed contrapuntal pieces for the organ called *tientos*, a form of prelude, as well as composing a series of themes and variations.

Francisco de Salinas (1513–90) of Burgos, a blind musician trained formally in Italy, became a professor of music in Salamanca, ca. 1567. He adapted modern theories of composition and collected Spanish folk music.

CUSTOMS AND SOCIETY. Castile once was known for its *casticismo*, which may be defined simply as the very essence of being Castilian. Such traits as a haughty autocratic manner, to the point of being domineering, or a meditative quality of preoccupation or concentration characterized the earlier Castilian personality. The title *hidalgo*, coveted especially in the sixteenth and seventeenth centuries, literally meant the "son of a noble" and offered the security of a social status essential for the pursuit of distinction independent of economic status. *Caballero* was a lesser noble who had usually performed military service to obtain a title and land.

On the other hand, Castilian egalitarianism, as V. S. Pritchett has noted, caused them to live their national life more in castes than classes. For members of many castes, nobility was less important than individual character. This quality, which was highly prized, came to represent personal social virtue—the absolute quality of a person. Manners, respect, and honor knew few social limits. In time, the growth of a more urban society has diminished many of these courtly aspects of behavior, but a residue of formality and respect still is noticeable among the Spaniards.

HISTORIC SITES. The cathedral in **Burgos**, which one writer has characterized as a gnarled, dour, idiosyncratic building, dominates the skyline with 275-foot twin towers and many lesser spires. The present structure was begun in 1221 according to plans drawn up by Bishop Maurice of Burgos for a French Gothic cathedral in Castile. The roof is not as steep as those of French cathedrals, and the interior decoration by Juan de Colonia (c. 1440) and the bas-reliefs on its exterior and towers are more like those of the Cologne Cathedral. The interior has a nave with two aisles, transept, ambulatory, and a vaulted dome. The greatest French influence is in the south transept portal with its many sculptured details. Christ is surrounded by evangelists, supported by apostles in the lintel, and adored by angels in the voussoir. In the center of the cathedral is the grave and memorial to El Cid Campeador. High on the wall of the sacristy stands the rusty old iron-bound chest called the Coffer of the Cid, which the knight filled with sand to represent the gold he promised to his early backers.

Nine chapels add a great deal of interest to the cathedral. The Condestable Chapel is an octagonal structure integrated within the cathedral at one end, an unusual example of German late Gothic style. Begun in 1482, the chapel honors Pedro Fernández de Velasco, *condestable* (constable) of Castile, and his wife, María de Mendoza; it was designed by Simón de Colonia, the master architect's son. The sculpture on the tomb shows the constable still holding his sword. The chapel of Santa Tecla is the decorative work of José Churriguera. A large cloister with a number of sculptures leads to a museum and chapter house adjacent to the cathedral. In the chapel of Santísimo Cristo hangs the miraculous Christ of Burgos, said to have been done by Nicodemus, who had known Christ in Jerusalem. The main figure looks extremely lifelike.

Other landmarks of Burgos include the churches of San Nicolás, San Gil, Santa Gaeda, and San Lesmes. Alfonso VI allegedly broke off relations with El Cid at Santa Gaeda, forcing the Cid to campaign independently against Aragón and Valencia.

Many buildings remain from Burgos's era as the capital of Castile. The church of the Real Monasterio de Las Huelgas (1187), burial place for early Castilian monarchs, contains only the tombs of Alfonso VIII and his wife,

Eleanor of England. The chapter house has a spectacular Muslim battle standard captured at the battle of Las Navas de Tolosa (1212). The Hospital del Rey (also 1187) served the poor and pilgrims on the route to Santiago. The Carthusian monastery of Miraflores, founded by Isabel the Catholic's father, Juan II, was decorated by Simón de Colonia on orders of Isabel the Catholic. The tombs and altar-piece are by Gil de Siloé. La Casa del Cordón, palace of the *condestable* of Castile, dates from 1482.

Elsewhere in the province, the convent of San Pedro de Cardeña outside the city of Burgos is the grave site of El Cid's prized mare Babieca. Northeast of the city of Burgos, **Briviesca** possesses many religious buildings or institutions such as the art-filled Renaissance monastery of Santa Clara, San Martín, the domed Santa María, and Santa Casilda, a pilgrimage chapel. Much further north, near the Ebro, **Medina de Pomar** owes its public buildings to the Velasco family, who built a church and endowed the Convento de Santa Clara with its large collection of art.

Approximately twenty miles southeast of Burgos, **Covarrubias** has a very large Gothic church of the fourteenth century, with three art-filled chapels and the nearby tenth-century doña Urraca tower. The Castilian administrative archive, the Adelantamiento de Castilla, also is located in Covarrubias. Further southeast, **Peñaranda de Duero** is site of the Miranda Palace, a fine example of Renaissance architecture. **Lerma**, directly south of Burgos, once was an important dukedom built by the duke of Lerma, Philip III's corrupt favorite. It contains the ducal palace, the church of San Pedro, and the monasteries of Santo Domingo, San Blas, Santa Teresa, and Santa Clara, all of the seventeenth century.

CUISINE. The old practice of *asado*-style slow roasting of meat still is practiced here. *Cordero asado* (roast lamb), *chuletitas* (lamb cutlets), *manitas* (lamb's feet), *mollejas* (sweetbreads), *riñones* (kidneys), *sesos* (brains), and *cocidos* (vegetable stews) are typical winter fare. Baby lamb is prepared as follows:

LECHAZO ASADO

4 lbs. lamb	salt and pepper to taste
⅛ lb. butter	1 Tbs. thyme
1 bay leaf	1 Tbs. vinegar
1 clove garlic	1 cup white wine
2 Tbs. chopped parsley	

Rub lamb with butter, spices, and vinegar and roast at 425°F for a half hour, then pour wine on the roast and cook at 200°F for an additional 2 hours, basting often.

LEÓN

VITAL STATISTICS. Pop., 517,973. Area, 15,581 sq. km. Capital: León (pop., 131,134), also regional capital. Diocesan sees: León and Astorga. The province is the largest of Castilla y León and lies between Asturias and Zamora on the north and south, with Lugo and Orense (Galicia) to the west, and Palencia and a corner of Valladolid to the east. The Río Esla runs north to south, and the hills of the Cantabrian Pyrenees occupy the northern section of León. The Leonese consider Salamanca and Zamora (and perhaps even Palencia and Valladolid) to be part of León.

ECONOMY. León is second only to Galicia in the cultivation of root crops such as beans and lentils. Barley is a leading grain crop, and sugar beets are also important. Wool is produced by the area's large herds, and León ranks third after Galicia and Asturias in mining iron ore, largely in the Astorga and Ponferrada fields adjacent to Asturias. About 30 percent of Spain's anthracite comes from the Bierzo, Fabero-Bembibre, Villablina, and Caboalles valleys in León.

HISTORY. (Legio [Roman]). The once-large Celtiberian population, colonized by the Romans during the Cantabrian War, lived in the villages of Lanca, Astorga, and Legio, with mining, the wool trade, and specialized agriculture dominating their economy. Muslim society touched the area only very lightly, and after Ordoño I of Asturias (850–66) annexed León it provided a base for the slow conquest of Palencia, Salamanca, Valladolid, and Zamora. Alfonso III el Magno (886–911) styled himself emperor and moved his neo-Gothic court from Oviedo to León.

After Ramiro II (931–51) won at Simancas (939) and Talavera (950), expansion slowed down when Almanzor sacked Burgos, León, and Zamora between 985 and 1002, and then because King Alfonso V (970–1028) died in battle while campaigning in Andalusia. The delay allowed Castilian nobles time to organize an independent principality and Navarre to intervene in Leonese affairs. Sancho el Mayor (1000–1035) of Navarre put Castile under his protection in 1028, and Sancho's second son, Fernando, claimed León as the dowry of his wife, the late Alfonso V's daughter Sancha, and defeated her brother Vermudo in 1037 to reign as Fernando I of Castile. Because Sancho el Mayor divided his empire among his sons, Fernando was free to pursue the aggrandizement of Castile, which soon dwarfed both León and Navarre.

Yet for more than a century and a half, the Castilian dynasty, still nonimperial in mentality, treated León as a separate royal property. It was ruled by the sons of Fernando I from 1065 to 1072, reunited with Castile under Alfonso VI (1065–1109) and Alfonso VII (1126–57), and separated again during the reigns of Sancho III (1157–58), Alfonso VIII (1158–1214), and Enrique I (1214–17) of Castile when Fernando II (1157–88) and Alfonso IX (1188–1230) ruled León. The two states finally merged in 1230 when Fernando III of Castile inherited León. Castile, just on the verge of great power status as Andalusia's conqueror, did not separate the two until 1978.

Power in Leonese society fell to the nobility, a powerful elite dominated by the condes de Luna (whose palace in León still exists) and the condes de Oñate, the marquises of Villafranca, and the Enríquez family (ultimately admirals of Castile), who bridged the two principalities to become some of the largest landowners in Castilla y León. They provided leadership of the royal council, an institution that had passed from Asturias to León as a consultative judicial tribunal. The council tended to curb absolutism and to take legislation beyond the narrowly dynastic. The Council of León in 1091, for instance, officially decreed substitution of Latin for Visigothic script in all ecclesiastical documents and writings, a process that elevated León to a position of national leadership in the reformation of the Spanish Church.

In addition, by consolidating their sheep herds into a collective flock to drive them from winter to summer pasture in the north and south, the lords of León created a prototype for the Honrado Concejo de la Mesta, an institution with royal protection and national status that in 1273 became Europe's greatest grazing institution. Herders and growers of the province supervised the drive, administered pastures in Extremadura, and often filled the office of the judge attached to the Mesta to hear cases of trespass and damage.

Although the Mesta gave León much of its later power and prestige, herding also depopulated the province and destabilized settled agriculture. The city of León possessed a population of only 3,000 by 1700. Efforts to industrialize in the eighteenth century created a new linen industry, but the Mesta's final collapse minimized economic growth. Peasant life slowly recovered in the nineteenth century as new experiments in grain farming produced a cash crop and rural areas managed to preserve their municipal commons.

New industrial jobs in the iron and coal mines of the Bierzo Valley greatly increased prosperity and population but also introduced new social and political grievances. Violence exploded in 1917 and again in October 1934, the second time as an offshoot of the Asturian insurrection. Buenaventura Durruti (1896–1936) of León, a militant in 1917 and an international desperado before 1936, commanded the militia army of Aragón during the first months of the civil war until his death during the siege of Madrid on November 20, 1936.

Many socialist miners met the same fate. Some died defending the republican government in Madrid, while others fell to the various forces supporting Franco that seized the province after an extremely bitter battle on July 20, 1936. Atrocities against republicans in Ponferrada caused guerrilla bands to roam northern parts of the province until the fall of 1937.

In the postwar era, the Franco regime placed great stress on the antiquity of Leonese society but also invested in mining and manufacturing. Its active economy created one of the most prosperous areas within Spain, although the rural nature of León often disguises the relative degree of prosperity.

LITERATURE. Early provincial literature occupied an important role in the emergence of letters and learned professions. The monk **Vimara** and the painter **Ioannes,** by using Visigothic and Muslim decorative sources, produced one of the earliest Christian illuminated manuscripts, the so-called *Bible of León* (ca. 1050). A legal treatise in Latin, the *Forum Iudicum,* was produced, ca. 1025, as a summary of Gothic law. Such thirteenth-century ecclesiastical writers as **Martín of León** (d. 1203) and **Lucas of Túy** (d. 1249) chronicled religious struggles such as the Albigensian Crusade in Latin. The anonymous *Crónica de Alfonso III* (ca. 1200?) may have been one of the first books in Castilian Spanish.

New signs of intellectual life did not reappear until the eighteenth century. Fray **Martín Sarmiento** (1695–1772), a disciple of Fray Benito Feijóo y Montenegro, defended his master in *Demonstración crítico-apologética del Teatro crítico universal* (1732). Sarmiento's other work, *Memorias para la historia de la poesía y poetas españoles* (1775), is an inexact but ambitious study of early Spanish letters.

The best-known regional literary figure of this period, Padre **José Francisco de Isla** (1703–81), also followed the enlightened Feijóo. Isla's major work, *Historia del famoso predicador Fray Gerundio de Campazas, alias Zotes* (1758–68), is a satire on the pedantry and emptiness of religious education, sounding some typically eighteenth-century themes. The main character, affectionately called Zotes, is a vacuous and illiterate youth who rises within the religious hierarchy to become a famous preacher, so often confused that he rarely has any idea what he preaches. Isla wrote other satirical pamphlets against the nobility, the Church, and the middle class, becoming one of the most important figures in the Spanish Enlightenment.

Leopoldo Panero (1909–62) of Astorga has been called the most skilled lyric voice in Spain since the civil war. *La estancia vacía* (1944) discusses God in terms of man's existence. Life becomes a constant search for belief, always leading backwards toward youth and greater simplicity. His prize-winning *Escrito a cada instante* (1949) is an ode to the province of León and to the town of Astorga, a nostalgic review of those things that hold greatest meaning for the individual.

Two other writers have lived and done significant work in León. As prior of the cathedral of León, the creator of Renaissance drama in Spain, **Juan del Encina** of Salamanca concluded his career in León. **Juan Benet** (1928–92) of Madrid, who worked as an engineer in the province for more than a decade, wrote brilliantly about León, which provided the setting for a quartet of his novels about the civil war collectively titled *Herrumbrosas lanzas* (1980–87). Of these, *Volverás a Región* (1974) is particularly effective in using a stream-of-consciousness narrative to illustrate how all Spaniards reacted to the experience of the war. His most recent book is *La construcción de la torre de Babel* (1990).

ART. León is a center of early Mozarabic art and architecture, characterized by primitive Romanesque churches built in the form of a Latin cross with Muslim decorative details. The area's leadership during the early Reconquest attracted Christians from all over the peninsula, and here Spanish Catholicism began its own architectural history.

During the early fifteenth century, a painter of French origin, **Nicolás Francés** (ca. 1430), introduced a more general Gothic style. He created the stained glass and retablos in the cathedral of León, which show subtlety and great harmony of color. The plateresque style of Spanish architecture is most noticeable in the façade of the convent of San Marcos in the city of León, a significant building of the late sixteenth century.

In Astorga, the cathedral of Santa María has several chapels decorated by Rodrigo Gil de Hontañon, a statue of the Immaculate Conception by Gregorio Fernández, altarpiece sculptures by Gaspar Becerra (1520–68, a Spaniard who studied with the mannerist Vasari in Italy), and a *Pietà* by Rogier van der Weyden. Its eight chapels, dedicated to kings, saints, and the Virgin, have a decorative style rich with Flemish carvings, silver shrines, monstrances, a throne, and other artworks. Of particular importance is *Nuestra Señora la Blanca*, an ivory figure similar to that of the Virgin of Rheims in France. The lintel above the Virgin is covered by a happy scene of the religiously blessed holding a fiesta. The Diocesan Museum has a wooden reliquary of Alfonso III.

CUSTOMS AND SOCIETY. Since the Bierzo Valley in northwestern León is one of the most rugged parts of the pilgrimage road to Santiago de Compostela, local folklore is filled with the suffering of pilgrims, their dogged devotion, and the miraculous rescues some experienced in the mountains.

León is also the real beginning of northern Spain. Wood or stone granaries, called *hórreos*, dot the countryside as the most typical structure of northern Spanish rural society. In the early twentieth century, these rural districts of León remained so isolated that a group known as the Maragatos, who lived near Astorga, maintained the legend that they represented a fragment of the original Celtiberian population. On the other hand, mainstream Spanish society considered them to be descendants of the Moors or Jews. In their traditional role as muleteers or teamsters who transported Galician seafood to Castile, the Maragatos wore distinctive primitive clothing and refused to marry outside their clans.

The mountaineers of León traditionally dressed in heavy wool with leather gaiters and *abarcas*, a type of sandal that laced up the leg. Sheepskin jackets and a blanket or small rug worn like a *serape* protected them against winter weather. Urban men, on the other hand, often wore embroidered waistcoats and wide-brimmed felt hats, while women of the towns made and wore wide embroidered waistbands over white wool skirts, protected by two aprons covered with sequins. Long winter cloaks were plain black for married women, or black edged with red for unmarried women.

The old dances came from Asturias and the Basque region, particularly those that used a double circle of dancers, men outside, women inside. Males performed spectacular solos, and certain dances used an ending with the Basque call of "hi-ju-ju." The *Giraldilla*, in which each man had two female partners, was characterized by the women's turns and the man's leaping choreography.

HISTORIC SITES. The Colegiata de San Isidoro is an important early Reconquest period church in the city of **León**. San Isidoro's dramatic history began in 988 when Almanzor destroyed an earlier church on the site. Reconstruction and expansion came in 1063 during a time of growth and importance in the Kingdom of León. To celebrate the rise of a northern Spanish Christian nation, the remains of St. Isidoro (570–636) were moved from Seville to León, where they were buried in a special tomb. The building is starkly Romanesque, forming a Latin cross with a nave, two aisles, three apses, and three chapels, one of them in the apse. Its ceiling frescoes, done in the late twelfth century in white and other natural colors, are Byzantine-inspired and include an *Annunciation* and *Last Supper* based on local scenes.

Next to San Isidoro, the Panteón de los Reyes, another historical building, is a cryptlike portico with groin vaults containing the remains of eleven Kings of León and family members. The structure has unusual frescoes and ornamental capitals.

The cathedral of Santa María de Regla, begun in 1254 and under construction for 300 years, is French Gothic to commemorate the abbey of Cluny's role in the pilgrimage of St. James. Many of the workers who built the cathedral of Burgos also worked on Santa María. The cathedral forms a Latin cross with a nave, two aisles, and a tripartite transept. The west façade has two 200-foot towers and a massive rose window over the portico. The interior is lit by three other large rose windows and sixty smaller stained glass windows, unusually light and colorful for a Spanish cathedral. A large cloister adjoins the cathedral, and the museum is larger than most. What makes this cathedral especially interesting is the maintenance of its original plan. There have been no later additions to alter its original thirteenth-century design.

Another religious building, the convent of San Marcos, is important as the birthplace of the military Order of Santiago, formed in 1173 to defend Christianity against the Muslims and to protect pilgrims traveling to Santiago de Compostela. Before Isabel died, the Catholic Kings designated San Marcos as a ceremonial center to convey Spain's thanks to the Order of Santiago for its role in the Reconquest. Construction lasted from 1513 until the eighteenth century and created a very tall, 328-foot-long spectacularly ornate plateresque façade. Inside are a cloister, chapter house, and church. The monastery no longer exists, and a hotel and the provincial archaeological museum now occupy its space.

Many other interesting parish churches exist in León. The oldest is the tenth-century Salvador de Palaz de Rey, while the church of San Martín has a considerable art collection.

Elsewhere in the province, between León and Astorga on the west at **Valencia de Don Juan**, the large castle of Oñate has double walls and six towers, while the Nuestra Señora del Castillo Viejo is the burial site of the counts of Valencia de Don Juan and the location of an important statue of the Virgin Mary. A few miles south of Valencia de Don Juan, **Sahagún** is a good example of a Reconquest frontier town, and its churches of San Tirso, San Lorenzo, Santuario de Peregrina, and the San Benito monastery all have Mozarabic features.

Further west, **Astorga** contains the cathedral of Santa María, which unfortunately contains little of the original church consecrated in 1069. Construction on the present cathedral began in 1471. It has a plateresque west façade, chapels, choir stalls, and a diocesan museum that has a good collection of ecclesiastical art. The churches of San Estéban and Santa Marta are also richly decorated, but the oddest is the Art Nouveau archbishop's palace built between 1889 and 1913 by the famous Catalan architect, Antoni Gaudí. It is a free Gothic rendering with turrets, spires, and arches made of white stones and black concrete. The Catalan-born bishop who commissioned the design died in 1893, construction stopped due to the project's unpopularity, and it was finished in 1913 only on a much reduced scale. Astorga also has a museum that commemorates the pilgrimage to Santiago de Compostela.

Further to the west is **Ponferrada**, dominated by the historic twelfth-century Templar Castle built to protect the pilgrims' way to Santiago de Compostela. The church of Santo Tomás de las Ollas (ca. 925) is a rare combination of Visigothic and Muslim features with horseshoe arches. At the confluence of the Brubia and Valcárcel rivers, French pilgrims traveling to Santiago de Compostela built the village of **Villafranca del Bierzo** with a number of Romanesque churches and a castle of the marqués of Villafranca. The nearby hamlet of **Cacabelos** surrounds a very old Asturian fortress in one of the highest portions of the pilgrimage route south of the Pyrenees.

In the other direction, not far east of León, **Gradefes** contains the church of San Miguel de Escalada, now part of a monastery but still one of the finest Mozarab churches in Spain. An exiled Benedictine community from Córdoba began the construction of San Miguel in 913. It has three horseshoe-shaped apses and painted interior walls covered by colorful textiles and *azulejos*, the glazed tiles used in Muslim architectural decoration. The altar, in the manner of the early Middle Ages, is hidden by a screen to evoke the mystery of the mass.

In the northeast, **Mansilla de la Mulas** is a walled city on the Río Esla. Nearby **Lanca** was once an important Roman town, the ruins of which have been excavated.

CUISINE. León's varied menu includes *pescados al horno* (baked fish), *trucha* (trout), salmon, and *ternera* (veal).

TERNERA

2 lbs. veal	1 onion, chopped
flour	1 cup tomato sauce
4 oz. butter or margarine	salt and pepper
½ cup meat stock	

Flour the veal and brown it in butter or margarine. Cover with stock and cook over low heat for 1½ hours. In another pan, combine onion and tomato sauce. Pour over the veal 5 minutes before it is served. Add salt and pepper to taste.

Picón (blue cheese) or the semisoft *queso de León* and wine from the El Bierzo and Cacebelos valleys also are popular products of León.

PALENCIA

VITAL STATISTICS. Pop., 186,512. Area, 8,052 sq. km. Capital and diocesan see: Palencia (pop., 74,080), sometimes called the granary of Castile. The province is a fertile plain bounded by Burgos and León on the east and west and Cantabria and Valladolid on the north and south, watered by the Río Carrión.

ECONOMY. Palencia is a wheat, oats, and barley growing center and also raises sheep. The modern capital has a Renault automobile transmission factory and other small technical industries. The once important mining of anthracite coal has declined considerably.

HISTORY. (Pallantia [Celtiberian and Roman]). The name Palencia is derived from Palantuo, an important chief of the Celtiberian Vaccaeis tribe. Romans made the town provincial capital of Citerior in place of Numancia (Soria), and it later became an early Christian bishopric. Theodoric's Visigoths settled the area in A.D. 457; some areas are still called *campos gó-*

ticos. The adoption of Christianity climaxed with King Recceswinth's founding of the basilica of San Juan de Baños in 661.

After 715, Muslims controlled the area loosely until Ordoño II of León freed some northern regions in the early tenth century. Sancho III of Navarre later took Cea and Bernesga, but the entire province came into Castilian control in 1037. Rodrigo Díaz de Vivar was one of many Castilians well known in the province. El Cid married his Palencian wife Jimena at the church of San Miguel, and both of his sons-in-law came from Carrión de los Condes.

The bravery and service of Palencians to Castile at Navas de Tolosa in 1212 caused their province to be chosen as the site of Christian Spain's first university, opened by Tello Téllez de Meneses (d. 1240), a member of a leading clan who later married into the Castilian royal family. The university was soon over-shadowed by Salamanca, created only a year or so later. The Cortes of Castile often met in Palencia during the thirteenth and fourteenth centuries, and a number of Palencian nobles filled offices in the Honrado Concejo de la Mesta, the large Castilian herding organization.

The province strongly backed Isabel of Castile against her rival and half-sister, Juana la Beltraneja, but its support for Isabel's daughter Juana in the Comuneros struggle caused Felipe II to permit ecclesiastics and nobles from Valladolid to absorb many local sees and noble property. The area also lost its representation at the Cortes of Castile until it was allowed to repurchase the right in 1666. These economic difficulties stimulated immigration to the New World. Pedro de la Gasca (1533–91) of Palencia played an important role in the pacification of Peru (ca. 1577–86).

Economic growth resumed in the eighteenth century. Small grain farmers obtained favorable prices and had no difficulty finding markets once Spain's population began to grow more rapidly after improvements in health care and public sanitation. Liberal land reform in the nineteenth century had little impact, since Palencia was not an area of large estates. The railway era enabled grain to be brought to market more cheaply and stimulated iron and coal mining. Labor politics had some impact when the development of coal mines created an industrial work force, but the province supported a minor Catholic agrarian party in 1931 and the Confederación Española de Derechas Autónomas (CEDA) in the provincial elections of 1933 and 1936. Socialist miners, who staged a general strike in sympathy with the Asturian insurrection in 1934, fell to local Franco supporters in July 1936. The province never saw an organized military campaign, but the mining communities suffered some vigilante justice.

LITERATURE. The *Proverbios morales* of **Sem Tob** (1290?–1369?), one of the first Jews to write in Castilian, combines a sense of despair over the predicament of Jews in Spain with a beautiful lyric use of Castilian. **Manrique Gómez** (1413–91) of Amusco wrote an early play, inspired by the marqués de Santillana, entitled *La representación del Nacimiento de Nues-*

tro Señor, a Christmas story set at the convent in Calabazanos. The drama, religiously tolerant, is unusually sophisticated for its time.

Jorge Manrique (1440–79), son of the conde de Paredes (Master of the Order of Santiago), wrote courtly romances and poetry. His major work, the elegy *Coplas a la muerte del Maestre don Rodrigo, su padre*, remembers his father's death. The work, a meditation on the transitory nature of life, condenses into one poem all of the important sentiments of a medieval man. Its format, *pie quebrado* verse, created the standard two eight-syllable lines followed by a half line of four syllables so often found in Spanish verse. The elegy has been set to music by several Spanish composers and influenced the poetry of the Frenchman François Villón. Henry Wadsworth Longfellow translated the elegy into English. Manrique himself died in the religious war with Granada.

Since then, the province has produced only **Michael de Carvajal** (1502?–76?) of Palencia, an early playwright. Little of his work survives.

ART. The Gothic cathedral of Palencia, begun in 1321, has a wooden plateresque altarpiece by Jan Joest de Harlem (1505), sculptures by Juan de Flandes, and retablos by Juan de Balmaseda. Alejo de Vahia, a local sculptor, carved statues of Mary Magdalene and of St. John the Baptist for the high altar. The museum of the cathedral contains El Greco's *St. Sebastián* and other paintings by Pedro and Alonso Berruguete, Mateo Cerezo, Nicolás Francés, and Valdés Leal, and sculptures by Gil de Siloé, Juan de Balmaseda, Alonso Cano, Martínez Montañes, and Pedro de Cuadra. Juan de Flandes (?–1519), a painter trained in the Ghent-Bruges school whose masterpiece is the *Temptation of Christ* (now at the National Gallery of Art in Washington, D.C.), did ten paintings for the cathedral's altar, of which *Christ Carrying the Cross* is the best known.

The lively later artistic tradition of the province began with the Berruguete family, natives of the province. **Pedro Berruguete** (1450?–1503) of Paredes de Nava, a town north of Palencia, was trained in Italy. His work synthesized the styles of Flanders and Italy and showed the increasing influence of the Renaissance, particularly in his work at the cathedral of Toledo. Pedro's son **Alonso Berruguete** (1485–1533?), also of Paredes de Nava, followed his father to Italy, but the influence of Ghiberti, Donatello, and Michaelangelo turned his vocation to sculpture and he became the chief sculptor of the Royal Chapel in Granada. Some of his sculptures are in the National Sculpture Museum in Valladolid, and there is a sculpture of him in the city of Palencia.

Just outside Palencia, the church of San Juan de Baños has three rectangular apses and three aisles, separated by columns supporting horseshoe arches. It is the best of the few remaining examples of seventh-century Christian Visigothic architecture.

MUSIC. One of the earliest composers of liturgical music in Spain, **Conancio** (607–38), also began the formal training of choirs. Later, the choirmaster of the cathedral, **Antonio Rodríguez de Hita** (d: 1787) of Palencia, assumed the directorship of music at the royal Convent of Incarnation in Madrid, ca. 1755. His musical works included the *zarzuelas Las Segadoras de Vallecas* (1768) and *Las Labradoras de Murcia* (1769), the latter work a masterpiece of the genre. In Enlightenment fashion, his works extolled the virtue of the common people.

CUSTOMS AND SOCIETY. One traditional dance indigenous to Palencia, the *baile de Santo Toribio*, is a civic event in which long lines of dancers accompany city officials to the cathedral for a blessing of bread to insure prosperity. The city of Palencia celebrates its patron saint San Antolín with bullfights in the old plaza.

HISTORIC SITES. Built on the ruins of a seventh-century Visigothic basilica, the cathedral in **Palencia** incorporates the old church's remains as the crypt of the medieval Gothic cathedral. It has a nave and two aisles with an ambulatory, groin vaulting, and an uncompleted tower. There is also the large church of San Pablo, part of a thirteenth-century Dominican monastery; the church of San Lázaro, built ca. 1050; and San Bernardo with a plateresque façade.

Elsewhere in the province, the church of San Martín in **Frómista**, like so many of the structures in the north along the pilgrims' trail, is Romanesque with an apse composed of three interlocking stone rings. Also far to the north in the province, **Aguilar de Campoo** is an ancient town that still has the ruins of its medieval walls, the monastery of Santa María la Real (founded in 822), and several ancient Romanesque churches. **Paredes de Nava** is the birthplace of the medieval poet Jorge Manrique, the painter Pedro Berruguete, and his son, Alonso Berruguete. Some of their paintings can be found in the Santa Eulalia parish museum.

To the northeast, **Carrión de los Condes** briefly housed the Council of León. Its largest church, Santa María de la Victoria, and the convent of San Zoilo are both tenth century. In the south, Fernando and Isabel first met at **Dueñas**, and there is a fifteenth-century Gothic castle and church in **Ampudia.**

CUISINE. Like much of Old Castile, Palencia uses the *asado* technique of roasting meat. *Lechazo* (roast lamb) and *tortilla de patata a la española* (potato omelette) are as popular here as everywhere else in Spain.

Tortilla española has nothing to do with the Mexican tortilla; "tortilla" simply means omelette in Castilian.

TORTILLA ESPAÑOLA

2 potatoes	4 eggs, beaten
2 onions	salt to taste
⅛ cup olive oil	

Peel and chop the potatoes and onions into small bits and mix together (small pieces of ham may be added as well). Then cook for 15–20 minutes over low heat. Heat oil to moderate temperature in a frying pan and add the eggs, lightly salted. When the omelette begins to stiffen, add the vegetable mixture and smooth. Cook for 3–4 minutes, remove from heat, and place a plate upside down over the pan. Flip both so that the omelette comes out in one piece.

SALAMANCA

VITAL STATISTICS. Pop., 368,055. Area, 12,350 sq. km. Capital: Salamanca (pop., 167,131). Diocesan sees: Salamanca and Ciudad Rodrigo. The University of Salamanca and the Pontifical University draw thousands of students to Salamanca. The main river is the Tormes.

ECONOMY. The ranches of Ciudad Rodrigo raise bulls. Wool is still an important commodity, and Béjar markets and processes wool.

HISTORY. (Salamantica [Roman]). Salamanca originated as an early Celtiberian trading center on the western plateau of Castile. Primitive fortresses at Candelario indicate a well-organized, skilled society. Romans, attracted by trade, entered the area during the Second Punic War and maintained a connection throughout the imperial age.

Vandals replaced the Romans about A.D. 420, followed by the Visigoths in the sixth century and the Muslims in the eighth. Ramiro II of León defeated Abd ar-Rahman III at Alhandega in 933 and gave Salamanca a municipal charter two years later, but Almanzor severely damaged and looted the town in 977, leaving Salamanca as a no-man's-land for more than a half century. In 1057, Fernando I of Castile reoccupied the town, and in 1085 Alfonso VI of Castile finally freed most of the province. Missionary efforts by the archbishops of Santiago de Compostela brought more settlers, and Alfonso IX of Castile created the University of Salamanca in 1220.

Royal patronage and the frequent presence of Alfonso X enhanced Salamanca's rise to the level of a great European university. Students belonged to *colegios mayores*, which were smaller selective colleges of the university. The humanists Peter Martyr and Lucio Marineo Sículo, the grammarian Elio Antonio de Nebrija, and the jurist Juan Ginés de Sepúlveda spent their careers at the university, and the staff's quality attracted many visitors. During Christmas season 1486, Christopher Columbus made his most important early argument for a western voyage as a new, direct route to the Orient at a meeting in Salamanca. Hernán Cortes, St. Ignacio Loyola, and Lope de Vega studied at the university, and Francisco Vázquez Coronado

(1510–54), the explorer of North America, came from the town. A woman, Beatriz de Galindo (1475–1534), may have briefly taught Latin at the university before becoming a lady-in-waiting to Isabel the Catholic.

The quality of education initially attracted many foreign students as long as Latin remained the scholarly language of the day, but expulsion of Jewish students in 1492, international conflicts that cut off the flow of foreign students, and adoption of Castilian instead of Latin reduced the university's scope. After the Council of Trent, the Counter-Reformation's strictures punished Fray Luis de León, who began serving a jail term of six years in 1572 for having questioned the accuracy of Latin biblical translations. Intellectual topics were influenced by the Reformation, but the arts and literature kept Salamanca a lively place.

The city of Salamanca joined the Comuneros movement in 1520 to demand justice against noble misrule. Perhaps by way of punishment, its bishopric was lost to Valladolid in 1593. The War of Independence turned the area into a frequent battle site, since Salamanca had the misfortune to be on the route from France to the Portuguese border. Napoleon invaded Portugal through Salamanca in November 1807 to attack the Anglo-Portuguese alliance, but the British reoccupied Salamanca until General John Moore evacuated Allied forces on December 11, 1808. The French remained until July 1812.

In 1835, a new national university in Madrid weakened the University of Salamanca. Liberal cabinets solicited bribes to enroll students and sometimes failed to deliver tax revenues needed to expand university facilities. Change did not come until the Basque philosopher and writer Miguel de Unamuno became rector in 1900. The unpopularity of General José María Primo de Rivera stirred unrest during his dictatorship, and service as "pedagogical missionaries" in 1932 radicalized some students. During the Second Republic, peasant riots in the surrounding province and anarchist demonstrations in the city were common.

General Franco's forces captured Salamanca during the first week of the civil war. Unamuno remained as rector of the university until October 12, when he had his famous exchange with a rebel general, José Millán Astray, whose motto, "Down with intelligence! Long live Death!" caused Unamuno to make his famous "temple of intellect" reply. He commented sadly that while the army might win, they could never persuade intelligent people because they possessed neither reason nor the right to dominate society. Unamuno, quickly relieved of office, died on December 31, 1936.

Throughout the remainder of the civil war, Salamanca was the site of Franco's Ministry of Defense. A military college added to the university in the postwar era enrolled Juan Carlos as a student when he began his college education in 1955. Emergence of student unrest in 1956 led to demonstrations in Salamanca and eventual appointment of Antonio Tovar as rector, a Falangist intellectual. Tovar modernized the university but later resigned his membership in the Falange.

LITERATURE. Salamanca's first patron, **Alfonso X**, el Sabio, king of Castile, is credited with some of the earliest scholarly work at the university. Scribes helped him produce a series of important collections and works: the famous compilation of laws, *Las siete partidas*, which harmonizes Christian, Hebrew, and Muslim law; *El fuero real*, a summary of the most basic royal laws; *Cantigas de Santa María*, a large collection of Gallo-Portuguese poems; and other works on astronomy, chess, and history. Carlos Fuentes argues that Alfonso consciously imitated St. Isidoro of Seville in trying to revive culture in a new period of Christian domination.

The origins of **Bartolomé de Torre Naharro** (1476?–1531?) are unknown, but he studied at Salamanca before becoming a priest and spending the rest of his life in Italy. He wrote *Propaladia* (1517) in Spanish to provide rules for composition of drama according to classical principles. **Juan del Encina** (1469–1529?), born near Salamanca, also was crucial in the creation of Spanish Renaissance drama as a playwright, musician, and poet. His works, *Égloga de Christino y Febea* (1499?), *Égloga de las grandes lluvias* (1507), *Zambardo y Cardonio* (1504?), and *Égloga de Plácida* (1506?) are all short pastoral plays that added comic peasant speech to dialogue. In particular, the *Églogas* (Eclogues) reproduce peasant conversations by using stylized rustic buffoonery and quaint language designed to amuse aristocrats. Patronized by the duke of Alba, Encina often spent time in Rome, where he was a member of a minor order. He eventually rose to be prior of the cathedral in León.

A professor of music, **Lucas Fernández** (1474?–1542) of Salamanca, wrote *Auto de la Pasión*, one of the finest *autos sacramentales* (one-act religious plays). He also created a number of secular plays, but his writing differs from Encino's by being more comedic and realistic. He also produced seven *Frasas y églogas*, the best known of which is *Plácida y Vitoriano*. His most original work, *Auto de la Pasión*, is a Holy Week drama set during the Roman period concerning the conversion of a pagan.

The eighteenth century became a special time of creativity in Salamanca. **Diego Torres Villarroel** (1693–1770), best known as an almanac-maker, wrote a picaresque work, *Vida*, invaluable for period and place because he taught so long in Salamanca. **Francisco Sánchez Barbero** (1764–1819) of Moriñigo, a poet of secular works and friend of José Moñino, the marqués de Floridablanca (1728–1808), founded the newspaper *La Constitucional*. During the Restoration, his advocacy of Floridablanca's ideas of reform caused Fernando VII to have Sánchez Barbero jailed in 1817.

José Iglesias de la Casa (1748–91) created the Arcadia Agustiniana, the first school of poetry in Salamanca, specializing in a style satirizing humankind's earthly efforts. Other members included Fray **Diego Tadeo González** (1733–94), **Juan Meléndez Valdés** (1754–1817), and the Asturian statesman **Gaspar Melchor de Jovellanos** (1744–1811). A second poetry group, Academia Cadálsica, became active later in the eighteenth century by strongly criticizing the period's cold French lyric poetry. Other writers of the time included the pre-romantic **Nicasio Alvarez Cienfuego** (1764–1809); **Manuel José Quintana** (1772–1857), nationalist poet during the War of Independence; and **Juan Nicasio Gallego** (1777–1853), also a nationalist poet. A third poetry group, the Parnasis Salmantina, flourished briefly at the end of the century.

In the modern era, **José María Gabriel y Galán** (1870–1905) of Frades de la Sierra, a poet, tried to popularize archaic Castilian. **Carmen Martín Gaite** (b. 1925) of Salamanca is part of the "wounded generation" of the post-1945 period. Her works include *Entre visillos* (the 1957 Nadal Prize winner), *Ritmo lento* (1963), and *El cuento de nunca acabar* (The Never-Ending Story, 1983). Gaite's technique takes themes of popular Spanish sentimental novels, called *novelas rosas*, and changes them into psychologically defining works for women. In 1988, she won the Prince of Asturias Prize.

Many professors or writers such as **Miguel de Unamuno** and **Clarín** wrote in Salamanca. The popular anonymous novel *La Vida de Lazarillo de Tormes* and **Fernando de Rojas'** *La Celestina* were both probably written in Salamanca as well. Spaniards from other regions frequently wrote about the city. **Cervantes** wrote *El Licenciado Vidriera* about a bizarre student and his misadventures in Salamanca. **Lope de Vega** did the drama *Las Batuecas del Duque de Alba*, about poor peasants, on the duque de Alba's land in the province. A major picaresque novel set in the city, *Vida del buscón, llamado don Pablos* by **Francisco Gómez de Quevedo y Villegas** (1608?) concerns the lives of boardinghouse dwellers. *El estudiante de Salamanca* by **José de Espronceda** is the vivid story of a debauched student. Others who wrote in and of Salamanca include St. John of the Cross, Calderón, Góngora, and St. Ignacio Loyola.

ART. Salamanca is a center of good art and architecture. Two of the greatest works are the design of the Plaza Mayor by **Alberto de Churriguera** and the altarpiece in the chapel of San Bartolomé and scenes from the Last Judgment on the choir vault by **Nicolás Florentino**.

A third masterpiece is the "new" cathedral of Salamanca (there are two) designed by Juan de Alava, Rodrigo and Juan Gil de Hontañón, Juan Gil Mozo, Juan de Ribera, and Joaquín and Alberto de Churriguera. **Rodrigo Gil de Hontañón** (1523?–77?), who came from Salamanca, particularly linked Gothic, Mudéjar, and plateresque details in this work. The cathedral's diocesan museum has a collection of fifteenth-century paintings that includes several important works by **Fernando Gallego** (ca. 1466–1505), a Salamanca native and one of the first Castilian painters to adopt the Hispano-Flemish style. His paintings for the altarpiece of the Virgin and of St. Andrew and St. Christopher are in the old cathedral.

Paintings by **Jusepe de Ribera** (1591–1652), a Valencian-born, Italian-trained naturalistic painter who lived most of his life in Naples, can be found in several churches. One of Ribera's masterpieces, *Virgin of the Immaculate Conception*, is at the convent of Agustinas Descalzas, which also has paintings by Claudio Coello, Rubens, and Nicolás Florentino, and sculpture by Luis Salvador Carmona. Asisclo Antonio Palomino, a sixteenth-century artist from Córdoba whose work is mainly in Salamanca, did the baroque frescoes at the church of San Esteban.

The University of Salamanca's art includes paintings by Juan de Flandes in the Salinas music room, Fernando Gallego, Felipe Bigarny, and Jusepe de Ribero. A painting of Carlos IV by Goya hangs in Paraninfo Hall.

Elsewhere in the province, St. Teresa, who died at the Carmelite convent in Alba de Tormes (1582), is honored with works by Luis de Morales and many others.

MUSIC. The master of ceremonies in the household of the second duke of Alba, **Juan del Encina**, wrote *representaciones*, pastoral playlets accompanied by songs that can be found in the collection *Cancionero de Palacio*, which are among the first secular songs to be preserved. *Endechas* lamented death; *ensaldas* burlesqued madrigals; and *villancicos* were rustic songs performed by peasants at village festivities.

Much later, **Tomás Bretón** (1850–1921) of Salamanca, an outspoken foe of the Italian musical influence in Spain, popularized the need to create a national lyric theatre. For this purpose, he composed the operas/zarzuelas *Los Amantes de Teruel* (1899), *Garín* (1892, with a Catalan setting), and *La Dolores* (1895), which ran for a record-setting 112 performances in Barcelona and was later performed in Milan, Vienna, and Prague as a full-scale opera.

CUSTOMS AND SOCIETY. Small groups of student street singers known as *la tuna*, dressed in medieval student robes, are particularly prevalent in Salamanca and frequently engage in competitive songfests that can last through the night. In La Alberca, Assumption Day (which marks the ascent of the Virgin Mary to heaven) is celebrated with great ceremony in the folk pageant called *Ofrenda a la Virgen* (A Gift to the Virgin).

The countryside, devoted to equestrian activities and bull raising, is *charro* (literally, the peasant culture of Salamanca, although it means *vaquero* or cowboy culture in Mexico). Not surprisingly, the traditional dance is called *charrada*, a couple dance in which the upper body is held stiffly while the feet are very active. One observer compares the steps of this dance to those of the Russian Cossacks. Another dance, the *rosca*, is a male-female chase frequently performed around the feast table at weddings.

The gala *charro* costume is very different from the same dress in Mexico. Men wore short velvet breeches decorated with gold or silver buttons on the side of the leg, a velvet coat, and a wide-brimmed hat with a peaked crown. *Charras* wore a bell-shaped skirt richly embroidered and covered with sequins, jet, or fine gold braid, crossed in the back to form a bow of cloth. Embroidered aprons decorated with silk flounces, velvet jackets, and black dancing slippers completed the ensemble. Modified cowboy boots with narrow toes and Cuban heels are more Andalusian than Castilian.

HISTORIC SITES. Built between 1729 and 1733, the Plaza Mayor of **Salamanca** is one of the most important, beautiful, and large (243 feet by 269 feet) baroque squares in Spain, often compared with St. Mark's in Venice or the Zócalo in Mexico City. Its edges are covered by a continuous arcade, decorated by bas-reliefs between the arches of the arcade. It joins the old and new cathedrals into a single omnibus ecclesiastical structure incorporating many other cloisters, chapels, and religious buildings.

The old cathedral of Santa María, built, like so many other important Spanish churches, on the site of an earlier religious center (this one of the eighth century), was begun in the twelfth century. The Torre de Gallo dome, four turrets, and Romanesque arches surround the nave, two aisles, and three apses. Like so many other church buildings of the high Middle Ages in Spain, this part of the cathedral complex is a combination of Romanesque and Gothic design, but the Torre de Gallo adds a Byzantine quality to the simple but diverse aspects of Santa María.

Among the many details within the old cathedral is the meticulously detailed statue over the central altarpiece of the *Virgen de la Vega*, patron saint of Salamanca. Several guidebooks suggest that it is Spain's finest work of art. The altarpiece of the chapel of San Bartolomé, off the cloister of Catedral Vieja, contains fifty-three painted and carved panels from the life of Christ and the Virgin Mary.

Catedral Nueva was attached to the old by removal of the north transept near the Torre de Gallo and the attachment of two chapels side by side, with a large cloister forming a T at the side of the old cathedral, edged by five more chapels to form an amazing complex of religious architecture. The new cathedral's interior has a nave, two aisles, a number of chapels, stellar vaulting, and a dome. Built between 1513 and 1700, it has a basic Gothic style with Romanesque and baroque details. The exterior is remarkable for its three portals lined by fine ornamental moldings, an abundance of carvings on the tympanum above the main portal, and baroque statues along the walls.

Fifteen other churches of note and nine convents or monasteries can be found in the city. Most of the churches are twelfth or thirteenth century: San José, San Julián y Santa Basilisa (with an altarpiece by Joaquín Churriguera), San Juan de Barbalos, San Marcos, San Martín, Santa María de los Caballeros, Santiago, and Santo Tomás Cantuariense (the first church to be dedicated to St. Thomas à Becket). Their dominant style is Romanesque with Gothic additions. Alberto Churriguera designed the eighteenth-century San Sebastián, and his brother Joaquín did the church of La Vera

Cruz. Juan Gil de Hontañón designed Sancti Spiritus, a sixteenth-century church incorporating plateresque and Mudéjar elements.

Salamanca's monasteries and convents possess a rich history. The Carmelitas Descalzas Convent of San José, where St. Teresa experienced her religious ecstasy in 1571, is properly plain, while the convent of Agustinas de la Concepcíon, founded in the early seventeenth century, used the colonial riches gathered by the count of Monterrey to complete excess. The convent of Estéban, designed by Jusepe de Ribera (ca. 1590) at the peak of the Golden Century, has a plateresque external façade, interior gilded columns, and splashy artwork. One writer calls it the best expression of the religious fervor so frequently encountered in early modern Spain.

The university, an 800-year-old institution, is itself an architectural jewel, although only parts of the Colegio Viejo still exist. The courtyard of Escuelas Minores stands in back of a large fifteenth-century wall that has an elaborate plateresque façade. One of the larger rooms off the courtyard is the aula, today a museum. The Frater Luis de León lecture hall and the old library have been left in their original style and are good examples of the ancient university. The modern university is best seen at the Patio de las Escuelas on Calle de Libreros. Other colleges affiliated with the university include the Colegio de Anaya (1411), the Colegio de Calatrava (1522), and the Colegio de los Irlandeses (1521).

Salamanca also has some interesting secular architecture. The Casa de Conchas (built in 1514 to honor St. James) is often cited by the guidebooks, as are the palaces of Monterrey and Salina de Fonseca. In addition, a large Roman bridge crosses the Río Tormes. Of more contemporary interest, a new museum has opened in an annex of the National Historical Archives to focus on Masonic history in Spain.

To the south, **Alba de Tormes** is a popular pilgrimage site. St. Teresa died here in 1582 at the convent of Discalced Carmelite Nuns that she had created in 1571, and pilgrims come to see relics of her life and the art dedicated to her. The village also has two twelfth-century churches of San Juan and Santiago, both with abundant Mudéjar detail. The ancestral home of the dukes of **Béjar** contains their ducal palace, dominated by three towers, now housing the Museo Municipal and a collection of paintings; a Roman bridge; and the early medieval town wall. The village of **La Alberca** is a perfectly preserved medieval town (now a national monument) that displays folk crafts and arts and has an ancient farm demonstrating medieval agriculture.

To the west, **Yecla de Yeltes** has one of the oldest castles in Spain. Nearby is the Ermita de Nuestra Señora del Castillo, founded by Fernando and Isabel.

CUISINE. The native dish is *chanfaina salmantina* (fricassee of rice, chicken giblets, lamb sweetbreads, and *chorizo*), but as in much of Old

Castile, Salamanca's general cuisine features meat. *Lechazo pierna asado* (roast suckling pig) and *sopa de rabo de buey* (oxtail soup) are frequently served. *Farinato* sausages are bar food along with *tapas* such as *croquetas de jamón y queso* (ham and cheese croquettes) or *corteza de cerdo con anchoa* (fried pork skins with rolled anchovies).

SEGOVIA

VITAL STATISTICS. Pop., 149,286. Area, 6,921 sq. km. Capital and diocesan see: Segovia (pop. 53,237). The Eresma and Clamores rivers run through the province, with the city of Segovia sitting on a rocky rise between them. The province borders Valladolid and Burgos to the north, Soria and Guadalajara to the east, Madrid and Avila to the south, and Avila and Valladolid to the west.

ECONOMY. The most important economic activities are tourism and the production of wool and wheat.

HISTORY. (Segobriga [Roman]). Several Celtiberian villages occupied the northern slopes of the Guadarrama Mountains in the area when Roman occupation began in 80 B.C. A military post patrolled the trade routes and the silver road. Construction of the picturesque and famous aqueduct over the center of town came ca. A.D. 100, while the beautiful and often photographed Alcázar, sitting on the cliff overlooking the confluence of the Eresma and Clamores rivers, was built by the Muslims sometime in the ninth or tenth century as a fortress used to guard the town market.

The metropolitan see of Toledo played a crucial role in establishing monasteries such as Paular (1190) to farm the land and provide spiritual leadership. In 1166, the synod of Segovia united all Castilian bishops in a holy war against the Muslims during Alfonso VIII's regency. With their help, the wool industry flourished. The Mesta's sheepwalk from Logroño to Extremadura linked Segovia to the new prosperity of the thirteenth and fourteenth centuries. Townhouses of wool merchants and Mesta officials clustered around the cathedral of Segovia.

Several noble families rose to importance; the Fonsecas of Coca took the Alba dukedom, and Mendoza possessions spilled over into Segovia from neighboring Guadalajara. Enrique de Trastámara, bastard son of Leonor de Guzmán and Alfonso XI (1312–50) and victor over his half-brother, Pedro the Cruel (1350–69), made Segovia a semiofficial residence after becoming Enrique II (1369–79). When his great niece, Juana Enríquez, married Juan II (1458–85) of Aragón and bore Fernando the Catholic, collateral branches of the Trastámara family occupied the thrones of both Aragón and Castile, and in 1469 they were joined together in the marriage of the Catholic Kings, Fernando and Isabel, who were second cousins. The

Alcázar in Segovia became the ceremonial site of Fernando's oath to uphold the *fueros de Castilla* in 1469 before his marriage and also the place where Isabel negotiated to succeed her half-brother, Enrique IV (1454–74). She was crowned ruler of Castile at the Alcázar in 1474.

The Hapsburg dynasty replaced the Trastámaras in 1517 when Carlos, son of Juana of Castile (daughter of Fernando and Isabel) and the Hapsburg Philip the Fair, inherited the throne. Three years later, on May 30, 1520, the Comuneros rebellion broke out in Segovia against Carlos with the murder of Rodrigo de Tordesillas. Behind the act lay declining royal reliance upon the brotherhood of towns and rising noble power in provincial affairs. Segovia was a leader among the towns involved in the Comuneros, but a royal counterattack destroyed the cathedral and subjected the town to severe punishment by the Inquisition. By 1561, construction of the Escorial outside Madrid reduced Segovia's role in Castilian affairs even further by making the Alcázar superfluous.

Segovia revived in the eighteenth century when the Bourbons rejected the Escorial as too Germanic and built the palace of San Ildefonso de la Granja east of Segovia. The area remained an aristocratic enclave until construction of a railway from Madrid in the late nineteenth century transformed Segovia into a tourist center. The town remained conservative, and the political instability of the Second Republic caused one resident of Segovia, Dionisio Ridruejo, to become a member of the Falange in 1933. He rose to become political chief of the whole region in the civil war. The Falange captured Segovia without much bloodshed at the start of the war, but a republican offensive in May and June 1937 threatened it as part of the desperate and futile republican effort to aid the Basque Provinces.

After 1945, Segovia became the headquarters of the military high command. The contemporary boom in tourism continues to make it an important stopping point in central Castile north of Madrid, reached by day trips from the capital.

LITERATURE. The Comuneros rebellion is a major topic of Spanish historiography. The assumption made by nineteenth-century liberals that they followed in the footsteps of the Comuneros rebels was rejected by **Manuel Davila** in *Historia crítica y documentada de las Comunidades de Castilla* (1884). He viewed the uprising as little more than the product of noble and municipal economic self-interest threatened by the rise of a modern, progressive monarchy. Later, however, **José Antonio Maravall** pointed out in *Las Communidades de Castilla: Una primera revolución moderna* (1963) that the Comuneros, by introducing nationalism and constitutionalism to Spain, produced strong ideological overtones important in the later centuries.

Among provincial writers, **Antonio de Herrera y Tordesillas** (1549–1625) of Cuéllar, the official historian of the Indies and Castile under Felipe II and III, wrote *Décadas o Historia general de los hechos de los castellanos* *en las islas y tierra del mar océano* to interpret the conquest of the Indies as a Christian crusade. **Antonio Enríquez Gómez** (1600–1663) of Segovia, a novelist, poet, and playwright of the Calderón school, wrote a satirical novel, *El siglo pitagórico, y Vida de don Gregorio Guadaña.*

The poet **Antonio Machado y Ruiz** (1875–1939) of Seville lived in Segovia from 1919 to 1921. The Basque **Miguel de Unamuno** (1846–1936) also spent long periods in Segovia and once wrote that the Alcázar looks like a golden stone steamship sailing through an ocean of wheat.

ART. Muñoz de Pablos designed the Alcázar's windows and did the painting of Isabel's coronation. Antonio Bermejo reconstructed the Alcázar after it was damaged by fire in 1882.

Juan Gil de Hontañon and his son **Rodrigo Gil** designed the reconstruction of the cathedral of Segovia in the sixteenth century. Pierre de Chiberry, Francisco Herranz, and Juan Danis created the stained glass windows, while Diego Casado, Pedro Bustilli, and Juan García designed the Capilla Mayor in 1614 and Juan de Juni did the altarpiece in the Capilla del Santo Entierro. Elsewhere in the cathedral are found a triptych by Ambrosio Benson, paintings by Sánchez Coello, and the Cross of the Lozoyas by Manuel Pereira. The cathedral museum contains paintings by Pedro Berruguete, Alonso Cano, Morales, and Van Eyck, and a reliquary by Benvenuto Cellini. The cathedral's reconstruction took place just before the building of the Escorial and influenced its architect, Juan de Herrera, to follow a similar style for the larger building.

The palace of La Granja has a large tapestry collection, while the Farnese Palace has paintings and frescoes by Bayeu, Canducci, Houasse, Jordán, Maella, and Ribera, and *La Caza* by Velázquez.

CUSTOMS AND SOCIETY. Segovia had a reputation for maintaining classical Castilian dress until the end of the nineteenth century. Women's wide skirts (worn over many petticoats), black velvet bodices laced in front over a white linen waist or camisole, and black velvet aprons set the traditional style, although the most noticeable feature was the black velvet bonnets worn instead of mantillas. Male dress featured short velvet or cloth trousers over white stockings and cloth or skin gaiters, a smock made of sheepskin or cloth and fastened by a leather belt from which hung a large outside pocket used as a purse.

Traditional dances include the oddly named *habas verdes* (green beans), a couple dance done with castanets with other partners cutting in on the couple. Round dances also were popular.

There have been occasional reenactments of royal history or earlier Spanish military history in Segovia, and sound-and-light programs for the Alcázar and aqueduct.

HISTORIC SITES. The town of **Segovia** is dominated by the picturesque Roman aqueduct and the Alcázar. The former, still in use, extends half a mile to the foothills on 165 arches, some as high as 96 feet, especially at the Plaza del Azoguejo in the center of town, where it is double-decked.

The Alcázar is all turrets, conical towers, and troubadour windows sitting on the edge of a precipice. It not only housed royalty but also served as a temporary prison for Juana of Castile and was the site of Felipe II's marriage to Anne of Austria in 1570. Alfonso X the Wise originally recognized the Alcázar for its beauty and had Mudéjar elements added. Juan II built two halls, El Solio and Las Pinas. Felipe II took time away from the Escorial to add a slate roof and the inner courtyard and to redo the portals. The building later became an artillery academy until a fire in 1862; today it is a military archive and tourist site.

The cathedral in Segovia is late Gothic (the last to be built in Spain) to replace the old structure destroyed in the Comuneros uprising. Juan Gil de Hontañan, designer of the Salamanca Cathedral, began its construction in 1525 and was succeeded by his son, Rodrigo Gil de Hontañan. Stellar vaulting and the golden color of the stones make the cathedral warm and spacious. Galleries above the chapels on each side run around the interior, which has a nave 352 by 168 feet long with two aisles. The marble and bronze altarpiece in the Capilla Mayor was a gift from Carlos III. The twelve chapels are heavily decorated.

The cathedral's exterior is dominated by the largest ecclesiastical tower in Spain, 352 feet high, although now reduced by a lightning strike to 295 feet. The cathedral's center dome is 225 feet high, and on the side walls flying buttresses, carvings, and tall windows make the building one of the most graceful cathedrals in Spain. A cloister, a chapter house, and a good museum are found next to the cathedral.

Other Segovian churches include the Romanesque San Esteban, San Juan de los Caballeros, San Justo, San Martín, and San Millán. In the valley below the Alcázar, the Knights Templar founded the twelve-sided church of Vera Cruz, modeled on the Holy Sepulcher in Jerusalem. Area monasteries include El Parral, which has a rich architectural heritage; San Antonio el Real, with Mudéjar paneling; and the most important, Santa Cruz la Real, founded by St. Dominic in 1218.

Significant secular architecture may be found in the Canonjía district of Segovia, where the wool merchants and provincial nobility built substantial townhouses in the late Middle Ages. The houses are still well preserved and handsome.

Elsewhere in the province, approximately sixty miles east, **Ayllón** has a wall and several beautiful gates. Contreras Palace is a striking Gothic fortification, while the monastery of San Francisco is said to have been founded by St. Francis of Assisi. Due north from Segovia, the church of San Juan Bautista in **Carbonero el Mayor** is another beautiful structure. Further north, **Pedraza** is an interesting town with the castle of Pedro Fernández de Velasco, a magnificent Plaza Mayor, and town walls. **Cuéllar** has a castle built by Beltrán de la Cueva, favorite of Enrique IV of Castile, four Mudéjar churches, and the Santuario de Nuestra Señora del Henar, which celebrates a medieval sighting of the Virgin.

Coca (Cauca [Roman]), approximately forty miles north-northwest of Segovia, is the site of the beautiful and often photographed fifteenth-century Fonseca Castle, built by the duke of Alba in Mudéjar style. The castle forms a square within a square, built on an irregular hillside site, with beautiful brickwork and elaborate pinnacle-like battlements. Part of the castle's beauty comes from the fact that it was never damaged or besieged. **Santa María la Real de Nieva** has a fourteenth-century Gothic church with a gilded Renaissance altarpiece.

East of Segovia, partly in the province of Madrid, Enrique IV's mid-fifteenth-century hunting lodge was given by Fernando and Isabel to the monks of El Parral for a chapel and hospice site, but the Bourbon king Felipe V liked the area and in 1711–34 built the **Palacio Real de la Granja de San Ildefonso** in a French chateau style of slim spires, mansard roofs, and two inner courtyards. Seven large formal rooms for display or business lead to the throne room and the church where Felipe V is buried. The gardens are more impressive than the small palace and outdo Versailles in their use of water. An artificial lake at the top of the mountainous site feeds a large cascade and twelve basins of fountains, which are surrounded by sculptures. One fountain reaches a height of 155 feet.

In the village of **San Ildefonso**, a glass factory was created to provide the palace with glass and crystal. Nearby **Riofrío** contains the Farnese Palace, built in 1745 by Felipe V's second wife, the Italian Isabel Farnese. The palace is Italian baroque with beautiful marble and wood details and a large art collection.

CUISINE. Segovia stresses the traditional Castilian cuisine. One restaurant, Mesón de Cándido, founded in the late fifteenth century, is famous for its huge *hornos* (roasting ovens). The recipe for roast suckling pig follows.

COCHINILLO ASADO DE SEGOVIA

1 suckling pig (6–9 lbs.)	½ tsp. mint
1 Tbs. salt	1 Tbs. sage
½ tsp. pepper	1 tsp. celery salt
1 loaf bread	½ cup hot chicken stock
1 clove garlic, chopped	1 cup red wine
1 Tbs. onion, chopped	1 whole apple
½ lb. seedless raisins	

Remove the pig's insides and rub cavity with salt and pepper. Crumble the bread and mix it with garlic, onion, raisins, mint, sage, and celery salt, moistened with stock, to make the dressing. Stitch up the pig's cavity and roast for about 3 hours at 350°F, never basting but occasionally puncturing the roast. When finished, pour red wine over the roast and put an apple in the pig's mouth.

Sopa de castellana (garlic soup, sometimes called *sopa de ajo*) is served in winter, or *gazpacho serrano* (cold tomato soup with egg, onions, garlic vinegar, oil, and bread) and *canelones de legumbres* (vegetable crêpes) in summer.

SORIA

VITAL STATISTICS. Pop., 98,803. Area, 10,306 sq. km. Capital: Soria (pop., 32,309). Diocesan see: Osma. Soria and Teruel have the lowest population density in Spain at ten persons per sq. km. Soria lies between Zaragoza, Burgos, and Segovia on the east and west, and Logroño (La Ríoja) and Guadalajara on the north and south. The Duero River rises in the province to flow 485 miles west to the Atlantic.

ECONOMY. Soria, an isolated and rural province, is almost entirely dependent on grazing of livestock and small-plot agriculture.

HISTORY. (Numantia [Celtiberian], Doria [Roman]). Prehistoric Numantia on the upper Duero River was an important center of Celtiberian life, more densely populated than it is today. Excavations reveal fragments of Astral cult designs and statues of gods similar to those found in areas such as Wales.

Numantia resisted Roman conquest in the first Celtiberian War (143–138 B.C.), which began when an inept Roman praetor provoked the revolt of Numantia. Fighting continued for several years before a new Roman commander, Publius Cornelius Scipio, youngest of the Roman family famed for their role in the Punic Wars, put down the revolt by months of intense campaigning. The historian Polybius believed that Numantia was the most difficult campaign of the Roman Republic in Spain. The guerrilla tactics used by Numantian tribesmen passed into legend as the first demonstration of a ferocious Spanish military spirit, but starvation finally forced the Numantians to accept a truce, and they were massacred.

The modern town of Soria began with Roman establishment of a new administrative center. Under the Visigoths, the area's open spaces permitted tribal grazing of common herds. Muslims continued this practice, but their influence remained minor, and a revolt led against Córdoba by a local noble, Sulayman ben Abdus, destroyed Muslim control in A.D. 869. Christian infiltration in the area of Osma and San Esteban de Gormaz attracted

Almanzor, whose battle at Calatañazor (ca. 1002) may have been his last. The province was finally pacified by Alfonso I the Battler (1104–34), but with the rise of Castile, Alfonso VII (1126–57) and Alfonso VIII (1158–1214) incorporated Soria by the end of the twelfth century.

In 1350, the Cortes of Soria codified the *Fuero real* and ratified their ties with Castile. Informal power lay in the hands of the counts of Medinaceli, a line begun by Alfonso de la Cerda (el Desheredado), grandson of Alfonso X and perennial claimant of the Castilian throne in the late thirteenth and early fourteenth centuries. The town of Medinaceli, in fact, often rivalled Soria as an important center. Other important nobles included the counts of Gómera, the Mendozas (who built the Hurtado Palace in Almazán), and the marqués de Berlanga and dukes of Frías in Berlanga de Duero, birthplace and frequent meeting point of the Honrado Concejo del la Mesta, the Castilian herding organization.

During the fourteenth century, Soria created a system of social-class representation effective for more than four centuries and good enough to keep Soria from joining the Comuneros revolt. Later in the sixteenth century, the province's wool interests urged conciliation during the war with Holland, the most important woolen finishing center in Western Europe. After 1648, the loss of Holland and Austrian control of the Spanish Netherlands caused the wool industry to decline. In part, Soria withdrew into otherworldly spiritual concerns, centering around a major religious figure of the area, Aloysius Gonzaga (1568–91), a Jesuit volunteer nurse who lost his life during a plague outbreak in Italy after performing devoted work. His example popularized charitable religious vocations, and a cult later celebrated his abandonment of aristocratic life for the single-minded nursing of the ill. He was canonized in 1726.

Inflation during the seventeenth century cut into the yields of municipal bonds (*censos*) used to finance capital improvements. The long decline created pent-up reformist desires leading to creation of the Económica Numantina de Amigos del País as a self-help group to promote economic development in the late eighteenth century, but after the Napoleonic occupation expropriated property and decimated sheep herds, Soria was left nearly destitute. Growing root crops in the dry, stony fields did not provide enough food, and thousands of peasants departed, until population fell below medieval levels. Agriculture today is still largely composed of tiny *estancias*, or small ranches and farms.

LITERATURE. The *auto sacramental* form of drama (one-act religious plays) may have been created by **Hernán López de Yanguas** (1470?–1540) of Soria, a playwright about whom little is known.

Obscurity also surrounds the childhood of Gabriel Téllez, better known as **Tirso de Molina** (1583–1648). Rumored to be the illegitimate son of the duke of Osuna, he became a friar of the Mercedarian Order and eventually master of a monastery in Soria. He spent his life in the province and in

1648 was buried at Almazán in the Mercedarian monastery. Yet the Council of Castile rebuked this provincial cleric in 1625 for the obscenity and vice in his plays. Clearly a man of paradox, his prodigious energy allowed him to write more than 400 plays in his lifetime, second only to Lope de Vega, his hero.

Many of Tirso's plays have been lost, but what remains includes *El vergonzoso en palacio* (1621), a comedy of inexperience about a young man who tries to further his career in the royal court. *La prudencia en la mujer* (1633) is a historical play about a fourteenth-century queen mother. *El condenado por desconfiado* (1635) is a religious play about two men: one a person of faith too unfeeling and bound up in ritual to be saved, the other a sinner who nevertheless performs good works. This work is often mentioned as the best religious play written by a Spanish author, but Tirso produced an even greater masterpiece in *El Burlador de Sevilla y convidado de piedra* (1630), which introduced for the first time the famous character don Juan Tenorio. The great mocker (which is the literal meaning of *burlador*), unable to repent his sins, is a unique character in Spanish fiction, a brave, almost foolhardy libertine. Tirso's message rang out clearly: divine mercy is not infinite, and those who do not repent shall be punished. The doomed don Juan is one of the greatest characters in Spanish fiction, inspiring many other explorations of the theme, including José de Esponceda's *El estudiante de Salamanca*, José Zorrilla's *Don Juan Tenorio* (1844), Jacinto Grau Delgado's *Don Juan de Carillana* (1913), and other works by Martínez Ruiz, Marañon, and Ridruejo.

A woman of the province, Sor **María Coronel de Jesús de Agreda** (1602–65), entered religious life in 1619. Her major work, *Mística ciudad de Dios*, particularly stressed the doctrine of the Immaculate Conception, and her patriotic visions during Felipe IV's reign stirred Spaniards overwhelmed by the religious wars to make her into a national heroine.

In the nineteenth century, **Julián Sanz del Río** (1814–69) of Torrearévalo came from a peasant background but was educated by his uncle, canon of the cathedral in Córdoba. With a doctorate in canon law from Granada, he taught legal philosophy at the University of Madrid. Encountering the ideas of Georg Wilhelm Friedrich Hegel and Friedrich von Schelling in the writings of the German philosopher Karl Christian Krause (1781–1832), whom he never met, Sanz developed a passion for secular philosophy that led him to seek to revitalize Spanish education by proposing many democratic reforms. Fired from his teaching position in 1868, he became the hero of many later reformers.

In the modern period, **Dionisio Ridruejo** (1912–75) of El Burgo de Osma went from provincial chief to head of national propaganda for the Franco regime in the civil war. Afterwards, he began writing verse in *Primer libro de amor* (1939) and volunteered to fight against the Soviet Union in Franco's volunteer unit, the Blue Division. *Poesía en armas* (1945) is an interesting memoir of his experiences on the eastern front. Another work of verse, *En once años*, won the Premio Nacional de Literatura in 1950, but after 1956 he became disillusioned with Franco's Spain and grew increasingly outspoken, going to prison for a year as a result. Later, he spent much of his life in exile, where he wrote *Dentro del tiempo* (1960), *Hasta la fecha* (1961), *Escrito en España* (1962), and *Castilla la Vieja* (1973).

Numantia's heroism inspired **Cervantes** to write *El cerco de Numancia*, sometimes simply called *La Numancia*, as an allegorical play. **Rojas Zorrilla, Gerardo Diego, Becquer, Unamuno**, and **Azorín** also wrote of Soria. The poet **Antonio Machado y Ruiz** (1875–1939) taught at the College of Soria between 1913 and 1919 during the most productive period of his career. His marriage to Leonor, a woman of the region who died quite young of tuberculosis, inspired some of his best poetry.

ART. The earliest expression of Mudéjar architecture is the cloister of San Juan de Duero in Soria, done in the early thirteenth century. The Mudéjar style is distinguished by the use of Islamic elements such as the horseshoe arch and by a marked tendency toward ornamentation based on geometrical motifs. Brick was the favorite construction material, rather than stone.

CUSTOMS AND SOCIETY. Sorian folk culture is distinctive. Villages of the Agreda district possess forested *tierras comunes* (municipal common lands, once widespread throughout many parts of Spain) that inspired creation of the *ejido* (lands shared by a community) in colonial Mexico. As late as 1961, an annual drawing among village inhabitants determined the right to harvest trees, the so-called "pine luck." This example of medieval municipal solidarity, even in the contemporary period of rural collapse, is typical of the old traditions of Sorian village society.

According to some studies, Sorian pastoralists played important roles in the Mesta and later in long-range hauling of freight by oxcart. Noted for their work ethic and literacy as much as for their rustic appearance and primitive manners, they were considered a race apart like other isolated rural groups in Cantabria, León, and Cáceres.

HISTORIC SITES. The twelfth-century Romanesque cathedral in **Soria**, rebuilt in 1573 after its collapse in 1520, has Renaissance and plateresque altarpieces and a Flemish triptych. Other churches include Santo Domingo, the best Romanesque architecture in the area; San Juan de Duero, a church left from a former Templar monastery; and San Juan de Rabanera.

None of Soria's churches is as large as the palace of the counts of Gómera, a sixteenth-century complex. The Jesuit College has a baroque façade, while the provincial Museo Numantino is particularly strong in its Celtic and Roman collections. The ruins of Numantia, the famous Celtiberian settlement, are on the northern edge of the city of Soria.

Elsewhere in the province, due east, almost to the border with Zaragoza province, **Agreda** provides one of the most sensational settings in Spain.

The village sits on a cliff overlooking a ruined castle with Roman and Muslim architectural details. The church of Nuestra Señora de la Peña is Romanesque, while the church of San Miguel is Gothic and plateresque. The convent of Concepción contains the tomb of Sor María de Agreda.

In the southwest, **El Burgo de Osma,** founded by the Visigoths, is one of the oldest diocesan towns in Spain. Its thirteenth-century cathedral has a nave and two aisles that form a Latin cross. Other details include an eighteenth-century tower and fine interior detail. Nearby **Osma** (Uxama Agralae [Roman]) is where St. Dominic was born.

Directly south of Soria, **Almazán** contains the Mendoza family's Hurtado Palace, Renaissance in style with beautiful stonework. The church of San Miguel is Romanesque with Mudéjar decorations. Near the bottom of the province in the south, **Medinaceli** is a very old town often fought over during the Reconquest. It has a Roman triumphal arch and the Hieronymite monastery of San Ramón, once an old synagogue. The Medinaceli Palace and other buildings have not been restored, but the Plaza Mayor is historic and interesting. On the far southeast, **Santa María de Huerta** has a beautiful monastery founded in 1162. Its chapel contains frescoes celebrating the battle of Las Navas de Tolosa. **Berlanga del Duero** is dominated by the palaces of the marqués of Berlanga and the dukes of Frías. The church of La Colegiata is a good example of late Gothic/Renaissance style. The grave of the great Golden Age playwright Tirso de Molina is in the Mercedarian monastery.

CUISINE. Spain still has free-range turkeys, used in *pavo asado* (roast turkey), which is prepared the standard way except that the dressing is similar to that used in making *cochinillo asado*. Basting is done with sherry. *Patatas consetas* (mushrooms and potatoes) is another popular dish.

VALLADOLID

VITAL STATISTICS. Pop., 489,636. Area, 8,110 sq. km. Capital and diocesan see: Valladolid (pop., 330,242), a large university town. The area is part of the Duero Basin and consists of meseta land not unlike steppes. Valladolid is in central Old Castile, surrounded by Palencia and Avila to the north and south, Zamora to the west, and Burgos and Segovia to the east.

ECONOMY. The city of Valladolid manufactures automobile parts and assembles cars for Renault and trucks for Renault and Mercedes Benz. The province is very much like the rest of Old Castile in that it is far more dominated by sheep grazing than field agriculture, although viticulture is rather large.

HISTORY. (Belad-Walid, "land of the governor" [Arabic]). This territory, lying along the Roman road linking Burgos, Palencia, and Zaragoza, remained relatively undeveloped by the Romans or Visigoths. Muslims lightly settled the area, and in A.D. 1074, as northerners moved into the region, Count Pedro de Ansúrez became the first Castilian provincial governor. Valladolid grew into a town of 20,000 by 1200, prosperous as a center of viticulture and livestock raising.

Expansion of Castilian boundaries to the south made Valladolid more central to the region and in time enabled it to challenge Burgos as the principal city of Castile. Major events over the centuries in Valladolid included Alfonso X's establishment of a university, ca. 1260; Fernando III's coronation in 1217; the beheading in the main square of Juan II's chancellor of Castile, Alvaro de Luna, in 1453; the marriage of Fernando and Isabel in 1469; the exile and death of Christopher Columbus in 1506; and the births of Felipe IV and Anne of Austria (daughter of Felipe III and Louis XIV's mother). The latter events came about during the reign of Felipe III (1598–1621), when his favorite, don Francisco Gómez de Sandoval y Rojas, the duke of Lerma, persuaded the court to move to Valladolid in 1600, inflation having made Madrid too expensive. Many visitors, including Titian in 1603, visited the town during this period, but Lerma's greed and corruption caused court costs to surpass those of Madrid, and so the king and court returned to the former capital in 1606.

Another major town of the province is Medina del Campo. In the fourteenth century, it became the site of an important fair that sold the Mesta's wool. Merchants and bankers from France, Germany, the Low Countries, and Italy set up shop to buy wool and to sell a wide range of trade goods. The fair developed commercial practices such as letters of exchange and credit, deposit banking, and sale of futures contracts very early in the history of capital exchange. Most rulers visited the fair often, since its economic importance could not be overlooked, and Isabel the Catholic died at the Mota castle in Medina del Campo on November 26, 1504. Rebels burned the town to the ground when it remained loyal to the monarchy during the Comuneros revolt, but Carlos I financed its rebuilding, and Felipe II gave Medina del Campo a monopoly as the only Castilian fair in 1564, which lasted until 1605 when Medina del Campo lost out to Burgos. The town declined and suffered extensive damage in the War of Independence.

For several centuries afterward, control of provincial land remained firmly in the hands of the Church and wealthy provincial nobles such as the counts of Benavente (in Portillo), the Pimentels, and the condes de Ansúrez of Carretero. After 1837, liberals challenged their prestige by alienating approximately 60 percent of all provincial ecclesiastical property. Distribution of religious estates created many individual farms, expected to generate greater agricultural wealth by improving dry-land farming. The effort, led by liberal *cacique* and free trader Germán Gamazo (1838–1901), dissolved into a quarrel with the Catalans over protectionism. Gamazo thought that high tariffs would destroy the market for Castilian agricultural exports and block import of European technology that Catalonia could not provide. He helped plan and finance the Valladolid-Burgos railroad to bring the province's crops to market, and an agricultural school was established in 1881. Unfortunately, aridity and drought proved to be difficult problems, and grain growing remained an extremely risky business.

Economic uncertainty and local conservatism dominated Valladolid's politics during the Second Republic. The main political figures, the authoritarian Onésimo Redondo and Ledesma Ramos (both 1905–36), created the Juntas de Ofensiva Nacional Sindicalista (JONS) as a right-wing group to agitate against the Republic. JONS merged with the Falange in 1933 to form the Spanish fascist movement. In the Popular Front elections of February 1936, Valladolid gave the Falange its largest vote. The area continued to support Franco in the civil war, housed part of his government, and never faced a threat from republican forces. In return, Franco made Valladolid a zone of economic development in 1966.

LITERATURE. In the Middle Ages, **Alfonso de Valladolid** (d. 1346), a converted Jew, used vernacular Castilian to defend his new faith. **Juan de Valladolid** (1403?–52), a blind *converso* poet, managed to travel throughout the Mediterranean and contribute to the late medieval ballad tradition. **Bernal Díaz del Castillo** (1492–1581) of Medina del Campo spent much of his life in Mexico, where he wrote the *Historia verdadera de la Conquista de la Nueva España*, the first major history of Mexico's conquest by Spain. Its heroic account contrasts vividly with Las Casas's black legend of Spanish cruelty.

Cervantes spent the last period of his life here, and the house he lived in has been turned into a museum. Olmedo and Medina del Campo provide the setting for **Lope de Vega's** play *Caballero de Olmedo*. Medina del Campo is also the setting for the anonymous *La Abencerraje y de la hermosa Jarifa* (ca. 1551), a love story between a Muslim and a Christian.

The soldier **Hernando de Acuña** (1520?–80?) became a poet influenced by Petrarch. **Juan de la Cruz** (1542–91) of Ciudad Real met Santa Teresa in Medina del Campo while working as a nurse in a paupers' hospital. Padre **Luis de la Puente** (1554–1624) of Valladolid, a Jesuit, wrote inspirational works such as *Obras espirituales* (1690). **Antonio de Escobar y Mendoza** (1589–1669), another Jesuit, wrote baroque poetry and inspirational works such as *San Ignacio* and *Historia de la Virgen Madre de Dios*. The English and Irish College at the University of Valladolid produced many writers and priests, including **John Lloyd** (1630–79), a Welsh priest executed by English authorities and canonized in 1970, and **John Roberts** (1576–1610), a Benedictine martyr who returned to Protestant England in 1602 to carry out missionary work until his arrest and execution as a Catholic in 1610.

The nineteenth century produced a minor romantic poet, **Miguel de los**

Santos Alvarez (1817–92), a friend of Esponceda who ignited a new interest in creative writing. His contemporary, and the province's most important writer, **José Zorrilla y Moral** (1817–93), was a major romantic poet and playwright with a vivid view of past Spanish glories, perhaps best typified by *Granada* (1841) or *La leyenda del Cid*. His most noted play, *Don Juan Tenorio* (1844), is an interpretation of the don Juan myth, the story of a sinner who is saved by the love of a pure woman. The play became the most popular work of the Spanish stage in the nineteenth century. Zorilla also wrote *leyendas* as long narrative and dramatic poems. In this genre, *Cantos del trovador* (1841) is one of his better works. Despite such success, Zorrilla never escaped poverty, bankrupt by many personal and family problems that forced him to become the director of the National Theatre of Mexico during the era of Emperor Maximilian. He escaped the emperor's fall in Mexico City with little more than his life.

Another figure of this period, **Gaspar Núñez de Arce** (1832–1903) of Valladolid, a dramatist, journalist, politician, and poet, wrote some of the most popular verses of the late nineteenth century, although they were not critically acclaimed. **Leopoldo Cano y Masas** (1844–1936) created popular patriotic and moralistic plays.

In the modern period, **Jorge Guillén** (b. 1893) is a pure poet similar to T. S. Eliot or Paul Valéry. He studied in Paris, translated Valéry and other leading modern poets, and later taught at the University of Seville. *Homenaje* (1922) and *Cántico* (1928) are two of his finest works on intellectual themes, with an impersonal but simple and elegant style. Critics praised their message that life is worth living, but faulted their cold, almost dehumanized tone and language. Guillén left Spain in 1936 to teach in the United States, where he continued to write poetry and studies of Spanish literature and civilization.

Another writer, **Rosa Chacel** (1898–1994), encouraged by her editor and friend José Ortega y Gasset, wrote a series of novels, of which *Memorias de Leticia Valle* (The Memories of Leticia Valle, 1945) and *The Maravillas District* (1992) have been translated into English. She remained in exile in Argentina and the United States before returning to Madrid in 1974. **Darío Fernández Flórez** (b. 1909), a novelist and historian who supported Franco, is noted for his anti-avant-garde opinions. **Miguel Debibes** (b. 1920), a contemporary novelist, won the Nadal Prize in 1947 for *La sombra del ciprés es alargada*, a bitter account of postwar society. Many of his stories deal with the problems of censorship and other restrictions in the Franco era, such as *Las guerras de nuestros antepasados* (The War of Our Ancestors, 1977) or *Aún es de día* (1982). *The Path, The Hedge,* and *Five Hours with Mario* have been translated as well.

ART. One of the chief artistic aspects of Valladolid is the concentration of Isabeline decorative style in the province. This late fifteenth-century development used the more flamboyant elements of the Gothic in the carving of wooden retablos, or decorative motifs such as escutcheons, heraldic animals, or sculpture placed against intricate backgrounds. The style is seen to its best advantage in the façades and interiors of the church of the monastery of San Pablo and the Colegio de San Gregorio. Important designers and artisans such as Colonia and Siloé developed the Isabeline style.

The plateresque also made an appearance in Valladolid in the sixteenth century. The Mendoza family commissioned **Lorenzo Vázquez** (1497?–1545?) to design the Colegio de Santa Cruz. At a time when the pointed arch was replacing round arches, Vázquez kept the horseshoe arch, Mudéjar woodworking, and the unrestrained ornamentation of the earlier Isabeline to create the plateresque style. The word comes from *platero*, or silversmith, since silver was often used to create highly decorative surfaces.

The sixteenth-century Valladolid Cathedral contains a considerable collection of art, particularly a retablo by Juan de Juni (1572), choir stalls by Francisco Velázquez, and a painting attributed to Goya in the chapel of San Pedro Regalado within the cathedral. Other religious objects in Valladolid's parish churches include the *Virgin del Cuchillo* by Juan de Juni in Las Angustias; a statue of St. Dominic by Gregorio Fernández in San Pablo; a Renaissance retablo by Francisco Giralte in the chapel of Los Corrales; three paintings by Goya at the convent of Santa Ana; and a retablo dedicated to St. Francis of Assisi by **Juan de Juni** at Santa Isabel. The French-born, Italian-trained Juni arrived in Spain about 1533, working first in León and then settling in Valladolid. His sculptures, spiritual in their full and beautiful forms, are natural in proportion but become declamatory in their distortion of gesture.

The former monastery of La Mejorada is now the National Museum of Sculpture with works by Juan de Gúas, Diego de Siloé, Juan de Juni, Alonso Berruguete, Pedro de Mena, José de Mora, Salvador Carmona, Francisco Salzillo, Pompeo Leoni, Pedro de Cuadra, and Jorge Inglés. There are also paintings by Gregorio Martínez and the Italian Vicente Carducho (1576–1638), who lived in Valladolid between 1601 and 1606 at the court of Philip III; Felipe Gil de Mena, Lucas Jordán, Juan Rizi, and Francisco Bayeu. The convent of Santa Ana has three paintings by Goya and three by Ramón Bayeu, and sculptures by Gregorio Fernández and Pedro de Mena. The monastery of Portacoeli has a sculpture of Christ by Juan de Juni and several altarpieces by the Italian student of Caravaggio, Orazio Borgianni (1575?–1616).

In Medina del Campo, the collegiate church of San Antolín has a relief by Juan de Juni, while the San Juan de la Cruz Chapel has works by Rodrigo de Dueñas.

MUSIC. The Russian composer **Mikhail Glinka** (1803–57), deeply fascinated by Spanish culture, spent part of 1845 in Valladolid listening to popular music, from which he later produced two Spanish overtures, *Jota*

Aragonesa and *Summer Night in Madrid*. He also visited Granada, Seville, and Madrid during his stay in Spain.

CUSTOMS AND SOCIETY. Valladolid stages the most important Semana Santa in Castile during Easter Week. Artwork by Gregorio Fernández and Juan de Juni are paraded before a silent crowd, followed by the sermon of the seven words ("[Father], into thy hands I commend my spirit") given in the plaza.

At Tordesillas in early September, the Toro de la Vega ceremony is a part of an annual fiesta. A bull is let loose on the streets of the town and chased to the Plaza Mayor, where it is attacked and killed by men on horseback or on foot. The ceremony began in 1355.

Traditional dance includes many other regional patterns, since the town society of Valladolid traveled more widely than usual due to their commercial interests. The only indigenous dance is the comic *zandango*, a line dance where men and women face one another, moving back and forth to the rhythm of castanets, until they turn and violently bump into one another.

HISTORIC SITES. Work on the cathedral in **Valladolid** started in the sixteenth century under the direction of Rodrigo Gil de Hontañon and Francisco de Colonia. Juan de Herrera, architect of the Escorial, continued the construction from 1578 to 1582, and in 1729 Alberto de Churriguera began work on the exterior, but the building is so massive that it remains incomplete, with only one of the two towers finished and the Latin cross design unrealized. The large diocesan museum has a *Pietà* by Juan de Juni.

There are ten other large churches in Valladolid. The town's late development means that only the tower of San Martín is Romanesque. Santa María la Antigua and San Benito are early Gothic; while the church of Santa Magdalena (originally designed by Rodrigo Gil de Hontañon), the chapel of Los Corrales, and the church of Santiago are Renaissance. The baroque prevails at San Martín and Vera Cruz. Simón de Colonia designed the doors and façade of San Pablo.

Other religious establishments in Valladolid are the convent of Las Huelgas Reales, established in 1282 by the wife of Sancho IV; the convent of Santa Ana, late sixteenth to late eighteenth century in style; and the monastery of Porta Coeli, which has a good art collection. The Colegio Santa Cruz (founded in 1474) contains a handsome library.

Valladolid has a profusion of other museums and palaces. Besides the diocesan museum already mentioned, the National Museum of Sculpture contains one of the largest collections of art outside Spain's largest cities. The Casa de Cervantes possesses many artifacts of his period, while the Palacio de Pimentel is quite elaborate and of some historic importance, since Felipe II was born here in 1527. The palaces of the archbishop, Vivero, and Benavente, and the castle of Fuensaldaña (a square defensive structure with tall towers) just outside town, all lend interest to the architectural heritage.

Elsewhere in the province, **Simancas**, not far south of the city of Valladolid, is an old Roman and Muslim settlement whose castle has become the Archivo General de Simancas, an important source for historical research on Castile of the early modern period. The location of the archive here commemorates the defeat of Abd ar-Rahman III's army by Ramiro II and Fernán Gonzaléz that preserved Castile's freedom. A short distance further southwest, **Tordesillas** is an old Muslim town, with the important Real Monasterio de Santa Clara, where the famous Treaty of Tordesillas divided the Western Hemisphere between Spain and Portugal in 1494. Juana la Loca, Isabel the Catholic's daughter and the mother of King Carlos I, was imprisoned at the Santa Clara monastery in Tordesillas from 1509 until her death in 1551, freed only briefly during the Comuneros revolt.

A bit further south, **Medina del Campo** was a famous wool market and fair site in late medieval Spain. The royal castle of La Mota, built by Juan II and rebuilt by Fernando and Isabel, overlooks the town. The outer wall is designed for defense against artillery, but the castle itself is austere. Isabel died at La Mota in 1504, and her disturbed daughter Juana initially was held prisoner here. The Dueñas Palace is a town mansion built for a wealthy wool merchant.

CUISINE. Food in Valladolid is classically Old Castilian cuisine. *Sopa de ajo al huevo* (garlic soup with egg) is one staple starter.

SOPA DE AJO AL HUEVO

5 Tbs. olive oil	salt and pepper to taste
2 cloves garlic	2 eggs
6 thin slices whole wheat bread	1 Tbs. paprika
4½ cups chicken bouillon	

Preheat over to 450°F. In a pan, heat olive oil until it smokes, then cool. Fry the garlic until brown and remove. Using the same oil, fry bread in chunks until brown. Pour bouillon on the bread, add salt and pepper, and cook at low temperature for 20 minutes, stirring the mixture. Pour into an uncovered casserole, then beat the eggs, add paprika, and spread mixture over the surface of the soup, and cook in the oven until they thicken. Other variations use cheese or peppers.

The Ribera del Duero, an area of demarcation for wines of Valladolid grown along the Duero River, produces some of central Spain's best red and rosé wines, pressed by cooperative wineries that were created in the

1920s. Rueda produces white Verdejo grapes, grown at a relatively high altitude, which are used in the marqués de Riscal white wines.

ZAMORA

VITAL STATISTICS. Pop., 224,369. Area, 10,561 sq. km. Capital and diocesan see: Zamora (pop., 59,734). The Duero River and the Sierra de Culebra in the northwest are important physical features dividing the area into wet and dry zones of forests and plains. The province is between León and Salamanca to the north and south, while Orense and Portugal are on the west and Valladolid is on the east.

ECONOMY. Zamora is agricultural except for some production of tin.

HISTORY. (Ocellum Duri [Roman]). Evidence of human habitation goes back to 2500 B.C., as dated from megaliths found in the area, probably created by Basque and Cantabrian people who established villages in the area. Romans built the provincial capital as a stop on the Roman silver route from Asturias to Mérida. Less growth took place under the Visigoths or Muslims, but Mozarabs who resettled in Zamora from the south created the largest Mozarab community in Old Castile.

Asturians raided Zamora as early as A.D. 747, and Alfonso III staged a major campaign in 893. Orduño II of León defeated the Muslims at San Estaban de Gormaz in 917 to dominate the Duero Valley, but Almanzor sacked Zamora in 987. Fernando I of Castile created a base in the area, and the final conquest of Zamora followed the Castilian envelopment of León. Zamora was part of the Mesta's route from León to Badajoz, and industries such as wool weaving and hat manufacturing began in the late thirteenth century. The Duero Valley's fertility encouraged field agriculture and decreased land holdings in size.

Zamora occasionally played a role in national events. In 1475, Afonso V of Portugal invaded the province and made the town of Toro the battleground over a disputed succession in Castile between Enrique IV's half-sister, Isabel the Catholic, and his daughter Juana, who was engaged to Afonso. Isabel's husband, Fernando the Catholic, defeated Afonso in September 1476, thus securing her right to the throne of Castile.

In the Comuneros revolt, Zamora initially sympathized with the populist position opposing the power of the Church and the great nobles, resisting further bureaucracy and taxation. Bishop Acuña of Zamora raised his own peasant army, but when rebel forces burned Medina del Campo he changed sides and accepted the Hapsburg dynasty. Zamora later was used as a place of internal exile for persons in disfavor. The best example is the conde-duque de Olivares, who lived in Zamora from 1643 to 1645 after he fell from power.

By the end of the eighteenth century, the city of Zamora's population fell below 2,000 as wool spinning and other textile manufacturing all but disappeared. War and revolution washed across the area during the following century. French occupation in 1808–13 and later liberal land reforms disrupted farming and grazing. As a result, the province of Zamora often lacked rudimentary government services or a basic educational system until the early twentieth century. By 1904, peasant unrest had spread widely, creating a reaction that strengthened conservatism. Ramiro Ledesma Ramos (1905–36), a native of the province and an early fascist in Valladolid and Madrid, strenuously opposed the Second Republic and rose to leadership in the Falange until he was imprisoned and executed early in the civil war. The city and province, after initial confusion, fell quickly to Franco's forces during the rising of July 1936. Scores of village battles saw hundreds of republicans killed or executed, including the wife of novelist Ramón Sender. General Mola's army occupied the area for the remainder of the war.

LITERATURE. In the Middle Ages, **Juan Gil** (ca. 1300) composed a number of works in Latin on the Virgin and the saints. During the early modern period, **Luis de Ulloa y Pereira** (1584–1674) of Toro, a poet, playwright, and friend of Olivares, became the *corregidor* of León. In the nineteenth century, **Miguel Ramos Carrión** (1845–1915), a journalist and musician, wrote popular *zarzuelas*. In the twentieth century, **León Felipe** (1884–1968), a surrealist poet, lived in exile in Mexico and the United States after 1939.

The dialogues of Juan del Encina may have been based on an amusing gibberish known as *sayagués*, which comes from the local dialect of Sayago, a village near Zamora.

ART. The Romanesque cathedral in Zamora contains paintings by Gaspar Becerra and sculptures of the Virgin Mary and Nuestra Señora la Calva by Bartolomé de Ordóñez. At the Colegiata Santa María la Mayor in Toro, a painting, *La Virgen de la Mosca*, is thought to be of Isabel the Catholic.

CUSTOMS AND SOCIETY. The Holy Week processions of Zamora are among the most lavish in the north and resemble those of Seville. Hooded participants carry figures of saints through the streets accompanied by drumming.

The town of Benavente conducts the *toro enmaromaro* ritual at fiestas. A bull is tied to a long rope and pulled by the townspeople to a pole in the central plaza, where the rope is twisted until the bull strangles.

Marriage arrangement by parents, commonly practiced in Zamora until thirty or forty years ago, meant that the marriage ceremony sometimes represented a joining of total strangers. This traditionalism could also be seen in dress, where the style was very close to that of urban Salamanca.

HISTORIC SITES. The city of **Zamora** is highly acclaimed as a center of the Romanesque. The cathedral, completed in 1171, is a good example. It has a simple nave and two aisles and one rather stubby tower. The dome, supposedly modeled on the Hagia Sophia in Constantinople (Istanbul), has four small towers surrounding it, very much like the Torre del Gallo of the old cathedral in Salamanca. The portals are simply decorated but not surrounded by sculpture in the usual Romanesque fashion. Groin vaults and plain capitals on interior pillars continue the style. The main altar and grill are eighteenth century in origin, but the two altars in the crossing are thirteenth century. On the right is a well-known Madonna and Child, *Nuestra Señora de la Calva*. The five chapels of the cathedral are Gothic, and there is a cathedral museum with a collection of Flemish tapestries.

Many other churches, mostly Romanesque and small, dot the city of Zamora. El Cid supposedly was knighted in the church of Santiago el Viejo. Santo Cipriano, built in 1025, may be the oldest church. There is also the sixteenth-century Convento de las Dueñas, a college (Colegio de Nuestra Señora del Transito), and three ruined monasteries.

The city walls and its five major gates date from 893. Puente Viejo (eleventh century) and Puente Nuevo (thirteenth century) bridge the Ebro River. The Museo Provincial de Bellas Artes has good ancient and medieval collections, and a religious museum gives the history of Holy Week processions in Zamora.

Elsewhere in the province, to the west, **Toro** is the site where Portugal and Spain confronted one another in 1476. It contains the Colegiata Santa María la Mayor, similar to the Zamora Cathedral with a nave, two aisles, three apses, and half-barrel vaults. The church's columns are richly sculpted. San Lorenzo is a Romanesque church, while San Salvador is Mudéjar. Rodrigo Gil de Hontañón designed the church of San Julián de los Caballeros.

In the north, the oldest Cistercian abbey in Spain, the monastery of Santa María, sets the Romanesque tone of this area. Due north of Zamora, **Benavente** is the setting for the Romanesque churches of Santa María del Azoque and San Juan del Mercado. Alonso de Pimentel designed the Hospital de la Piedad. Almost all the churches in the villages around Benavente are ancient and interesting, as befitting one of the best Romanesque districts in Spain.

CUISINE. As in other provinces of Old Castile, *asado* dishes are common. *Sopa de ajo* or *sopa castellana* is made with water, garlic, pimentos, bread, and sometimes a poached egg. Seafood is available from Galicia and the Bay of Biscay. Benavente is the vineyard of the province and produces various types of sparkling wines.

Chapter 17

LA RIOJA

REGIONAL CHARACTERISTICS. Pop., 253,295. Area, 5,045 sq. km. Regional capital: Logroño. The region is south-southwest of Navarre and Araba (Alava), north of Soria, northeast of Burgos, and west of Zaragoza. Smallest of all regions except for the Balearic Islands, Canary Islands, and Ceuta and Melilla, it occupies a strategic location dominating the western reaches of the Ebro Valley at the intersection of Basque, Castilian, and Aragonese culture.

The region had no prior history of regionalism, but its Basque minority favored unification (along with the larger Basque minority in Navarre) with Araba, southernmost of the Basque provinces. The possibility of future Basque independence made La Rioja's Castilian majority incline toward Old Castile, but the downsizing of that region blocked such a move. Since La Rioja's intensive agriculture differs dramatically from its neighbors, regional autonomy became a viable alternative despite the lack of regionalist sentiment.

The new regional flag has four horizontal bands from top to bottom of red, white, green, and yellow.

The region ranks fifth in personal income.

LOGROÑO

VITAL STATISTICS. Pop. and area: see above. Capital: Logroño (pop., 110,980). Diocesan see: Calahorra. The province is divided between the

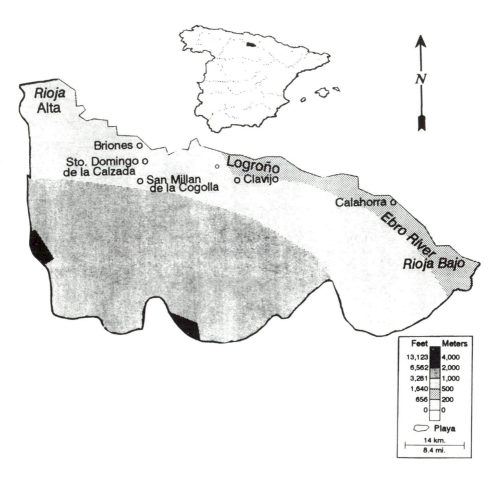

Rioja
Alta

Briones o

Sto. Domingo o
de la Calzada

o San Millan
de la Cogolla

Logroño
o Clavijo

Calahorra o

Ebro River

Rioja Bajo

Feet	Meters
13,123	4,000
6,562	2,000
3,281	1,000
1,640	500
656	200
0	0

⬭ Playa

14 km.
8.4 mi.

LA RIOJA

hilly Rioja Alta of Harro and Santo Domingo de la Calzada on the Río Leza and Rioja Bajo on the Ebro.

ECONOMY. Logroño is one of Spain's richest agricultural and viticultural areas, generally with low unemployment rates. The two major agricultural products are wine and white asparagus. White asparagus, very tender and tasty, is a lucrative cash crop, created by mounding soil around the plant to prevent sunlight from turning the stalks green.

Other economic strengths are an important wool region in Rioja Alta and manufacturing in Logroño, which produces tobacco products and automobile components.

HISTORY. (Río Oja [Spanish], named for the river). La Rioja, settled by the Verones group of Celtiberians, emerged with the founding of Calagoricos, a small trade center where Calahorra stands today. Romans recognized the valley's agricultural potential and fortified Calahorra in 189 B.C. to guard the frontier. Viticulture began ca. A.D. 100, about the same time as the establishment of Logroño (Varea Lucrosus [Roman]).

The Roman emperor Theodosius I (347–95), son of a Legion general commanding the region, was born in Logroño. He ruled East Rome (the later Byzantine Empire) from 379 to 392, negotiating a truce with the Goths in 382 that gave them land in return for service in the Roman Legions. He also called the First Ecumenical Council of Constantinople to denounce the Arian heresy. In 387, after the death of the Western emperor, Gratian, Theodosius reunified the two parts of the Roman Empire, a difficult task made more complicated by his excommunication by St. Ambrose, bishop of Milan, over the issue of his use of excessive violence in doing so. Theodosius offered public penance to get the ban lifted but died soon afterward.

After the collapse of Roman power in La Rioja, a local religious figure of the fifth century, St. Millán de Suso of Vercejo, Aragón, solidified the hold of Christianity on the area and provided a religious life and cultural identity for the surviving romanos. Outside the towns, tribes of migratory sheep herders lived in the surrounding hill districts. In the mid-eighth century, a sizeable Muslim population introduced irrigation and planted root crops that began to realize La Rioja's agricultural potential.

Christians scored a major victory over the Muslims at the battle of Clavijo. Legend says this battle saw the first appearance of St. James. It took place just south of the modern city of Logroño on May 24, 844, when a large body of Muslims ambushed warriors from Asturias led by Ramiro I (842–50) near Albelda and forced the Asturians to take refuge under the crag of Clavijo. According to later accounts, St. James the Apostle appeared in a dream that night to the sleeping king and announced that Christ had commissioned him to take Spain under his protection. The next day, astride a huge white horse and brandishing an enormous sword, St. James led Ramiro's army to victory, becoming Santiago Matamoros (St. James the

Moor-Slayer). After the capture of Calahorra, Ramiro ordered Christians to make an annual offering (*voto de Santiago*) so that St. James's church in Santiago de Compostela, Galicia, could be built.

Modern interpretation suggests that ancient Roman myths were adapted by the archbishop of Cantabria, Dulcidio, to create a reconquest ideology by putting a local victory over Muslim forces at Clavijo into the larger context of Roman folklore, particularly the stories of Castor and Pollux, which provided much of the lore attributed to St. James. In fact, Asturias seized La Rioja only as far south as Nájera during Ramiro's campaigns. The remainder did not fall until after Almanzor's campaigns, and all of the area came under Christian control only during the reign of Alfonso VI (1065–1109) of León and Castile.

St. James especially caught the imagination of French Christians. When the famous abbey at Cluny began organizing pilgrimages to Santiago de Compostela, construction of bridges and roads linked Logroño to the east and west and brought thousands of French immigrants down the pilgrim's way (*calzada*) to Galicia. St. Dominic and St. John of Ortega built churches and monasteries, and French merchants accompanying the pilgrims settled in Logroño's *barrio de francos* and began improving La Rioja's viticulture.

The area remained disputed by Asturias and León until León formally absorbed it in 1072. As late as the reign of Sancho VII (1194–1234), Asturias tried to reannex the area, but Castile realized that La Rioja had the necessary agricultural resources to provide food and so paid close attention to it. This did not deter Navarre from seeking to claim Rioja, and in 1367, aided by Edward, the Black Prince of England, Navarre briefly held Logroño. The proclamation of Enrique II of Trastámara as king of Castile, which took place in Calahorra, marked the beginning of a new Castilian revival.

The market for land within the province soon grew active and profitable, with large estates created in the early fourteenth century by the count of Haro and Leonor de Alburquerque. As late as the eighteenth century, the conde de Floridablanca of Murcia invested heavily and encouraged Manuel Esteban Quintano y Quintano to introduce French techniques of viticulture, aging, and transport of wine. Quintano began the *rioja alavesa* technique of aging wine in oak barrels and clarifying it with egg whites for transport. The Napoleonic era and the later Carlist troubles stopped this initial effort to improve the industry.

During the mid-nineteenth century, confiscation and sale of Church properties by the liberals caused a land rush by private purchasers. Práxedes Mateo Sagasta (1825–1903) of Torrecilla de Cameros, the region's major politician, sought to encourage middle-class acquisition of land without radicalizing Spanish society or threatening the enjoyment of private property. Sagasta rose to become premier briefly in 1871 and again in 1874, but he derived greater power from his partnership with Antonio Cánovas del Castillo between 1881 and 1897. Sagasta held the premiership seven times in rotation with Cánovas. Both grew increasingly authoritarian and corrupt when confronted by issues of regionalism, the *fueros*, and labor militancy. Sagasta's last cabinet fell on December 6, 1901, and when he died several years later he was remembered as an unpopular symbol of liberal failure.

Before Sagasta's era, La Rioja had produced only white and light red wines for the national and colonial markets. Spain's loss of empire, however, forced the area's vintners to compete in the European red wine market. The marqués de Riscal (Camilo Hurtado de Amézaga) hired an oenologist from the Médoc, Jean Pineau, who introduced new varieties of grapes and techniques of destemming and crushing, double fermentation in large oak vats, and aging in oak casks. Riscal's French-style *bodega* opened in 1860, about the same time that another oenologist, Luciano de Murrieta, adopted modern French techniques for his employer, the duque de Victoria. A viticulture and oenology station at Haro developed new techniques for grafting indigenous local roots to phylloxera-resistant American roots. These efforts prevented a total collapse of the industry during the phylloxera epidemic of the late nineteenth century.

In recent times, La Rioja has experienced little political turmoil. General Mola's forces seized the area without major fighting at the start of the civil war, and during the postwar period of Spanish diplomatic and economic isolation, the wine industry gradually improved its quality and quantity until the lower prices of La Rioja's wines gradually revived prosperity. Recent membership in the European Community has brought further modernization, and today the region is a world-class wine producer.

LITERATURE. The few creative figures of this region are scattered over a long span of time. The Roman writer **Quintilian** (ca. A.D. 35–100) of Calahorra spent most of his life in Rome teaching rhetoric and developing concepts of education that he discussed in his multivolume work *Institii*. Gerald Brenan compares Quintilian with Luis Vives and Francisco Giner de los Ríos as a great educator. His fame, given his indigenous Celtiberian roots, makes him unique among Iberian Romans.

The first poet to use Castilian, according to some authorities, was **Gonzalo de Berceo** (1195?–1265?), a member of the Benedictine monastery of San Millán de la Cogolla. He combined classical, ecclesiastical, and minstrel rhetoric into the development of the legend of St. James. For many centuries, he was also the first Spanish poet known to us by name, an important representative of the "learned" school of poetry who wrote stanzas of four fourteen-syllable lines with a single rhyme. None of his works can be dated precisely, but *Vida de Santo Domingo* and *Vida de Santa Oria* began the practice of hagiography. His chief work, *Milagros de Nuestra Señora*, provides a fundamental basis for Marian literature.

Much later, **Manuel Bretón de los Herreros** (1796–1873) of Quel was a

distinguished essayist, major playwright, and secretary of the Real Academia Española. **Francisco Alcántara** (b. 1922) of Haro is a novelist who
won the 1952 Nadal Prize for *La muerte le sienta bien a Villalobos*.

ART. Martín de Beratúa designed churches in Logroño and Santo Domingo de la Calzada, and Juan de Riba designed Logroño's Santa María
del Palacio, which also contains an altar by Arnao de Bruselas and paintings by Pero Ruiz and Francisco Hernández. Master Guillén (ca. 1535)
created the plateresque alabaster altar in the San Pedro Chapel of Calahorra.

MUSIC. The pianist **Pedro Albéniz** (1795–1855) of Logroño studied piano at the Paris Conservatoire. He became a professor of piano at the
Madrid Conservatory in 1830 and composed a large number of piano
works, becoming one of the foremost Spanish pianists.

CUSTOMS AND SOCIETY. The traditional dress of La Rioja, worn by
peasant women, included short skirts and heavy bodices of serge, a very
large scarf around the neck and shoulders, and a white cotton head covering. Males wore short leather or sheepskin work trousers and woolen
leggings in colder weather. Typical dances usually included some variation
of the *pasiegas*, in which rows of men and women stepped back and forth
before swinging their partners vigorously to steadily faster music. The
dance evolved into male kicks, jumps, and other solos, with the women
swaying in time to the music.

The wine fiestas of La Rioja almost equal the San Fermín Fiesta in Pamplona. The most impressive, with strong religious overtones, is the Fiesta
of Santo Domingo de la Calzada in mid-May, a true spring festival. The
most riotous is the "wine battle" of Haro each June 29 with a wine-
spraying bacchanal, followed by a running of the bulls.

HISTORIC SITES. Two important sites of the early pilgrimage era in
Logroño are the Puente de Piedra across the Ebro and the church of San
Bartolomé. There are two cathedrals, including the older Santa María del
Palacio, built on the former palace of the Castilian kings and given by
Alfonso VII to the Knights Templar. Few eleventh-century details have sur-
vived, but the chapel of Nuestra Señora de la Antigua is impressive.

The other cathedral, Santa María la Redonda, is a fifteenth-century structure with three polygonal apses, a nave, two aisles, and many chapels.
Among the smaller churches, Nuestra Señora de la Paz has a sixteenth-
century plateresque retablo and some impressive tombs. The nineteenth-
century military leader and premier, General Baldomiro Espartero of
Ciudad Real, is buried in the church, and his palace is now the provincial
museum.

Elsewhere in the province, **Clavijo**, only a short distance south of Logroño, is the legendary site of St. James's miraculous battlefield appearance.
His victory is celebrated in the very historic French Basilica des Laturce,
decorated with mementoes of ancient pilgrims. Several other towns have a

close association with the pilgrimage. **San Millán de la Cogolla** is the birthplace of the saint venerated as the first religious leader in the region, and a monastery celebrates the saint and the pilgrimage. To the west, **Santo Domingo de la Calzada** provided pilgrims with a hostel, hospital, and cathedral, while **Briones** has a Renaissance church decorated with a number of early paintings. To the east, **Calahorra** is a center of plateresque architecture.

CUISINE. The availability of asparagus, beans, and potatoes makes vegetable stews like *menestra riojana* very popular. These include combinations such as *patatas riojanas* (potatoes and *chorizo*) or *pochas riojanas* (haricot beans, *chorizo*, and peppers). The basic *menestra* (vegetable stew) is begun by cooking cucumbers, green or red peppers, and tomatoes on a hot grill. An olive oil dressing, seasoned with salt, crushed garlic, and parsley, is poured over the vegetables when the mixture has cooked.

In the wine trade, La Rioja is second only to Jerez and parts of Catalonia. The industry, begun by the Romans, improved when medieval French merchants brought pinot noir vines, ancestors of the *tempranillo* grapes used today. Later innovations in the eighteenth and nineteenth centuries greatly improved the industry.

Altogether, 37,500 hectares of vineyards stretch along the Ebro and Oja rivers and grow *tempranillo*, *garnacha*, *mazuelo*, *graciano*, *viura*, and *malvasía* grapes. Reds are produced three times more than whites. The most important *bodegas* are Marqués de Riscal, Murrieta, and Cáceres.

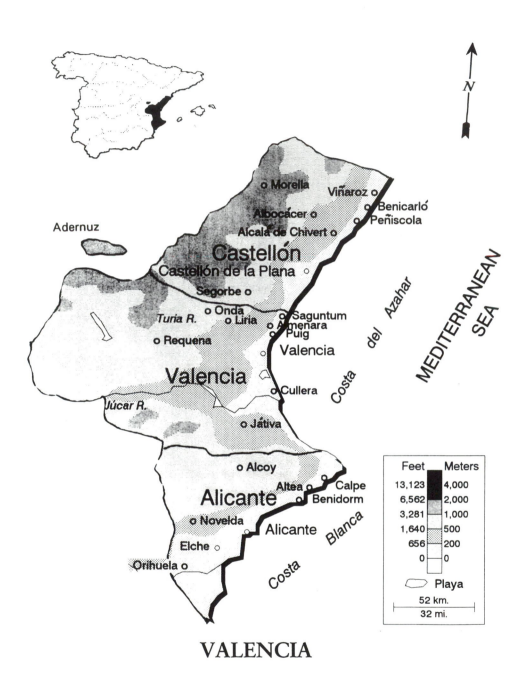

Adernuz

Morella
Viñaroz
Benicarló
Albocácer
Peñiscola
Alcalá de Chivert

Castellón
Castellón de la Plana

Segorbe

Onda
Saguntum
Turia R.   Liria
Almenara
Requena
Puig

Valencia

Valencia

Júcar R.
Cullera

Játiva

Alcoy

Altea   Calpe
Alicante   Benidorm

Novelda   Alicante   Blanca

Elche

Orihuela   Costa

N

MEDITERRANEAN SEA

Costa   del   Azahar

Feet		Meters
13,123		4,000
6,562		2,000
3,281		1,000
1,640		500
656		200
0		0

Playa

52 km.
32 mi.

VALENCIA

Chapter 18

VALENCIA

REGIONAL CHARACTERISTICS. Also called the Levant (East). Pop., 3,646,765. Area, 23,255 sq. km. Regional capital: Valencia. The region borders the Mediterranean between Catalonia on the north, Murcia on the south, and Teruel (Aragón), Cuenca, and Albacete (New Castile) on the west.

As a region, Valencia contains some complex linguistic patterns. While the term *Becavés* is occasionally used to indicate a composite of Balearic, Català (Catalan), and Valencian speech, the most common interpretation is that the region speaks a special regional dialect called Valenciano, based upon Castilian. The words and accents of Català dominate local dialects in northern areas close to Catalonia, but Valenciano Castilian is the official governmental language and common tongue. While there is enough diversity to preserve strong local patterns of life and a sense of separate regional feeling, the region's coastal location, separated by mountains dividing the region from the interior of the peninsula, may be more responsible for this sense of separation than linguistic differences. The *valencianos* possess neither the Basque sense of ethnic separatism nor the same degree of Catalan cultural separatism.

Nevertheless, the region's political history has often emphasized separatism. As an important part of Muslim civilization until the thirteenth century, Valencia already contained strong cultural differences not entirely repressed by federation with Aragón and Catalonia under the Crown of

Aragón. In 1707, new complications arose when the Nueva Planta decree destroyed Valencia's traditional *furos* or *fueros*. The Carlists were defeated before foral law could be restored in the nineteenth century, but a new wave of regionalist activity began in 1921 with the appearance of the Agrupación Regional de Acción Católica. For a brief time it was eclipsed by the Partido Social Popular, which put Christian social policy ahead of regionalism, but a splinter party, Derecho Regional Valenciana (DRV), appeared in 1930 to support a foral type of regionalism and oppose the rise of democracy in the Second Republic. The DRV later joined the larger, more conservative Confederación Española de Derechas Autónomas (CEDA), but the huge anarchosyndicalist Confederación Nacional de Trabajo (CNT) picked up the issue of regionalism in 1931, fighting the DRV and CEDA in the process. Polarized over the controversy, the region was unable to reach a basic understanding before the outbreak of civil war.

In the postwar era, Franco's economic autocracy often frustrated Valencian export interests. New rounds of autonomy talks during the early constitutional monarchy focused primarily on the degree to which Basque and Catalan autonomy would harm Valencian economic growth and tax revenues. To guarantee equal treatment, the region approved limited autonomy over continued centralized rule in the first referendum of 1978 by a 62–26 percent margin. Final autonomous status was approved on January 7, 1982.

The three provinces of Alicante, Castellón de la Plana, and Valencia now call themselves the Valencian Community. Their elaborate flag has a medium blue field and yellow pronged designs of different sizes attached to a vertical red stripe that divides this area from the remaining three-fourths, which is covered by vertical red stripes on a field of yellow.

Valencia ranks seventh among the regions in personal income.

ALICANTE

VITAL STATISTICS. Pop., 1,148,597. Area, 5,817 sq. km. Capital: Alicante (pop. 251,387), a university town on the Costa Blanca (White Coast). Diocesan sees: Orihuela, Albacete, Valencia. This coastal province is below Valencia and above Murcia, with Albacete (New Castile) and a section of Murcia to the west.

ECONOMY. Alicante has a diverse economy based on agriculture, tourism, and manufacturing. Lucrative crops such as early tomatoes and almonds make food processing very important, and while fishing and tourism have declined slightly, the area now ranks fifth in manufacturing and produces shoes, toys (half the national total), clothing, and curios.

HISTORY. (Akre Leuke [Greek], Lucentum [Roman], al-Lucant [Arabic]). The original Neolithic Iberian tribes built cave sanctuaries and animal sculptures at Denia and attracted contacts with the Phoenicians, Carthaginians, and Greeks. Hermeroskopeion, one of the first Greek settlements, was settled in the sixth century B.C. Hamilcar Barca built the Carthaginian fortress of Santa Bárbara on Mt. Benacantil in 238–229 B.C. The beautiful *Dama de Elche*, unearthed near the coast, is an Iberian bust still bearing traces of polychrome which shows the influence either of a Greek fertility goddess or the Carthaginian goddess Tanit of the fifth or fourth century B.C., although recent allegations claim that it is counterfeit.

After the Second Punic War, the town of Alicante exported agricultural products from southern Spain to Italy. Little is known about the later Visigothic period, but the town of Denia became a Christian bishopric late in the period. Muslims initially coexisted with the Hispano-Gothic population in al-Lucant, and a former governor, Theodomir, retained military command until A.D. 779, when Aben Hud, king of Murcia, absorbed the area. Those who accepted Islam lost little, so the Arabs made great inroads.

The Christian Reconquest by Jaume II of Aragón and Catalonia in 1226 brought harsh, fragmented rule by Christian nobles. Denia grew into a duchy under the duque de Lerma, while Fernando III of Castile ruled Elche. Both Aragón and Castile claimed the whole province, but Castile fortified it against attacks by Granada, and in 1490 Fernando the Catholic relinquished Aragón's claim on Alicante to Castile. The University of Santiago in Orihuela, created by the bishop of Orihuela, became a new center of Christian life.

The Hapsburg monarchs, fearing Ottoman raids on this section of the coast, strengthened its fortifications, particularly at the castle of Santa Bárbara. Muslims expelled from Spain used Alicante as a chief port of embarkation in 1609–10, but the only major attack came from the English, who seized the port briefly in 1706 during the War of Spanish Succession.

Bourbon free trade policies allowed Alicante to begin trading with Latin America in 1778, successfully organized by the Consulado de Mar y Tierra, established in 1785. The large mercantile class made the area a center of liberalism during the nineteenth century. Alicante's best-known liberal, José Canalejas y Méndez (1854–1912), was a relatively honest leader who rose to be national premier in 1910 after a long parliamentary career, only to be assassinated two years later.

The railroad arrived in 1858. Manufacturing grew rapidly but also brought large labor disturbances. The metallurgical center of Alcoy briefly created an independent revolutionary canton during the First Republic (1873–74), and later both the socialist Unión General de Trabajadores (UGT) and the anarchosyndicalist Confederación Nacional de Trabajo (CNT) cultivated a large membership in the city of Alicante itself and in the countryside. As a result, the area grew to be a hotbed of political radicalism, strongly supporting the Second Republic and remaining republican throughout the civil war. Alcoy, Elche, and Sagunto gravitated more toward anarchism, while Alcira and Elda favored the socialists. The city of Alicante was a communist stronghold.

The civil war's most important local episode concerned the imprisonment of José Antonio Primo de Rivera, founder of the Falange, jailed originally for violating parliamentary immunity just prior to the outbreak of the civil war. Despite elaborate efforts to rescue him that included use of German naval forces, he was executed on November 20, 1936, in reprisal for the death of a prominent anarchist on the Madrid front. Alicante receded from the headlines and did not surrender until March 29, 1939. Sweeping military trials held by the Franco regime later jailed thousands. Alicante remained under strong controls until the tourist boom relaxed the political climate several decades later.

LITERATURE. During the Golden Age, **Cristóbal de Virués** (ca. 1600) used Seneca as a model to write tragedies such as *La cruel Casandra*.

In modern times, **Carlos Arniches y Barrera** (1866–1943) wrote popular one-act plays often made into *zarzuelas*, while **Rafael Altamira y Crevea** (1866–1951) was a major historian of Hispanic civilization.

By far the best known writer of the province, **José Martínez Ruiz** (1873–1934?) of Alicante, known by his pseudonym **Azorín** (meaning a hawk), first won a reputation as a journalist. His politics, which favored the radical republicans, led him to write works such as *La ruta de Don Quijote* (1905) to chronicle daily life and glorify the common people. He also produced semi-autobiographical novels such as *La voluntad* (1902), but he later grew enamored with Castile and developed a poetic vision of everyday life in the region.

One of Azorín's admirers, the novelist **Gabriel Miró** (1879–1930), used themes of psychological analysis and sensual modernism in such works as *La novela de mi amigo* (1908), *Las cerezas del cementerio* (1910), *El libro de Sigüenza* (1917), and *El humo dormido* (1919). Perhaps the work of his that drew the most attention, *Figuras de la pasión del Señor* (1916), is an unorthodox life of Jesus.

Miguel Hernández (1910–42) of Orihuela escaped his early life of poverty by pursuing a career of journalism and poetry. Strongly influenced by the classics, his dramatic poem *Quien te ha visto y quien te ve y sombra de lo que eras* (1934) makes a morality play out of the human struggle to avoid sin. Hernández won the national prize for poetry for *Viento del pueblo* (1937), a description of the civil war as a patriotic struggle for the people. This theme continues in dramas such as *Teatro de la guerra* (1937) and *El labrador de más aire* (1938), but at the end of the war his collections entitled *Sin sangriento y otros poemas* (1939), *El hombre que acecha* (1939), and *Cancionero y romancero de ausencias* (1939–41) indicate disillusionment and sorrow. His republicanism was punished by a sentence of life imprisonment, but after poor medical treatment he died of tuberculosis in a prison camp at the age of thirty-two.

ART. The archaeology museum of Alicante contains the sphinx of Agost, an Iberian work that shows Greek influence. The museum also contains several other early collections of jewels and weapons.

The church of Santiago in Orihuela has paintings by Juan de Juanes and a statue of Christ attributed to Benvenuto Cellini. Several paintings by Velázquez and Ribera are in the Episcopal Palace.

MUSIC. New sacred music in a polyphonic and monodic style composed by **Juan Gínez Pérez** (1555?–1609?), choirmaster of the cathedral in Valencia, allowed the famed folk play *Mysterio de Elche* to be resumed in 1603.

The talented **Ruperto Chapí Lorente** (1854–1909) of Villena composed one opera, *Las naves de Cortés* (1867), about the colonial era. Much of his career was given over to the writing of *zarzuelas* such as *La bruja* (1887), *El rey que rabió* (1891), and *La revoltosa* (1897).

The self-taught pianist and composer **Oscar Esplá y Triay** (1886–1969?) of Alicante wrote *El Misterio de Elche*, three operas, and a great deal of music celebrating the eastern areas of Spain, including *Suite Levantina* and *Levant*.

CUSTOMS AND SOCIETY. The battle of Moors and Christians, celebrated in Alcoy each April, is an important reenactment that celebrates the Muslims' defeat and the triumph of Christianity. The summer fiesta of Denia, according to local folklore, is of Phoenician origin. The town, named in honor of the goddess Diana, still makes the goddess a central figure in the celebration.

Elche stages the *Mysterio de Elche*, a medieval mystery play done by an all-male cast, on Assumption Day, August 15. This liturgical drama is based on the legend that the *Virgen de Elche* drifted ashore on an ark from unknown origins sometime between 1266 and 1370. The play, developed in the Middle Ages, continued to be performed until 1568, when Felipe II objected to its paganism. The addition of new sacred music allowed the play to be revived in 1603.

The feast of St. Juan is celebrated in Alicante during the last week in June. The *palmera del fuego* is a fireworks display that ends the festival. The traditional dance of these celebrations is simply called the *danza*, a slow fandango. A century ago, peasant dress at the smaller fiestas would have included wide white pants pleated at the waist and cut off at the knee, a silk sash, and a linen shirt. Women still wear silk dresses of beautiful colors, sashes of a floral design, and brocade blouses.

HISTORIC SITES. The old-town district of Santa Cruz in **Alicante** suffered damage in the civil war. Of the surviving churches, Fernando and Isabel commissioned the baroque Santa María. The Herrera-styled San Nicolás is dedicated to Alicante's patron saint, Nicholas of Bari. San Nicolás, a fourth-century pope active in fighting the Arian heresy, has been the patron saint of Alicante since the Byzantine Empire introduced icons dedicated to him in the sixth century. There is an archaeology museum that covers the province's ancient past.

Elsewhere in the province, **Alcoy** is an inland industrial town in the Sierra de Montcabrer. Ruins of a Hellenistic sanctuary and other remains are displayed in the local archaeological museum. **Denia** is a northern hill town high above the sea that for a short time in the early Middle Ages ruled the Balearic Islands. The village has an impressive ancient citadel/castle where Viceroy Diego Hurtado de Mendoza found refuge in 1520 from the Germania riots in Valencia. The old quarter of Les Roques is an arts and crafts center. On the coast near Cabo de la Nao, **Benidorm** is a popular beach resort of the Costa Blanca, close to the old and beautiful fishing villages of **Altea** and **Calpe.**

In the south, **Elche** (Helice [Greek], Colonia Julia Ilici Augusta [Roman]), inland and due west of Alicante, is famed for its palm forest planted by the Muslims, which now supplies fronds for Palm Sunday to all of Spain. This fertile oasis of almond, date, olive, orange, and pomegranate trees is also the archaeological site where the famous *Dama de Elche* (now in the National Archaeological Museum of Madrid) was found. There is a small branch museum at the site with information on the find. A few miles north of Elche, the Mola Castle in **Novelda** was once the prison of Alvaro de Luna before he was executed in Valladolid. Further southwest of Elche, **Orihuela** has a Gothic cathedral with a nave, two aisles, rib vaulting, and a domed altar. Donations by Fernando and Isabel helped finance the building of the Santiago Church in the late fifteenth century. The Episcopal Palace has a museum and a collection of paintings.

CUISINE. Seafood such as *lubina con costra* (baked bass) or hake (turbot) is common fare in the province, but *turrón*, a nougat candy introduced by the Muslims, is most closely associated with Alicante. *Turrón de Alicante* (or *Turrón de Jijona*) can be made as follows:

TURRÓN DE ALICANTE

½ lb. whole almonds	1 pint water
3 Tbs. olive oil or almond oil	4 egg yolks, beaten
½ lb. sugar	

Blanch and skin the almonds and grind in a blender. Cook in oil for 3 minutes. Mix sugar and water in a pan and boil until mixture begins to turn hard. Remove from heat and stir in the almonds until a thick paste forms. Blend in the beaten egg yolks and pour the mixture into an ice tray lined with waxed paper. Cover the top and let cool.

Wines of the province include the very strong aged red wines of the Manchuela and Almansa demarcations.

CASTELLÓN DE LA PLANA

VITAL STATISTICS. Pop., 431,755. Area, 6,662 sq. km. Capital: Castelló de la Plana. Diocesan sees: Segorbe, Tortosa. The eastern coast is the Costa del Azahar (Orange Blossom Coast). Much of the area lies in the fertile *huerta*, an area of intense gardening. The province is south of Tarragona (Catalonia), above Valencia, and to the east of Teruel (Aragón). The Maestrazgo Hills rise to the west. About a fourth of the population speak Català.

ECONOMY. The alluvial soil and semitropical climate are perfect for growing oranges, lemons, figs, sugar cane, and rice. Commercial fishing is important, and some mercury mining, oil refining, leather curing, and shoe manufacture are carried on. In the past decade, deep wells have been sunk to irrigate new groves of orange trees, greatly increasing citrus production but causing commodity prices to fall.

HISTORY. (Spanish). Ancient small villages of the Iberian people, of which Peñíscola, with a double harbor, was the largest, attracted Phoenicians, Greeks, Carthaginians, and Romans. Romans and Muslims developed the fertile Castellón *huerta*, which provided large yields of cotton, rice, and sugar irrigated by *al-sagyut* (Arabic) or *acequias* (Spanish), ditches that bring water from the mountain rivers.

Under the Muslims, the *huerta* grew so valuable that it attracted Christians from Catalonia and Aragón. After the fall of Córdoba, nominal suzerainty of the emir of Zaragoza ended when he refused to pay tribute to Fernando I of Castile. Fernando invaded in 1065 but died before he could establish control. The same fate overcame El Cid, and short Almoravid forays and the later Almohad military frontier south of Peñíscola in the twelfth century managed to restore a degree of Muslim rule.

Christian success began with Jaume I (1213–76) of Aragón, whose army of crusaders from southern France and military orders (Temple, Hospital, Santiago, Calatrava) seized northern Valencia in the summer of 1232 and made the village of Castellón de la Plana (now most frequently called Castelló) a military camp. Catalan peasants, ruled by a few Aragonese nobles, resettled the area to replace the Muslims who had fled. The Catalan *furos*, or system of local rights, provided the basis for local government.

Peñíscola fell the next year to the Knights Templar, who continued to govern the district until replaced by the smaller Order of Montesa in the fourteenth century. Yet the border between Christendom and Islam remained open. Labor shortages kept many Muslims in place but sometimes led to religious riots. The Church became responsible for keeping order by 1268. "Friars of the Sack" contravened provisions in the *furos* of Valencia against transfer of royal property to the Church and began an informal crusader kingdom of Valencia, a religious state supported by a heavy tithe.

This new burden caused serious riots in 1275 in Peñíscola and other towns and created a steadily widening ethnic cleavage.

While Christian clerical rule eventually subdued the most dangerous outbursts of ethnic violence, it occasionally led to other crises. After the Avignon Papacy (1309–77), when Italy, Castile, and France agreed to restore the papacy to Rome, a section of the Church nevertheless pursued the schism for their own national purposes. The archbishop of Aragón, Cardinal Pedro de Luna, elected as the schismatic Pope Benedict XIII in 1413, was supported only by Martí I (1395–1410) of Aragón. Benedict refused to resign and continued his schism for about a decade, setting up court in a small castle on the promontory that divides the harbor of Peñíscola, the Spanish "Rome" from 1415 until Benedict's death in 1424.

His successor, Clement, resigned at the urging of Alfons de Borja, Benedict's former chamberlain who, having dealt with many of Europe's high churchmen, himself soon experienced a meteoric rise within the ranks of the Church. Made bishop of Vic (Catalonia) and then Valencia, he rose further by becoming a cardinal in the Roman curia, changing the spelling of his name Borja to the Italian Borgia. In 1455, he was elected Pope Calixtus III (1455–58), becoming the first Spanish pontiff since the early Middle Ages. The new pope, of a poor family from the village of Borja in the Ebro Valley that had resettled in Játiva, made his relatives extremely powerful throughout the province of Castellón de la Plana.

In the meantime, Alfons's nephew, Rodrigo (also of Játiva), the father of Lucrezia and Cesare Borgia, held bishoprics in Gerona, Oviedo, and Valencia, and succeeded Alfons (Calixtus) as Pope Alexander VI (1458–1503). He favored Spain in the division of the Americas, but proved to be so venal and secular that until recently only Italian popes were chosen.

During the sixteenth century, the Ottoman Turks' rise in the eastern Mediterranean introduced a period of uncertainty along the coast. Pirate scares became so common that harbor defenses had to be strengthened. In the eighteenth century, the War of Spanish Succession saw Peñíscola support the Bourbon monarchy and hold off a seventeen-month siege by Karl of Austria. In 1812–13, the French held the fortress at Peñíscola against Spanish rebels until late in the Napoleonic War. Violence also flared during the First Carlist War when many would-be regionalists joined guerrilla bands in the Maestrazgo Hills.

Overpopulation led to a series of land disputes in the later nineteenth century, and after 1926 the newly founded Federación Anarquista Ibérica (FAI) gained considerable support for their anarchist schemes. During the Spanish Civil War, they collectivized rural areas in the province and organized agrarian communes. The first few days of civil war were violent, but military campaigning did not start until Francoist forces reached the coast at Vinaróz on April 8, 1938, dividing the Republic into two separate parts. Now suddenly on the front lines, the town of Castelló de la Plana fell on June 14 after much of it had been destroyed.

In the subsequent postwar period, rural migration to neighboring cities eased discord over land. Specialty agriculture and tourism, particularly in Peñíscola, have brought greater prosperity to the province during the past thirty years.

LITERATURE. While there are no noteworthy provincial authors, two works have been written about the area. **Benito Pérez Galdós's** novel *La campana del Maestrazgo* dramatized nineteenth-century Carlist campaigns in the province. **Manuel Azaña,** premier and president of the Second Republic, left an unfinished and unproduced play in his papers entitled *La velada en Benicarló.* The play, a memoir about a trip Azaña made to this area while president of the Republic, finally reached the stage in the 1980s.

ART. The Remigia Cave at Ares del Maestre near Castelló de la Plana has wall paintings similar to those at Altamira. The paintings date from the Mesolithic period from 10000 to 3000 B.C. They are remarkable for the variety of animals portrayed and the ability of the drawings to convey motion and setting.

Francisco Ribalta (1555–1628) of Castelló de la Plana studied painting in Naples, where he adopted the chiaroscuro style pioneered by Caravaggio. His frescoes are in the museum of the Diputación building in Castelló de la Plana, which also contains paintings by Bartolomé Bermejo (1430?–98?).

In Segorbe, the cathedral has a retablo by **Juan Vicente Macip** (1490?–1550?), who introduced Raphael's style into Valencian art. The cathedral museum also possesses works of El Greco, Ribalta, and Jerónimo Jacinto Espinosa (1600–1680).

CUSTOMS AND SOCIETY. In areas where Catalans and Aragonese first settled, a local version of the *jota* is danced slowly, accompanied by songs known as *albaes*, with musicians playing the *dulzaéna* (a primitive oboe) and the *tamboril* (a small drum). Only the drum is used to accompany the singer. Another popular dance is the *bolangera* (also done in Tarragona and elsewhere in Catalonia). It is danced by four couples in a rather staid fashion, except for the *aranilla* (little spider) section, where the male tries to step on the woman's feet as if there were a spider on the floor.

The Fiesta de la Magdalena in Vinaróz is quite spectacular, especially as a bull is run at midnight and again at 4 A.M. using the practice of *toro embolado* (literally, burning bull). A metal contraption containing oil is fitted over the horns and set on fire, creating a vivid image of a blazing bull running through the darkened streets of the town. During the day, a makeshift arena for bullfights is created by blocking off the main square of the town. Similar *corridas del pueblos* are held all over Spain, but unlike many other areas the town of Castelló de la Plana does not allow the bull to be killed.

HISTORIC SITES. The old town of **Castelló de la Plana**, damaged in the Spanish Civil War, has been rebuilt, especially the fourteenth-century Gothic church of Santa María. Some paintings of a famous native artist, Francisco Ribalta, are exhibited in the church. The unattached bell tower of El Fadri is opposite Santa María, and a museum in the Diputación houses paintings and prehistoric artifacts.

Elsewhere in the province, north to south along the Mediterranean coast, the Knights Templar once owned **Vinaróz**, the walls and towers of which still stand. **Benicarló**, originally a Greek colony, is another attractive beach community. **Peñíscola** is a beautiful seaside town familiar to cinema fans as the locale in the film *El Cid*. The castle of Benedict XIII occupies the promontory between Peñíscola's two harbors. Next to the castle is the small church of the Virgen de la Ermitana, which contains a small painting believed to be a relic of St. James. The contemporary town has a national parador and many beach resort tourist hotels. **Alcalá de Chivert** has an eighteenth-century baroque parish church with a handsome tower.

In the Maestrazgo Hills overlooking the Mediterranean, **Albocácer** contains the castle of the local Knights of Montesa. The Stone Age caves of Cueva Remigia, Barranco de la Gazulla, and Cueva del Civil are nearby. **Morella** is in the mountains about forty miles west of the Mediterranean. It was important during the Carlist War as a center for guerrillas. **Segorbe** commands a strategic location inland over the southern coastal plain as an ancient vantage point with Celtiberian and Roman fortifications. Its cathedral is Gothic with a Renaissance gallery and two towers, and there is also an interesting Plaza Mayor.

CUISINE. The main ingredients of cooking in Castellón de la Plana are rice, seafood, shellfish, and spices. All are combined in paella with chicken, sausage, and the expensive spice, saffron. Paella is Spain's national dish.

There are many types of rice dishes. *Arroz a la Valenciana*, the simple Valencian rice, uses small Levant sausages (*blanquillos*) or Catalan pork sausage (*butifarra*) instead of shellfish. *Arroz con pollo a la alicantina* is made with rice, chicken, green peppers, and artichokes, but shellfish paella is the most popular and expensive. *Arroz con alcacofa* includes artichokes and ham, but various combinations of zucchini, eggplant, and potatoes stuffed with ground meat in an almond, herb, and garlic sauce are also served. Dessert is usually fresh fruit.

The viticulture of Castellón de la Plana is the least important of the Valencian region, but the white wine of Cheste is among the best in the immediate area.

VALENCIA

VITAL STATISTICS. Pop., 2,066,413. Area, 10,776 sq. km. Capital and diocesan see: Valencia (pop., 751,734), located on the Río Turia at its mouth on the Mediterranean. Slightly northwest of the main province is the county of Ademuz in the Magro Valley, completely surrounded by the territory of Cuenca (New Castile) and just below Teruel (Aragón). It was attached to the province of Valencia in 1851.

The main province is south of Castellón de la Plana and north of Alicante, while Cuenca and Albacete (New Castile) lie to the west. The Turia and Júcar rivers provide water necessary for large-scale irrigation of Valencia's agricultural plain. The Costa Blanca and Costa Azul, two main tourist coasts, are both south of the city of Valencia.

The city is the third largest in Spain and home of the University of Valencia.

ECONOMY. The province of Valencia is one of Spain's most prosperous regions. The Valencian orange originated here, and citrus is an old and important industry now revitalized by the introduction of the larger navel oranges. More than 200,000 hectares are devoted to citrus production, while 900,000 produce other types of fruit, including apples, pears, apricots, cherries, plums, peaches, and figs. Vegetables and rice are other important products, and Valencia is the sixth-largest commercial fishing province in Spain.

Paper, steel, cotton spinning, woolen clothing, silk (in Burjasot and Valencia), and food processing (6 percent of the national total) have been important industries for a long time, but heavy industry has grown spectacularly since 1973, when Ford established a plant at Almusafes to produce over a thousand cars a day. IBM and other electronics companies are recent arrivals, and Spain's newest stock exchange opened in 1981.

HISTORY. (Thurias [Greek], Medina bu-Tarab [Arabic]). Bronze Age culture by Iberian tribes from the south of France created a society by 1200 B.C. that developed simple river bottom irrigation along the coast and sheep raising with seasonal transhumance in the hills west of the coast. Liria developed high-quality pottery by the third century B.C. Greeks founded Thurias (Valencia) in the sixth century, soon the largest colony of the eastern Mediterranean coast. According to Livy, the disputed possession of Saguntum (Saguntoia) between Rome and Carthage caused the Second Punic War when Rome began settling legionnaires to develop the region. By 138 B.C. a major colony had emerged. The town of Cullera at the mouth of the Júcar River is typical in having been held by Celtiberians, Phoenicians, Greeks, Carthaginians, and Romans.

At the end of the Roman period, Visigoths lacked the agricultural skills necessary to maintain this level of civilization, but herding flocks did increase and Saetabis (Jávea) became the seat of a Visigothic bishop. Saetabis was renamed Medina Xateba by the Muslims and became thoroughly Mozarab. As a region, Valencia trailed only Andalusia in size and prosperity during the caliphate of Córdoba. Arab technical sophistication enabled riparian expertise from the Nile and Tigris-Euphrates valleys to be used throughout the Valencian *huerta*, including introduction of water wheels and extensive irrigation canals (*al-sagyut* or, in Spanish, *acequias*). The use of water tribunals to apportion flow to individual properties, based on a complex set of customary laws, later became a part of the Spanish heritage in the Río Grande Valley of New Spain and is still used today in the southwestern United States. This vastly developed irrigation society enabled horticultural transfer of many new fruits and vegetables not previously grown in Europe.

Muslim Córdoba's decline began with the Umayyad collapse in A.D. 1031. The region briefly came under Seville's Abbadite dynasty, but in 1085 Toledo's capture by Alfonso VI of Castile and León threatened Valencia. A Christian ally, al-Kadir, held the area until challenged in 1087 by the ex-emir of Murcia, al-Hajib. In desperation, al-Kadir allied with El Cid to forestall the approach of strong Almoravid reinforcements. *Valencianos* rallied to El Cid, and the Almoravids retreated on June 15, 1094. El Cid ruled for five years until his death on July 10, 1099, and his wife, Jimena, ruled an additional three years before the Almoravids regained the area.

Reestablishment of Muslim rule created a principality first led by Muhammad ibn Said that lasted until Jaume I of Aragón reached Valencia in 1238. The Reconquest of eastern Spain closed with an agreement between Fernando III and Jaume, by which Castile waived all claims to Valencia in exchange for release of Aragonese claims on Murcia, putting aside the so-called division of Wamba, an earlier bequest by a Visigothic king that had caused both the archdiocese of Tarragona and that of Toledo to claim ecclesiastical control of Valencia.

Aragonese rule in Valencia created a Cortes and extended *furos* to the Christian community. As an informal crusader kingdom that depended heavily upon Muslim labor, it used Saracen slaves to create a plantation society. Christian commoners rose rapidly into the petty knighthood (*caballeros ciudadanos*) as lessees of crown properties. The *caballeros* treated Muslims harshly by refusing to grant them independent charters, excluding them from the local *furos*' protection and creating Moorish ghettos (*morerías*).

In this tense situation, the Church was asked to mediate between these ethnic and religious groups so often that its power came to rival that of the Crown. Popes offered indulgences to attract Christian settlers, and parishes became the basic administrative structure, handling tax collection, new land grants, and debt collection. Two men from each parish church made up the Valencia City Council. Only a third of the tithe went to the state, and the remaining revenues made the Valencian church rich.

Valencia offered unparalleled opportunities for an ambitious Christian, as shown by the Borja (Borgia) family. Alfons de Borja's nephew Alexander VI gave a large papal loan to Fernando the Catholic in order to obtain Gandía and Játiva for the Borja family in 1485. Only such largess could attract men in arms to hold in check the huge Muslim population. Another example is provided by the Dominican friar Vincent Ferrer (1350–1419), born in Valencia to a *valenciana* mother and an English father. After becoming an advisor to Benedict XIII, he organized a fervent open-air preaching campaign in 1391 to convert Muslims and Jews, aided by the ex-rabbi Paul, later the bishop of Cartagena. Ferrer broke with Benedict when the latter failed to reconcile with the Roman Pope Urban VI and persuaded the Kingdom of Aragón to abandon the schismatic pope as well.

The sixteenth century witnessed several new crises. With the advent of the Hapsburg monarchy, the Germania revolt of 1520 further strained the area's social stability. At the heart of the revolt, the Germania (which took its name from a military brotherhood) had vague republican origins, perhaps originating in Italian Renaissance politics, but soon veered into attacking the Muslim community. While the Germania never reached the same level of revolt as the Comuneros, it destroyed Christian-Muslim relations and damaged dynastic ties by seeking greater autonomy for the region.

Another crisis involved the rise of the Ottoman Turks as challengers to the Mediterranean-wide strategy and far-flung interests of the Hapsburg dynasty. Suleiman the Magnificent (r. 1520–60) was a formidable opponent, particularly since Valencia remained within reach of Turkish naval power and contained a large population of potentially rebellious Muslims. In an attempt to control this section of society, 200,000 Muslims underwent forcible conversion in 1525 and many others were enslaved.

The Christian religiosity of this age is best exemplified by St. Francis Borja (1510–72), son of the duke of Gandía, great-grandson of Pope Alexander VI and of King Fernando V of Aragón. Francis began serving Carlos I at age twenty-nine when he was appointed viceroy of Catalonia, but an unpopular judicial reform forced him to retire to his estates. After his wife's death in 1546, he pursued a religious vocation and secretly joined the Society of Jesus, receiving ordination as a priest in 1554 and entering the circle around Ignacio of Loyola. Francis later founded many Jesuit institutions in Spain and Portugal, but he returned to Rome in 1561 and four years later, after Loyola's death, was elected general of the Jesuits. Always zealous against the Turks, during his term he also expanded missionary activity in Poland, France, the entire Mediterranean, and Latin America, where he initiated the Jesuit ministry to the Americas. In the same era, St. Luis Bertrán (1526–81), distant relative of St. Vincent Ferrer, emerged as one of the most successful Dominican missionaries in the New World, later being elevated to become the patron saint of Colombia.

The climax of this religiosity came when St. Juan de Ribera (1527–1611), archbishop of Valencia from 1568 to 1611, took an intense dislike to the Moriscos (converted Muslims), believing them to be a threat to the Church because of their ignorance of religious doctrine, and preaching ardently that they be expelled. Felipe III and the court debated the proposal and in 1609 forced a total of about 280,000 Moriscos to leave Spain—135,000 from Valencia alone. Silk production collapsed, and the irrigation system lost many of its technicians. The Hapsburg kings tried to lessen the damage by lowering taxes and increasing Valencia's regional freedom, but their own popularity suffered.

Not so surprisingly, Valencia rose in support of the new Bourbon dynasty during the War of Spanish Succession. Only Játiva, with its Borja links, remained loyal to the Hapsburg dynasty until Felipe V sacked the town. But when the Bourbon regime ended the federated Aragonese empire and its foral laws by the Nueva Planta decrees, chaos appeared throughout the area along with a sense of betrayal. Not until the 1770s, when Carlos III spent huge amounts of royal funds to improve Valencia's agricultural productivity, did confusion abate and the new monarchy's popularity increase.

During the War of Independence in the early nineteenth century, the city of Valencia, twice occupied by invading Napoleonic armies, had little option but to continue supporting the Spanish Bourbon cause, but during the later liberal era the northern areas of Valencia supported the Carlists, urged on by a leading Valencian politician, Antonio Aparisi y Guijarro (1815–72), an outspoken Carlist. The Valencian middle classes, while religiously conservative, proved to be more eager to own *huerta* properties confiscated from the Church and generally inclined toward liberalism. The rich Church lands constituted more than a third of the province, and land fever gripped many mercantile townsmen. In time, the province of Valencia was changed greatly by the abolition of entail and mortmain, and commercial agriculture boomed as new citrus orchards and rice plantations contributed significantly to rising agricultural production.

Even during this period, however, politics remained diverse. Sagunto's sympathy for the Bourbon cause during the First Republic (1873–74) led Alfonso XII to proclaim himself king from the town, replacing his mother, Isabel II, who had abdicated in 1868. During the later Restoration, federal sympathies reappeared in reaction to late nineteenth-century centralization, but socialism and anarchism spread even more rapidly among urban workers and peasants. Their grievances created general support for the Second Republic in 1931 and resistance to the rebellion against it in 1936.

During the civil war, the city of Valencia suddenly became the capital of republican Spain on November 4, 1936, when the army's siege of Madrid forced the republican cabinet to relocate. Valencia, itself cut off from Catalonia when Franco's army broke through to Castelló de la Plana in the spring of 1938, saw the republican government flee to Barcelona less than a year later. The city of Valencia surrendered on March 30, 1939, after Barcelona had fallen.

Trade with the Axis Powers caused the region to be militarized during World War II. Valencia struggled in the postwar period to reestablish foreign produce markets, but until the Cold War eased isolation, Valencian exports faced enormous difficulties. High population growth made industrial expansion crucial, and although Valencia was made into an economic development zone in 1966, excessive bureaucracy and corruption tarnished this project. Both management and labor supported the constitutional monarchy between 1975 and 1977, but a bitter opponent of democracy, General Jaime Milans del Bosch, commander of the Valencia military district, led a coup d'état that briefly held the national Cortes in Madrid captive on February 23, 1981, until King Juan Carlos, in a brave speech, calmed fears and destroyed the uprising. The incident catapulted the Partido Socialista Obrero Español (PSOE) into power during the 1982 national elections.

LITERATURE. The Valencian towns of Jérica, Onda, Almenara, Saguntum, and Valencia are locales in *Cantar de mío Cid*. During the later Middle Ages, **Pere March** (1338?–1413) of Gandía began a deeply religious poetic tradition. His son, **Auziás March** (1397?–1459), was the first poet to write exclusively in Català. Influenced by Dante's concentrated style, March's *Cant espiritual*, an early expression of religious crisis in European poetry, exposed fear that man's free will might prevent salvation. In his collection of tormented love poems, *Cants de Amor*, he assails his love, a married woman, for having accepted his suit, thus threatening their chance of salvation. March's craving for a pure and ideal love expresses an ambiguous view of women both as objects of lust and models of virtue.

During the Renaissance, **Joanot Martorell** (1413?–68) of Gandía wrote *Tirant lo Blanc* (1460?), a romance of chivalry. Educated in Paris, **Juan Luis Vives** (1492–1540) of Valencia was a talented humanist who taught at Bruges and in England. Friendship with Erasmus sparked Vives's interest in religious reform, and his major work, a commentary on St. Augustine's political ideas, opposed many policies of the sixteenth-century Church. As a philosopher, he argues that experience is crucial to knowledge but often leads to individualist extremes which must be curbed if knowledge is to be used effectively.

The Golden Age produced **Joan Timoneda** (1520?–83) of Valencia, a man of letters who by editing and publishing the works of Alonso de la Vega and Lope de Rueda made the city into an early printing center. He also wrote dramas and collected ballads, stories, and folklore. His *Patrañuelo* collected stories told by many characters. In *Tres comedias*, he adapted classical Greco-Roman drama to the Spanish stage. Timoneda also is the first dramatist to use the word *entremeses* to describe comic interludes later so popular in Spanish drama. **Francesc Agustí Tárrega** (1554–1602) of Segorbe, canon of the Valencia Cathedral, wrote more than a dozen religious works and belonged to Guillén de Castro's Nocturnos group.

The great **Guillén de Castro y Bellvís** (1569–1631) served in the coast guard and became a Knight of Santiago before he turned to writing. His overwhelming success, *Mocedades del Cid* (1608?), is one of the most popular plays of the Spanish stage and revitalized El Cid's status as a national hero. Castro also wrote comedies such as *El Narciso en su opinión* and adapted stories such as *Don Quijote de la Mancha* by Cervantes for the stage. In general, his outstanding accomplishment as a writer came in adapting the *romancero* to Golden Age drama. He also founded the most famous literary group in Valencia's history, the Academia de los Nocturnos, active from 1591 to 1593 (later followed by another group, Los Montañeses del Parnaso).

Other creative figures of this period include **Gaspar Honorat de Aguilar** (1561–1623), a dramatist and poet; **Gaspar Gil Polo** (1519?–85), a novelist whose *Los cinco libros de la diana enamorada* (1564) is considered one of the best Spanish pastoral novels; **Carlos Boyl Vives de Canesmas** (1577–1617), a playwright of the Lope de Vega tradition; and **Andrés Rey de Artieda** (1549–1613), whose tragedy *Las amantes* (1581), set in Teruel, provides the first serious portrayal of tragic love on the Spanish stage.

The Enlightenment produced **Antonio Ponz** (1725–92) of Bechí, a travel writer who visited most of Spain during his lifetime and wrote *Viaje de España*, a good source for the period. **Francisco Pérez Bayer** (1714–94), an educator and Hebrew scholar at the University of Valencia and Salamanca, later was made director of the Royal Library.

The nineteenth century saw **Josep Bernat y Baldovi** (1810–64) of Sueca become a folklorist and playwright who contributed to the Catalan revival. **Enrique Gaspar** (1842–1902), a diplomat and playwright, wrote works denouncing middle-class decadence. **Julián Ribera y Tarragó** (1858–1934) of Carcagente, a scholar of Arab affairs at the University of Zaragoza and the University of Madrid, did scholarly research on Muslim society in Spain that revitalized studies of early medieval Valencia.

The best-known Valencian writer of recent times, **Vicente Blasco Ibáñez** (1867–1928), a controversial and sometimes bombastic novelist, wrote in a realistic and naturalistic style. *Arroz y Tartana* (1894) deals with merchants in pursuit of easy money in Valencia. *Flor de Mayo* (1895) presents a romantic and moving story about the fishermen of El Cabañal. Two novels, *La Barranca* (1899) and *Entre Naranjos* (1900), tell the story of Valencian rural life. Another, *Cañas y Barro* (1902), is set among the fishermen in the marshes of Albafuera. His so-called sociological novels, or political tracts, are derived from Karl Marx and Pierreare Proudhon. *La Horda* (1905) describes Madrid's underworld with brutal realism in the style of Zola, but without subtlety. National works such as *La maja desnuda* (1906) or *Sangre y Arena* (Blood and Sand, 1908) cover various regions of Spain. His international works, a product of Blasco Ibáñez's five-year-long travels in the Americas, include *La tierra de todos*, set in nineteenth-century Argentina, and his later best seller of World War I, *Los cuatro jinetes del apocalipsis* (*The Four Horsemen of the Apocalypse*, 1916), which was made into a melodramatic but extremely popular early

Hollywood movie. Through these various stages, he maintained an almost revolutionary anticlericalism and showed great sympathy for peasants.

Other Valencian writers imitated Blasco Ibáñez. **Manuel Cignes Aparicio** (1873–1936) of Enguera, a radical novelist, wrote about the illiterates of rural Spain, and **José Más** (1885–1940) of Écija extensively examined the Andalusian peasant question, particularly in Córdoba. Today, a leading poet of the area is **Francisco Brines** (b. 1932).

ART. In the fifteenth century, close contact with Italy created a considerable artistic tradition for Valencia. **Dello di Niccoló Delli** (d. 1471) initiated the Italian influence, and Cardinal Rodrigo Borja (the future Alexander VI) encouraged **Paolo da San Leocadio** (1445?–1520?) to work in Valencia. Little remains of San Leocadio's frescoes, but his *Virgin and Child with Sts. Benedict, Bernard, and a Donor* now hangs in the Prado.

Around the same time, Hispano-Flemish art also entered Spain through Valencia, largely through the work of **Luis Dalmau** (ca. 1445) of Valencia, who painted in both Valencia and Catalonia. His work embodied perspective adapted from Van Eyck of viewing a subject through an optical instrument.

At the cathedral, there are panels by Hernando Yáñez de la Almedina (n.d.) and Fernando Llanos (ca. 1506), both influenced by Leonardo da Vinci. Yáñez's *Madonna and Child with Infant St. John* is in the National Gallery of Art in Washington, D.C. Other paintings in the cathedral are by Ribera, Juan Vicente Macip (1490?–1550), and Nicolás Florentino (1404–71). There are also two works by Goya.

Valencia is a major area of the baroque in Spain. The Colegio de Corpus Christi built for Archbishop Juan de Ribera, who held the office from 1569 to 1611, is early baroque. The walls are covered by frescoes done by the Genoese mannerist Bartolomé Matarama. Archbishop Ribera also possessed one of the earliest copies of Caravaggio's work in Spain, and he sponsored Francisco Ribalta (1555–1628), a painter from Castelló de la Plana whose *Martyrdom of St. James* and *St. Francis Comforted by a Musical Angel* are at the Prado in Madrid.

Another important baroque structure is the Palacio del Marqués de Dos Aguas, which has an alabaster portal by Ignacio Vergara. The building houses the Spanish National Ceramics Museum, a good collection of Valencian ceramics, which is still a highly developed artisan industry. Also baroque is Nuestra Señora de los Desamparados, an eighteenth-century parish church decorated with frescoes by the painter-theorist **Antonio de Palomino** (1655–1726), who executed them in the Italian baroque style.

Rococo had little place in Spanish decorative schemes, excess having already been explored by the plateresque and churriguesque. What little exists in Spain can be found in Valencia with the rococo façade added to the cathedral in Valencia and the later additions to the Palacio del Marqués de Dos Aguas by the German Conrad Rudolf.

The Museo Provincial de Bellas Artes has an important collection of paintings by such Valencian artists as Fray Bonifacio Ferrer (ca. 1450), Marçal de Sax (ca. 1460, of German origin), Vicente Maçip (1475?–1550?), and his son, Juan de Juanes (1510–79), both strongly influenced by Raphael. Most of these artists fall into the Hispano-Flemish school, but Joaquín Sorolla (1863–1923) followed an early modern style. In addition, there are works by Murillo, Zurbarán, El Greco, Velázquez, Hieronymus Bosch, and van Dyck.

The Colegiata Church of Gandía has a beautiful retablo by Damián Forment (1408?–1541). There is a small museum in Jávea (Játiva) of the native painter **Jusepe de Ribera** (1591–1659), who won his reputation in Naples. A good draftsman, Ribera used realistic models and picked up tenebrist techniques from Ribalta by adding glitter to his paint to create a silvery light color of flesh tints in dramatic scenes.

MUSIC. The *Cancionero General* of Hernando del Castillo, published at Valencia in 1511, is a prime collection of the *romances*, or ballads, derived from old epics of chivalry and put to music, which attained great popularity in Valencia. The verses lacked scores until **Luis Milán** (1500–1561?) wrote *Libro de vihuela de Mano intitulado el Maestro* as an introduction to guitar tablature. The *vihuela*, or guitar, adapted from the ancient Egyptian lute, was less delicate and had curved sides introduced by Muslim instrument-makers. Milán wrote music for four- to seven-string guitars that made the guitar so popular in Spain.

In the early modern period, **Juan Bautista Comes** (1568–1643) typified the Valencian school of music by using grandiose concepts and violent contrasts in his religious compositions. As part of the Age of Enlightenment, **Vicente Martín y Soler** (1756–1806) of Valencia received his musical training in Florence, where he wrote his first opera, *Ifigenia in Aulide*. He later taught music in Vienna and composed *Una Cosa Rara* (1786), anticipating Mozart's *Le Nozze di Figaro*. In 1788, he became director of the St. Petersburg Opera, where he remained until his death.

In the modern period, **Manuel Penella** (1880–1939) was a highly successful writer and composer of the *zarzuela*. His work *El Gato Montés* (1916) is one of the great masterpieces of *zarzuela* and contains *paso doble* music familiar to anyone who has gone to bullfights or heard the music of the *corrida*. The story reworks the *Carmen* theme of a gypsy girl loved by a matador and a bandit. Its Puccini-influenced score compares favorably with Bizet's *Carmen*. Penella's other *zarzuelas* include *Las Musas Latinas* (1913) and *Don Gil de Alcalá* (1932), set in eighteenth-century Mexico.

A contemporary musician, **Joaquín Rodrigo** (b. 1901) of Sagunto, has been blind since the age of three. He studied music in Valencia and Paris but has lived in Madrid since 1939. His most popular work, *Concierto de Aranjuez*, is a concerto in three movements for orchestra and solo guitar. He wrote *Fantasía para un gentilhombre* in 1954 for Andrés Segovia. Rodrigo's guitar pieces are some of the most famed serious works in this literature.

CUSTOMS AND SOCIETY. In Valencia, the festival of San José on March 19 honors St. Joseph. Many of the events are usually held during the middle of Lent. The unique *fallas* built for this fiesta are huge papier-mâché and wooden effigies of grotesque animals or persons featured in a series of parades and then burned in the *cremá*, a huge fire, at the end of the ceremony. Gandía also has a *falla* festival.

In Bocairente, the festival of Moors and Christians lasts for several weeks with fireworks, parades, and a reenactment of the Reconquest that climaxes when a stuffed effigy of Muhammad is destroyed.

The bells of the cathedral in Valencia at one time regulated the irrigation of the *huerta*, and the famous Tribunal de las Aguas traditionally met once a week on the steps of the cathedral's west portal. The Holy Grail (chalice of Christ) in the chapel of Santo Cáliz of the cathedral is venerated during Holy Week.

Traditional dance is dominated by the *jota valenicana*, a slower variation of the bolero, a term taken from the Spanish word *volar* (to fly). Couples using castanets divide the dance into three parts (*coplas*). The first is the *paseo* (walk or strut), the second, the *bien parado* (a set of poses), and the finale, a wild dance that exhausts the dancers.

Dress traditionally tended to be finer in Valencia than in the other provinces of the Levant. Silk, a major local product, added distinction to both male and female costumes. Women also may have been more expertly coiffured than elsewhere in Spain. The most popular nineteenth-century hairdo was two bobs, caught with silver pins at the sides and kept in place by a high silver or gold comb. Jewelry was worn conspicuously, and Valencian women favored large pearl and gold earrings, gold or silver chains, and pendants on silk ribbons.

HISTORIC SITES. The central Plaza del Ayuntamiento in the city of **Valencia** has a large musical fountain, government offices, and the municipal museum. In the center of the old town, the historic Plaza de la Reina adjoins the cathedral, built between 1252 and 1482.

The cathedral's basic style is Gothic, but it has a baroque façade. The south portal is the Puerta de Hierros with a large iron gate. The freestanding octagonal Micalet Bell Tower stands 223 feet high. Inside the cathedral, two prominent features are the *cimborio* dome over the crossing and the Capilla Mayor, a fifteenth-century chapel with a beautiful altar. The most revered Spanish religious relic in the Santo Cáliz chapel is the Holy Grail, the chalice said to have been used by Christ at the Last Supper or to have held his blood after crucifixion.

Six other major churches are in the city of Valencia: Nuestra Señora de los Desamparados (Our Lady of the Forsaken), the city's patron saint; Santa Catalina (a hexagon tower), Santo Domingo (Gothic with unique palm-sculpted decorations), San Agustín, San Martí, and San Nicolás. The Colegio del Patriarca is pure Renaissance in style. Many of Valencia's churches have blue tiled domes.

Interesting secular buildings include the Lonja de la Seda, a fine Gothic building that is the silk exchange and once served as the Consulado del Mar to administer shipping and hear maritime claims and cases. The Palacio de la Generalidad is a fifteenth-century Gothic building where the Cortes met. The Palacio del Marqués de Dos Aguas is decorated with baroque naturalistic designs. The Jardín Botánico is one of Europe's finest gardens.

Elsewhere in the province, not far north of the city of Valencia, **Sagunto** is a large coastal city with an ancient castle high above it thought to date from the First Punic War (ca. 237 B.C.). There is a restored Roman theatre, a temple of Artemis, and a local archaeological museum with many Roman artifacts. Closer to Valencia, the Entenza Castle in **Puig** was Jaume I's base for the capture of Valencia. **Llíria** (Lauro [Roman], Líria [Castilian]) is an ancient Celtiberian town where early mosaics (now in the National Archaeological Museum in Madrid) have been found. The Iglesia de la Sangre is a transitional Romanesque-Gothic structure, while the Ayuntamiento occupies the former palace of the dukes of Alba. **Chelva** is an isolated but lush inland village with a very tall Roman aqueduct and a nature preserve that protects the natural beauty of the Valencian *huerta*.

At the mouth of the Júcar River in the south, the coastal town of **Cullera** is surrounded by terraced agricultural plots on the hills near town. The Torre de la Reina Mora is a Muslim tower, and there is also a Muslim fortress. On the Serpis River south of Cullera on the coast, **Gandía** is the main town of the Costa Blanca and the site of the Borjas family palace. This luxurious ducal palace, built in 1600, is now owned by the Jesuits. Of particular interest is a small museum dedicated to St. Francis Borgia (1510–72), who abdicated his title as duke and resigned as viceroy to become a general of the Society of Jesus. The Colegiata Church is an example of Catalan Gothic with a single aisle but a long interior. It is a church filled with interesting religious artifacts. The original Borja center in Valencia, **Játiva,** home of the family's founder, Domingo de Borja (l340?–l428), contains his Torre de Canals, a fortified manor that overlooks the town. Játiva's main church is Tuscan-Renaissance in design; Archbishop Juan Borja's tomb is in one of the chapels. The municipal museum in Játiva has a fine collection of Muslim and Mudéjar decorative items.

On the Castilian border in the western Magro Valley, **Requena** is thought to have been the primary base of El Cid in his conquest of Valencia. Even though it did not become a part of Valencia until 1851, its ties with El Cid made the province of Valencia demand its inclusion.

CUISINE. Valencia is synonymous with paella. The origin of the word is illusive. *Patella*, Latin for pan, is one possibility, but since most paellas are prepared in *cazuelas*, a brown earthenware dish glazed only on the inside, the etymology may be incorrect. Whatever the term's derivation, the choice of paellas is large. The basic recipe is a mixture of fresh vegetables with rice, chicken, shellfish, *chorizo*, and saffron, the expensive dried stigmas of the *crocus sativus*, the autumn crocus, which has a wonderfully astringent taste. Saffron is the key element in paella. It is a costly spice because it must be hand picked, usually from fields along the eastern Mediterranean. It is gathered and dried following a traditional process also used in India and China. Since a little saffron goes a long way, it is usually sold by the gram, which makes it affordable. Saffron produces the bright yellow color of paella.

Putting together a paella is a labor-intensive process involving a number of stages.

PAELLA A LA VALENCIANA

½ lb. ground pork	3 cups Valencian or hard rice
2 large *chorizos* (sausages)	1 gram saffron
2 cloves garlic, peeled	½ cup peas
¾ cup olive oil	½ lb. large shrimp
1 green pepper, chopped	½ lb. clams, cleaned
1 onion, chopped	4 cups chicken stock or bouillon
2 tomatoes, cut into chunks	1 oz. sherry
1 deboned chicken, cut up	6–10 mussels
2 tsp. paprika	6 pimento strips

Cook pork and *chorizos* in a pan until done. Then cook the garlic in the olive oil until brown. Cook the green pepper and set aside. Lightly cook the onion, tomatoes, and chicken for 10 minutes. Slowly add the paprika and rice and slightly raise the temperature for 2 or 3 minutes. When the rice begins to soften, stir in saffron until rice turns yellow. Remove pan from the heat and add peas, shrimp, clams, and chicken stock or bouillon. Cook this mixture an additional 15 minutes before removing pan from the heat. Sprinkle the paella with sherry and add the mussels. Cover the pan for 1 or 2 minutes to allow the mussels to open. Garnish with pimentos.

Citrus fruit is used in many drinks, confections, and candies. Valencian oranges are particularly popular. Wine is another important product. More than half the wine exported from Spain each year goes through the port of Valencia, much of it from local sources. But Valencian wine is sold more in bulk than by individual brands, and much of it is blended for commercial sangria drinks or used in spritzer wines.

GLOSSARY

Adelanto mayor: the council or agents of a provincial governor.

Apostólico: a very devout Catholic.

Audiencia: court of appeal.

Caciques: political bosses, often rural, who manipulated political life.

Caciquismo: system of political manipulation, usually dependent upon the lack of an effective opposition.

Capilla: chapel.

Català: the Catalan language.

Caudillo: political or military dictator.

Churriguesque: Spanish form of baroque architecture developed by the three Churriguera brothers.

Consulado: a special government body to pursue some particular purpose, usually economic.

Conversos: Jews forcibly converted to Christianity.

Corregidor: chief magistrate, often with administrative duties, almost like a governor.

Cortes: legislative body.

Costumbrista: genre dealing with manners, customs, and national habits.

Desamortazación: liberal land reforms of the nineteenth century that destroyed religious (mortmain) controls placed on the sale of lands.

Diputación: local government council.

Disentailment: liberal land reforms freeing land of feudal restrictions.

Euskara: the Basque language.

Flamenco: music of southern Spain, gypsy in origin, accompanied by guitar and voice, which accompanies the special flamenco dance style.

Fuero: a socioeconomic privilege governing local life and institutions, or providing traditional law for many parts of Spain. *Foru (foruak,* pl.) in the Basque language; *furo* in the Catalan language.

Hectare: unit of land measure that equals 2.471 acres.

Hermandad: brotherhood serving some special purpose—a league or guild.

Huerta: irrigated land; a truck-garden area of great fertility.

Jornalero(s): those whose landholding exceeded one hectare but did not exceed three, or those who were agricultural day-laborers.

Latifundia (latifundistas): large landholdings, sometimes used to indicate large landowners.

Manos muertas: called mortmain in English. A special title for land donated to the Church. Liberals changed the laws and allowed the land to be sold in 1837.

Mesta, Honorable Society of the: a collective Castilian sheep herding organization, long controlled by the monarchy.

Moriscos: Muslims forcibly baptized to Christianity.

Mozárabs: Christians living in Muslim principalities.

Mudéjars: Muslims living in Christian principalities; also an architectural style (*see* Plateresque).

Muladíes: Christian converts to Islam.

Patronado real: royal control of high Church offices.

Picaresque: style of literature having a roguish hero or describing sharp-witted vagabonds.

Plateresque: style of architecture derived from Mudéjar artisanship; excessively decorated.

Real: royal.

Refranes: sayings; a genre of literature.

Retablo: altarpiece.

Ricohombres: landowners with more than fifteen hectares.

Romancero: collection of ballads.

Romanesque: European architecture of the eleventh and twelfth centuries, based on earlier Roman styles and characterized by use of the round arch and vault, with thick exterior walls.

Serranilla: rustic songs that became a part of poetry.

Siglo de Oro: roughly the period from 1575 to 1681 (date of Calderón's death) that saw Spanish art and literature become highly developed. Usually referred to in English as the Golden Age.

Taifa: small Muslim states that emerged after the fall of the caliphate of Córdoba in the early Middle Ages.

Tapas: small dishes served at bars in the evening.

Vega: tract of unusually fertile land.

Viceroy: governor of a country, region, or colony, ruling in the name of the king.

Zarzuela: lyric or comedic opera.

CHRONOLOGY

I. ANCIENT IBERIA

1. PREHISTORY
   20000–1000 B.C.

2. ERA OF SETTLEMENT
   1100–539 B.C.—Phoenician colonies
   814–201 B.C.—Carthaginian colonies
   218–201 B.C.—Second Punic War

3. ROMAN EPOCH
   143–138 B.C.—First Celtiberian War
   83–71 B.C.—Second Celtiberian War
   29 B.C.–A.D. 409—Roman Empire
   97–117—Trajan
   117–139—Hadrian
   387–395—Theodosius I

4. GOTHIC EPOCH
   414—Visigothic invasion
   550–601—Byzantine occupation of the Southeast
   507–711—Visigothic Kingdom of Iberia proclaimed

II. ISLAMIC IBERIA, 711–1036

1. UMAYYAD SPAIN, 750–1000
    756–788—Abd ar-Rahman I
    822–852—Abd ar-Rahman II
    912–961—Abd ar-Rahman III
    929—Caliphate of Córdoba created

2. SUCCESSOR ISLAMIC REGIMES: TAIFA PERIOD
    976–1008—Amirid dictatorship
    977–1002—Almansor (al-Mansur the Victorious)
    1039–1147—Almoravid Empire
    1130–1269—Almohad Empire
    1248–1492—Nasrid dynasty of Granada

III. MEDIEVAL SPAIN

1. ASTURIAS
    710?–737—Pelayo, Battle of Covadonga
    739–757—Alfonso I

2. CATALONIA
    878–897—Guifré el Pilós of Catalonia
    1035–1076—Ramón Berenguer I
    1131–1162—Ramón Berenguer IV

3. NAVARRE
    918?–1134—Iñigo Arista's dynasty
    1250–1512—French dynasties
    1515—Castilian control

4. ASTURIAS–LEÓN
    834?—Battle of Calatrava
    850–866—Ordoño I
    886–911—Alfonso III
    970–1035—Sancho the Great

5. CASTILE
    930–970—Count Fernán González
    1035–1060—Fernando I
    1065–1109—Alfonso VI unites León and Castile

1158–1214—Alfonso VI

1212—victory at Las Navas de Tolosa

1217–1252—Fernando III, nephew, prince of León

1230—León incorporated into Castile

1243–1248—conquest of Murcia, Jaén, Seville

1252–1284—Alfonso X (El Sabio, the wise)

6. ARAGÓN–CATALONIA

1035–1063—Ramiro I

1063–1094—Sancho Ramírez

1113–1131—Ramiro II

1137—marriage compact between Aragón and Catalonia

1162–1196—Alfons II creates federated empire

1213–1276—Jaume II

1229–1244—conquest of Balearics and Valencia

1287—Privileges of Union

7. GALICIA

1073—Castilian annexation of Galicia

1121—cathedral of Santiago de Compostela

IV. SPANISH RISE TO WORLD POWER

1. CHANGING DYNASTIC AND DIPLOMATIC CRISES, 1300–1480

A. *Castile*

1312–1350—Alfonso XI

1350–1369—Pedro the Cruel (civil war)

1369–1379—Enrique II (new Trastámara dynasty)

1406–1454—Juan II (defeated by nobles)

1454–1474—Enrique IV (continuing noble problems)

B. *Aragón*

1336–1383—Pedro IV (Pere)

1360—invasion of French and English

1412—Compromise of Caspe

1412–1416—Fernando I (Trastámara cousin)

1416–1458—Alfonso V conquers Corsica and Naples

1458–1479—Juan II opposed by Remença

2. CATHOLIC KINGS
    1469—marriage of Fernando and Isabel
    1474–1504—Isabel of Castile as queen of Castile
    1479–1516—Fernando II as king of Aragón
    1492—Conquest of Granada
    1504–1516—Fernando as regent of Castile

V. CARLOS I, 1517–1556

    1519—Charles V elected emperor of Holy Roman Empire
    1519–1521—Germania revolt of Valencia
    1520–1521—Comuneros uprising
    1521–1526—French-Spanish Italian War
    1542–1544—Second French-Spanish War
    1552–1556—Third French-Spanish War in Saxony
    1555—Peace of Augsburg

VI. FELIPE II AND THE SPANISH CRISIS, 1556–1598

    1566–1609—revolt of the Low Countries
    1568–1569—Alpujarras Muslim revolt, Granada
    1571—Spanish naval victory of Lepanto
    1580—Felipe inherits Portugal
    1586–1603—war between Spain and England/Holland
    1588—Spanish *Armada* defeated
    1589 and 1596—English raid Cádiz

VII. DECLINE OF THE SPANISH HAPSBURG DYNASTY

1. FELIPE III, 1598–1621
    1600–1602—bubonic plague
    1600–1618—duke of Lerma as favorite
    1609—truce with Holland
    1618—beginning of Thirty Years' War

2. FELIPE IV, 1621–1665
    1621—truce with Holland expires
    1624—Union of Arms proposal
    1633—Holland's final revolt

1637—France invades Catalonia

1640—revolt of Catalonia and Portugal

1643—Olivares falls from office

1648—Treaty of Westphalia ends Thirty Years' War

1652—France retreats from Catalonia

1659—Peace of Pyrenees between Spain and France

VIII. CARLOS II AND THE END OF HAPSBURG SPAIN, 1665–1700

1667–1668—War of Devolution over Spanish Netherlands

1668—Portugal regains independence

1700—Karl (Austria), then Phillipe (Anjou) as heir

IX. EIGHTEENTH CENTURY

1. FELIPE V, 1701–1746

1701–1713—War of Spanish Succession

1714—rebellion of Catalonia

1718—war over Sicily with Austria and Great Britain

1727—Spain fails to recapture Gibraltar

1733—Treaty of Escorial with France

1739—Anglo-Spanish War (Jenkins' Ear)

1740–1742—War of Austrian Succession; Italy lost

1743—Second Bourbon Family Pact

1745–1890—*foro* crisis in Galicia

2. FERNANDO VI, 1746–1759

1753—concordat with Rome

1756—founding of Amigos del País

3. ENLIGHTENED DESPOTISM AND CARLOS III, 1760–1788

1761—Third Bourbon Family Pact

1763—first restriction of ecclesiastical mortmain

1767–1814—Jesuits banished from Spain

1768–1771—educational and agrarian reform

1776—conde de Floridablanca as chief of government

1779—Spain aids U.S. in Revolutionary War

X. SPAIN IN THE FRENCH REVOLUTIONARY ERA

1. CARLOS IV, 1788–1808

    1792–1797, 1800–1808—Manuel Godoy as favorite

    1794–1795—war with republican France

    1801–1808—alliance with France

    1805—Battle of Trafalgar destroys Spanish fleet

    1807—French-Spanish partition of Portugal

2. WAR OF INDEPENDENCE, 1808–1813

    1808—Joseph Napoleon made king of Spain

    —Madrid uprising, Dos de Mayo (May 2)

    —Juntas de defensa resist Napoleon, Bailén, June 8

    1808–1809—siege of Zaragoza

    1809–1813—battles of the War of Independence

    1810–1812—Cortes of Cádiz writes Constitution of 1812

XI. NINETEENTH CENTURY

1. FERNANDO VII, 1814–1833; AND REGENCY

    1820–1823—Liberal Triennium and French intervention

    1827—revival of liberal influence

    1829—Fernando marries María Cristina de Borbon

    1830—female inheritance of crown confirmed

    1832—birth of Isabel II

    1833—regency of María Cristina

    1833–1839—First Carlist Civil War

    1834—Royal Statute defines constitutional monarchy

    1837—Constitution of 1837 seizes church property

    1839—Truce of Vergara

2. ISABEL II AND PRAETORIAN LIBERALISM, 1834–1868

    1858–1863—Unión Liberal cabinet of General O'Donnell

3. REVOLUTIONARY INTERLUDE, 1868–1874

    1869—democratic constitution

    1868–1870—leadership of General Prim y Prats

    1871–1873—constitutional monarchy of Amadeo I

    1873–1874—First Republic

1873–1876—Second Carlist Civil War

4. RESTORATION AND REGENCY, 1876–1902

1876–1885—Alfonso XII

1879—creation of socialist party (PSOE)

1881—*Turno del partidos*: liberal *caciquismo*

1885–1902—Regency: Cánovas and Sagasta hold power

1887–1896—José Rizal seeks Filipino independence

1890—universal manhood suffrage

1892–1895—José Martí seeks Cuban independence

1894—creation of Basque Nationalist Party

1895—Cuba seeks independence from Spain

1897—Cánovas assassinated, August 8

1898—Spanish-American War, April 24

XII. TWENTIETH CENTURY

1. ALFONSO XIII, 1902–1931

1914–1918—Spain neutral in World War I

1919–1926—colonial war in Morocco

1921—Anwal Disaster in Morocco, July 22

1923–1930—dictatorship of General Primo de Rivera

1931—Alfonso abdicates

2. SECOND REPUBLIC, 1931–1936

1931–1933—radical era led by Manuel Azaña

1933–1936—right-wing control of Republic

1934—Asturian insurrection, October 4–20

1936—left wins Popular Front elections, February 16

   —Azaña as president of the Republic, May 10

3. SPANISH CIVIL WAR, 1936–1939

1936–1937—Popular Front cabinet of Largo Caballero

1936–1939—Franco creates nationalist government, October 1

1937—nationalist capture of Málaga, February 7

   —bombing of Guérnica, April 26

   —fall of Bilbao, June 16

1938—nationalists capture Teruel, February 22

   —Ebro campaign, July–November

1939—Republican surrender, April 1

4. FRANCO ERA, 1939–1975

    1939—Spain joins Axis, April 7

    1942—Blue Division sent to fight in Soviet Union

    1945—UN bars Spain's membership, June 19

    1947—national referendum approves Franco's rule, March 31

    1952—Spain joins UNESCO, November 19

    1953—U.S.–Spanish military bases agreement, September 26

    1955—Spain admitted to UN, December 14

    1956—student protests against regime, February–April

    1962—creation of Workers' Commissions (CCOO), April 17

    1963–1965—massive worker and student strikes

    1966—Organic Law approves restoration of monarchy

    1973—assassination of Admiral Luis Carrero Blanco, June 8

    1975—death of Franco, November 20

5. CONTEMPORARY PERIOD, SINCE 1975

    1976—Adolfo Suárez as premier, July 3

    1978—democratic constitution approved, September 28

    1980—Catalan home rule begins, January 11

    1981—Suárez resigns, January 29

          —unsuccessful military coup d'état, February 23

    1982—socialist PSOE wins Andalusian election, May 23

          —Spain invited to join European Community, May 30

          —PSOE wins national elections, October 28

          —Felipe González new socialist premier, December 2

    1983—Supreme Court upholds regional autonomy, August 10

    1984—new Spanish-French offensive against ETA, January 24

    1985—Spain votes to join European Community, September 11

    1986—Spain becomes member of European Community, January 1

          —PSOE wins national elections, June 22

    1987—end of bases agreement with U.S., November 13

    1990—PSOE wins narrow victory in national elections

    1992—Expo '92, Seville

          —Olympic games, Barcelona, August

          —Madrid "cultural capital of 1992"

    1994—Partido Popular wins EC elections, June

BIBLIOGRAPHY

INTRODUCTION

Garreau, Joel. *The Nine Nations of North America.* Boston: Houghton Mifflin, 1981.

REGIONS

Aulestia, Gorka, and Linda White. *English-Basque Dictionary.* Reno: University of Nevada Press, 1989.

Bell, David S., ed. *Democratic Politics in Spain.* New York: St. Martin's Press. 1983. (See chapter by Mike Newton, "The Peoples and Regions of Spain".)

Bonime-Blanc, Andrea. *Spain's Transition to Democracy.* Boulder: Westview Press, 1986.

Delamaide, Darrell. *The New Superregions of Europe.* New York: Dutton, 1994.

Diccionari Vox: Anglès-Català, Català-Anglès. Barcelona: Biblograf S/A, 1988.

Fusi Aizpurua, Juan Pablo, ed. *España autonomías.* Madrid: Espasa-Calpe, 1989.

Graham, Robert. *Spain: A Nation Comes of Age.* New York: St. Martin's Press, 1984.

Gunther, Richard, Giacomo Sani, and Goldie Shabad. *Spain after Franco: The Making of a Competitive Party System.* Berkeley: University of California Press, 1988.

Pérez-Diaz, Victor M. *The Return of Civil Society: The Emergence of Democratic Spain.* Cambridge: Harvard University Press, 1993.

VITAL STATISTICS

Enciclopedia Universal Ilustrada. Madrid: Espasa-Calpe, 1966.

Entwistle, William J. *The Spanish Language, Together with Portuguese, Catalan and Basque*. New York: Macmillan, 1938.

Estadística, Instituto Nacional de. *Anuario Estadistico de España*. Madrid: Pich Editorial, 1992.

Gran Enciclopedia de España. Madrid: Enciclopedia de España, 1990.

Gran Enciclopedia Rialp. Madrid: Rialp, 1976.

El País.

Spaulding, Robert J. *How Spanish Grew*. Berkeley: University of California Press, 1943.

ECONOMY

Anderson, Charles W. *The Political Economy of Modern Spain: Policy-Making in an Authoritarian System*. Madison: University of Wisconsin Press, 1970.

The Economist.

Salmon, Keith G. *The Modern Spanish Economy: Transformation and Integration into Europe*. New York: Pinter, 1991.

Vicens Vives, Jaime. *An Economic History of Spain*. Princeton, N.J.: Princeton University Press, 1969.

Wall Street Journal.

HISTORY

Artola, Miguel. *Enciclopedia de Historia de España*. Madrid: Alianza Editorial, 1991.

Bard, Rachel. *Navarra: The Durable Kingdom*. Reno: University of Nevada Press, 1982.

Carr, Raymond. *Spain 1808–1939*. Oxford: Clarendon Press, 1966.

Carr, Raymond, and Juan Pablo Fusi. *Spain: Dictatorship to Democracy*. 4th ed. London: George Allen and Unwin, 1985.

Collins, Roger. *The Arab Conquest of Spain 710–797*. Cambridge: Basil Blackwell, 1991.

———. *Law, Culture and Regionalism in Early Medieval Spain*. London: Variorum, 1992.

Cuenca Toribio, José Manuel. *Historia de España*. Barcelona: Ediciones Danae. 1973.

Domínguez Ortiz, Antonio. *The Golden Age of Spain 1516–1659*. New York: Basic Books, 1971.

Douglass, William A. *Basque Politics: A Case Study in Ethnic Nationalism*. Reno: Basque Studies Program, University of Nevada, 1985.

Freedman, Paul. *Church, Law and Society in Catalonia, 900–1500*. London: Variorum, 1994.

Fuentes, Carlos. *The Buried Mirror: Reflections on Spain and the New World*. Boston: Houghton Mifflin, 1992.

Gerber, Jane. *The Jews of Spain*. New York: Free Press, 1992.

Gilmour, David. *The Transformation of Spain*. London: Quartet Books, 1985.

Heiberg, Marianne. *The Making of the Basque Nation*. Cambridge: Cambridge University Press, 1989.

Holmes, George, ed. *The Oxford Illustrated History of Medieval Europe*. Oxford: Oxford University Press, 1988.

Johnson, Marion. *The Borgias*. New York: Holt, Rinehart and Winston, 1981.

Johnson, Paul. *A History of the Jews*. New York: Harper and Row, 1987.

Kamen, Henry. *The Phoenix and the Flame: Catalonia and the Counter Reformation*. New Haven, Conn.: Yale University Press, 1993.

Kaplan, Temma. *Red City, Blue Period: Social Movements in Picasso's Barcelona*. Berkeley: University of California Press, 1992.

Kern, Robert W. *Liberals, Reformers and Caciques in Restoration Spain, 1875–1909*. Albuquerque: University of New Mexico Press, 1974.

———. *Red Years/Black Years: A Political History of Spanish Anarchism, 1911–1937*. Philadelphia: Institute for the Study of Human Issues, 1978.

Lannon, Francis, and Paul Preston, eds. *Elites and Power in Twentieth-Century Spain: Essays in Honour of Sir Raymond Carr*. Oxford: Clarendon Press, 1990.

Linehan, Peter. *Spanish Church and Society 1150–1300*. London: Variorum. 1983.

Liss, Peggy K. *Isabel the Queen*. New York: Oxford University Press, 1992.

Lynch, John. *Bourbon Spain 1700–1808*. Oxford: Basil Blackwell, 1989.

———. *The Hispanic World in Crisis and Change 1598–1700*. Cambridge: Basil Blackwell, 1992.

———. *Spain 1516–1598*. Cambridge: Basil Blackwell, 1991.

Malefakis, Edward E. *Agrarian Reform and Peasant Revolution in Spain: Origins of the Civil War*. New Haven, Conn.: Yale University Press, 1970.

Payne, Stanley G. *A History of Spain and Portugal*. 2 vols. Madison: University of Wisconsin Press, 1973.

———. *The Franco Regime 1936–1975*. Madison: University of Wisconsin Press, 1987.

———. *Spain's First Democracy: The Second Republic, 1931–1936*. Madison: University of Wisconsin Press, 1993.

Reilly, Bernard F. *The Medieval Spains*. Cambridge: Cambridge University Press, 1993.

Richardson, John S. *Hispaniae: Spain and the Development of Roman Imperialism, 218–82 B.C.* Cambridge: Cambridge University Press, 1986.

Sánchez, José M. *The Spanish Civil War as a Religious Tragedy*. Notre Dame: University of Notre Dame Press, 1987.

Share, Donald. *The Making of Spanish Democracy*. New York: Praeger, 1986.

Tanner, Marie. *The Last Descendant of Aeneas: The Hapsburgs and the Mythic Image of the Emperor*. New Haven, Conn.: Yale University Press, 1993.

Thomas, Hugh. *The Spanish Civil War*. 3d ed. New York: Harper and Row, 1986.

LITERATURE

Alcina Rovira, J. F., and others. *Historia de la literatura española*. Madrid: Ediciones Catedra, 1990.

Alvarez-Emparanza, José Luis, and others. *Cultura vasca II.* San Sebastián: Ediciones vascas argitletxea, n.d.

Ano literario español 1974–1979. Madrid: Editorial Castalia, 1980–1991.

Aullón de Haro, Pedro, Javier Huerta Calva, Juan Palette, Pío E. Serrano, and Carlos Tirado. *Historia de la literatura española.* Madrid: Editorial Playor, 1981.

Bell, Aubrey F.G. *Castilian Literature.* Oxford: Oxford University Press, 1938.

Brenan, Gerald. *The Literature of the Spanish People.* 2nd ed. Cambridge: Cambridge University Press, 1953.

Burckhardt, Titus. *Moorish Culture in Spain.* New York: McGraw-Hill, 1972.

Chandler, Richard E., and Kessel Schwartz. *A New History of Spanish Literature.* Baton Rouge: Louisiana State University Press, 1961.

Crow, John A. *Spain: The Root and the Flower.* 3rd ed. Berkeley: University of California Press, 1985.

Hughes, Robert. *Barcelona.* New York: Alfred A. Knopf, 1992.

Linehan, Peter. *History and the Historians of Medieval Spain.* Oxford: Clarendon Press, 1993.

Pritchett, V. S. *The Spanish Temper: Travels in Spain.* London: Hutchinson, 1954.

Río, Angel del. *Historia de la literatura española.* 2 vols. New York: Columbia University Press, 1949.

Schwartz, Kessel. *Studies on Twentieth-Century Spanish and Spanish-American Literature.* Lanham, Md.: University Press of America, 1983.

Ward, Philip, ed. *The Oxford Companion to Spanish Literature.* Oxford: Oxford University Press, 1978.

ART

Brown, Jonathan. *The Golden Age of Painting in Spain.* New Haven, Conn.: Yale University Press, 1991.

Campoy, Antonio Manuel. *Diccionario crítico del arte español contemporáneo.* Madrid: Ibérico Europea de Edicions, 1973.

Corredor-Matheos, José. *Seis Artistas Catalanes.* Santander: Sur, 1978.

Dyckes, William, ed. *Contemporary Spanish Art.* New York: Art Digest, 1975.

Gudiol, José. *The Arts of Spain.* Garden City, N.Y.: Doubleday, 1964.

Levenson, Jay A. *Circa 1492: Art in the Age of Exploration.* New Haven, Conn.: Yale University Press, 1991.

Malet, Rosa María. *Joan Miró.* New York: Rizzoli, 1983.

Mehling, Franz N. *Spain: A Phaidon Cultural Guide.* Oxford: Phaidon Press. 1985.

Stokstad, Marilyn. *Medieval Art.* New York: Harper and Row, 1986.

Ureña, Gabriel. *Las vanguardias artísticas en la postguerra española, 1940–1959.* Madrid: Colección Fundamentos 73, 1982.

MUSIC

Chase, Gilbert. *The Music of Spain.* New York: W. W. Norton, 1941.

Demarquez, Suzanne. *Manuel de Falla.* Philadelphia: Chilton, 1968.

Hamilton, Mary Neal. *Music in Eighteenth-Century Spain*. New York: Da Capo Press, 1971.

Hoppin, Richard H. *Medieval Music*. New York: W. W. Norton, 1978.

Land, Paul Henry. *Music in Western Civilization*. New York: W. W. Norton, 1941.

CUSTOMS AND SOCIETY

Anderson, Ruth Matilda. *Spanish Costume: Extremadura*. New York: Hispanic Society of America, 1951.

Behar, Ruth. *Santa María del Monte: The Presence of the Past in a Spanish Village*. Princeton, N.J.: Princeton University Press, 1986.

Brandes, Stanley H. *Migration, Kinship, and Community: Tradition and Transition in a Spanish Village*. New York: Academic Press, 1975.

Carreras y Candi, Francisco, ed. *Folklore y costumbres de España*. 2 vols. Barcelona: Casa Editorial Alberto Martín, 1944.

Collins, Larry, and Dominique Lapierre. *Or I'll Dress You in Mourning: The Story of El Cordobés and the New Spain He Stands For*. New York: Simon and Schuster, 1968.

Davis, J. *People of the Mediterranean: An Essay in Comparative Social Anthropology*. London: Routledge and Kegan Paul, 1977.

Douglass, William A. *Echalar and Murelaga: Opportunity and Rural Exodus in Two Spanish Basque Villages*. New York: St. Martin's Press, 1975.

———. ed. *Essays in Basque Social Anthropology and History*. Reno: Basque Studies Program, University of Nevada, 1989.

Ford, Richard. *A Handbook for Travellers in Spain*. 2 vols. London: John Murray, 1855.

Freeman, Susan Tax. *Neighbors: The Social Contract in a Castilian Hamlet*. Chicago: University of Chicago Press, 1970.

———. *The Pasiegos: Spaniards in No Man's Land*. Chicago: University of Chicago Press, 1979.

Gilmore, David D. *The People of the Plain: Class and Community in Lower Andalusia*. New York: Columbia University Press, 1980.

Hughes, Russell Meriwether. *Spanish Dancing*. Pittsfield, Mass.: Eagle, 1967.

Lisón Tolosana, Carmelo. *Belmonte de los Caballeros: A Sociological Study of a Spanish Town*. Oxford: Clarendon Press, 1966.

———. *Invitación a la antropología cultural de España*. La Coruña: Editorial Adara, 1977.

Mitchell, Timothy. *Passional Culture: Emotion, Religion, and Society in Southern Spain*. Philadelphia: University of Pennsylvania Press, 1990.

Palencia, Isabel de. *The Regional Costumes of Spain*. London: B. T. Batsford, 1926.

Peristiany, J. G., ed. *Mediterranean Family Structures*. Cambridge: Cambridge University Press, 1976.

Pitt-Rivers, Julian. *The People of the Sierra*. Chicago: University of Chicago Press, 1961.

Salisbury, Joyce E. *Iberian Popular Religion 600 B.C. to 700 A.D.*: Celts, Romans and Visigoths. New York: Edwin Mellen Press, 1985.

Sobrer, Josef Miguel, ed. *Catalonia: A Self-Portrait*. Bloomington: Indiana University Press, 1992.

Valle, Teresa del. *Korrika: Basque Ritual for Ethnic Identity*. Trans. Linda White. Reno: University of Nevada Press, 1994.

Vittucci, Matteo, with Carola Goya. *The Language of Spanish Dance*. Norman: University of Oklahoma Press, 1990.

HISTORICAL SITES

Atlas Nacional de España: Indice toponimico. Madrid: Instituto Geográfico y Castastral, 1965.

Butler, Reg. *Where to Go in the Canary Islands*. New York: Hippocrene Books, 1990.

Casas, Penelope. *Discovering Spain: An Uncommon Guide*. New York: Alfred A. Knopf, 1992.

Court, Alex, ed. *Baedeker's Spain*. London: Jarrold and Sons, 1992.

Cowell, F. R. *The Garden as a Fine Art: From Antiquity to Modern Times*. Boston: Houghton Mifflin, 1978.

Ellingham, Mark, John Fisher, and Graham Kenyon, eds. *The Rough Guide to Spain*. London: Routledge and Kegan Paul, 1983.

España: atlas e indices de sus terminos municipales. Madrid: Confederación Española de Cajas de Ahorros, 1989.

Grunfeld, Frederic V., with Teresa Farino. *Wild Spain: A Traveler's and Naturalist's Guide*. Englewood Cliffs, N.J.: Prentice-Hall, 1989.

Guía del Viajeros, various provinces. Madrid: Susaeta ediciones, 1990–92.

Jacobs, Michael. *Northern Spain: The Road to Santiago de Compostela*. San Francisco: Chronicle Books, 1991.

King, Mona. *Driving Tours of Spain*. New York: Simon and Schuster, 1992.

Lowe, Alfonso. *The Companion Guide to the South of Spain*. London: Collins, 1973.

Mitchell, Angus, and Tom Bell. *Spain: The Best of Spanish Interiors, Gardens, Architecture, Landscapes*. Boston: Little, Brown, 1990.

Morris, Jan. *Spain*. New York: Oxford University Press, 1979.

Tucker, Alan, ed. *The Berlitz Travellers' Guide to Spain 1992*. New York: Berlitz, 1992.

CUISINE

Andrews, Coleman. *Europe's Last Great Culinary Secret: Catalan Cuisine*. New York: Atheneum, 1988.

Bettónica, Luis. *Cocina regional española*. Barcelona: Ediciones Hymsa, 1981.

Casas, Penelope. *Tapas: The Little Dishes of Spain*. New York: Alfred A. Knopf, 1985.

MacMiadhacháin, Anna. *Spanish Regional Cookery*. Harmondsworth: Penguin Books, 1976.

Norman, Barbara. *The Spanish Cookbook*. New York: Bantam, 1967.

Read, Jan, Maite Monjón, and Hugh Johnson. *The Wine and Food of Spain*. Boston: Little, Brown, 1987.

CHRONOLOGY

Cortada, James W., ed. *Historical Dictionary of the Spanish Civil War, 1936–1939.* Westport, Conn.: Greenwood Press, 1982.

Kern, Robert W., and Meredith D. Dodge, eds. *Historical Dictionary of Modern Spain, 1700–1988.* Westport, Conn.: Greenwood Press, 1990.

Olson, James S., ed. *Historical Dictionary of the Spanish Empire 1402–1975.* Westport, Conn.: Greenwood Press. 1992.

INDEX

Note: Main entries appear in boldface page numbers. The provincial location of entries are contained in parenthesis.

About the Author

ROBERT W. KERN is Professor of History at the University of New Mexico. He is the author of eight other books, five of which are about Spain, including *Historical Dictionary of Modern Spain* (Greenwood Press, 1990). He has spent some time living in Spain.